FISHERMEN'S DIGEST

9th EDITION

Edited by
Erwin A. Bauer

DIGEST BOOKS, INC., NORTHFIELD, ILL.

FISHERMEN'S DIGEST STAFF

Erwin A. Bauer
 Editor
Peggy Peters
 Executive Editor
Mary MacDonald
 Art Director
Deborah James
 Production Assistant
Sheldon L. Factor
 Associate Publisher

ISBN 0-695-80400-6   Library of Congress Catalog #75-148727

An Editorial

In this era of unrest and violence around the world, it often seems that there is no escape from the unhappy headlines—no place to turn and at least briefly be apart from it all. A good many citizens believe they are trapped in an existence they did not plan and certainly do not enjoy. Peace and serenity seem very elusive—if they exist at all.

To all these "trapped" Americans—and in fact to all Americans—we suggest a fishing trip.

The sport fisherman's world has always been a refuge and a tonic. Angling takes a person to some of the most beautiful and least developed places on our continent. Except for such natural sounds as wind, waves, rapids and seabirds, it is a comparatively quiet world where a man can unwind and recuperate.

You do not have to be rich to enjoy angling. Nor do you have to be young, handsome, or very experienced. Kids love it and so do their great grandparents. Fishing can be either a challenge or a relaxation; you can play the game as seriously or as casually as you like it. It's your choice. You can fish alone (the perfect time for contemplation) or with old friends and selected companions. Either way a day hip deep in a cold mountain stream or a lukewarm lagoon is always a rich experience.

But like almost everything else nowadays there is trouble in paradise as the angler's world is more and more threatened. The recent awareness of a world-wide ecology crisis has in no way halted (or even slowed down) the increasing pollution of our waterways. The same industries which dumped mercury, acids and other poisons into our rivers are still doing it. The same strip mining companies which have completely despoiled running streams in Appalachia have now moved westward and are beginning the pillage of eastern Montana and Wyoming.

Unnecessary dam building is still an ugly specter across the land and a good example of that is the proposed T.V.A. impoundment of the Little Tennessee River, the last free-flowing trout stream in the entire watershed. It would seem that we could spare that one at least. The U.S. Soil Conservation service continues to wipe out river after river with their channelization programs.

Perhaps the most discouraging aspect of all is the total lack of concern by the President of the United States, his administration, and far too many politicians at all levels, about the deteriorating American environment. Keep in mind that as the total environment goes, so goes fishing.

But exactly what can the American fisherman do to save his sport?

First—and this is not always easy—is to elect the best possible candidates to all offices from village and township level all the way to the highest office in the country. Vote the straight conservation ticket because it is as crucial to our eventual survival as well as to our fishing right now.

Be active in conservation organizations. Join and contribute generously to one or more of the following: Sierra Club, Trout Unlimited, National Audubon Society, Environmental Defense Fund, National Wildlife Federation or the Wilderness Society.

Personally set a good example as a sportsman. Keep only the fish you need, do not litter or deface the waterways, introduce others to the greatest sport on earth.

Erwin A. Bauer

TABLE OF CONTENTS

SADDLE UP FOR HIGH ANGLING ADVENTURE

by JOE JACKSON

Sure you sometimes encounter bad weather and flood waters on pack trips, but it's all part of the game.

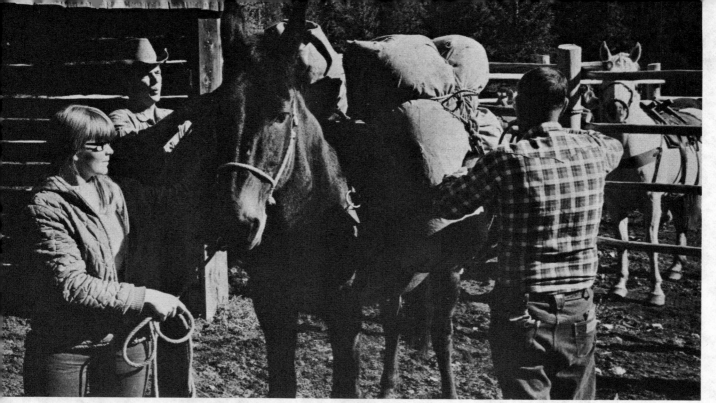

Loading up a pack mule at the Canyon Creek Ranch near Dillon, Montana. Departure soon follows for the high country——and fishing.

SOME adventures simply do not have auspicious beginnings. Some never come off at all. But according to my young son Bob, who is the original Eternal Optimist, it's how they end that counts. His firm philosophy is "all's well that ends well" and last summer's pack trip is his favorite illustration.

Almost from the moment we assembled in Massacre Meadows to saddle up the horses and to pack the mules it began to rain, although only softly at first. That didn't make loading up our camping gear on reluctant animals any easier. Even outfitter Mac Masterson's purple bunkhouse vocabulary didn't seem to help. He swore magnificently. Still one balky pack mule, Maxwell, unloaded our sleeping bags and skillets all over the landscape only minutes after the gear was diamond-hitched to the pack saddle. One of my flyrods was busted in the melee. Altogether it was a spectacle to make anyone weep.

"The next trip that #$%*@& animal makes," Mac swore, "will be to the glue factory."

But Maxwell notwithstanding, we eventually were underway. Only now the rain was falling harder . . . and harder.

For most of the morning the thin trail climbed steeply within sight of Massacre Creek. Now and then it would stray from the stream via switchbacks long enough to detour around waterfalls or ledges of rimrock. It could have been a scenic ride into the high country, but I shivered and tried to hunch down deeper inside a foul weather suit. Still I couldn't escape the rain.

First a thin trickle of water found a way down the back of my neck. Then brushing against evergreen branches along the trail made small punctures in my parka. Before long I was soaked clear to the skin—and that is when Maxwell decided to throw his cargo a second time. Half an hour was lost while Mac caught the animal (he would have shot it then and there, but had no gun) and the three of us reloaded it. When the chore was finished, I thought I knew how drowned rats feel. Bob alone didn't seem to mind the downpour.

"Remember," he joked in the manner of a pious preacher, "that no matter how black the cloud up above, there's blue sky just beyond."

My first inclination was to snarl back at the boy, but he had broken the tension and I had to laugh instead. So did Mac.

And believe it or not, within the next hour we rode out above the rain cloud which had hung over Massacre Creek and into a bright new world above timberline on top of the Rockies. Now I find it nearly impossible to describe the sudden dramatic change, but old hands in the mountains will understand. Not long after that a warm sun had dried us completely and we were feeling human again. Even Maxwell seemed contented—well, *almost* contented —with the load on his back.

By mid-afternoon we gained a windy alpine meadow called Lupine Ridge and there dismounted to stretch. Below us and extending far into the distance was a necklace of azure lakes. Beyond and below the lakes was the cloud bank we'd left behind.

"This," Bob pointed out, "is the blue sky up above." I couldn't think of an appropriate reply.

What followed that damp, unpleasant beginning was adventure—a very high adventure—which none of us could ever forget. And that includes Mac Masterson, even though pack tripping is his business and he is inclined to take a blasé view of scenery, sunshine and similar things.

We pitched a comfortable camp beside the nearest of the mountain lakes. This consisted of two light tents—one for sleeping and the other for cooking and eating in case bad weather drove us under canvas. (It never did rain again on this trip.) After the horses and mules were unsaddled and hobbled to graze in the meadows nearby, there was a frantic race to set up fishing tackle.

I cannot recall who won and that makes no difference anyway; we easily caught enough fat, foot-long cutthroat trout for dinner. I could see them come far up out of the gin clear water to strike my flies.

And how delicious the trout were! That night I fell

This pack string pauses in passing spectacular scenery of Montana's Beartooth Mountains.

Outfitter of this pack trip in Canadian Rockies uses Indian-type tepee for fishermen.

First step after unloading gear is to set up camp. Note lake close by and sparkling in the background.

asleep as if drugged and never stirred again until much too late the next morning. The last sounds I'd heard were Bob and Mac chatting and laughing beside a crackling campfire. Bells on hobbled horses trailed into the distance. Paradise Found.

For the next few days we explored the nearby lakes, caught plenty of fish in some and others were apparently barren. Elk sign was abundant all around and often we saw herds of cows with calves born only months before. Once we had a glimpse of a fine muley buck in the velvet. Instinctively Bob had thrown a spinning rod to his shoulder and aimed it at the deer, pulling an imaginary trigger.

"I'd like to meet that one come fall," he said.

Yellow-bellied marmots were abundant in the meadows around our camp and their burrows completely encircled us. At first they were shy of us, but they soon decided we were harmless. Finally one bold marmot was eating bread crusts which Bob offered.

But there was one other unpleasant aspect about this pack trip which I must mention. It ended. However, as Bob firmly believes, all's well that ends well.

In North America today there are almost as many ways to enjoy the great outdoors as there are outdoorsmen. But there is no adventure which exactly matches the trail ride or wilderness pack trip. Except for backpacking, which isn't practical or possible for all outdoorsmen, it is the only

possible means to reach many of the most beautiful and awesome wildernesses on this continent.

Packing is the only means to visit some of the best hunting areas; some species of big game are not at all available from traveled roads. The pack trip also offers the best opportunity for sportsmen to sample some of the best, most undisturbed fishing waters still remaining. In addition to all these, a trail ride is anyone's greatest chance to *escape*.

There is nothing new about pack tripping. It is as old as man's association with animals of burden—with camels, oxen, yaks, the Old World asses as well as with horses. Marco Polo remains the best known of the early packtrippers, having devoted a good chunk of his life to his fantastic trip from Venice to China and return. The first pack trippers in America were the soldiers, prospectors, settlers, trappers, scouts and even itinerant clergymen who won (or lost, depending on how you look at it) the wild "Wild West." Although other modes of travel have changed almost beyond human comprehension, American pioneers used virtually the same saddles, lashings, techniques and sometimes even the same knots as did Marco Polo. So do outfitters today.

If it seems that pack tripping is purely all-American, it is only natural. Nowhere else on earth is it done almost 100 percent for sport or pleasure. Nowadays tens of thousands of Americans and Canadians enjoy holiday pack trips, even in an era called the jet or space age, and the number increases every year. The main reason is that these trips are such wholesome and rewarding experiences. That is doubly true if the pack tripper is a fisherman. But equally

Main reward of summertime packtripping is having a beautiful alpine lake all to yourself. This one is in the Pioneer Mountains.

important is that today they are easy to organize and some sort of pack trip or trail ride is within reach of anybody's budget.

But exactly what is a pack trip?

Any pack trip is an expedition into faraway country inaccessible by other means. Pack trippers ride horseback and all necessary gear for their living in the field is transported on pack animals. A trip may be of any duration—overnight, several days, a week, a month or even more. Experienced horsemen may organize trips on their own, but most are led by outfitters who devote full-time to the business or who are ranchers devoting part-time to it.

Normally the outfitter furnishes everything except his customer's personal gear. Specifically that includes good safe riding and pack stock, riding and pack saddles, tents, kitchenware, all food, saddle bags. Besides outdoor clothing, riders are expected to furnish their own sleeping bags, air or foam mattresses, toilet articles, fishing tackle or hunting gear. Youth, great riding ability or top physical conditions are not essential for taking pack trips, although of course the last two are helpful.

Of a lifetime spent vagabonding in the outdoors, past pack trips are among the easiest and happiest adventures to recall. My first one was a post-World War II reunion of old hunting buddies into the Bob Marshall Wilderness of Montana. The main purpose then was elk hunting and in that we were not completely successful—two bulls bagged for four gunners. But the companionship, the fishing and the mountain scenery was superb enough that all of us have been hooked ever since. We have lived from one trail ride to the next.

The next trip, with the same cast of characters, now addicted, lasted for three weeks into the British Columbia Cassiars. On this one both the hunting and fishing were more than any trail rider could really hope for. We fished in many streams which might never have seen a fly or lure before; at least that's how the trout responded. Other pack trips have taken me to Mt. Assiniboine (one of the world's most spectacular peaks) in B.C., to Horseshoe Lake (huge rainbow-cutthroat hybrids) and Egypt Lakes (a whole chain of trout waters) in Banff National Park; Alberta's Highwood Mountains for bighorn sheep; three times into Montana's spectacular Beartooth Primitive Area with hundreds of lakes; the Mogollon Mountains of New Mexico's Gila Wilderness; the list could go on and on. But of all these, two trips with Gene Wade and his Hiland Guide Service of Cooke City, Montana, stand out alone.

The first of these was also the first pack trip for both of my sons, Joe and Bob, then 11 and 15. It isn't any wonder, then, that I should recall it with nostalgia. Beginning the first day out, both boys became as crazy about high country as the old man and that is saying a great deal.

For this trip, Gene selected to take the route over Daisy Pass and to follow a faint, little-used trail into the northeast corner of Yellowstone Park. His destination was a lonely, lush meadow along Slough Creek, which must be (or have been) among the best dry fly waters for cutthroat trout in the world.

It's true that Slough Creek is easy of access by highway and in fact meanders right through a public campground. But the upper portion of Slough Creek which we visited on this occasion might have been a different waterway altogether. The only other fisherman we ever saw was an otter. And we never before enjoyed any faster trout fishing until . . . another pack trip with Gene Wade.

This second venture was also within Yellowstone Park. About two million tourists visit the Park each year. But only a handful have ever even seen Broad Creek, although it is a mere day's ride or hike from Canyon Village.

Gene had truck-trailered six horses from Cooke to the stables at Canyon and there we saddled them up for the trip. We crossed the Yellowstone River not far from Upper Falls and then began a slow climb through a dry forest which showed considerable evidence of past thermal activity. Here and there steam still hissed from the ground and hot yellow water trickled from tiny springs. It was not particularly scenic country so we pushed the horses hard until by late afternoon when Gene led the string down a long grade to the valley of Broad Creek.

At first impression, Broad isn't a classic stream in the sense of Slough Creek. To begin, it is smaller and more shallow. But never before that golden day have I found so many trout of such large size in so confined a waterway. On the first three drifts of a dry fly he had tied himself, Bob hooked trout. Each was better than two pounds.

"You're my witness," the exuberant lad called out to me, "that I've designed The Super Fly."

"Any fly is super here," I answered—and also caught fish on three successive casts with an entirely different pattern.

During dinner at dusk that evening, a pair of elk passed our camp and paid little attention to us or to our conversation. And in the morning, the fresh paw prints of a grizzly were etched in the soft earth along Broad Creek. The big bruin had passed our camp during the night.

Trails everywhere in the Rockies are well marked to assist packtrippers.

Pack trip camp high on Jorden Lake in Beartooths. Horses are hobbled to graze nearby, ready to ride to next lake.

Rainbow trout is netted from Rocky shore of high mountain lake. Horseback is most convenient way to reach spots like this.

Even in midsummer, snow might fall and keep the gang confined to camp, but summer squalls soon end.

It's warm and bright now as pack string heads out and up along Canyon Creek and into Montana's Pioneer Mountains.

Luckily we had hung all of our food in canvas sacks high in trees some distance from the tents.

Next morning Gene made a bet which it seemed he couldn't possibly win. "I'll saddle my horse," he offered, "ride through that pool just below camp and then cast back into it. I'm wagering that I hook a trout on that first cast."

"A dollar says you don't," Bob replied.

Gene won the dollar.

Planning a pack trip is neither a difficult nor complicated matter. Contact with reliable outfitters can be made through the where-to-go sections of *Sports Afield, Outdoor Life* or *Field & Stream*. Also, each year the Wilderness Society (4260 East Evans Ave., Denver, Colorado 80222) sponsors many (21 in 1972) non-profit, group trips from New Mexico to Canada. Still others are organized annually by the American Forestry Association, by the Sierra Club and Trail Riders of the Canadian Rockies.

The cost of a trip will vary a great deal depending on the number of riders and on how much of the work and chores the riders are willing and/or able to do themselves. A family of five, for example, might get along for $15 to $20 each per day by doing their own cooking and by helping with the horse wrangling. But if the outfitter must hire a cook and extra cowpokes as guide-wranglers, the individual cost could more than double.

Consider also some typical costs quoted by the Wilderness Society for the all-expense trips on which riders only enjoy themselves; the cooking, dishwashing and stock wrangling is done by the pack trip staff. Ten days in the Absaroka Wilderness of Montana costs each person $360 or $36 per day. It almost costs that much to stay at home nowadays.

Other Wilderness Society rates for summer excursions are as follows: Pecos Wilderness, Arizona, 10 days for $320; Weminuche Wilderness, Colorado, eight days for $275; Selway-Bitterroot Wilderness, Idaho, 11 days for $375; Bob Marshall Wilderness, Montana, 10 days for $385; North Cascades Wilderness, Washington, 10 days for $355; San Juan-Rio Grande Wilderness, Colorado, 10 days for $280; southern Yellowstone Park, 11 days for $385; Banff Wilderness, Alberta, ten days for $285.

Keep in mind that autumn pack trips for hunting will run much higher because parties are necessarily smaller and more gear must be packed into hunting areas for colder weather. In some regions it is even necessary to pack in hay for the horses. Figure $60 to $75 per man, per day in Wyoming, Montana, Colorado and the Southwest. The farther north you hunt, the greater the cost. In northern British Columbia and the Yukon, for instance, the tab may run as much as $100 to $150 per day.

Pack trips invariably involve minor hardships—riding out sudden squalls, coping with balky horses and saddle-soreness. But as the adventure goes on, the soreness has a bittersweet quality which riders remember with warmth long after the trip has ended.

Mostly, though, pack trips mean crossing ridges and traveling toward distant horizons, breathtaking scenery all around, sudden encounters with moose or coyotes, indelible evenings with friends around campfires and trout rising on lonely alpine lakes. On most pack trips I live 14 days a week and that is a precious thing in a hurry-up age when time passes so quickly. So very, very quickly.

The New Art of SURFBOAT FISHING

A 14-foot "tin boat" can be manhandled. Oars are used in launching. Then the helmsman takes over with his outboard motor.

by FRANK WOOLNER

THE definition of a surf caster is a man clad in waders, foul weather jacket, armed with an impossibly long rod and a strange compulsion to challenge big combers while he throws baits or artificial lures to various fishes roving a given sea rim. Right?

Wrong!

Small boats on inshore grounds now challenge the ancient art of surf casting, often driving beachcombers off their dunes and practically out of their cotton-picking minds. This is, depending upon your convictions, a blessing or a curse. Nowadays, only the big-surf areas are reserved for true squidders: in mild wash and manageable waves it's boats away!

Of course some will contend that there's nothing very revolutionary about pushing off from shore in order to hunt fish; dorymen have been doing it for several hundreds of years.

The difference lies in new techniques and launching for sport, no hard labor, on the green pastures of inshore seas. Our current boom in surfboat sport fishing began 20-odd years ago.

At that time, in the late 40's and early 50's a small group of derring-do beach buggy surfers on the outer tip of Cape Cod got sick of chewing their fingernails every time striped bass and bluefish rushed bait well beyond their best casts. The thing was almost spontaneous, although greying regulars argue endlessly about who was first.

On Cape Cod it might have been Jim, Gus and Pete Kissell of Worcester, Massachusetts. They launched at Race Point, Provincetown where the surf is normally light, caught striped bass on eelskin rigs and managed to corral a few school tuna. The Kissells pushed a small boat into the suds, but they weren't really surf-launching, because in their chosen area the ground swells rarely threatened.

Down on the North Truro shore, where combers often boom ashore, the beach buggy clans went to a succession of plywood rowboats, most of them custom-made with enough freeboard to insure more safety than that offered by an inland skiff. Arnold Laine, the legendary rod-and-line commercial, was among the first with a 10-foot scow shaped like a pumpkin seed. Johnny Clark, Charley Whitney and Warren Williams soon appeared with 12-foot plywood row-

16

Still great sport, surf casting will endure—particularly in areas where wave action prevents the easy launching of small boats.

An experienced operator can make it alone. This is a mild surf, and yet—right on the shore, such waves can swamp a small boat.

A shocker to those seeing it for the first time, boats drive ashore at full throttle. This is a 17-foot Boston Whaler.

Practically all of the tin boat skippers use extension operating handles, so that they can stand while under way.

boats, and I got into the act with a similar craft.

In those days surf launching was a mite hairy. We operated with a two-man crew: having manhandled the boat down into the suds, with its bow just awash, one man seated himself at the oars while the other prepared to push off. It was necessary to second-guess the waves and go just after a big one had crashed in and the next in succession seemed smaller.

As the bow lifted in the wash of that big wave, the push-off man shoved mightily and then scrambled aboard while his companion bent to the oars and tried to beat that oncoming juggernaut to the safety of deep water. It was hard work and it was exciting. Now and then we'd misjudge and get swamped, wet and bruised. There were no fatalities, but the surf launching of that time incurred a full share of wounded egos.

Then, of course, the "tin boat" came on strong and, with it, the outboard motor for propulsion. An oarsman still took his position amidships, and the push-off man again heaved mightily and scrambled over the transom. Thereafter, it was the helmsman's duty to fire up that kicker the moment its

lower unit could be dropped, and to thread a way over the advancing swells. Motors that were recalcitrant, in those days, weren't very popular.

Motors soon aided recovery. With the old rowboats, we found it necessary to back in because the sharper bow entry presented less surface to advancing ground swells. A big swell, developed while we were out there tonging bass and blues, caused worry wrinkles and—very often—undignified landings where everybody aboard got wet, tackle was lost, and the shoreside gang laughed until their bellies ached.

Very shortly canny surfers found that it was possible, with so little as a 10-horse motor, to pick a wave and come ashore bow-first. The trick then—and now—consists of picking the right wave, following it, and then applying full power at that precise moment when the advancing ground swell hits the beach and blows up in a smother of spray. Properly executed, a small boat operator can drive his craft high and dry, skidding up the shingle on the wash of that last wave.

Inevitably the tin boat—really an aluminum planing skiff —added refinements. There was the matter of the Ritefit

Tools of the trade often include a live-in beach buggy (note the TV antenna), a four-wheel-drive prime mover such as this Jeep Wagoneer, and a 16- to 18-foot boat.

extension operating handle. With it, you could stand in the sternsheets, once under way, and better trim a small boat. By standing, a thing often scored as dangerous by land-locked authorities, the helmsman also gained a high vantage point to thread his way over shallow bars and to search for fish. The extension operating handle not only permitted standing, it also served as a clumsy cleat or brace.

Power swiftly escalated. Where the first tin boats used motors in the 10 horse bracket, their successors went to 15, 18—and finally 25. My present 14-foot Aerocraft is pushed by a 25 horsepower Johnson and it is a very comfortable little craft in anything but a wild sea.

Incidentally, the 14-foot aluminum boat and 25-horse-power outboard is just about maximum where manhandling is necessary. A couple of brawny fishermen can skid this rig down the beach and then pull it out of the wash upon recovery—assuming, of course, that the bow-on, full-throttle landing is perfectly executed. Nowadays there is always a four-wheel-drive vehicle such as a Jeep Wagoneer to provide aid.

Such a craft can be operated by one man, where waves are not threatening. You simply position it with bow in the water, wait for the proper moment between waves—and then push off with oar or pole. Almost immediately, fire up the outboard and climb over those oncoming swells.

The little boats, meaning those that can be manhandled, can be cartopped or trailered with relative ease. Don't expect them to perform miracles, for they were never meant to challenge big seas. However, when the ocean is reasonably benign, such craft are practical.

While the tin boat revolutionized surf fishing in the Northeast, West Coast salmon fishermen were launching in a somewhat similar manner, although they used big, Amesbury dory types with high bows to defeat those oncoming swells. The operation was never so extensive as that on Cape Cod.

By the early 60's no North Atlantic beach buggy angler felt himself properly equipped without a surfboat, and practically all of these were aluminum skiffs powered by 18- to 20-horsepower outboard motors and fitted with extension handles. They launched at all hours of the day and night to cast or troll lures over the offshore bars and the inshore surf. Shore casters were understandably irked, but aside from the occasional sinker thrown at a helmsman who ventured too close, the net result was a rapid increase in tin boats. Progressively, the surfman was going to sea.

Nor did it end there. Although the small aluminum planing craft which is light enough to manhandle still flourishes along the entire Atlantic Coast, the Gulf of Mexico, and along the Pacific from Baja to British Columbia, there has been a noteworthy move to much larger fiberglass hulls. Since these can't be manhandled, due to excessive weight, they require trailers and prime movers. It is no longer startling to see a 16- to 19-foot craft bounding along on the sand behind a four-wheel-drive buggy. Some specialization is involved.

Uninformed observers always wonder why such "big" boats are not launched on hard pan ramps. The answer is obvious: in many prime fishing areas there are no ramps. Besides, surf launching—provided that you have the necessary equipment—is a very simple operation. You're right on the spot, able to sally forth at the first sign of surface-

When fish are well out beyond a surf caster's best heave, the small boat skippers enjoy double-headers.

feeding fish or working birds. You become a latter-day equivalent of the old corsairs.

The equipment includes first an aluminum or fiberglass boat in the 16- to 19-foot range fitted with a suitable motor, which may be anything from 25 horsepower for the small hull, up to 100 in the big one. You will want to bracket or stow a smaller kicker for a spare in the event of breakdown. Such a craft must be trailered behind a beach buggy, and so the trailer is fitted with large, soft, oversized tires—both to provide clearance and to track over soft sand.

The four-wheel-drive prime mover—mine is a Chevy Carryall fitted with high-walled 950x15 four-ply nylon tires deflated to about 13 pounds—becomes a workhorse. With it you push the boat into the suds, and with it you haul the craft high and dry after a landing. It works like this.

You arrive on site, the trailered boat—thanks to those oversized tires—towing easily. Back it to the high tide mark and unceremoniously dump the rig off its bunkers. Now you have a hull that weighs a lot of pounds perched stern toward the surf. It would be difficult for a crew of husky surfmen to move this package with muscle power alone, yet there is no problem.

A line is quickly bent to a stern cleat and, in turn, fastened to the prime mover's trailer hitch. With power, you simply spin that big baby on her axis, so that the bow points seaward. The rest is elementary.

Remove the line and swing the beach buggy around so that it contacts the boat's starboard transom edge. I forgot to mention that a prime mover's port bumper is always fitted with a padded wooden contact engineered to snug up against the transom. This pad is positioned on the left front bumper, so the driver can see what he's doing.

Now simply push the boat down and into the water. Back the prime mover up on the high dunes. Choose a proper ground swell to get under way—and you're in business. Incidentally, a push-pole is an awfully good idea for this final operation in launching, and the larger surf boats are far less likely to veer in an oncoming ground swell or broach when hit by a wave. Achieve sufficient depth to drop the lower unit, and fire up.

Recovery is a far simpler matter with the big boats than the smaller ones, because you deal with greater power and weight to flatten rolling seas. Enthusiasts have found that glass hulls slide better than aluminum, so they zip farther up on the dune after a full-throttle landing.

It is still wise to pick a wave and come in behind it at full bore, choosing the right moment to arrive on shore. One must also learn to cut the gun and allow the motor's lower unit to tilt as it touches down. On a sand beach damage to the wheel is negligible. Recovery on a rocky shore is only essayed in dire emergency, when sea conditions dictate landing or a chance of joining one's ancestors.

There are no-no's. An outboard motor must never be in the locked-down position when landing at full bore, else the hull's transom may be torn off. Never try to power over a towering ground swell right at the beach, for this may mean a crashing descent—followed by a wall of water slamming into the cockpit. The trick is to hit it just right in order to slide high and dry.

Some slight damage is inevitable. Small aluminum planing boats, racked in successive beach landings, tend to leak because the rivets in their hulls are jarred loose. Glass boats, during the course of a season, may wear a layer of gel-coat off their bottoms—a thing easily repaired. Since a few rocks are always concealed in the average sand beach, wheels get nicked and must be filed smooth or occasionally replaced. The game is still worth the candle.

With larger surf boats, anything from a 16-foot Boston Whaler which lands beautifully on its three point hull, on

Bow man braced, a small tin boat comes ashore under full throttle.

Jack Townsend exhibits a 49-pound striped bass from Provincetown on Cape Cod.

The author with a two-man night catch of blues and stripers at Provincetown.

up to the 19-foot Mako and similar craft, a "surf fisherman" enjoys a very stable platform, plus room for a lot of sophisticated aids. Nobody, other than the cartop adventurer, now goes to sea without a workable compass, and even the cartoppers carry some sort of an instrument, even if it is no more than a woodsman's pocket model. Where hulls provide space, a depth sounder, which also serves as a fish-finder, is indispensable. CB radios are much used, both for communication with shoreside beach buggies and for checking on colleagues working a ground.

If salt water game fish had a voice, they'd curse that aforementioned depth sounder/fish-finder. It is a deadly tool. With it, you can follow a drop-off, find a bar or wreck, pick up schools of fish or even individuals and, generally, call your shots. With the flickering dial it is often possible to predict a strike while trolling. For example, you read the dial upon reaching a drop-off known to harbor bass or blues, compute the length of line streamed—and begin a count-down.

Five, four, three, two, one—He's on!

Surf casting still remains one of the world's most exciting fishing methods, and yet it is phasing out wherever water conditions permit the launching of small boats. There just isn't any future in plugging rollers when the whole inshore sea is swarming with boats of all descriptions. On popular grounds, night or day, the activity can resemble a Gold Cup race.

Yet it's still surf casting. The small boat gives an inshore angler seven league boots. He can work right up against the creaming breakers, or move out to the twinkling spray of a breaking bar. Outboard propelled, it is possible to visit areas where hikers are few and beach buggies baffled by dune conformation. The big rips are prime hunting grounds. Armed with modern electronic equipment, fog and deep night are seldom very threatening, although it's still a mighty good idea to respect the sea and stay ashore when Neptune begins to roar.

Addicts use the same rods, reels and end tackle they'd use in casting from a beach. Often they drift off a breaking bar and heave to its edges. There are nights when the big stripers swarm in a creaming wash and will grab plugs thrown from a position offshore. Light spinning tackle and fly rods come into play too, for the surf boat is nothing but a casting platform—even though it is often used to troll when heaving fails to pay off. Therein lies its versatility —the little critter can do just about anything.

Joe Townsend and the basic combination, a big glass boat and a four-by-four to aid in launch and recovery.

Some confirmed beach men are bitter about the surfboat invasion, maintaining that such craft spook their game fish. They're probably right; certainly stripers and blues are likely to be chased offshore by a mosquito fleet zooming around the shallows. Regardless, the trend is toward greater use of boats and less emphasis on the classic method. Sometimes shore casters forfeit a game.

One recent midnight, Jack Townsend and I outboarded into the rips off Race Point, Provincetown, to find striped bass very eager. We caught them until our arms ached, nice fish in the 15 to 30 pound class and each was hooked by casting plugs or by trolling the same lures when we were too weary to cast.

The important thing is the fact that our pod of stripers was located not 50 yards off a strand where dozens of beach buggies were outlined against the sky. Boats were secured on the beach, but not one surf caster was plying his trade! All hands were asleep, convinced that shore casting would be a waste of time.

Jack and I prefer surf casting from a beach to the same sport in a small boat, and we toyed with the idea of going ashore. We voted against it for one very good and selfish reason—had we done so, the sleeping multitudes would have awakened and offered competition. It was very pleasant to hook a bass on every cast or every trolling swing. We were very much alone and triumphant. That night we loaded up.

At dawn, shorebound casters viewed our catch and vowed to buy boats so that they could duplicate it. Truth is, they could have bettered our haul by wading. We didn't elaborate.

Usually the surfboat, where it can be used safely, is a very potent weapon. It offers a host of options and covers much ground. It is a casting platform supreme, yet it can be employed in trolling. With modern aids to navigation, you can go out in pea-soup fog or dark of night. You have instruments to gauge depth and even to pinpoint individual fish, plus radio communication. There is no difficulty in launching or recovery, providing an efficient prime mover is used. The inshore sea is all yours and you become a mobile surf caster whose targets can't swim out of range.

Big rig in the surf? Not if you have equipment to move it, and know how. Here, Jack Townsend and his son, David, are rigging an unlimited outfit which will be used to fish for giant tuna.

There is one important difference. Anyone who assumes that an angry sea can be treated with disdain will either learn better through a terrifying experience, or wind up a Coast Guard statistic. Smart operators understand that "seaworthy" is a slippery word, with definition hinging on a lot of variables. A surfboat skipper had better watch weather and water conditions, and he'd better go ashore very rapidly when the ocean kicks up.

A good friend of mine, a fellow laborer in the vineyards of outdoor writing and a fine small boatman, nearly lost his life when he tarried too long in a blow. Since he had written a great deal of copy on safety at sea, I gave him considerable flak.

But only in a personal letter—because I am quite as guilty, having just about paged Davey Jones on two separate occasions! Shore-bound surfmen have always pulled the weedy beard of Neptune and those who now go into his domain with small boats are no exception. They catch a lot of fish and they dare the shambling sea.

This happens when a helmsman errs. The glass inboard-outboard came in too slow and was caught in the line of breakers. Water and sand poured into the cockpit and the expensive craft was soon rendered close to a total loss.

OFFER 'EM

Here's a close up of an Okie Drifter, one of the most effective of all artificial steelhead lures. This is the way I rig my own. Note the little fluff of fluorescent yarn I've inserted in the leader loop behind the Okie ball.

Here's what the Okie was originally designed for. Note the two hooks, one above and one below the ball. The original idea was to use salmon eggs in the leader loop on that top hook. Pacific Northwest anglers soon discovered they could get fish just as well without adding eggs.

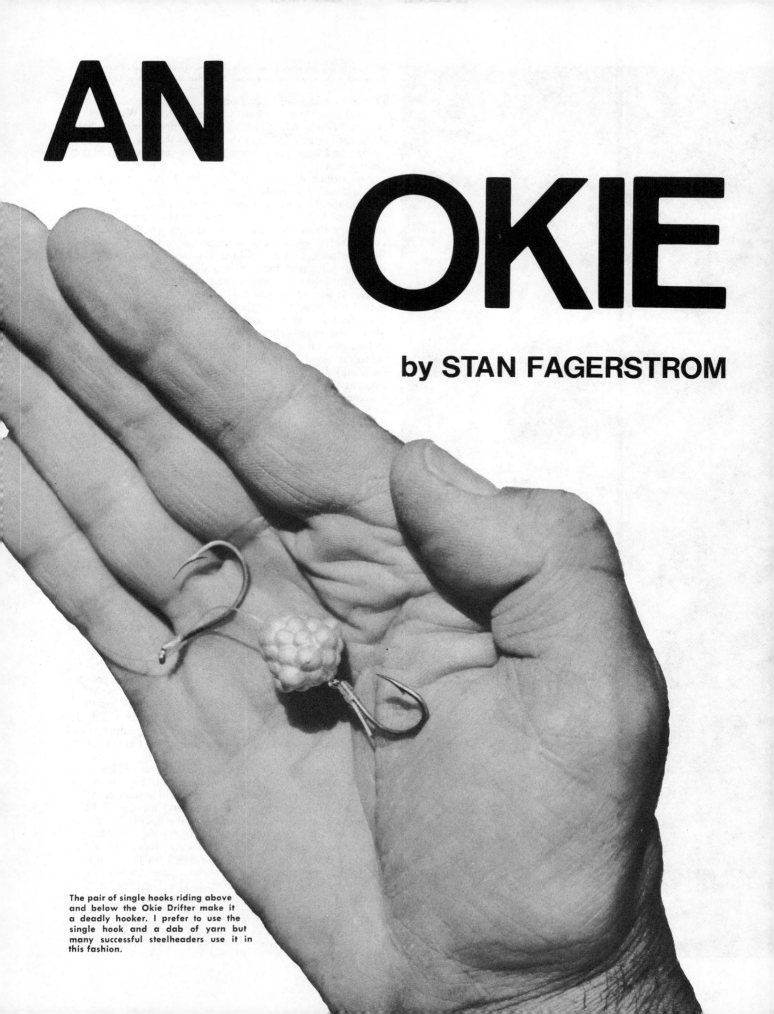

AN

OKIE

by STAN FAGERSTROM

The pair of single hooks riding above and below the Okie Drifter make it a deadly hooker. I prefer to use the single hook and a dab of yarn but many successful steelheaders use it in this fashion.

◄ This husky steelhead was taken on a number three Okie Drifter, the most popular of the five sizes in which the lure is produced.

IT was almost time to go home.

I had been up to my boot tops in southwest Washington's popular Toutle River fishing for steelhead since daylight. A steady January rain had the river on the rise. Water conditions had been poor when I arrived and were gradually getting worse.

The stretch of river did hold fish. I had seen a couple roll and one had nudged my bait of fresh steelhead eggs but dropped it before I could set the hook.

I reeled in, examined my eggs and realizing it was time to change them, debated for a moment whether or not to continue fishing. Instead of changing my eggs I reached into the pocket of my fishing vest and pulled out a new lure I'd purchased the previous day.

The little lure was about the size of the end of my forefinger. It was round and had a lumpy finish much like an actual bait of salmon eggs. It was a reddish-orange color. The one I'd purchased was rigged with two hooks, one tied above, the other below the marble-sized plastic ball.

I attached the lure to my leader, then dropped it into the water at my feet to note what it would do. The highly buoyant little ball bobbed right up in the shallow water and even at the river's edge where there was little current its buoyancy made it move around on the surface.

Figuring there was no harm in trying it for a few minutes before heading home, I cast across the drift and slightly upstream, I felt the sinker bump bottom and then it was moving downstream, threading its way through the pebbles, rocks and boulders where the winter steelhead would be holding. Suddenly there was one slight tug at the rod tip and then wham! My rod jerked so savagely I actually stumbled forward a couple of feet. Along the far shore, outlined against the darkness of the dripping fir trees, a beautiful silver steelhead came bursting up through the surface. Even from 50 feet away I could see the bright little red-orange ball hanging from its jaw.

That was my introduction to the Okie Drifter, one of the most popular and most effective steelhead lures employed by anglers on the white waters of the Pacific Northwest. It was to be an introduction that changed rapidly from a friendly acquaintanceship into a full-blown love affair. Me and those Okies have been going steady ever since!

There was a time not so many years ago when I'd have just as soon not gone steelhead fishing if I didn't have a supply of good fresh eggs. The Okie has changed my attitude, and thousands of fishermen just like me. How can I be so sure? Well, the Maxwell Manufacturing Company of Vancouver, Washington, is the outfit which developed the Okie Drifter. This year the company will produce and sell more than three million of the fish-catching little lures.

Steelhead fishermen all over America are missing a bet if they fail to try the Okie. The Maxwells have made extensive tests of the Okie on the steelhead waters of Michigan. Apparently it is just as effective for Great Lakes steelhead as it is on the fast waters of the Pacific Northwest.

It's great buoyancy is one key to the success steelhead anglers have enjoyed. There are exceptions, but almost always steelhead are going to be down on the bottom of the rivers they travel. The lure which takes them must get down where the fish can get at it. This is where the Okie excells. Pacific Northwest fishermen use it just like they

Look closely and you'll see an Okie Drifter pinned to the lower jaw ➤ of this nice winter steelhead. The Okie will take both winter and summer fish and has proven effective on the Pacific Northwest.

A Washington state steelhead angler punches his steelhead card after landing a nice winter steelhead on an Okie Drifter. The angler is Dorian Lavier, veteran biologist with the Washington State Game Department and himself an ardent steelhead fisherman.

Husky steelhead like this 18-pounder I'm cleaning will pick up a bait of salmon eggs ever so easily. That's not the way they hit an Okie Drifter. They slam the Okie so hard you'll need to have a firm grip on your rod to keep from losing it.

There was a time when Pacific Northwest steelhead anglers didn't want to go out unless they had fresh eggs like those this angler is holding. The effectiveness of the Okie Drifter has helped change that attitude.

would if they were drifting a bait of salmon eggs. A sinker is attached from 12 to 24 inches above the Okie ball. The sinker takes the Okie down and its extreme buoyancy lets it ride just up from the bottom in the most favorable position for the steelhead to grab it.

The length of the leader and the weight of the sinker are both of special importance for the most effective use of the lure. The leader must be matched to water conditions and to the season of the year. In my part of Southwest Washington we have steelhead in our rivers all year around. Anglers use longer leaders, 18 to 24 inches mostly, when they are after summer steelhead. The summer fish will move farther to take a lure than their winter counterparts and longer, lighter leaders help hook more in the first place. The longer the leader the higher in the water the Okie Drifter is going to run.

In the winter most fishermen use a much shorter leader.

← See that little Okie Drifter just below and to the right of this lunker steelhead's eye? It's the lure which caught this 18-pound beauty. The lucky fisherman is Emmett Easterly from the Seattle area.

There are steelhead in certain streams of Washington state all year long and the Okie Drifter will get them in any season. Here I wrestle a good one out of the Toutle River near my lakeside home on Silver Lake.

My own choice is about 15 inches. I'll vary that, of course, if conditions dictate but 15 is a good average. There have been occasions in the dreary dampness of the Washington winter when 10 or 12 inches of leader have worked even better. There have been times when the fish were right down on the bottom and one had to put the lure directly in front of their scaly snouts to get action.

Selection of the right sinker size is important to any kind of steelhead fishing. You just aren't going to get many fish unless you have the proper weight. How do you know when you have it? A little practice will soon show you. The sinker weight must be such that it takes the lure down and holds it there throughout the drift. It must be light enough to let the current tumble it on downstream and it can't be so heavy it digs in behind the pebbles and rocks and is hanging up all the time. If your sinker is the right size you'll feel an almost constant series of bumps and thumps coming up your line and transmitted into the rod tip as you work the water of a steelhead drift.

Even the hard-headed old timers who still stick to their fresh eggs for steelhead will admit the Okie is ever so much easier for the newcomer to learn to use than egg clusters. The main reason is because of the way the fish hit. The newcomer to steelheading finds it difficult to believe how gently even a big steelhead will often pick up a bait of eggs. There is just a stopping or maybe a sort of nudging of the bait. Sometimes it's about like the way a small bass nibbles at a plastic worm. In no way does it resemble the savage chomp you'd expect from a fish which might run 20 pounds or more.

That gentle biting changes when the steelhead tackles an Okie. You may get just one heartbeat of warning then— whamo! You better have a good grip on your rod and a sound nervous system because both will get a workout before the battle is over. It used to take at least a couple of seasons for a beginning steelheader to learn what was happening to his salmon eggs and to distinguish between sinker bumps and an actual pickup. When a steelhead sails into

An Okie Drifter fished right along the bottom is one of the best ways for taking beautiful steelhead like this one I display.

an Okie Drifter you get the picture, but quick.

The Okie is molded from styrene plastic. It figures that any lure as popular as this one has been would be copied and there have been many imitations of the Okie. Few have been successful. Most of the duplicates turned out by either American or Japanese copiers have had faults in the design of the air chamber, aren't watertight or fail in some other fashion.

One always hears how gullible the American angler is. Don't kid yourself. That weatherbeaten gent out there hunched over in his boat or up to his hind-end in some river ain't all-over dumb. I can cite the development of the Okie Drifter lure to prove my point.

The Maxwell people introduced two new lures the year they brought out the Okie. One was a plug called a "Firefish." The company really expected the Firefish to sell much better than the Okie and almost all of the promotional money was put behind that product. What happened? Fishermen bought the Okies by the tens of thousands be-

cause it caught fish. The other lure didn't do much. All the advertising money in America isn't going to move lures off tackle shelves very long if they don't produce results. That's why more than three million Okies will be manufactured this year. The lure really is one of the best ever for steelhead.

Okies are now produced in 16 different colors. The colors range from a deep red raspberry to white pearl. Here, again, I like to think the indication of the best color can be found in sales statistics. Fishermen buy far more Okies in what the company calls its flame finish than anything else. The flame color is a bright reddish-orange and it has also been my own personal best producer.

Steelhead, like bass, sometimes show a preference for different colors. That's why it's wise to have a selection of shades when you employ this lure. Other top colors in the Okie line have been orange, pink, pink-pearl, clown and luminous peach.

There are a couple of tricks I like to use with the Okie

Fish like this winter steelhead are fresh from the Pacific Ocean and full of fight. The Okie Drifter is one of the most effective means of taking them. I show my catch to Dorian Lavier.

which can be highly effective, especially during the winter run in the Pacific Northwest from late November on through March. This is a time of year when western Washington or Oregon streams are often high and discolored. You need something the fish can see easily because water visibility is so low.

I carry a tube of fluorescent chartreuse yarn in the pocket of my fishing vest. When I rig up my Okies I always tie on the hook with the knot attached to the shank, allowing me to push the leader back from the eye to form a loop. This is the same sort of egg loop used by the fishermen who drift with eggs. I snip off a ½-inch length of the chartreuse yarn and cinch it down in the little loop to ride behind the Okie ball. This bright red-green combination has high visibility and has been a real killer for me during the winter season.

Another trick I'll employ now and then in roily water is to insert a small gob of salmon eggs in the leader loop. That way one has the scent of the eggs and the buoyancy of the Okie both working for him. Actually, that's what the Okie was designed to do originally. It's designers rigged it with two hooks, one above and one below the ball. The leader could be pushed back from the top hook leaving the loop to hold salmon eggs. The Okie ball was shaped like a gob of salmon eggs itself and the result was sort of

You'll seldom see brighter winter steelhead than this pretty pair. ➔ I took these two on Okie Drifters during December.

This is the kind of water where the Okie is most effective. I cast across and slightly upstream, working the bouyant lure down along the bottom of the river where the steelhead will be holding.

a half artificial-half natural bait-lure. It didn't take fishermen long to discover the Okie would get fish without the eggs just as well or better than it would with them.

Most pre-tied Okies still come with the two-hook set up and there's no doubt that the single hooks riding above and below the ball really make a deadly hooker out of the lure. Lots of steelheaders, myself included, prefer to tie up their own.

The Okie ball is manufactured in five sizes. The most popular size is the number three. I'll usually rig the number three with a 2/0 hook and just use the one hook below the lure. As I've indicated, I'll tie that hook on with the knot on the shank so I have that little leader loop to attach either the yarn or the eggs if I choose.

Anything a steelhead man can do in advance to eliminate

fumbling around with half-frozen fingers when he's on the river in the wintertime is to his advantage. I make up all my Okie rigs in the comfort of my own workshop before I go out. Once the hook and ball are in place, I tie a small barrel swivel on the upper end of the leader. I'll add a small sinker drop line to the forward end of this barrel swivel. That way I can clip the Okie leader and lure into the snap at the end of my line when I reach the river, add a sinker, and be all ready to go. If I break off on a snag or lose my rigging some other way it's just a matter of seconds to pull out another pre-tied set up and get back to fishing. I keep the Okies I have tied up in little plastic bags in a pocket of my fishing vest so they are separated and easily available.

I'll admit to being on the stubborn side when it comes

Sinker selection is basic to successful steelheading. The angler must carry pliers to cut and pinch shot or pencil lead sinkers into place. The lead can't be too heavy or too light. It should allow the Okie Drifter to work along naturally just off the bottom.

More than 3 million of these little lures will be manufactured and sold this year, the best evidence of all that they are a highly effective steelhead lure. I inspect the hook on this one before offering it to the steelhead I'm after.

to fishing and things connected with it. I'm sure my wife of 30 years would agree! That's why it was terribly tough to admit to myself there actually was a lure which was as effective as those fresh salmon and steelhead eggs I'd prepared with such tender loving care for so many seasons. It's sort of like telling the bass angler who has caught most of his fish on one beat up old plug that there really is another lure which will work as well as his faithful "Old Dynamite."

One morning last January I stood in mixed rain and snow and hooked five steelhead, a couple of them in the 14-pound class, without ever moving my boots and every last one of them on that bouncing little Okie Drifter. That's enough to change the thinking of most anybody, even an old hardheaded fisherman of Swedish ancestry!

I'll be back on that same rock this winter, working the Okie down through the rocks of my favorite steelhead stream. If your future travels take you around the steelhead waters of either the Pacific Northwest or the Great Lakes you'll be missing a bet if you don't do the same thing.

ANY FISH IS A GOOD CATCH

by CHARLES E. MOST

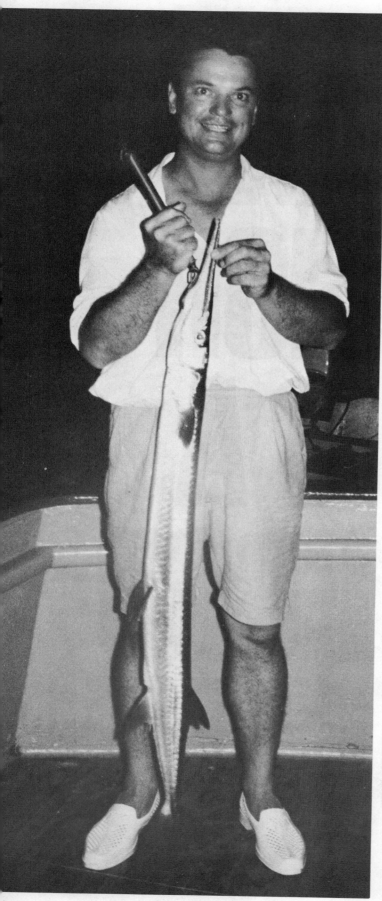

THE effort required in bringing a fish to hand is undoubtedly one of the characteristics that gives a fish a preferred status. Some are simply tougher to catch than others, and the sporting way dictates that such fish become the most eagerly sought.

I believe this is as it should be.

The brown trout, noted for its wariness and probably the most prized trout among fly-fishing advocates, is a good example. I recall a stream in Pennsylvania, primarily brown trout water, where the fish are so "educated" that to have one or two just examine your offering during a day's fishing seems ample reward. Tiny flies, gossamer leader tippets, and great finesse in casting are believed vital to success on this beautiful stream. Just because I caught a 16-inch brown trout on a monstrous grasshopper imitation the first time I fished there has nothing to do with it.

Or does it?

Actually sport involves overcoming obstacles of our own making, and some fishermen tend to make their sport more demanding with tighter and tighter ground rules. If an angler feels that fairy-wand rods, microscopic flies, and leaders like spider webs are necessary to his success (and I can't say they are not), then those are the rules under which he chooses to play, and more power to him. But let's not forget that our objective is still a fish—a rather primitive creature, with a well-developed instinct for survival, but far from human intelligence.

I'm not saying that brown trout aren't difficult to catch. They do require extra effort, but the same goes for carp, a species reviled by many anglers. Those in the know realize how frustrating fishing for carp can be. These fish are so spooky that any clumsiness by the angler is likely to ruin the fishing for hours.

One of the cagiest anglers I know has developed his carp fishing to an art. He spends hours concocting various doughball baits designed to be the undoing of the huge carp that patrol the river near his home. I suspect he even goes through a few strange chants as part of the bait-making ceremony.

Whatever he does, it works; some of the scaly monsters he lands are downright frightening. This man realizes that carp are wary, that their small mouths, in relation to overall size, make them hard to hook, and that they are finicky about which baits will entice them to bite. He uses light lines to prevent frightening the fish and small hooks that aren't likely to be detected inside a doughball.

A 20-pound carp caught by this old riverman, who devotes much effort to his fishing, is as great a prize to him as a hefty brown trout would be to an angler using the most refined tackle. If you can't believe this, then the effort required to catch a fish is not a suitable measure of its value.

There are other attributes of various species that perhaps increase their value to anglers. Some taste better than others. Trout and large- and small-mouth bass are among our most popular freshwater fish and are delicious table fare. On the other hand, catfish are not overly difficult to catch, they are hard to clean, and they would hardly win any beauty prizes. Yet many people with a taste for fish —myself included—consider the lowly catfish as tasty as any American freshwater species.

Then there's the fast-stepping bonefish, one of the most prized fish sought by light-tackle saltwater anglers. I've never seen a mounted catfish, but almost everyone catching a bonefish wants it mounted so he can brag about it later. Yet bonefish are not considered edible at all. It doesn't

◄ Even the strange and exotic houndfish makes an excellent adversary in salt water when taken on light tackle. It's a thrilling jumper.

Dick Kotis lands a largemouth bass on the Rainbow River, Florida. This is among the most sought-after species in fresh water.

seem that the table qualities of a fish are a good yardstick for measuring its value to anglers.

Perhaps it's the fighting ability of a fish when hooked that determines its sporting qualities and consequently its value to the angler. Strength that can put a strain on modern tackle is a factor that adds value to a catch. We all like to boast about the great skill needed to subdue a strong fish. Chinook salmon, the various tunas, lake trout, and red drum are good examples of fish noted for the strength they can pit against an angler's rod.

And yet a bluegill, for its size, can throw tremendous strength against a fisherman by turning the broadside of its body against the pull on the line. A professor of mine once described the fighting quality of bluegills as "holding onto the water as though they had claws." Many knowledgeable fishermen think bluegills, particularly when tackle is scaled to suit, are adversaries worth any angler's interest.

Neither can we discount the carp in any discussion of strength in fish. These brutes are not flashy fighters, but stopping their bull-like runs with anything less than heavy saltwater tackle is practically impossible. If bluegills and carp are not considered prize catches by sportsmen, then strength alone is not the basis for judging sporting qualities of fish.

Speed is one attribute that the more popular species of fish seem to have in common, to a varying degree. Salmon and trout, including the rambunctious sea-run steelhead, display considerable speed when hooked. The elusive bonefish, which ghosts across the shallow flats of the Florida Keys, the Bahamas, and other tropical areas will, when spooked, turn on an awesome burst of speed to reach deeper water. I have heard that the big billfish, particularly marlin, are the speediest of game fish. I frankly can't say—I've never fished for marlin or sailfish.

I remember, as a little boy, accompanying my grandfather on a sucker-snagging trip to an Ozark creek. Redhorse

The saltwater permit is an excellent gamester wherever it's found—and many anglers consider it the greatest fish of all on light tackle.

To some anglers, the setting is almost as important as the fish and fishing. These men are trying for bass among the cypresses of a Florida lake.

suckers were moving upstream to spawn, and grandfather would toss a line strung with alternating hooks and sinkers across a narrow part of the stream and wait for a big one to swim by. When the fish moved over the line, grandfather would give a violent yank, and more often than not, snag the fish on one of the hooks. I helped by keeping watch for fish moving toward the lines.

Strangely enough, the one thing I remember best about this trip was the fish grandfather missed. I couldn't tell if they swam upstream or down because they simply disappeared. Several years later I tried my own variation of sucker-snagging, by lowering a weighted hook into a spring-fed Arkansas stream, to see if I could snag a big sucker resting on the bottom. As soon as the hook touched the fish, there was an explosion of speed as it moved to the lower end of the pool. I was younger then and more impressionable, but the speed of that fish impressed me just as much as that of the last bonefish I spooked in the Florida Keys.

Many fish sought by sport fishermen leap when hooked, and this certainly adds to the thrill of catching them. The noble Atlantic salmon is prized for its jumping ability as well as other sporting qualities. Probably the most aerial-minded of all trout is the rainbow, whose sea-run version, the lordly steelhead, is particularly notorious for wild leaps.

Both largemouth and smallmouth bass tend to jump when hooked, with the smallmouth, in my experience, taking to the air more often.

The tarpon is probably the champion jumper of all fish sought by sportsmen. These overgrown herring throw themselves around with an unholy abandon when hooked and have broken overhanging, broomstick-size mangrove limbs during their frenzied leaps. Should one happen to land in the boat after one of its jumps, discretion calls for immediately abandoning ship. Their tremendous strength and total wildness makes them a threat to life and limb at close quarters.

That certain something that makes a fish leap when hooked is highly desirable to sportsmen, but that doesn't explain the popularity of bonefish, walleyes, and cutthroat trout, which seldom if ever jump. And what about the flying-fish? Will we someday have a sport fishery for these creatures which seem to feel they are more bird and fish?

A big fish of a given species is always worth bragging about, and the lucky angler catching an unusually large specimen is sure to get his picture in the hometown paper. Such a fish has survived longer, under a barrage of fishing lures and baits, escaped more natural enemies, and has developed its protective instincts to a keener edge, than lesser members of its tribe.

More and more the northern pike has become a favorite of fishermen who head toward northern lakes for their vacations. This is Reed Lake, Manitoba.

But when we cross tribal lines and compare a species of fish that never gets very large with another noted for bulk, size begins to lose some of its meaning. A 20-pound carp may be a prize to my doughball-mixing friend but it's not likely to be honored by an ultra-purist trout fisherman.

Some species of fish seem to have studied knot-tying. At least I've hooked quite a few that knew just how to tie a line around the most convenient underwater obstruction. Some anglers say these fish are smart, others that they possess animal cunning. But such fish are actually just seeking shelter; and rocks, brush, and other obstructions are an automatic choice. On finding that the pull of a fisherman's lure persists after reaching such shelter, a fish will usually move on to other cover, tangling the line in the process.

Fish, such as rainbow trout and their sea-going steelhead brethren, Atlantic salmon, or shad, capitalize on the strength of moving water to try and escape the fisherman. Any angler hooking a big steelhead above a long, fast riffle needs track shoes or lots of line. These fish seem to always run downstream when hooked, and the fisherman must either make a record-breaking dash down the bank or, with enough line on the reel, let the fish run to the next pool and then follow at a more leisurely pace.

The first steelhead I hooked headed downstream with a savage rush, while boulders and logjams on the shore prevented me from following quickly enough. The fish hit the end of the line going full tilt, and that was the end of that. Now when I fish steelhead there's plenty of line on the reel, and I try to pick spots with the fewest obstructions along the shore.

There are many species of saltwater fish that live in and around coral reefs. Snappers and groupers in particular like the reef habitat, and catching them midst such hazards can be a trial. Some of the groupers are extremely powerful, and when hooked, generally swim into one of the coral caves. A fisherman's line, even of heavy test, cannot last long against sharp coral.

Fish that use every advantage offered by their environment, be it snags, coral, or a heavy current, offer a challenge that enriches the fishing experience. I've hooked brown trout that wedged themselves so tightly in thick mossbeds that I had to reach in and haul them out, moss and all. And just thinking of the largemouth bass I've lost to stumps and snags is enough to make me weep. When I do lead a fish through a series of underwater hazards, however, the suspense makes it a moment that lives forever.

Some fish are lovely to behold; others seem to be somewhat lacking in physical beauty. Most trout, for example,

A good many anglers go out looking for the trophy fishing only—as does this bass angler.

are colorful, especially at spawning time, and their stream-lined conformity, evolved to breast heavy currents, gives them an overall attractiveness to sportsmen. The brookie is probably easiest of all trouts to catch, but it is also among the highest prized by anglers. I suspect the primary reason for this is the brookie's wild, exotic beauty. I consider it the most colorful among America's commonly caught trout.

Even fish that are not very colorful or otherwise attractive have their following. Northern pike, chain pickerel, and muskellunge are far from winning any piscatorial beauty contest, but hordes of fishermen travel thousands of miles each year to fish for them. These fish have been called "water tigers" from the way they pounce from hiding.

Perhaps it's their wicked appearance and a reputation as efficient killers that attract anglers. Their vicious strike is a thrill few fishermen soon forget.

And then some fish just live in more beautiful surroundings than others. I've caught bluegills in Okefenokee Swamp, snook in Florida's Everglades, smallmouth bass in pastoral Ozark rivers, and trout in mountain streams of the West. In every case, I have thoroughly enjoyed both the scenery and the fishing.

There are anglers, however, who are more provincial. A southern swamp may appear foreboding to some, while a western stream, fishing across a sagebrush flat, lacks appeal to others. A river that's polluted or whose banks are littered with trash certainly detracts from any fishing experience there. So the esthetic qualities of a fish's home, as seen through the eyes of an angler, can add to the popularity of a particular species.

Why a certain species of fish should have greater appeal to a particular angler is a nebulous thing. The presence, or lack, of the various qualities I've discussed certainly influences such thinking, but there's no overlooking the personal attitude of the fisherman as a factor. And who can figure this out? I am not even sure I understand my own attitudes.

For example, I claim not to be particularly interested in eating fish—it's the sport of catching them that counts. Yet two experiences, one in freshwater and one in the salt, points up the hypocrisy of such an attitude.

Several years ago, while surf fishing on North Carolina's Outer Banks, I felt a sharp tug on the bait, and something powerful began taking out line. I was sure it could only be a good-sized red drum. After a lengthy seesaw battle, punctuated by moments of inactivity when I couldn't budge the fish, I finally landed the creature, and to my chagrin saw it was a big skate, a species of ray.

Sure I was disappointed—but why? The beast had given me a thrilling battle, and after all, I was certainly not interested in catching something to eat. Instincts are sometimes a better barometer of motives than thinking processes are.

Once while float-fishing Pennsylvania's Juniata River, I had a hard strike and saw a good-sized fish dash through a shallow area and into deeper water. I had apparently hooked a whopper smallmouth bass. After a hard fight that actually tired my arm, I boated a good-sized fallfish—a trash fish in most eastern streams.

Here was a fish that struck savagely at an artificial lure and then gave me a tremendous battle. Was my disappointment because fallfish are not as good to eat as bass? Perhaps I just wanted a fish I could brag about.

The soul-searching following these two experiences taught me not to be a fishing snob. I'm now convinced that any species of fish is a good catch—a prize worth the effort—and that an angler should go fishing when and where he can.

Because the finest fish I know just happens to be the one I'm currently trying to catch.

Reprinted from *Sport Fishing USA*. (The entire book may be obtained from the Superintendent of Documents, U.S. Government Printing Office, Washington, D.C. 20402. Price $10)

Giant tortoises once roamed in abundance on all of the Galapagos Islands, but now only a pitiful few remain.

GALAPAGOS ADVENTURE
The Wildlife Islands Nobody Knows
by Erwin A. Bauer

ON A still, steaming morning late in September 1835, the H.M.S. *Beagle* dropped anchor off San Cristobal Island and soon put ashore a small party of seamen. Farthest east in the Galapagos archipelago of the eastern Pacific, Cristobal then as now, was an island nobody knew. In the longboat, which a heavy swell carried onto a black cinder beach, was a 26 year old, chronically seasick, young naturalist, Charles Darwin.

What Darwin found ashore was unlike anything he had ever seen or ever even expected to see in a nightmare. Hordes of "hissing black lizards" slithered over brittle lava floes which had solidified into hideous shapes. He thought he could detect the smell of something burning, perhaps because he could feel the hot lava sand searing through the soles of his boots. A myriad of volcanic cones under an ugly, threatening sky reminded Darwin of the iron foundries back home in England.

"Nothing," Darwin wrote about that occasion, "could be less inviting than that first appearance."

But during the next 30 days the *Beagle* sailed among the 15 other Galapagos Islands and the naturalist landed to explore on a number of them. What Darwin found entirely changed his first impression. In addition to the stark land, reptiles and savage seascapes, he also found great undisturbed beauty. Millions of strange, theretofore unknown seabirds nested and paid no attention to humans who walked among and even touched them. Finches and mockingbirds perched on his shoulder. Darwin encountered tortoises which weighed as much as 500 pounds and marveled at the exotic vegetation.

In the bays and channels many kinds of fishes, sharks and green sea turtles were extremely abundant. At every anchorage the *Beagle's* sailors soon had their baited lines over the sides. "This sport," Darwin wrote, "makes all hands very merry; loud laughter and the heavy flapping of fish on the deck are heard on every side."

Summed up, probably no sea expedition since Columbus's discovery of the New World has been so important to mankind's knowledge as the voyage of the *Beagle*. From the unique wildlife he observed, collected and studied here, Darwin later wrote "Origin of the Species"—his radical new theory of evolution which enlightened people of the world today accept. But nowadays anyone can duplicate almost exactly the voyage of the *Beagle,* minus most of the hardships and uncertainties of almost a century and a half ago. Traveling in Darwin's wake can be the great adventure of anybody's lifetime. And oh, what fishing!!

Late last spring I made the Darwin-Galapagos trip with Joe Cross and Frank Sayers on the *Golden Cachalot,* a fine sailing vessel which is available for charter there. Joe and Frank are old hunting and fishing friends with whom I have wandered around the globe. Like the *Beagle,* the *Cachalot* is a 190-foot, 390 ton, 3-masted schooner. But launched in 1875 as a cargo ship and refitted (with modern plumbing and an echo sounder, for example) in 1969, it carried only 17 crew and passengers compared to the 75 officers and seamen jammed aboard the *Beagle*.

We flew Pan American to Guayaquil, Ecuador, and then hopped the 600 miles over water by Ecuadorian military flight to Baltra where exists the only airstrip in the Galapagos. The landing site was built as a U.S. base during World War II to protect against submarine attacks on Panama Canal shipping. Soldiers stationed here considered themselves on the most isolated of all military outposts. We boarded the *Golden Cachalot* at Baltra and soon were head-

← While trolling close to shore, we pass pair of Galapagos penguins, the only penguins in existence above the Equator.

ing eastward across an unbelievably calm sea. Destination: the north side of Isla Santa Cruz or Indefatigable Island. Take your choice because all islands have both Spanish and English names, the latter having been given during early whaling days.

From our anchorage in early morning, this part of Santa Cruz might have been somewhere in the Bahamas or Florida Keys. Dense mangrove forests fringed a maze of tidal lagoons, but there the similarity ended. At the lagoon entrance our landing boat had to squeeze past giant turtles and shoals of spawning rays. Deeper in the lagoon night herons flushed from mangroves and schools of fish cruised underneath. Frank and I recognized them immediately as snook.

There was only one casting outfit in our boat and I snapped a surface plug onto a metal leader. On the first cast several snook charged the lure, one caught it and danced a wild ballet on top to get rid of it. But a second snook caught the plug almost in the air and that four-pounder we boated.

I have never seen snook fishing to match what followed in these Santa Cruz lagoons. Maybe it cannot be matched anywhere. It was only necessary, we proved a number of times, to poke the rod tip in the water and maneuver a lure—any lure—under the boat. A snook would strike it and then come cartwheeling out of the water, sometimes

We catch vast assortment of colorful groupers wherever we anchor among the islands. That's Joe Cross holding a golden.

Land iguana thrives on a few islands of the archipelago. The only marine iguanas anywhere on earth are very numerous.

Waved albatross flies past our ship far out at sea. This huge bird nests only on Hood Island.

up into the mangrove limbs. Anyway, we could have filled the boat with enough snook to sink it if that had been our goal. Instead we kept enough to feed crew and guests.

Tower (or Genovesa), northeasternmost of the Galapagos, required an all-night cruise from Santa Cruz. We arrived on choppy seas at daybreak and, escorted by a pod of porpoises, sailed into the suddenly smooth harbor which is really the inside of a mountain crater. Tower is a flat-topped volcanic peak surrounded by Pacific Ocean, but long ago the surf had broken through one portion of the crater wall to permit entry into the nearly circular sanctuary by small ships. Let me try to describe the scene "inside."

The white-frosted black cliffs loomed high above the masts of the *Golden Cachalot* which lay almost motionless at anchor. Fur seals literally dropped out of caves in the cliffs and swam out to investigate us. A crew member with a hand line overboard hooked a fish, but a huge shark inhaled the fish, and the man, suddenly with more than he could handle, pulled in nothing. Boobies circled overhead and then large numbers landed in the rigging to watch us enjoy al fresco breakfast on the deck below. But a school of fish exploded on the surface nearby and the boobies hurried away in search of their own breakfast. After coffee, we lowered the skiffs to go ashore.

Tower is among the toughest places to land because it lacks the splendid beaches of most other islands. Instead we scrambled ashore on slippery rocks and then used ropes to climb up through a deep fissure to the top of the cliff.

There it is flat, brushy and seething with birds—actually with a million or more birds, both in and out of sight. Their calls create a constant loud din.

Underground in cracks and crevices were shearwaters and petrels. On the edges of cliffs were the exquisite swallow-tailed gulls, known only to the Galapagos. Above ground nested the boobies, doves and frigates, the latter in such concentrations that their swollen red throat pouches resembled a vast berry field. Some birds were incubating; others were feeding tiny, grotesque chicks. Tower is an immense bird spectacle.

But when cruising in the Galapagos, the spectacle never really ends. On remote Hood Island, the main attractions are the giant waved or Galapagos albatrosses with 7-foot wingspans and without fear of human visitors. Cormorants which cannot fly and the only penguins north of the Equator live here. The world's only marine iguanas frequent most rocky shorelines and are beautiful or horrible to see, depending on how you look at primitive reptiles.

Troll close to any shoreline and you will catch fish—both such familiar ones as bonitos and dolphin, as well as species seldom seen and perhaps not even yet cataloged by science. In a busy afternoon off Bartolome Island, we caught five species of groupers, including one pure yellow-gold in color. Try to find that one in any fish identification volume!

Tiny Plaza Island is the home of brightly colored land iguanas which will pick cigarettes from your pocket. On

Great frigate bird displays inflated ruby chest during courtship on Tower Island.

Young frigate bird sits on Tower Island nest and waits to be fed.

Floreana Island we mailed letters (delivered 3 months later) in a barrel mail box which has been used by mariners since 1792. Any boat which happens along picks up any mail going in its direction, but too often the interval between boats is very long.

When diving in James Bay we found a treasure of amphorae scattered over the rocky bottom. Some were broken, a few were intact. Most likely a Spanish buccaneer had jettisoned the earthen wine or water vessels at least two centuries before us. On James Island a hermit, the only inhabitant of a salt mine ghost town abandoned long ago, guided us far up into steep mountain forests where we found giant land tortoises. Once these existed in astronomical numbers, but for over a century every whaler and pirate in the Pacific stopped long enough to capture them for fresh meat. The tortoises could live on board until ready for slaughter; other fresh meats wouldn't keep under the hot sun. Nowadays the tortoises are in short supply and on some islands, gravely endangered.

Without the abundant and wonderfully confiding wildlife, the Galapagos Islands would probably be completely unknown today, as far as they are from the important travel and shipping lanes. But now there is another magnet besides the birds and reptiles to attract more and more visitors. It is complete escape.

Where else can you go today and, except in a few bleak, scattered communities, go fishing and see no one else except those in your own party? Only four of the islands are inhabited. The Galapagos are not as lush and tropical as Hawaii or Tahiti, but where else can you enjoy miles of golden sand beaches with no other swimmers or divers except a few curious sea lions and fur seals.

In truth, the fishing around the islands has never really been explored. Probably there are cruising billfish. While traveling one night a sudden collision rocked the boat and all hands feared we were aground. But the water was deep. In the morning a crew member found where a marlin had rammed into the hull, breaking off its bill and leaving it imbedded in 10″ of wood. Diving equipment was necessary to repair the "wound."

Bill of marlin which rammed *Golden Cachalot* during night. This part was extracted from the hull.

◄ Frank Sayers casts shoreward from foredeck of *Golden Cachalot*. Note the strange volcanic shore in the background.

Our 3-masted schooner, which is similar to Darwin's *Beagle*, at anchor off Indefatigable Island. We caught groupers close to the foreground rock.

The archipelago remained a blank space on navigation charts until 1535 when Tomas de Berlanga, a bishop of Panama, found it by accident during a storm. Since then the islands have been only the haunts of pirates, whalers, a few disillusioned colonizers and a good assortment of eccentrics, many on the lam from European gaols. Among the latter was a self-styled Austrian baroness who arrived in 1932 with two male escorts and not much else. She proclaimed herself Empress of the islands, but fell on hard times and is believed to have eaten at least one of her friends. Anyhow neither was ever seen intact again.

The Galapagos, which are bisected by the Equator, belong to Ecuador. The weather is always warm, usually dry, but except on lava flows when the sun is directly overhead, never unbearably hot. The seas average very calm and, being in a doldrums latitude, storms are rarities. However, the fertile Humboldt Current guarantees astronomical quantities of marine life around the islands. Altogether the situation permits cruising the year around by the *Golden Cachalot*. Now bookings for the schooner, as well as for visits to the Galapagos by steamship, are handled by Lindblad Travel Inc., 133 E. 55th St., New York, N.Y. 10022.

How to Cook Fish Deliciously

Deliciously

by PEGGY PETERS

...When You Don't Know How

Freshly caught fish make a superb meal. These are fried at Gates of the Mountains on the Missouri River in Montana.

ALRIGHT, let us assume the worst: you are in possession of a fish, or worse yet, several fish and it is your job to cover that series of steps which will culminate in the moment when the fish will be served. In short, *you* will cook the fish.

Your fisherman has already successfully completed his end: selection of the fishing area and the proper tackle: employment of his own knowledge and skill in its use and with patience, good humor and perseverence in evidence throughout. He has now arrived at your elbow grinning widely, slightly sun-burned and sporting an aroma which might be called "Essence de Poisson."

Now fear not, but advance boldly to attack the problem. First, look at the fish. He (?) is no doubt dead and therefore poses no threat to your physical safety. The purpose of this first step is to determine whether or not said creature is cleaned. Crouch down a bit and take a quick glance at his tummy. With any luck you'll note a slit from chin to tail indicating the innards have been disposed of. If you do not find such a slit I suggest you recall the aforementioned angler and confidently assert that the cleaning of fish falls within the responsibility of the catcher, not the

cooker. While you have him there tactfully inquire as to the species of fish you have.

Next you must make two judgments: one as to size and the other as to whether your fish is fat or lean. Fat, in this case has nothing to do with calories, exercise, over-eating, etc. Fish are *born* fat or lean depending upon the amount of natural oil in the tissue. Salt water fish tend to be fatter than fresh and these include bluefish, mackerel, grayling, tuna and trout (this family includes salmon and steelhead). The lean fellows are all the little "pan-fish": halibut, bass, pike and sole (flounder). In cooking "fat" fish the idea is to allow that oil to drain away from the cooking fish; therefore a large fat fish could be baked on a rack or grilled over coals, but would probably not taste its best fried or foil-wrapped or cooked in any manner which would trap it in its own juices.

Obviously, the lean fish require the opposite treatment. These could be fried, baked in a shallow pan under a coating of fat you apply, foiled roasted or grilled—*if* you can find a willing soul to stand in attendance and baste the flesh frequently with a magic potion you, you clever creature, have concocted. Let this magical substance be mainly melted butter with a little corn or peanut oil added. This raises burning temperature so you are less likely to incinerate the mixture. No one likes burned butter, especially on fish! While melting the butter, add small bits of onion and/or garlic and scoop them out just before the basting procedure begins. A wedge of lemon added to the finished dish would make it appear that you spent your early years studying under Dionne Lucas, James Beard and Julia Child. Tastes good too!

Now as the second judgment: size. The little fellows are best fried or grilled whole, the jumbos do well baked and most of those in between can be filleted and then pan-fried or grilled. Should you be confronted with a variety of fish, despair not. Think soup. We'll get to this shortly. It's easy and delicious and you'll love it.

The question of removing the heads and tails must inevitably come up. Now, as a novice fish-chef this is a distressing subject but nonetheless one that must be faced. Take heart in the knowledge that in the case of small fish, they're better left on. Sometimes it looks attractive for baked fish to have theirs too. On the other hand it is grimly true that at times the wretched things just will not fit in the pan, grill or whatever as they are and you'll just have to get a grip on yourself and do the job. A good, heavy, sharp knife will be your best friend. Tails are easy: just "thwock" right through. With the heads try to leave as much of the good meat as possible which will mean two or three good slices before you are done. Remember this is the worst part. Once done, you're almost home free. Courage! You probably will not believe right now that the day might come when you will actually save the heads, tails and bones for fish stock. Small quantities of stock in the freezer are grand for making fish soups, sauces and even as the liquid required in a mundane canned tuna casserole.

When frying the small ones you can use the same fat as described for basting grilled fish, or oil alone, or bacon fat. Get it quite hot, but not smoking. Make a few slits along the back bone so the little devils won't curl up fetal-fashion on you and it's done when the skin begins to wrinkle. If you really believe it couldn't possibly be done yet gently poke the fish with the tip of a sharp knife at

Even the kids can cook delicious foil-wrapped fish. Let young imaginations run free with seasonings for their own package.

the dorsal fin (that's the one which would be "up" when he was swimming) and twist a bit. If no juice runs, it is done. Whatever you do, don't overcook fish and remember it'll even cook a bit between pan and palate. Fish "flesh" isn't really flesh at all, but muscle and the cooking is done to firm up the muscle, not to tenderize as in red meats.

Baking fish could really be your speciality, especially if the catch at your place runs to the big ones, say over 2 to 3 pounds. First, you needn't bother removing the head and tail; second, it doesn't need your constant attention while it cooks; third, it tastes marvelous and fourth, and last, it looks so elegant. Good fish for baking are halibut, pike, striped bass, sea bass, blue fish and even cod. The simplest procedure is to season the cavity with salt, pepper (freshly ground, if possible) and some chopped onion or a favorite herb. Some of those dried herbs could topple Muhammad Ali when cooked, so be circumspect. I'm still trying to forget the night when my favorite fisherman was driven from the table due to an overdose of tarragon. Grease the creature in any manner that suits you and pop it into a hot oven. A 2- to 2½-pounder should be done in about 20 minutes. The test for doneness is simple and works no matter how you prepare fish. Put an ordinary dinner fork into the flesh and pull up gently. The fish is done when it flakes easily.

The second easiest way to bake fish is to split it almost all the way through and lay it flat skin-side down on a greased pan or baking dish. Season it, grease it (perhaps with dots of butter here and there) and bake in that hot oven for a very short time. Obviously in this method, the head and tail must be removed. I've done this more times than seems possible with blue fish caught off the south shore of Long Island. It tastes impossibly divine with a tomato and fresh basil salad, crisp French bread and a dry white wine or frosty beer.

For the master coup in fish baking try stuffing the fish. The stuffing is basically bread crumbs and for the "Plain Jane" variety just do what you would to stuff poultry. Dry the cavity of the fish, salt it, add the stuffing, and close the pocket using skewers, string, thread or whatever is handy. This, too, is baked in a really hot oven: 400 or 425 degrees. A 3- to 4-pounder will take 30 to 40 minutes and a 4- to 5-pounder about 45 to 50 mintues. Figure 4 pounds of fish will make about six servings.

An easy way to insure your masterpiece doesn't fall apart en route to the table is to line the greased pan with a double thickness of foil (grease this too) having the piece wide enough to dangle over the pan at the ends. Fold the excess into handles and use them when transferring the fish to the platter.

To make your stuffing really outstanding add some variety of shell fish to the basic mixture, even if it's canned or frozen! Try sea bass with crabmeat, striped bass with shrimp or freshly poached oysters or almost any fish species with a tomato, onion and mushroom combination. Be adventurous! Garnish the platter with all the color you can manage: parsley bunches, hard-cooked eggs, lemon wedges, carrot curls. "Marvelous" will describe both the looks and the taste of your creation.

One of the really basic ways to handle fish is to fillet it. I have even known people so fortunate as to regularly be presented with fish in this delightful condition. Once in possession of these headless, tailless, skinless and finless portions the cook is free to prepare them in numberless ways without further preliminaries. She could even freeze them. However it seems likely that you, like most of us, will have to fillet the finned friends yourself and, assuming the fish have already been gutted, here's how: slit along the backbone from head to tail loosening the meat all the way.

Then cut a notch just behind the head and from there slice down on a diagonal line toward the rear. Do this on both sides and then loosen the skin. Now comes the fun part. Grab the head with one hand and the loose skin with the other and peel off the skin from front to back. With a nice sharp knife slice off the fillet working from head to tail. Do this on both sides, of course. This is a lovely skill to acquire. You *look* so professional doing it and there are so many varieties to do it to! Consider all these: bass, haddock, flounder, blue fish, perch, bluegill and more, more, more. This art can make you a Fish Fixer Extraordinaire! You, who thought you couldn't manage to get a fish dinner together!

Alright, now you have these fillets and you may bake, broil, panfry or roll them in crumbs and fry in deep fat. You can also cook them out-of-doors over coals. One of those long-handled wire grills is handy. Do be sure, though, that if you have one of the oily fishes the oils don't drip right onto the coals and then smoke. It smells just awful and can even give the fish a bad taste. To avoid this scrape away the coals directly under the fish or catch the drippings in a pan and *don't* spill it during the emptying process! I happen to know first-hand the disasters which await the

spiller of fish oils. Picture a soft, summer evening. A congenial assemblage of family and friends gathered on a brick patio. Flowers bloom, libations flow, sun sets, husband grills main course (trout) over coals in new BBQ and I catch fish oils in a miserable tinny tray. Tray fills; I attempt to pour into near-by empty coffee can; miss. Bricks saturated forever with oil; shoes no charity will accept; hostess gown in rag bag. Friends, relatives and children amazed and startled by your grasp of the English language. Don't spill fish oil.

Gourmet magazine prints a recipe from Restaurante Fabiola on the Costa del Sol which might avoid disaster and sounds delicious: "Cut 1½ lbs. bass or sole fillets into serving pieces. Sprinkle the fish lightly with salt and pepper. In a skillet just large enough to hold the fish brown the fillets on both sides in 2 tbsp. butter and 1 tbsp. oil for 5 minutes. Sprinkle the fish with ¼-cup finely chopped parsley, 1 garlic clove, minced, and 3 tbsp. lemon juice and cook it over low heat for 5 minutes, or until it flakes easily. Serves four."

Since you are new to the fish business you may not know that it is estimated that there are 20 million freshwater fishermen (they count licenses sold) and probably about

A family camping-fishing vacation can easily be one that no member will remember without pleasure. Each family member can find it exciting and rewarding experience, one which may be repeated annually.

Trout seasoned with salt, pepper and dehydrated onion bits and lightly oiled will grill to a delicious doneness.

10 to 15 million more who fish the salt waters. Now 30 million fishermen can't all be wrong, and besides you can't fight numbers like that. Consider joining 'em. Honestly, it's good fun!

Ladies whose sanity has never been doubted and whose femininity has never been questioned are known to really enjoy the sport. They're right out there having a fine time. And don't you think it does everyone good to see mama on the other end of a fishing rod rather than a floor mop and on the other side of a campfire rather than a bridge table? You're darned right it does! If this continues we might even insist that the word "fishperson" be used.

If you do go along with your fishperson and plan to cook the fish on the spot there are just a few things you should bring along. Dehydrated onion bits, salt, pepper, salad oil, imitation bacon bits and an honest-to-goodness lemon. With these ingredients you can fry the catch over the fire, grill it over coals, or bake it in foil. My pre-teenage girls love to cook in foil, and really turn out delicious meals this way.

They place a fish on a double thickness of greased foil, sprinkle the inside with salt, pepper and onion and bacon bits, grease the outside of the fish and triple fold all the edges to seal. Each fish is a separate bundle and these are placed on glowing coals. A 2-pounder cooks in about 20 minutes. If the trip happens to be a first class type and we have real bacon, a strip wrapped around the outside of the fish is delightful. Another nice—almost chic—addition is wild chive snips. Once you can recognize the globular lavender flower heads, finding this delightful member of the onion family in the wild is easy. Don't use those flowering, though; choose the milder non-flowering leaves. Needless to say, if in a national park, Thou shalt *not* pick!

If the day's catch consists of small sized fish, there's another way to prepare them which you'll appreciate. Everyone does his own, and even the small fry (!) can manage it. Send the kids off to find themselves and you a hickory (or any hardwood) branch as long as his arm and slim. Do not accept piney stuff; it spatters. (Once again, if you're in

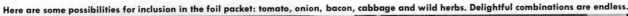

Here are some possibilities for inclusion in the foil packet: tomato, onion, bacon, cabbage and wild herbs. Delightful combinations are endless.

This large home smoker allows the angler to enjoy his catch weeks and months later. Obviously, there will be an abundance for distribution to delighted neighbors, too.

a national park this is a no-no.) Each person will also need a Y-shaped stick which is driven into the ground near the fire. Have each mini-chef impale his fish (whole and cleaned) tail to nose on his branch leaving about 6 inches protruding at the nose end. Rest this leading end in the crotch of the Y-shaped piece and slowly turn the fish a few inches above the coals until done. It's better by far for the soul and body than franks.

Aside from stews, soups probably allow the cook the most latitude for expressing herself and/or the ingredients available. Fish soup is no different. Whenever you don't know what to do with what you have: too little fresh, to little of yesterday's, not enough of anything etc., etc. . . . make soup. Fish soups are usually made with lean fish and using as many varieties as possible. That fits right in with that mixed bag you have on hand, doesn't it? The inclusion of some gelatinous types is desirable. These include bass, eel, flounder, haddock, halibut, perch, drum, snapper, trout and weakfish. For the base start with bottled clam juice or some of that fish stock you so cleverly have in the freezer, and add a can of tomato paste and some garlic. Toss in any fish bones you have and water, if necessary, and let this mixture cook for about 30 to 40 minutes. Then remove the bones and add something for body: spaghetti, vermicelli, potatoes or eggs. This is the time to "express yourself" by adding any

Smoking fish are examined by this expert. The right kind of wood, ➤ correct temperature and proper seasonings determine the quality of the finished product.

Freezing is what is usually done with fish not eaten shortly after they are caught; but smoking, which can be done at home too, is another fine way to preserve them.

likely-looking left-over from the refrigerator. When this is well along add the final touch: the fish, cut into 2-inch pieces. Do any stirring gently in order to keep the pieces whole and serve just as soon as the fish is cooked through. Served with crusty rolls and a green salad, this is a fine meal.

Another fine meal is one our whole family enjoyed on a beautiful Pacific Northwest beach not long ago. It was Potlatch, which is a salmon feast the likes of which none of us had ever seen, smelled or tasted before. The word Potlatch comes from the Chinook meaning gift or giving and it marked the tribe's communal feasts. The Northwest Indians have been preparing their magnificent salmon in this delectable way for centuries. They marinate chunks for several hours, then lash the pieces to sticks which are propped over a fire and the fish slowly cooks in the smoke of its own sputtering juices. The resulting aroma is indescribable and if it weren't for the availability of plump steamed clams I honestly fear that some members of our party would have succumbed to the proddings of their stomachs with disasterous results. We all ate far too much but never got to the "don't-ever-mention-Potlatch-to-me-again" stage. It was just too delicious for that. In fact I've even tried it at home and you may want to, also. I must admit that even at its best, it just never did measure up to the original, but even second rate is marvelous. The whole secret is the marinade, of course, *but* all I can tell you is the ingredients. The proportions were never revealed to me, so just obey your instincts. You can hardly miss. Use butter, garlic, salt, pepper, oregano, rosemary, paprika, dry parsley, celery seed (or celery salt) and Tabasco. Lashing the pieces to sticks is picturesque and probably the proper way to cook the salmon, but greeted with the limitations of civilization we must alter things a bit. Try placing the meat on a wire mesh frame over coals, slathering on some of the marinade, and covering with a sheet of aluminum foil. The marinade will drip down onto the coals and steam and smoke will rise up cooking the salmon and creating the same aroma we first smelled on that blessed strand in Washington.

It's bound to happen that one day someone will present you with a whole batch of small bluegills. At least I hope it will happen because then you can make use of this formula for deviled bluegill. Bill Gressard from Kent, Ohio, gave me the recipe and I've honored his name ever since. Bill's business is raising bass to sell for stocking, so he should know something about fish, and he does. With precious few motions Bill fillets his fish, skims off the scales, and proceeds thusly: 4 cups bluegill meat (drop fillets in boiling water, bring to boil again—remove and drain)

1 cup milk
4 thick slices white bread, crusts removed
¼-lb. butter
3 tbsp. chopped parsley
1½ tbsp. grated onion
¾-tsp. salt (or to taste) & dash pepper
dash Tabasco sauce
3 tbsp. Worcestershire sauce
1 tsp. dry mustard
1 green pepper and 1 pimento finely cut

Cook everything but the fish for 10 minutes, stirring. Then add the fish and cook 5 minutes. Put in a flat casserole and sprinkle crumbled corn flakes lightly over the top. Brown in a moderate (350 degree) oven 10 to 15 minutes. Serves six smiling people.

So here you are, cooking fish deliciously without knowing how. It's the best way.

Bon Appetit

Salad Bowl Bass

Fishing big bass bugs in heavy cover of grass and lily pads.

by CHARLES WATERMAN

AT FIRST glance it looked like a very short man walking through an alfalfa field. But he kept casting as he went along and finally there was considerable splashing, after which he rummaged around in the foliage and came up with a 5-pound largemouth. Until then I didn't know bass lived in stuff that thick but in the 40 years since then I have caught my biggest bass in what looked like poorly kept lawns.

Bass hide from people and the things bass eat hide from bass. You can lump all of it off as "cover" of one kind or another, ranging from coontail moss to old truck tires. Many fishermen have spent a lifetime fishing around the edges of such things without ever getting in where the landscaping is really dense. This is about the thick stuff.

This isn't light tackle fishing for when the fish is hooked you find yourself fighting both him and his habitat and you may have to land part of his environment along with him. Grass and weed fishermen lean toward 20-pound-test

baitcasting line, better than 10-pound line on spinning outfits, and the type of fly tackle most commonly seen in salt water or on steelhead rivers. This is no place for the delicate touch and if I had my choice for pure efficiency it would include a husky baitcasting rig with the heaviest line I could cast conveniently. The majority of grass, weed and bonnet (lily pad) fishermen use fairly large lures that can be chunked well with heavy outfits.

So what's the bass doing in there before your dingus comes along?

Well, in warm, sunny weather he may be loafing on the bottom, completely shaded by vegetation. He might be moving slowly along the more open underwater channels with an eye out for food. Although the bass is primarily a near-bottom resident, there are times when he travels above the tops of submerged grasses or even lies there quietly—and that's a time when he can be especially spooky and might even prefer a small lure presented daintily. That

Author nets good fish for Jack Gowdy who caught it on a shoreline eelgrass flat shrouded by hyacinths.

is the exceptional case which keeps me from making flat statements about the crudity of thick-stuff angling.

A bass on the bottom and surrounded by underwater grass has a very limited range of vision. He is most likely to go on the prod because he hears something that sounds like a meal or because he feels water or plant vibrations from it. When the flora is thoroughly tangled, the twitch of a single stem can be felt 10 or 15 feet away. Since it may take a while for the fish to thread his way through such a salad, many casters say the very slowly working lure is best. Otherwise, the poor old fish may not be able to catch up with it.

The other argument is that the fast-moving lure covers so much territory it's seen by a lot of fish at close range and they don't have far to go. There are days for both kinds of presentation. If you're skipping a spoon along the surface it's a good idea to make your casts close together so that you'll get a second crack at a fish which was aroused by a previous attempt.

Most of the baits used in heavy cover are intended to be weedless but it isn't always so. I once watched a guy launch an 8-foot homemade boat, paddle it out into a tangle that would discourage a watersnake and then throw out a big popping bug that appeared designed to snag everything in sight. Then he lighted his pipe and just sat there. Every little while he'd twitch the bug but he never moved it more than 3 inches. He couldn't. While I was snickering at this uninformed amateur there was an explosion and he hooked a bass 10 minutes after he'd made his cast. He was waiting for fish to come by and several of them did. I don't like to talk about this because I didn't catch anything by fishing the way any intelligent angler should.

Except for plastic worms, which are increasingly popular in the weeds, few of the most successful artificials are close imitations of anything that lives. Through the years my most successful weed and grass lure has been the "wiggler," generally a spinner up front, a heavy and streamlined body for casting, and a rubber or bucktail skirt. Sometimes a porkrind or pork frog is added. There are a number of such lures, some of them intended for rapid reeling across the

57

Big bass (largest, nine pounds) are taken by Walter Dineen in the Everglades. Dineen is a specialist in lightweight spoons and surface lures, somewhat smaller than those commonly used in heavy cover.

Forrest Ware, fisheries biologist, takes scientific advantage of large-mouths by using big popping bugs and a husky fly rod.

surface—call those "cluckers" if you want. Real experts on the topwater ones tune them very carefully by bending or remodeling the spinners to suit themselves. I've had more consistent success with the ones that work equally well on top or under the surface. With a fast reel you can keep them on top and throwing a little flick of water now and then, or you can keep them just deep enough to create a slight surface wake, or you can drop them down into the underwater greenery and yank them from hangup to minor hangup.

The user of such a lure has quite a repertoire. On the same cast he can retrieve rapidly on top, allow the thing to dive into obvious holes in the cover, and then keep it at mid-depth for a while. For that matter, he can let it sink clear to the bottom, rest for a few seconds, and then bring it to the surface with a rush. An expert wiggler jockey is apt to move his rod on the retrieve and one observer said he'd think a man could decide how he wanted to do it after all that practice and wouldn't have to make all those adjustments. But, the adjustments are part of the

game, and if one particular phase of the retrieve gets most of the fish, you can eliminate the other moves for the day.

I'd say that the wobbling spoon, with or without a spinner in front, is most popular of all weedy water baits. Most of these have a single hook with weed guard and I don't find them the best bass holders, even when they're the best strike getters, but losing an acrobatic client now and then is much better than not getting the strikes.

If a weedy water spoon is fished on top I've found that a pork frog is a big help, keeping the hook up and avoiding all sorts of weed snagging. The frog is an extra added attraction in most cases and has a stabilizing effect that minimizes line twisting as well as keeping the hook out of trouble. Wobbling spoons are fished much the same as the wigglers and there are days when it's almost impossible to be too violent with them, a healthy yank sometimes flipping one into the air like a jumping baitfish.

I have generally liked light colors in the wiggler skirts, using yellow about as much as anything else. White is fine and you can hedge your bets by mixing the two although

Nine-pound bass that took a wiggler for Debie Waterman in eelgrass.

When all of the growth is beneath the surface, conventional topwater baits are fine. With accurate casting you can work the open places, even when the grass sticks well above the water, but weedless surface baits aren't too common in most tackle lines. One disadvantage of the weedless surface bait is that a heavy weedguard fends off strikes that would be well-hooked with a lure moving rapidly. When a bait is being moved gently on top, the fish doesn't get as solid a shot as when the lure is going fast. When using a weedless surface lure you must be prepared to strike back hard—and with a stiff rod.

A big torpedo-shaped plug with fore-and-aft spinners that runs above sunken grass tops and makes a trace of wake is about the surest hooker I've ever used. It's coming fast, it has no weedguards, and the rod's stiff, but conditions have to be just right for its use—a nice open area above the lawn.

Although live bait fishing in the grass has its problems, I've seen it done effectively with large shiners, the operators using a float and allowing the bait to find its way through the cover. One of the most effective shiner users I've watched used a float and drifted across an eelgrass flat in a brisk breeze with the line running out behind the boat. Since the water was quite shallow and the boat usually passed over the fish before the bait arrived, that fisherman was as quiet as a waiting heron and liked to do his thing alone. He kept his float set so that the big shiner moved just above the submerged grass tops, usually no more than a foot down. That was in Florida, and although I don't know that it was necessary, he used a hyacinth bulb as a float, fearing a gaudy cork or plastic gadget would scare fish.

When you have to work your catch through a wet hayfield to get it to the boat you'll find that long casts are a handicap. The more line you have out the more leeway the fish has and the harder it is to set the hook. Bass accustomed to living in grass often burrow almost straight down when hooked and the quicker you can get the rod tip over him the better. If you use a net you're likely to land more pounds of greenery than pounds of fish at best. Also, a fish has a lot of things to hook your bait to when he's wallowing around down there. Such landings are certainly not spectacular, however exciting they can be, Frankly, there are many fishermen who don't like to play a fish in clogged water where there's little chance for quick runs or high jumps.

When I used to wade-fish for bass in some shallow, weed-choked Kansas ponds, I soon learned that business of getting the rod over the fish. I used fly-rod bugs and as soon as the fish took I'd flounder toward it while trying to maintain a tight line. The closer I got to the boils and splashes the more the upward pressure and I'd get the rod as high as possible. Many times the fish would simply give up and come up on his side. I have always used heavy fly rods for weed fishing and even when you don't hook any fish you'll find the extra beef is fine when you grab hold with both hands to pull out of the frequent hangups.

There's a rule that when a fish goes away from you in the grass you should lean on him with all the power the tackle will stand; when he heads toward you, let him pick his own way through the grass. If you hurry him too much when he's coming your way you'll simply yank him into a bad situation. I have seen bass of more than 10 pounds landed in less than 30 seconds in heavy stuff, simply because they headed toward the net and the fishermen let them come. That might be poor sportsmanship in open water but it's cool operation in the goop.

As the cigarette advertiser said, it isn't for everybody, but grass and weed fishing has its own unusual appeals—and it catches a lot of bass too.

local preferences make more sense than general rules. If you want the skirts to flare and present a wider silhouette, stick them on backward. The wiggler bodies are usually fairly small and I have no color preference there, although I've used yellow more than anything else. For many years, the nickel and gold spoons had things pretty much to themselves but they're using them in color these days and pure, shiny black has its days. I am convinced there are times when spoon color can change the score drastically.

The first time I ever saw a plastic worm used on the surface was over a forest of elodea and the operator twitched it along like any other surface bait, letting a striking fish take it well down before he set the hook. Other systems involve keeping the worm moving pretty fast and striking back the instant the fish takes. Then there's the worm worked clear down on the bottom and moved slowly through the stems, some of them using weedguards and others with the barb buried in the worm itself. Almost any worm tactics that work anywhere else can work in heavy vegetation and the ideal tackle is the same. If anything, the rod should be even stiffer than that for open water worm fishing for the weedless arrangement soaks up some of your strike and thick grass can hamper in other ways.

Tincup Lake Lodge, while unpretentious, offers anglers what they could find at few other places: unfished or nearly-unfished lakes and streams, proximity to Kluane National Park and an abundance of wildlife seldom seen by temperate zone denizens.

A YUKON GRAYLING HOT SPOT

by Karl Maslowski

AS THE raven flies, Tincup Lake Lodge is about 25 miles north of Milepost 1118 on the Alaskan Highway in the Yukon Territory. That would place the Lake about 160 miles due northwest of Whitehorse. My son, Steve, and I flew into Tincup Lake perhaps even more directly than the raven might fly it—via helicopter. A bird might want to detour around some of the 6,000 foot peaks over which we passed with ease.

The Lodge offers anglers a unique fishing experience inasmuch as the operator, Ray Conant, ferries his guests to a wide variety of sub-arctic waters other than Tincup Lake in his small chopper. Thus, one day might be spent fishing for northern pike at Wellesly Lake; another day he may drop you off at Sockeye Lake to search out rainbow trout and Kokanee; and on still another he might drop you off somewhere where you will do your own angling research to see just what kind of fish are at home in a rarely—if ever—fished stream or lake. At this point in time much of the area for a hundred miles around Tincup Lake is still being researched for its sport fishing potential.

When Steve and I arrived at Tincup in early June, prospects for any kind of angling other than ice fishing appeared remote because of a very late spring. Most of the lakes we passed over were still sheathed rim to rim with heavy ice, and Tincup itself had only a narrow 50 to 75 foot wide strip thawed around its upper 5 miles. The one exception was a 100 foot wide arc at the mouth of a small unnamed stream that flows into the lake within sight of the Lodge.

It looked like ideal grayling water and proved to be all of that. On his first cast with a black gnat, Steve hooked and landed a 2-pound Arctic grayling. It was a fine male with a high sail-like dorsal fin heavily spotted and tinged with pink along the outer edge. The body appeared to be cased in gleaming bronze when seen from one angle, and then from another it appeared to exude a lilac-like glow.

Steve, I, and other guests were to repeat this performance many more times at that precise spot in the next few days while we waited for more open water.

Naive Yukon grayling yield to the appeal of dull pattern flies. If these fish had ever seen a human they obviously did not associate him with danger.

Dall sheep rams race across the landscape of Kluane National Park, Canada's newest. The author was often able to get within 40 to 50 yards of the handsome white animals.

The wait was not a monotonous one. Ray arranged for Robert Dunbar, a fellow helicopter pilot, to take Steve and I into neighboring Kluane National Park to see its scenic grandeur and wildlife. The glaciers alone in this newest of Canadian National Parks are worth a trip to the Yukon Territory. And perhaps nowhere in the world will one find a heavier concentration of Dall sheep. We saw more than a thousand of these handsome white animals during our stay and had rare opportunities to film them both in motion pictures and stills. It was simply a question of landing on a flat mountain top and then cautiously working our way

Helicopter pilot Bob Dunbar and author Maslowski discuss the fishing potential at the lake chosen for the day's angling activities.

Joanne Jonzen, the camp cook, landed a lake trout which in pounds, is more than her age in years! Happily, her cooking ability matched or surpassed her angling skills.

The author's son, Steve, lands a 10-pound Tincup Lake trout. His obvious delight with the catch and his surroundings is understandable.

toward a band of from ten to 50 sheep maybe a mile away. Often we were able to get within 40 to 50 yards of the sheep.

In the course of our Dall sheep stalks we also encountered a whole menagerie of other wildlife: barren lands, caribou, moose, ground squirrels, weasels, golden eagles, willow ptarmigan, hawk owls, and even a single Toklat grizzly bear!

Tincup Lake itself proved to be a pretty fair fishing hole even though we were limited for a time to casting the narrow, thawed shoreline strip mentioned earlier. Small lake trout up to 3 pounds would rarely permit a spinner or spoon to be retrieved without being hooked. Such fish on a 4-pound test line provided constant action and the main course for superb meals.

Despite the lack of big expanses of open water, Tincup fairly swarmed with waterbirds during the early days of our visit. White-winged scoters, goldeneyes, oldsquaws, and bizarrely plumaged harlequin ducks dispersed themselves close to shore in the icy waters, along with Arctic loons and terns. Moreover, we found both Bonaparte's and mew

Kluane National Park where the glaciers alone make the trip to the Yukon worthwhile.

Barren lands caribou such as these, plus many other mammals and Arctic birds are to be seen at Kluane.

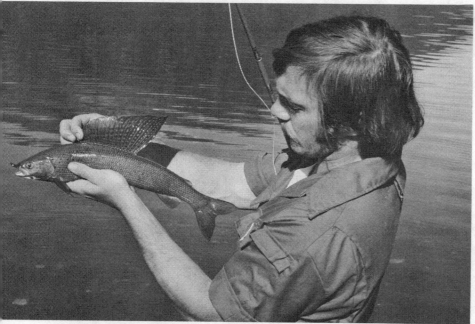

Steve Maslowski displays the dorsal fin of the grayling which many consider the most beautiful of all fresh water fish.

gulls already incubating clutches of eggs right along the water's edge.

Gradually as the lake thawed, bigger trout began to make their appearance, and for about 3 hours one day a 10-pounder Steve caught held the record for the year. But then the cook, a perky 22 year old blonde, Joanne Jonzen, who grew up on a mink ranch out in British Columbia and who has made a name for herself as a stock car racer in the Yukon Territory, went "fishin'." She caught a 26-pound lake trout, almost as finely proportioned as herself. Even though she decisively beat Steve's record and put all of us male anglers to shame with her catch, I am happy to report that her abilities as a cook matched or even surpassed her skills as an angler. You just do not know what good home-made bread, rolls, and pastries taste like until you have eaten some of Joanne's kitchen magic.

The one spot we "researched" for angling potential while we were at Tincup Lodge was nearby Dogpack Lake. It is not even a speck on the Yukon Territory travel maps be-

Bonaparte's gull found close to shore at Tincup Lake in spite of lake's almost completely ice-covered condition.

This mew gull (below), together with the Bonaparte's gull was already incubating during the icy June of the Yukon. The nests were at the narrow thawed edge of the lake.

Fly-fishing for grayling which abound here in perhaps greater numbers than anywhere else in the Northwest Territories.

Two other guests who fished the lake with us, Ray Roberts of West Chester, Ohio, and Robert Filey of Centerville, Ohio, had brought along chest high waders and those two fellows caught and released so many grayling they simply lost count. And, for every fish they caught they had at least four strikes. Bob even had the dubious distinction of catching a grayling on a backcast! They would have caught even more grayling but the water was so chilly that about every half-hour they had to wade ashore for a long thaw in the sun.

Steve and I found that it was not easy fishing for grayling from the brushy shore on Dogpack Lake. A canoe would have been ideal, but lacking that craft we started to explore and quite by accident started to follow along the edge of a small stream that drained the lake. If it has a name we could not find it on a map.

At no point that we investigated was the stream wider than 35 feet and nowhere did the pools appear to be deeper than 3 or 4 feet. At first as we walked casually along the edge, fringed with stunted black spruce and willows, we were not aware of the grayling that were thriving in this small stream. But once we learned the trick of staring intently for a few minutes at one spot we began to see the ghostly gray shapes as they swirled after an aquatic organism or dimpled the surface as they rose for insects.

We had only 90 minutes to fish that creek before the helicopter was due to pick us up. Here as elsewhere in that area a black gnat fly proved to be an irresistible lure. The grayling were so naive that again and again I could kneel directly over a pool and watch at a distance of 3 feet as husky fish sucked in the black-gnat flies Steve was offering. If these fish ever had seen a human being they did not associate him with danger. The grayling in the lake and stream were not record breakers—Steve's biggest weighed perhaps 2 pounds and the largest caught by Bob or Ray measured just over 18 inches. But for sheer numbers I have never seen anything like it, and I have made six other trips into some of the choice grayling areas in the Northwest Territories.

Steve and I made no attempt to keep score of the fish he took on his flyrod, but his father is never likely to let his son forget the number of times, on his backcast, that he wrapped the flyline around the willows and black spruce that hugged the streamside. Steve found exactly 22 of those traps. Happily for his old man, his son's all too frequent profanity was offset by the more soothing and harmonious sounds made by white-crowned sparrows, olive-sided flycatchers, and hermit thrushes living along the edge of the stream.

At present the only way to get into this area of the Yukon is by the helicopter service offered by Ray Conant at Tincup Lodge. Write him direct at Yukon Outdoor Adventures, Ltd., P. O. Box 4164, Whitehorse, Yukon Territory, for complete details. It is possible to drive directly to Milepost 1118 on the Alaskan Highway and have Ray pick you up at that point.

If you make the trip be sure to take a flyrod outfit and, for some incredible grayling fishing, lots of #12 and #14 black gnat flies or similar dull patterns. Incidentally, Ray told me that an angler from Oklahoma hooked what he thought might be a world's record grayling in Tincup Creek, which drains the Lake and is about 10 miles by boat from the Lodge. But you know, we were so darn busy that we never did go down to try to confirm that Okie's judgment. If he was accurate in his estimate, chances are that big fish is still waiting to be entered into the record books. It just might be worth your time to check on this—soon. If the rumor proves true the Yukon may soon experience a piscatorial type of "Klondike Gold Rush."

cause it is only 2½ miles long and ½-mile wide. It is just over the mountain from the Lodge and we got there via helicopter in about 5 minutes. The trip would make a hard, but interesting, half a day's hike.

As we hovered momentarily maybe 100 feet over the lower end of Dogpack, while the pilot selected a landing site, we could see hundreds of smallish-sized fish in the shallow, glass clear waters along the edge.

My first cast from shore with a small spinner revealed the identity of these fish. They were Arctic grayling and there must have been thousands concentrated in the lower end of that lake.

Boats You Can Carry

...or almost carry

Canoe is among oldest, traditional types of watercraft. It also has numerous uses for fishermen who like to escape the heavy fishing pressure.

by BARNEY PETERS

JUST IN CASE you get the urge to catch a striped marlin off Baja California while trolling aboard a miniature inflatable boat, Joe Peters of Florham Park, New Jersey is the man to see.

Joe recently returned from Cabo San Lucas on the southern tip of Baja California where he fished the Gulf of California from a 14-foot rubber boat. Although he didn't land a billfish personally, one of his companions successfully managed to boat a 130-pound striped marlin from the little craft.

Why the little rubber boat? Well, according to Peters, he recently wrote a story about offshore fishing from various types of sportfishing craft which appeared in *Outdoor*

Life magazine. In the story Joe related that inflatable boats, while fine for fishing sheltered waters, lakes and rivers, were impractical and out of the question for offshore fishing.

But as expected, B. Alden Smith, president of the Bonair Inflatable Boat Company of Merriam, Kansas, immediately took up the challenge and told Joe that inflatable boats are not only practical, but quite capable of performing successfully offshore when fishing for giant game fish. The challenge was quickly accepted by Joe who met Smith and his two sons in Baja California and the convincing session began.

"We used one of Bonair's 14-foot inflatable boats constructed with a V-bottom and three individual inflatable

Pontoons affixed to light canoes give much added stability—and this is in the angler's favor.

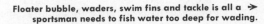

Floater bubble, waders, swim fins and tackle is all a → sportsman needs to fish water too deep for wading.

Canoe plus small outboard is the means to range far on wilderness camping trips. It's possible to use motor part way, then continue by paddling and portaging.

Lightweight aluminum boat is ideal for cartop carrying and can serve for many types of fishing.

compartments," said Joe, "and for three days fished the Gulf of California, ranging to 15 miles offshore daily.

"The inflatable boat carried a 35 horsepower outboard motor and we were accompanied during the venture by a conventional 40-foot offshore vessel which carried a crew of photographers who wished to photograph our strange antics.

"OK, we trolled 1½-pound flying fish for bait and had an initial streak of bad luck.

"However, early the third morning we were trolling some 12 miles offshore when all at once marlin seemed to go on a feeding spree—a marlin soon crashed our baits, but managed to elude the hook—it came back a second time

and cut the bait in half. We re-baited and as we dropped the bait astern the billfish appeared within yards of the rubber boat, instantly inhaled the flying fish and was solidly hooked.

"The marlin fought on the surface, leaping some 20 times before we had the tired fish alongside and gaffed it. The fish weighed 130 pounds and taped 8½ feet in length—we had the first striped marlin that, to our knowledge, was ever successfully caught from a rubber boat and Alden Smith had proved his point," concluded Peters.

Of course the greatest use for inflatable—or in fact any kind of light boats today—is in freshwater and in relatively small bodies of fresh water at that. Most popular, natur-

Pyrawa inflatable canoe is new favorite of backpackers. It can be lashed onto packboard and carried in to remote mountain lakes.

This inflatable rubber raft was even used to land a 130-pound striped marlin off Baja California.

be carried and they are still among the most useful. An angler with a small canoe—even one on which he can mount a small outboard—has the means to explore waters not accessible to other fishermen. He can, for example, portage to lakes beyond other lakes in a chain and can maneuver his way through narrow or shallow places where boats of deeper draft cannot go. It all adds up to fishing in places where the pressure is not heavy.

Today, canoes are built in a bewildering number of styles, models and designs—from one- or two-person capacity (and which weigh only 29 pounds) to large freighter canoes which can carry nearly a ton of cargo. But the latter cannot be carried far or easily by fewer than two strong fishermen.

Recently a small inflatable canoe called a Pyrawa and marketed by Sears, Roebuck & Co. has appeared on the market. It is very easy to inflate, ideal for one angler, slightly tippy for two, and is the absolute answer for backpackers who like to travel far and fish in lonely mountain lakes of the Rockies and High Sierras. Uninflated, the Pyrawa (plus paddles and pump) can easily be lashed onto a packboard and carried anywhere. Of course it also fits into very limited storage space either at home or in a car.

Also in the category of craft which can be carried is the floater bubble. This is simply a doughnut-shaped inflatable float with a canvas seat for an angler stretched across the hole of the doughnut. The fisherman sits inside and, wearing waders and swim fins, propels himself about the water, casting as he goes. Floater bubbles may be best on fairly calm lakes, but also are a good bet for drifting and casting leisurely downstream. No cartop racks or other carrying devices are necessary to take these floats from place to place.

What about the future of fishing craft you can carry?

The trend, obviously, is to lighter yet sturdier and safer equipment—and perhaps it is being accelerated by the American outdoorsman's desire to escape; to get farther and farther away from the pressure. New designs of ages-old canoes, for instance, make some models very difficult or almost impossible to overturn. Nor are the light designs as fragile as older, heavier craft. A recent innovation has been to install pontoons (light outriggers, really, which, again, are centuries old) for much added stability. These may be especially helpful when float-tripping and where an unfamiliar current makes the fisherman uneasy.

The fisherman's world is broader today because of the light fishing boats which are available. He might as well make the most use of them.

ally, are the cartoppers or collapsibles—models which are small, light or compact enough to be carried on top of an automobile or in the luggage compartment. To a bass fisherman who specializes in exploring farm ponds or the trout angler on beaver ponds, these mini-boats can be worth their weight in gold.

Canoes and kayaks are the oldest craft light enough to

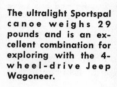

The ultralight Sportspal canoe weighs 29 pounds and is an excellent combination for exploring with the 4-wheel-drive Jeep Wagoneer.

IN THE spring of 1963, the Malaysian government shipped 70 adult fish to the Fish Farming Experimental Station at Stuttgart, Arkansas. These fish, the first white amur (also called grass carp) in North America, were imported to determine if release of this new wonderfish into public waters would be feasible.

In 1966, a modest spawn was achieved and the young amur were distributed to the Arkansas Fisheries Dept. and to Auburn University for testing and observation. As if on signal, this single event seems to have ignited more interest, pro and con, than any alien species since the common Ger-

their ponds that 113 of them were moved to Babcock Lake in the nation's capital.

Once before the public (and politician's) eyes, the carp boom really took off. Fishery representatives expounded upon the sporty nature and tasty flesh of the great new fish from Germany. Pond owners whose waters were weed-choked were told the first planting of carp would doubtless devour aquatic plants and clear the ponds in no time.

The furor rose to such a pitch that it seemed nearly every farmer with a pond, or even a plot to dig a pond, was demanding brood stock be made available so that they,

WHITE AMUR: BOON OR BOONDOGGLE?

Closeup of white amur and teeth used to grind up aquatic vegetation.

by DAVE BOWRING

man and Israeli carp. Before going further with this newest of carp imports it might be well to retrace the importation and ballyhoo surrounding the unbeautiful German and Israeli species.

Prior to 600 AD, the Asian (later German) carp had been moved to Europe, where it provided low-quality food. By fewer than 100 years ago, Rudolph Hessel, a U.S. Government fish culturist, decided America was missing out on a truly fabulous species, and shipped 345 carp by boat from Hochst, Germany to New York City.

First stockings took place in small ponds at Druid Hill, Boston. But, almost in prophecy, the carp so overpopulated

too, might reap the many benefits of this Asian-European wonderfish.

Never ones to miss the chance to please a constituency, Congress involved itself to the extent of distributing 260,000 German carp throughout 298 congressional districts. This single act is to blame for the infestation of the common carp to nearly every corner of America. Today we harvest what our overzealous and short-sighted ancestors sowed. Carp actually changed the face of the American landscape for the worse.

The results of this widespread dispersion of the German carp, later followed by other subspecies, have been cata-

The white amur, above, is here contrasted with Israeli carp. Introduction of the amur could prove a major tragedy to U.S. sport fishing.

strophic for much of the country's sportfishing. Common carp are bottom-dwellers, feeding on almost anything while keeping the water so turbid that gamefish—bass and panfish particularly—can neither spawn nor see to feed.

Carp grow quite large—50 pounders are not unheard of —and directly compete with more desirable species for living space, spawning beds, and food. In a great many impoundments which suffer from regular doses of siltation, and therefore become increasingly shallow, carp have become the water's dominant species, to the exclusion of all others. The high water temperature found in many shallow lakes decreases the gamefish population while actually enhancing conditions for carp.

Once a lake, pond or reservoir contains even a small carp population, more often than not the impoundment is on its way downhill as a provider of sportfishing. So hardy is the German carp that live-packed carp shipped in ice from Illinois to New York have not only arrived alive, but were revived to full vitality.

Carp have become a problem in many areas to the extent that state fishery agencies have had to spend large dollar amounts in often unsuccessful attempts at eradication. But the tough carp can withstand even large doses of rotenone and antimycin, two chemicals usually fatal to fish contacting them.

Spring Valley Lake, a manmade impoundment administered by the Ohio Division of Wildlife south of Dayton, is a good example. For years Spring Valley had become shallower due to siltation, and carp had become more numerous as other fish either died out or remained stunted. But in recent years, Wildlife fisheries personnel drained the lake, poisoned the few potholes still holding water, and refilled the lake. Word got out that Spring Valley, due to this extensive effort to improve the lake, would once again provide quality fishing, but it hasn't happened.

In spite of concerted efforts, the carp remains to foul Spring Valley. John Walker, district fisheries supervisor, admits that Spring Valley carp are there to stay. The only way to make sure that the carp are out, says Walker, is to completely drain the lake, leave it dry for a year or more, and then start over. Meanwhile, Ohio fishermen, whose license fees pay to maintain state waters such as Spring Valley, are, like the lake itself, left high, dry and fishless.

Michigan's Dept. of Natural Resources calls the German carp a "noxious trash fish" which "makes a muddy mess of lakes and streams." Most states with carp problems would term their unwelcome resident similarly.

The history of past carp importations and propagations would hardly lead the observer to consider bringing in yet another type of carp of the minnow family, but this is exactly what is being done. Arkansas, a land well known for its excellent smallmouth bass and stream trout angling, has for nearly a decade been experimenting with another great new "wonderfish," the Asian white amur, also called grass carp, ca cham, chow hu, sogyo ts'yu.

The Arkansas Game and Fish Commission evidently knows something about this wonderful new carp unknown to the rest of the states, because Arkansas is nearly alone in the expenditure of time, effort and money researching the grass carp. At least four states—California, Missouri, Nebraska and Michigan—have banned importation of the grass carp. The rest should follow suit.

Michigan's Fisheries Division (habitat protection specialist Thomas Doyle) suggested a reason for the sudden interest in this tongue-in-cheek "miracle fish."

"I am sure you are aware that the southern third of Michigan has numerous lakes, and virtually all of them are densely populated. The old septic tank tile field waste disposal system has not done a very good job of keeping the nutrients from our lakes; and when coupled with the runoff from agricultural fields and industrial additions, many of these waters have become culturally eutrophic. That is to say, man has rapidly accelerated their aging process."

Doyle goes on to estimate the grass carp to be what Arkansas considers an instant and inexpensive answer to its eutrophication problems. Just drop a few amur into your weedy lakes, and like aspirin applied to a headache, there goes the problem.

When civilization added extra nutrients to lakes and streams, the long term effects of these additions were not considered and today we suffer the problem. Arkansas fish biologist William M. Bailey, in a paper on the white amur published in September 1971, appears headed for the same mistake made earlier with the German and Israeli carp.

"Most of the information on the white amur came from other countries," writes Bailey, "and does not reflect the actual behavior of the fish in American waters . . . We will never know what effects the white amur will have in the wild until we plant it there." With this in mind, he continues, Arkansas is releasing the fish into public (and interstate) waters.

What quality does the grass carp possess which makes it so extraordinarily attractive to Arkansas?

The answer is appetite. The Arkansas research has shown that the amur has been known to consume up to twice its body weight daily in aquatic plants, and that these plants include as many as 35 different plant varieties.

Of immediate concern to trout fishermen throughout the eastern U.S. is the fate of Arkansas' White River, one of the most productive and popular trout streams in the entire south. The White River already contains white amur.

Here is something of a paradox. In that same paper, Bailey states, "If the white amur will spawn naturally in Arkansas, the White River best fits its requirements." Yet in the paragraph immediately preceding this, Bailey says the "White River is almost devoid of aquatic vegetation."

Taking these statements at face value, are we to believe the amur can thrive and spawn without eating? And furthermore, since Arkansas' published reason for experimenting with the grass carp was to control aquatic growth, why stock it in waters "almost devoid of vegetation?"

Richard Stroud, spokesman for the Washington-based Sport Fishing Institute (SFI), wrote in a recent SFI Bulletin about his wonderment over the Arkansas action:

"Unfortunately for the rest of the world, no scientific reports of such (grass carp research) work are known to

Arkansas fisheries personnel stocking amur in a reservoir of that state. They might as well be dumping poison in the water.

have been released by the Arkansas Game and Fish Commission. It is very much to be hoped that their closely-held scientific knowledge in the release will be shared with the fisheries science community."

SFI goes on to take note of the "unprecedented ballyhoo . . . generated by the commercial fish farming industry," and says "the potential risk of releasing this controversial species at this juncture into American waterways, in view of the abysmal ecological ignorance surrounding it, is totally unacceptable as we see it."

Quoting two marine biologists from an article in a recent *Bioscience* Magazine, SFI added: "The grass carp does indeed consume aquatic plants and is reputed to be a flavorsome fish, but it poses a special threat to waterfowl management, to rice crops and to endangered species such as the Everglades kite which feeds exclusively on the snail 'Pomacea paludosa' as it enters shallows and climbs emergent vegetation."

The carp's outsized vegetarian appetite has made it appear especially attractive to states whose waters are weed-choked and in need of immediate repair, yet that same Arkansas white paper gives what should amount to a warning. The amur is said to have a particularly short digestive system, and so the plant materials it eats are passed back into the aquatic environment with a good deal of the nutrients intact. Would it not be possible, then, for the addition of the grass carp to an already overly fertilized environment to actually enhance plant growth, rather than retarding it? Research has no answer to date.

Florida, a state already developing itself out of a former pristine condition, appears to be a slow learner when it comes to providing a home for miracle fish.

An Associated Press story published in 1972 said that Florida's Dept. of Natural Resources has asked the state cabinet for $103,000 "to test the feasibility of introducing Chinese grass carp into Florida's waters."

Randolph Hodges, executive director of the Florida Natural Resources Dept., says he hopes the grass carp might be the answer to getting rid of water hyacinths, a plant which has turned many Florida waters into thick carpets of greenery. But a Florida state biologist recalled with embarrassment the abortive introduction of another wonderfish, the plant-eating tilapia, into state waters in the mid-1960s.

"We thought we were getting a fish that would eat unwanted vegetation and provide excellent sport, but it turned out we got the wrong species of tilapia," the biologist lamented. "The one we got turned out to have a stomach like a bottomless pit. It would eat all the noxious weeds, then chew up all the needed vegetation as well."

If the grass carp, native to the Amur River between China and the Soviet Union, does indeed eat such tremendous quantities of aquatic plants, what will become of those plant's natural roles in the pond's ecosystem? Will the carp so harvest available plant growth as to inhibit the water's oxygen supply? What new diseases, for which native North American fishes have no immunity, does the white amur bring with its introduction?

Will the amur's great potential size (reported to reach 100 pounds) crowd native fishes out of contention for living space? And once the palatable vegetation is gone, will this great new carp feed on our smaller gamefish?

Those who stand to profit from the grass carp boondoggle appear to care less or nothing for these important questions.

Roy Prewitt, writing in the August 1972 issue of *The*

Seining amur at Joe Hogan Hatchery near Lonoke, Arkansas. The species is now at large in the Mississippi River.

The new "wonder fish" devours a great variety of vegetation, beneficial as well as harmful or noxious plants.

American Fish Farmer, quotes a member of the Exotic Fishes Committee as stating that "the laws prohibiting the possession of the famous 'walking catfish' were redundant because, he says, "It is already too late to eradicate it.' This is already true of the white amur," Prewitt concludes.

Prewitt's interest, of course, lies in selling fish, not in considering the effects of his remarks. But at least one state official, Ohio fish management supervisor Clayton Lakes, shares Prewitt's belief that further attempts to retard the grass carp's spread would be useless.

Lakes, in a letter dated August 9, 1972, said, "the amur is already present in the Mississippi River system as a result of stocking in Arkansas, so it is only a matter of time until it migrates into the Ohio River system."

Because of Arkansas' irresponsible act of permitting the grass carp to reach interstate waters, the following statements quoted from Illinois Fish Management leaflet No. 37 would appear late indeed: "The American Fisheries Society (1971) recommends that this species of fish (grass carp) *not* be released in any waters of the United States until careful evaluation is made to weigh the effective uses of the amur as a biological weed controller against the probable impact to the lives and habitat of the native freshwater species in the United States."

The leaflet continues with another recommendation, ominous because of its lateness:

"The Illinois Dept. of Conservation recommends that the white amur not be introduced into the state except for experimental testing by qualified state university agencies in waters that have *no outlets.*" (emphasis added)

So the grass carp, which Florida officials say fight so well that they hope it will become "the freshwater equivalent of the famous saltwater tarpon," is even now present in our largest river systems. But before fishermen rejoice, they should know that a federal fishery biologist at the Joe Hoagan hatchery, Lonoke, Ark., home of the amur, has said the fish is something less than a great battler on hook and line.

The amur is already gnawing away at plants, noxious or needed, and venturing into waters which may or may not have welcomed the invasion, thanks to the Arkansas fishery people.

There must come a time when our total environmental responsibility at least matches the headlong rush for quick and easy answers to lengthy and complex problems. The Asian grass carp is a good, or bad, example, depending on whether you sell fish, or merely enjoy catching them.

The author strains to pump a fish from the depths. Note progressive taper in the rod that takes the pressure right into the butt. A rod with "lifting power" makes it easier to move a big fish on light tackle.

HOW TO FIGHT A FISH AND WIN!

by Mark Sosin

WHEN YOU set the hook into a fish and someone tells you to keep your rod tip up, he may be giving you the wrong advice. And there's a good chance that a well-meaning angler will suggest that you take it easy and play the fish carefully because you have a trophy on the end of the line.

To the small core of specialists who consistently land big fish on any type of tackle, this type of advice is a popular fallacy and it only serves to *decrease* your chances of landing your quarry. Instead, the position of your rod depends on what the fish is doing at the moment and there's no substitute for rough-housing a fish instead of babying it. That's how big fish are landed consistently.

Learning to fight a fish properly starts long before you get out on the water. The place to begin is with the tackle you are using and the knots you tie. Your goal is the ability to apply the maximum pressure the tackle will withstand. You can't attain that goal unless the tackle can take the punishment and unless you learn the benchmarks of measuring pressure.

Most rods on the market today boast what manufacturers refer to as "store action." When you whip them from side to side in a tackle shop, they feel good. Yet, put pressure on the rod as if you were trying to lift a fish or even a dead weight and the rod simply won't have the guts. The type of rod you want is one that has what I like to call lifting power. When you lift, the strain is taken along the entire taper of the rod and right into the butt. You can feel something move at the other end. Remember that if you're going to land a fish, you have to literally drag its head toward you. Where the head of the fish goes, the tail will certainly follow. But, if a rod has a soft tip or fast taper, chances are that the tip will collapse under pressure and won't transmit the strain throughout the rod.

Reels are another item that require attention. Some of us rebuild the standard drags in reels to make them smoother. On a fast running fish, you need a drag that is smooth and won't bind. Otherwise, the extra pressure could break a light line. On spinning gear, the rollers should turn under pressure. Many require constant maintenance, but it's a worthwhile investment in time. In fact, many sophisticated anglers

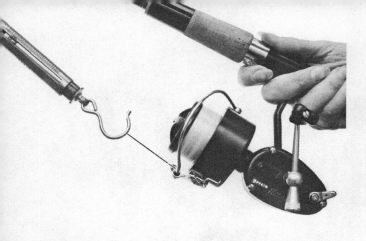

Drag should be set with a spring scale on a direct pull from the reel. Normal drag for light tackle is 15 per cent of the breaking strength of the line. Additional drag is added by hand pressure.

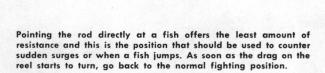

Pointing the rod directly at a fish offers the least amount of resistance and this is the position that should be used to counter sudden surges or when a fish jumps. As soon as the drag on the reel starts to turn, go back to the normal fighting position.

clean and lubricate light tackle reels before every major fishing trip.

There's a tendency among most anglers to ignore line, using the same monofilament over and over again. Unfortunately, monofilament deteriorates and it often becomes nicked or abraded. The nicks cause stress concentrations, greatly weakening the line. New fishing lines are the cheapest insurance you can buy and it makes sense to change them frequently. How often you actually change lines depends on how hard they were used, but some of us have been known to change an entire line after a single fish. Just keep in mind that the fishermen who are landing big fish consistently—and the word "consistently" is the key—don't take chances and don't cut corners.

No matter how good or how new a line may be, you cannot fish with it properly unless you learn to tie knots that are equal in strength to the unknotted line. Knot systems of this type are known as 100 per cent systems because they are just as strong as any other part of the line. If you cannot tie a 100 per cent knot system, you have no way of knowing how much pressure you can put on a fish without something giving. However, if you can tie knots as strong as the line, you can learn how much pressure to put on 10-pound test, 12-pound test, or any other rating of line. That's really the key to fighting a fish hard. Without 100 per cent knots, the line (or in this case the knot) could break anytime.

If you're going to become a specialist at hooking and landing fish, there's another point you should be aware of. Most hooks (even those just out of the box) should be sharpened, and that goes for treble hooks on plugs as well. Take a file or hook hone and triangulate the points so that they'll penetrate easily. You really want cutting edges that will slice right through the skin of a fish's mouth. And when you set the hook, don't try to yank the fish's head off. Instead, use a series of short, sharp, upward jerks—perhaps five or six in series—because you're only trying to bury the barb.

Fighting a fish is an art that is developed through experience. Unfortunately, the majority of fish taken are not large enough to tax either the angler or the equipment, and that is basically why fishermen get by with less than ade-quate tackle. But, periodically the law of averages will produce a fish or two of trophy proportions for every angler and that's the one you want to land more than anything in the world. There are definite procedures in fighting a fish that apply to all types of tackle and the majority of situations. Let's go through a typical battle.

Your first job is to set the adjustable drag on your fishing reel. This is done before you start fishing and it's a good policy to set it correctly in the beginning and then leave the setting alone. To arrive at the initial setting, you must consider the type of fish you will be catching. If you're fishing in open water where the fish will probably run a good distance, you want a lighter drag setting. But, if you're trying to wrestle a gamester out of heavy brush or there's a chance the fish will head for the nearest obstruction, the initial setting must be tighter.

To set a drag properly, rig the line through the guides on the rod and attach the end of the line to a spring scale. Have someone hold the scale while you point the tip of the rod directly at the scale. There should be no bend or flex in the rod. Specialists express the amount of drag in pounds and as a percentage. For normal situations, the drag should be set at 15 per cent of the breaking strength of the line. That means you would set 1.5 pounds of drag for 10-pound test line. When you have to stop a fish from reaching an obstruction, your initial drag might be as high as 30 per cent or 3 pounds for 10-pound test line.

Many factors affect drag. While you have the line attached to the scale, lift the rod to a typical fighting angle and have your helper read the scale to you. You'll find that although the initial setting with the rod pointing right at the scale might have been 1.5 pounds, you could get a reading as high as 3 pounds in the fighting angle. Now consider that it takes more effort to start a spool spinning than to keep it spinning. This is called starting drag and it adds to the total. The amount of line the fish takes out also is important. As the line on the reel spool decreases, the drag actually increases proportionately. And, there are many more factors that come into play. So, by setting a light drag, you can add additional resistance by hand, but you are also able to remove the drag instantly (by taking your hand away). With this method, you never have to adjust

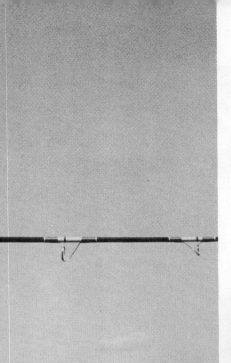

When a fish is being netted or gaffed, the angler should stay close to the scene where he can counter any sudden moves by the fish. Here the author is ready to drop the rod tip if the tarpon should suddenly make a last ditch bid for freedom.

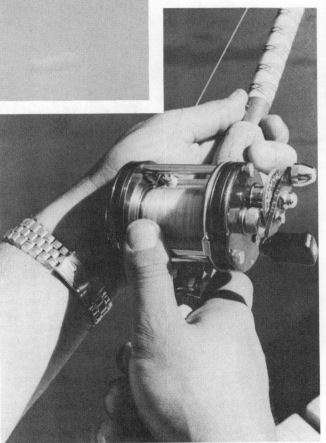

On a baitcasting reel, additional drag can be added by pressing the thumb against the spool.

the mechanical setting.

The best way to learn what affects drag and by how much is to use that spring scale and measure it. On an open face spinning reel, you need only cup the palm of your hand around the spool and you can add an amazing amount of extra pressure. With a bait casting reel, your thumb can add pressure. And, with any type of reel, you can push the line against the rod with one thumb and gain a pound or two of additional drag. On the other hand, you can go back to the drag setting by removing your hand from the line or the spool.

When a fish strikes, you know from experience that the fish is going to run. He's in a panic situation and he will try his best to get out of the area where he got into trouble. If the water is open, there's nothing you can do but let him go. Don't try to stop the fish. That's how break-offs occur

early in the game. The only time a fish has to be stopped is if he's heading for an obstruction and will cut the line away. The trick is to stop the fish before he ever gets started.

The very instant your quarry stops the initial run, you must start to fight and fight hard. If you're in a boat and the run was a long one, use the boat to get down on the fish quickly. Either way, you must start pumping the fish toward you to regain line. If you merely maintain pressure, the second run can strip the reel or the fish will be so far away that you cannot exert enough pressure.

As a general rule, you always want to fight a fish as close to the boat or to where you are standing as possible. The faster you regain line, the faster you can exert the type of pressure needed to beat the fish. Working a trophy fish demands determination, strength, and the willingness to continue slugging it out without a rest. If you stop to rest,

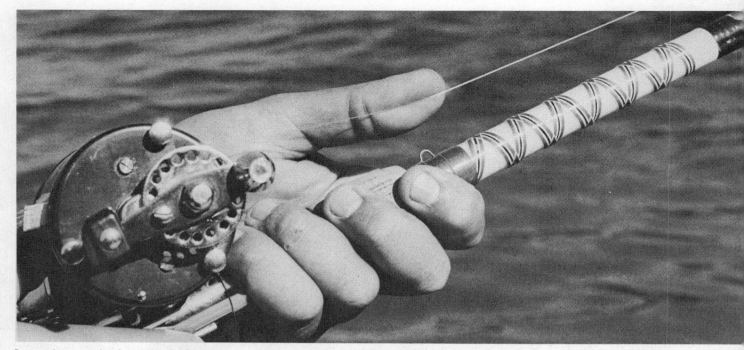

By pressing your thumb against the line, you can add up to a pound of additional drag. This is a valuable tool when pressuring a fish at close quarters. Even more drag can be added if the line is pressed against the rod blank.

the fish will regain its strength faster than you can get yours back. And every second the fish is in the water, your chances of landing the fish diminish. If the battle seems too quick for you, switch to lighter tackle, but use each type of tackle to the maximum.

Inexperienced anglers have the tendency to crank the handle of the reel continuously regardless of what the fish is doing. With a spinning reel, this only serves to twist the line and you can twist it so badly, it will have to be discarded. A fishing reel wasn't designed as a winch. It is a storage spool for line with an adjustable braking mechanism that allows line to slip at a predetermined pressure.

The trick of regaining line depends on pumping a fish toward you. But, how you pump is predicated by what the fish is doing. Pumping, by the way, is nothing more than lifting the rod smoothly and rhythmically and then turning the handle of the reel as you drop the rod tip.

Let's go over it in more detail. Point the rod tip at the fish and then lift the rod to almost a vertical position. At that point, you must lower the rod tip and regain the slack line created when the tip drops. Yet, when you learn to pump smoothly, you also learn to drop the rod tip at the same speed that you're regaining line. The two things to avoid in pumping is to drop the rod tip so that the line goes slack and to lift with a jerk instead of smoothly. You can practice this in your living room with a friend holding the end of the line.

If a fish is near the surface and some distance from you or the boat, the pumping motions can be rapid. Just as fast as you can raise the rod tip, you're ready to lower it. And the instant you complete one pump, you should be starting the next. Some fish have a habit of sounding or probing along the bottom when hooked. In that case, you want to get the boat right over the top of the fish. Pumping becomes a slower and more methodical procedure. You lift the rod very slowly until you reach almost the vertical position and then lower the tip rapidly while reeling. This continues without letup until the fish comes to the surface or starts to run again.

No battle is easy. The fish will come your way and then suddenly, without warning, it will scurry off in some direction. Whenever the fish runs, you must let it go. Don't try to pump. Instead, lower the rod tip and point it at the fish until the drag starts to give line. Then, instantly raise the rod tip to the normal fighting angle (about 45 degrees with the horizontal). When the fish stops, start pumping again.

Some species of fish are noted for their spectacular aerial acrobatics. They'll leap clear of the water repeatedly and if you're fishing with tackle under 50-pound test line, there's a definite procedure you should follow. As the fish clears the water, point the rod directly at the fish. This creates what we call controlled slack. It actually takes the pressure off the line. You can see the slack in the air.

Pumping a fish out of deep water is a slow, methodical process. The angler applies thumb pressure to the reel with his right hand and forces the line against the blank with his left, adding several more pounds of drag during the upward stroke.

Bob Stearns uses his left hand to cup the spool on a spinning reel to add more drag. By removing his hand from the spool, he can go back to the pre-set drag on the reel. This is a much better method than constantly adjusting the drag on the reel.

Now everybody tells you to keep a tight line, but if you do, you run the risk of having the fish land on a tight line and you also help a fish to dislodge a plug or lure. With controlled slack, the lure stays in the vicinity of the fish's mouth and if he lands on the line, there's a good chance it won't break. And don't forget that underwater a fish maintains neutral buoyancy and has very little weight. In the air, however, a 100-pound fish weighs 100 pounds. That in itself can be mighty taxing on light lines.

The harder you fight a fish, the faster you'll beat him. If you persist in babying your quarry, the odds quickly shift over to the fish and you can bet you'll never land really large fish with any degree of consistency. You might get lucky on occasion, but it's a gambler's bet that you'll be telling another fish story about the one that got away.

One of the most critical times in fighting any fish is when you bring the fish near the boat or prepare to land it. You know from experience that the fish will make at least one final bid for freedom, so be ready. When the fish sees the boat, net, gaff, or you, he'll lunge away. When that happens, push the rod directly at the fish just as you would if he jumped. That helps to counter the sudden surge and could save a broken line. When the drag starts to work, come back to the fighting position and bring the fish back toward you.

Using a net or gaff is easy if you follow a couple of basic rules. As the angler, your job is to stay right up front where you can handle your fish and counter any move. Don't back away to make room for your partner who is wielding the net or gaff. Maintain a position where you can see everything that is happening. With a net, the trick is to lead the fish into the net *head first*. A fish can't swim backward very well so any surge propels the fish into the net. Have your partner place the net in the water at a 45 degree angle and simply lead the fish into the net. Don't let him scoop the fish or touch the leader with the net.

A gaff is slightly harder to use. Each experienced gaffer

Charlie McCurdy is all smiles as he walks off the dock with his 35-pound jack crevalle taken on light plug gear. Catches like this are made possible because specialists have learned how to fight big fish on light tackle.

Twenty pounds of barracuda on a fresh water bait casting outfit can be great sport. The author landed this fish in less than 5 minutes in shallow water.

Bermuda's Pete Perinchief never rested for a moment until he landed this beautiful black fin tuna on an outfit that most people wouldn't even use for large-mouth bass. The secret lies in using the tackle to its maximum capability.

Rollers on spinning reels that fail to turn under pressure will destroy monofilament line on a single fish. That's why knowledgeable anglers lubricate the rollers constantly and keep their reels in top flight condition.

has his own technique, but a common procedure is to have the gaff placed in the water. Then swim the fish over the gaff and the man on the gaff can lift sharply, bringing the fish into the boat with the same motion. Preferably, the gaff should be moved into the water behind the fish so the leader won't hit it and the fish should be gaffed when its head is pointing away from the boat. That way, if the fish does lunge, he won't go under the boat and get cut off.

If you enjoy fishing light lines, you would be surprised how much pressure they can take. Try tying a line rigged through a rod to a door handle and pulling with the rod. You'll break the rod before you break the line. Think of fighting a fish as a boxing match. You have to counter when the fish swings and you have to swing when the fish is pausing. No matter how you used to fight a fish, try doing it twice as hard as you did before. You'll probably land a lot more fish in the process and have fun doing it.

Jim Thurston (left) helps the author hold up a pair of husky lake trout taken in Canada's Northwest Territories. It took less than 5 minutes apiece to land these fish because the author moved the boat to the fish where maximum pressure could be brought to bear.

WE FLEW NORTH FOR HONOR BADGES

By Ed Park

Colville Lake lake trout and, left to right, Ed Park, Herb Morey, Larry Chateauvert.

FOR THE umpteenth time Larry dropped his big red and white spoon right in close to the weeds and immediately began his retrieve. And for nearly the umpteenth time, he'd reeled only a few feet before the lure was smacked with a force that still—after days of fishing—startled me by the ferocity of the hit. That's one thing about those cold water northern pike; they certainly aren't shy about striking anything.

But instantly we could tell by the bend in the rod, and the line Larry was forced to give up, plus the hopeful smile on his face, that this was somewhat larger than anything he'd hooked so far.

"Wow, it looks like old fighter," I kidded, then added, "and I'll bet he'll go a whopping 14 pounds, 15 ounces and no more."

Larry held grimly to his rod and flashed me a dirty look, but refused to answer just then. He'd been fooled too many times.

"Well, I hope he's over 15," Herb added, "But under my top 17¼."

This also brought a nasty look from Larry and chuckles from Walt and myself. As soon as Larry had tied into this one, Herb and I had reeled in to get out of the way, and I was now manning the net while Herb stood by to take a few photos.

The big northern had given Larry a momentary tussle when it first tasted the hooks in its mouth, then had come rather easily toward the boat. But when within sight of the boat, all hell broke loose in a lather of spray.

Minutes later Larry managed to work the pike in close again and we got our first good look as it powered its way through the clear water. It was a nice fish alright, but I hated to guess on which side of 15 pounds it would be. Larry had his fears too, for he just played the fish quietly.

After a few more powerful rushes for freedom, Larry managed to work the tiring pike in close and I eased the net into the water.

"If he looks like he'll top yours, Herb, I'll try to knock his off," I joked.

On the next pass the fish rolled slowly over on its side and I netted it easily and lifted it into the boat.

"Get the scales," Larry ordered eagerly.

Walt handed them to Larry, who quickly hooked the fish on and held the scales aloft. The big pike was still flopping because we didn't want to pacify it with the club until we were sure it would top 15 pounds, so reading the scales was an effort.

But finally the fish hung limp for a few seconds and the look on Larry's face told the story. Not big enough! But he checked it again, had Herb look at it too, then unhooked

Summertime travel to the NWT is entirely by float plane. Here Larry loads duffel for flight to Hay River.

the fish and slipped it safely back into the water.

Herb, with an expression of one who'd just lost a dear friend, turned to us and muttered, "About 14½."

And that's the way it had been for the past couple days. We fished hard for big northern pike during most of the day, then spent the long evening hours tangling with the large and plentiful Arctic grayling. With grayling we had little trouble, and Herb and I had no trouble with the pike. But Larry and the pike just didn't seem to see eye to eye.

Take the first day for instance. My first cast for pike produced a tiny but scrappy little bugger that only went about 4 pounds. He was a real ball though, because a northern pike of any size thinks he can whip the world, and they all sure do try it.

Then I had a couple dry casts before tying into one that felt like I had snagged into a submarine. At first I was sure I'd hooked the bottom, but then felt that reassuring vibration that told me something more than weeds was on the other end of that line. Best of all I felt the strong muscular vibration of real size. I reeled back to move him and he didn't like that. For the next few minutes I was sure the

pike was going to have *both* ends of that line as the reel screeched out yards and yards of monofilament.

But the arch of the rod did its job and the line held. The first time I was able to bring it to the boat, the fish came easily as usual—then it saw the boat. Many fish can be brought into a boat fairly easily, but seldom the northern pike. This pugnacious guy will take on most anything he can get in that oversize maw of his, but boat-shy he definitely is. You just plain have to wear them completely out before you net them.

I've tied into big fish before, but I wasn't prepared for the length of that thing, and when I got my first look I got more than just a bit excited. I was sure Herb was going to net it all wrong, and proceeded to tell him all about how to do it.

He calmed me by extending the net in my direction with the casual comment, "Would you rather do it?" But I had my hands full and was in no mood to joke.

The first netting attempt was muffed because our net really wasn't deep enough for this fish and then I was even more nervous.

We even caught northern pike off of the float plane dock at Brabant Island.

Author Ed Park holds up large pike taken on red and white spoon.

Guide Walter Hupp releases average size pike hooked by Herb Morey.

Some NWT pike are great aerial performers, clear the water like this one.

Larry weighs pike which just barely misses 15-pound honor badge size.

Herb's cheerful comment, "sorry about that," didn't help a bit.

But the second attempt was good and we lifted the monster into the boat. We weighed it roughly with our hand scales in the boat, then checked the weight back in camp with the accurate scales. 23 pounds, 12 ounces for my second northern pike! And he measured a substantial 47½ inches long! That's one big buster anywhere.

Likewise Herb didn't have too much trouble getting a jumbo. That same day, near the mouth of a small stream, he picked up a pike that checked out at 17 pounds, 5 ounces. And then of course there were those nice 15- and 16-pounders Herb and I boated—and released—accompanied by snide remarks to Larry about his fishing ability. And to rub salt in the wounds I caught and released (with the comment, "too small") a husky 19-pounder shortly after Larry turned back the one that was only 14½.

"I'll qualify if I have to stay here all week," Larry blustered.

Yes, we were all trying to qualify—to qualify for one of the fishing contest honor badges awarded by *Field & Stream* magazine. Just as a hunter who has bagged many big game animals gets just a bit blasé about knocking over game, and hence often turns to serious trophy hunting, those of us who have caught enough fish over the years to fill many buckets, often turn to fishing only for the big ones to add new zest to the sport.

The ultimate of course is trying for world records—whether it be hunting or fishing. The hunting fraternity has the Boone & Crockett Record Book to aim for, and, believe me, *any* head listed in that book is a mighty fine specimen of that species. The minimum point totals have been adjusted over the years often enough that now even the bottom listing is a heckuva fine animal.

The fisherman doesn't have a counterpart to the Boone & Crockett book, but the various fishing contests in the country give various goals to aim for. The annual *Field & Stream* contest is probably the best known, and a check of the minimum weights will reveal that most of them are high enough to make it a real challenge. *Sports Afield* also offers awards for big fish of all species.

Oh sure, if you live in prime bass country, you've probably caught a few smallmouth bass over the minimum 4 pounds, but a 4-pounder is a big smallmouth in anyone's puddle. Likewise brown trout, a 2-pound crappie, or a 15-pound channel catfish. These are worthy goals, and any fisherman catching a fish larger than the listed minimums has done something well above average.

Thus a couple years ago I was infected with the bug to fish for big fish—*only* those big enough to meet those minimum weights. Since then I've caught fewer fish, but the average weight has gone up. Still, most of the really big ones have eluded me and began looking around for some new area in which I would stand a much better chance of getting a few monsters.

I discussed this with an old fishing buddy, Herb Morey, of Newport Beach, California. Herb is a retired school principal, and is now devoting his time to lecturing and taking movies of interesting places. Herb's also a great hand with a fly or spinning rod and immediately liked the idea of a safari for big fish. And he had the spot already picked out.

"Ed, I'm planning a movie on the Northwest Territories of Canada, including their tremendous fishing, the Eskimos and Indians, Wood Buffalo National Park, and the whole bit. They have some fantastic fishing up there and I'd planned to sample some of it myself anyway. And, I've met a fellow who lives up there who I'm sure will help."

The fellow turned out to be Larry Chateauvert, who lives in Fort Smith, NWT, has a passion for jokes, fishing, good food and fine Scotch—but not necessarily in that order. He's been over a good share of the western part of the huge Northwest Territories, and knows a few fishing holes that ought to do the job for us.

Herb had driven to Edmonton, Alberta, while I'd flown up from my home in central Oregon. Then Herb and I took a flight out of Edmonton for Fort Smith and were met at the airport there by Larry.

"Pike, grayling and lake trout, you say," were Larry's first words after the introductions. "I think we can fix you up without much trouble."

After talking with Larry for only a few minutes I became excited. The minimum we wanted for grayling was 2 pounds, and 15 pounds for either lake trout or northern pike. Now I've caught hundreds of grayling, but none over about 1¾ pounds. Even that's a nice grayling on a light fly rod taken from the crystal clear waters of some high lake in the Rockies. But never a 2-pounder. I was eager to do so.

I've also caught my share of northern pike and lake trout, but again never anything over 15 pounds. Twelve to 14 pounds, yes, but none over 15. So when Larry stated that he'd just about guarantee all three of us would pick up fish in each of the three species over the minimum weights, I was eager to have at it—right now.

We chartered a Cessna 206 for the flight to Hay River on the shores of Great Slave Lake and there met Walter Hupp, owner of Brabant Island Fishing Camp. Then a 2½ hour boat trip across the southern part of the lake, and we were there.

While unloading our gear I noticed just a bit too much

Top northern of the trip was this 23-pounder from Brabant Island, a lunker no matter where it's caught.

surface activity near a point less than 50 yards from the dock. I tried to resist, but couldn't, so begged out of my share of the work and slipped my flyrod together.

Walter mentioned that there were always grayling near that point, and I was hooked. I tied on a number 10 black gnat—a fly that has always been a good one for grayling.

Hurrying over to the point, I whipped out a short line and dropped the fly gently at the edge of the current sweeping by the point. The fly floated jauntily along for about two feet, then vanished with a slurp.

I set the hook and was fast to a real acrobat of a fish. It made a quick run downriver, then came crashing through the surface in one of those spectacular jumps for which grayling are famous. But the size of it! *This* was no pound and a halfer!

The grayling fought spectacularly for several minutes, but was no match for the limber glass rod and I soon eased him onto the shore. When I had my first good view of it, I felt a slight touch of buck fever because this was really a fine fish and by far the largest grayling I'd ever caught.

I hurried my prize to the dock and interrupted the unloading long enough to weigh him. When the pointer settled, my eyes really lit up. Two pounds and nine ounces! My first fish! On the first cast! And well over the minimum two pounds for a badge!

It was difficult to forsake the fishing for the next half hour while I pitched in to help carry gear to our cabin. But then I was right back at fishing. That grayling was the first, but by no means the only, and not even nearly the largest we took during the next few days. Before it was over, and my collection of flies had been reduced to a mass of badly chewed feathers and fur, we'd caught and released scores of large grayling.

Herb's largest topped 2½ pounds, Larry's was even larger at just under 3, while I managed to come up with one at 3 pounds, 1 ounce. And each of us hooked and released dozens of fish in the 2½-pound class, with actually very few going under the needed 2 pounds. Herb and I mainly used flies—dark patterns—while Larry did best with various small lures, including a pink lead-head hair jig. Herb didn't fish too much as he had a lot of movie footage to grind off, but I'm sure he got some excellent footage of Larry and me hooking and releasing 2½-pound grayling.

Since the grayling is near the tops for eating in my book, we did keep enough for several good feeds, but most of the fish were returned unharmed to the water, as Larry put it, "to grow up."

The northern pike fishing in that area was no less spectacular. We concentrated on the grayling during the evening, but spent the major part of the day chasing those plentiful northern pike. And this is the fish that was Larry's downfall.

Pipe-smoking Cree Indian lady come to visit anglers at Colville Lake camp.

Grayling fishing was great. All of these fish averages about 3 pounds and easily qualified for *Field & Stream* badges.

We fished hard; we fished long. We caught dozens and dozens of northern pike running from a few small 2- to 3-pounders, on up to my 23-pounder. Just for the information, I weighed one series of 20 pike I caught and released. The average came to just a little over 8 pounds! We all got bloodied up from the rows of sharp teeth that adorn the mouths of these fish.

Once while Herb was busy filming, he left his rod leaning against the gunwhale with the lure hanging in the water. Wham! A 7-pounder took the lure and almost took the rod too.

Another time I watched a feisty 6-pounder follow my spoon in toward the boat, slashing at it all the while, but never quite hooking himself. As the lure neared the boat, the pike turned aside, immediately spotted Larry's lure coming in, and slammed into it like an express train. Another to release.

The greatest barrier to catching the big northern pike were the smaller ones. We spent so much time catching and releasing 5- to 10-pounders that the lures weren't in the water long enough for the 15-pounders to grab it.

In fact Larry was getting a bit perturbed with all the "small" fish. One aggressive 10-pounder followed his lure in and when Larry spotted it, he jerked and reeled faster to get the lure away from the fish. This only antagonized the fish into making a rush for the spoon, but Larry was quicker and flipped the lure into the boat as the pike slammed head-on into the side about 4 inches below the gunwale. A bit higher and he'd have boated himself.

For several days the fishing was fast and furious. We fished mainly with large wobbling spoons, the red and white being the favorite. Herb and I kept fishing, hoping to top

the ones we'd already taken, although Herb did take lots of time to get much of the action on film. And Larry of course did his best to come up with a 15-pounder, but in the end our time ran out and we had to settle for five qualifying fish out of a possible six. We each had our grayling, and Herb and I had our pike.

In an effort to get that 15-pounder for Larry, we'd cut ourselves a bit short on time for catching big lake trout, but again Larry was convinced we'd have no trouble, so we left the pike and moved on.

Our lake trout water was north of Great Slave at the new Colville Lake Lodge, recently opened on the shore of that lake. This is about 500 miles northwest of Brabant Island Lodge and just north of the Arctic Circle.

"It's quite a long ways," Larry admitted, "But it's a newly opened lake and a downright cinch for big lake trout."

"Like 15-pound pike here?" I laughed.

The remark went unanswered.

The first day at Colville Lake we had only a few hours of fishing time, but we quickly discovered that Larry wasn't kidding about Colville Lake fish. Herb started off the parade with a 4-pounder caught trolling an orange spoon with black spots. Then within minutes I tied into my first one on a large red and white spoon. This monster took out many yards of line on several strong rushes before I could convince him that the place to be was in the net. Later back at shore we weighed him in at 24 pounds, 4 ounces, and I quickly became convinced Larry knew what he was talking about concerning Colville Lake lake trout.

After all the hullaballoo concerning my big one, we went back to fishing and Larry caught and released a couple 5- or 6-pounders. Herb then quickly added his name to the list

Two big fish on at once! For the next 15 or 20 minutes we had a ball. Both men worked their fish in slowly, not wanting to run the risk of pulling out or breaking off. Both fish fought with the deep-down power for which lake trout are famous and in this frigid lake about the Arctic Circle, they didn't seem to tire. Lose line, gain line, lose some more. Work them in slowly, carefully. Don't horse them.

Larry's came in first and Charlie netted it with no trouble, then turned his attentions to Herb. We almost lost this fish when it made a final rush for freedom at the net, but on the next go-around Charlie netted it also.

Both fish were big, this we knew, and the hand scales indicated both were over the minimum 15 pounds. The more accurate scales back at the lodge indicated they were for sure. Larry's just made it with a reading of 15 pounds, 2 ounces, while Herb's went a healthy 21 pounds, 1 ounce.

"I'll bet mine shrank a good 2 pounds before we got him in," Larry insisted. He didn't get too much sympathy out of us however.

We'd hoped to fish some more, but the weather socked in on us and we had to call it quits. Our actual fishing time while we were there was less than one full day, but was enough to make me realize the potential of a place such as that.

As Charlie put it so well: "You come back. Catch some *big* ones next time."

The twin Beechcraft came for us that evening, and we headed home—the fishing trip a complete success, except of course for Larry's northern pike. But any trip that can produce fish as big as those we caught would have to be considered a success. I was assured that this was only a sample of the fast and furious fishing that can be found in the many lakes and streams of Canada's vast Northwest Territories, and I sure intend to have another try at it soon.

Before this trip, the thought of taking fish of that size was pretty wild dreaming on my part. But Larry's boasts proved true, and now when I think about it I get to dreaming of things even higher. There may be world records to be broken up there and I'd love the opportunity to try.

The lakes of the Northwest Territories are huge, the land is vast, and there are many large lakes that have never been fished. The potential is astounding, and the possibility of a new world's record is always there when you fish waters where big fish can be considered common.

of qualifiers with a nice one that tipped the scales at 16 pounds even.

This left Larry out again, as usual, but he wasn't concerned. "We'll have more time tomorrow. You just watch."

The next day we hit bad weather with a strong wind and the lake kicking up wildly, so we spent the day sitting around the lodge telling each other fishing lies and giving Larry a bad time.

"Herb," I comment once, "I think we ought to wind it up and go home. You and I have bothered these fish enough."

"Aw Ed," Herb continued, feigning great sympathy, "I *really* think we ought to take the time to give poor Larry a few fishing lessons."

The next day was more calm, so with our Indian guide, Charlie Masazumi, we headed out to fish. The storm began to kick up later in the day and we eventually had to cut our fishing short again, but we managed to do alright in the short time we fished. Charlie had headed immediately for the far side of the lake, with the brief comment: "I know good place."

Charlie knew, alright. One of the great things about guides such as Charlie, men who have lived all their lives in the area, is that they do *know*. In the area Charlie specified, we were constantly busy hooking and releasing fish. Often we had two on at a time, including many in the 10- to 12-pound class. The lake trout fishing was wild.

Then shortly after our lunch stop Herb tied into one that we all knew was something special. As soon as Herb sang out, "fish on," Charlie cut the motor and Larry began reeling in.

Suddenly Larry struck, paused, then sang out himself: "me too!"

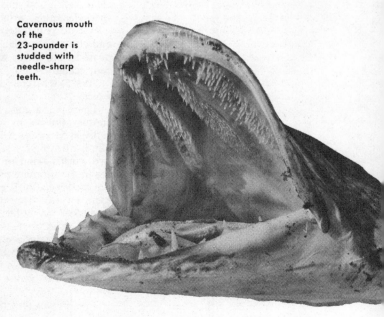

Cavernous mouth of the 23-pounder is studded with needle-sharp teeth.

ATTENTION
ATTENTION
ATTENTION
ATTENTION
ATTENTION
ATTENTION
ATTENTION
ATTENTION
ATTENTION anglers:
ATTENTION all sportsmen:
The Pillage of

by Erwin A. Bauer

"DO YOU," begins the sales pitch in a colorful brochure, "enjoy shining mountains towering over dark green forests? Are you a nature lover who yearns for fresh air, sparkling water, clear skies and the grandeur of unspoiled natural wonder?"

"Or do you require all the comforts and conveniences and a certain sophisticated flair along with your magnificent scenery?"

"Big Sky offers you the best of both worlds."

There are a good many anglers and conservationists in America, but especially in Montana, who believe that Big Sky is offering far less than the best of two worlds—and in fact may be leading in the ultimate pillage of that state. Big Sky is really Big Sky of Montana, Inc., a vast corporate promotion now embarked on building a $20 million, 10,647-acre "recreational complex" in a previously undeveloped valley of the Gallatin River, a famous trout stream. It is about 40 miles south of Bozeman and not far north of Yellowstone National Park.

The project was conceived by Chet Huntley, a New Yorker but Montana-born and until recently a commentator on N.B.C.'s Huntley-Brinkley Report. Because of his nationwide exposure on television, he is the board chairman. But the real owners are Chrysler Realty Corp. (a subsidiary of Chrysler Motors), Montana Power Co., Burlington Northern Railroad, Northwest Orient Airlines, Continental Oil Co., General Electric Pension Fund and Meridian Investing and Development Corp. of Coral Gables, Fla.

When it is finished in 1980, Big Sky will contain two complete communities separated by golf courses, an air strip, tennis courts, "trout fishing", bridle paths, ski slopes and lifts. The two "villages" will contain 1200 condominiums priced between $27,000 and $70,000 each, plus about 800 other more or less permanent homes. There also will be lodges, bars, shops of every kind and restaurants—all to help one enjoy "the grandeur of natural wonders." The promoters believe they can entertain between 6,000 and 10,000 visitors on winter weekends during the skiing season. That would

Montana is Underway!

require a huge service or catering population.

According to Huntley, "this is the greatest thing that ever happened to Montana."

Of the millions of Americans who have fished in the Gallatin River, who have hunted in "the shining mountains and dark green forests" surrounding it, or who have driven through the Gallatin Valley en route to Yellowstone Park, all will not agree with Huntley. Most who genuinely love the outdoors—or who hate to see our last wildernesses vanish—are likely to consider the project as "Big Eyesore" at best.

But how did it happen in the first place?

Perhaps it is only symptomatic of what is happening to many scenic regions of the United States. Everywhere, well-financed corporate enterprises have been quietly taking over wilderness areas because they well realize how in the future there will be a greater need, even a desperate need for humans to "escape." The value of that land will multiply over and over.

To date, Florida has been the best, or rather the worst, example of acquisition of these lands from private holders who cannot resist the inflated offers. But in Montana, Big Sky also acquired space by trading for public lands then under the jurisdiction of the U.S. Forest Service.

Such exchanges are not illegal, but U.S. law requires a *fair* exchange and that may not be what happened in the Gallatin Valley. At least 1,362 Montanans wrote letters claiming it was not. In addition, the trades were approved in June 1970 by Neal M. Rahm, a regional forester, without submitting an environmental impact statement as was required by our Environmental Policy Act which had been in effect since Jan. 1, 1970. Under growing pressure from Montana conservationists a statement was finally submitted in 1971. But it said nothing and amounted to nothing. Qualified ecologists and most sportsmen call it a whitewash.

Although Big Sky may seem to be only a small, 10,647 acre pillage in our fourth largest state which contains over 147,000 square miles, it is still a very ominous development. There is little to prevent Big Sky from spreading like a cancer over a much wider area. In fact speculators are acquiring as much land as is available around it, and over into nearby Paradise Valley of the Yellowstone River, another classic trout stream.

Perhaps Montana is especially ripe for exploitation. It is an immensely beautiful state, sparsely populated, where the air and water are comparatively pure and which surely deserves the Chamber of Commerce slogan of Big Sky Country. It may even be our most beautiful state and long has been every outdoorsman's promised land. No state, except possibly Alaska, can match Montana's wild trout fishing, its big and small game hunting. Many outdoor-oriented Americans who visit Montana wistfully wish that they lived there. One poignant example of the state's appeal has been the recent massive migration of eastern school teachers to Montana to seek *any* kind of teaching job, no matter that they are paid only a fraction of eastern salaries. They just want to live and work in a more attractive environment. It is hard for a fisherman not to fall in love with Montana as this writer, an Ohioan, has done long ago.

But there have been signs of trouble in paradise for some time. The Ana-

◄ The native grayling of Michigan disappeared long ago when forests along the Au Sable River were cut. Montana grayling, here, are also endangered by unwise land use practices.

conda Copper Co., mining in the Butte area, has never been the most conscientious custodian of Montana's environment. From time to time the stench of the air in Missoula, courtesy of pulp processing operations, has been deplorable. The once pure Bitterroot River was befouled. But not until the past decade, did things really begin to happen in Montana. Or maybe it is only that conservationists are more alert nowadays and the public in general is less tolerant of senseless pillage.

For example, the destructive clearcutting of our public forests—removing all the trees large and small as a timber harvest—is now being attacked all over America. But it was really in the Bitterroots of western Montana that conservationists forcefully focused attention on this awful matter and on other destructive forest practices. Still a good many of the national forest lands in Montana are terribly overgrazed and the uncontrolled mining practices (permitted by existing laws) have created a nightmare. This seems to be getting worse.

Montana sportsmen have had their share of shocks in recent years. They learned, for example, that they would lose a significant portion of the Big Hole River beneath Reichle Dam, a structure nobody needs. There are some serious anglers, such as Joe Brooks, fishing editor of *Outdoor Life,* who consider the Big Hole the greatest trout stream on earth, as it might be. But still it is to be sacrificed for a crazy scheme to pipe water over a mountain range far away.

Other bad news came late in 1969 when researchers discovered that Montana pheasants and Hungarian partridges contained excess amounts of toxic mercury in their bodies. In some cases the mercury content was several times the human tolerance level set at .05 parts per million by the World Health Organization. This high poison content comes from the organic mercury fungicides widely used to treat seed wheat and other grains in Montana, but which has been banned in other places.

"Still," complained Frank Dunkle, then the Montana Fish and Game Director, "the agricultural extension service isn't ready to stop recommending mercury fungicides." Fishermen naturally wonder how much has found its way into fishing waters.

By early 1971, Dunkle himself had become a major conservation issue in Montana. Nowadays men who are qualified both scientifically and as good administrators are all too rare in state conservation departments.

Dunkle was one of the good ones. He had managed the state's wildlife resources well, free of political taint and aggressively. Perhaps *too* aggressively to suit the growing number of those who would rather pillage and worry about wildlife and the environment later. Dunkle did not hesitate to speak out on important environment issues and as a result did not earn the gratitude of Governor Forrest Anderson.

Specifically, Dunkle had been in favor of preserving the Lincoln-Scapegoat Back Country region as a roadless, undeveloped wilderness area and has opposed any new mining schemes which pollute rivers and take a toll of fish life. The Lincoln Country is a fragile high mountain area unsuited for timbering or for mass recreation development as the U.S. Forest Service had planned. And mining along the Stillwater River would affect a population of native cutthroat trout and perhaps wipe them out. Gov. Anderson, on the other hand visualized Montana as a developing industrial state, of which we already have too many. It is therefore easy to understand his hostile attitude toward Dunkle—a thorn in the Governor's plans.

But it is not easy to understand Anderson's methods of trying to eliminate Dunkle, which included the introduction of new legislation (commonly called the "get Dunkle" bill) to permit firing the man. Otherwise Dunkle was protected by state law, unless he failed to do his job. In unprecedented harmony, every major conservation organization in Montana backed up Dunkle for his conservation philosophy as opposed to political expediency and pillage.

Strip mining of coal has been, until recently, an exclusive horror of the eastern United States, particularly in Appalachia which it has helped to destroy. But did you know that it is also a burgeoning business in Montana where operations at Colstrip in the eastern part of the state are quietly being expanded? Also the Montana Power Company has plans for a 400,000 kilowatt steam generating plant to be built near the surface coal. That is only another guarantee that the Big Sky will also be the Dirty Sky above polluted waters.

Speaking of dirty skies naturally brings up the subject of what may now be Montana's greatest horror of all. The scene of this is Columbia Falls in the northeast corner where the Anaconda Aluminum Co. daily releases a deadly mist of fluoride particles into the Big Sky. The total effect so far has been frightening, but the worst may be still to come.

This twilight scene on the Yellowstone River may be a thing of the past —unless sportsmen act fast to save Montana's streams from pillage.

Columbia Falls is a fairly tidy community of about 2,700 in the Flathead Valley and near beautiful Flathead Lake, an angler's favorite. It appears to be an ideal place for an outdoor family to live and many have gone there just to escape big city life in distant places. There is good hunting, fishing and skiing nearby. Every third or fourth bread-winner in the Falls works for Anaconda which has an annual payroll there of $8.5 million. If only *every* town in Montana was as "prosperous" as Columbia Falls. But what price prosperity!

A few years ago, it was noticed that ponderosa pines (the ponderosa is Montana's state tree) were turning brown and dying on Teakettle Mountain which looms just behind the Anaconda plant. True enough a forest fire had earlier killed most of the pines anyway and most local people considered the new blight on the surviving trees as only an aftermath. But that was just the beginning.

Obviously winds carry the fluoride mist from Anaconda chimneys to the Glacier National Park boundary which is only six miles away and to damage trees as far as 28 miles inside the Park, which is among the world's most exquisite scenic wonders. A U.S. Forest Service plant pathologist from Missoula, Clinton Carlson, found that needles of some coniferous trees inside Glacier contained fluoride levels 13 times greater than could come from normal sources. Some grass meadows in the Park were found to contain 70 parts per million of fluoride, or twice the amount allowed by Montana's liberal forage law. Carlson's report concluded that Glacier Park's matchless wildlife, vegetation, and fishing waters—which belong to all Americans—were threatened by the Anaconda plant.

As long ago as 1968, claims against Anaconda began to accumulate. Ranchers complained about sick cattle. A Christmas tree raiser said that 85,000 trees were damaged and the company bought both the trees and the livestock to quiet the incidents. But even more dramatic evidence of damage was revealed.

In 1971 Dr. Clancy Gorden, director of the University of Montana's environmental studies laboratory, found excessive fluoride deposits in both the teeth and bones of deer, chipmunks, rabbits, mice and ground squirrels nearby. Fluorides accelerate cell growth, causing bones and teeth to grow far too rapidly. The metacarpal bone of one 7-year old deer shot about 1500 yards from the Anaconda plant was twice as big in diameter as in a normal animal. Teeth of other deer were discovered to be malformed, scarcely able to permit browsing.

Lest enlarged bones and teeth of wildlife appear to be of little consequence, it should be reported that these prevent normal foraging, shorten the animal's life and render it less resistent of predators. It is also unrealistic to believe that large mammals such as deer could be affected—while the humans also sprayed by the mist would survive unharmed.

Anaconda admitted a daily fluoride emission as high as 7,500 pounds in 1968-69. With new cleaning equipment installed, they say it has been reduced to 2,500 pounds per day. The Montana Board of Health has ordered Anaconda to reduce further to 864 pounds per day by mid-1973. Company officials claimed that they cannot possibly meet that standard and as a result will then close down. Some conservationists in Montana have described that attitude as blackmail. Why should *any* company be legally allowed to pump even one pound—let alone 864 pounds—of poison into the Big Sky every day?

A little over a century ago a group of Montanans sat beside a campfire near the junction of the Madison and Firehole rivers, both well-known to every American angler. They had just completed an exploration of what is now Yellowstone National Park. What they had seen moved everyone present so profoundly that they agreed the region should forever remain a national park belonging to everyone. A year later in 1872, General Ulysses S. Grant made it official by establishing Yellowstone as the first such national area in the world. Today both the actions of the Montanans and Grant would seem to have had divine guidance. But what is really a shame is that the entire Montana Territory was not included in the Park. It is equally precious.

Our—and by that I mean all America's—Big Sky Country and its wonderful waterways deserves to be saved from the pillagers who threaten it from every side today.

Many rate the Big Hole River as the greatest trout stream in America. It is the home of large brown trout. But, part of the Big Hole is scheduled to die beneath a dam (Reichle) which no angler wants or needs.

YOU FISH TOO FAST!

by RUSSELL TINSLEY

Slow, precise fishing gives fisherman advantage with the element of surprise.

SOME THINGS a person never forgets. Like that lesson in bass fishing that the late Bill Moore gave yours truly, for example. Bill was a tackle representative and a bass plugger par excellence. On this chilly spring day on a lake near my home in central Texas he was doing his darndest to put me in contact with a bass.

"Try that stump there," he'd instruct patiently. "Throw close and bring a bass up. There's bound to be one there."

I'd work my lure in the vicinity and get nothing but exercise. Then Bill would follow up, playing a sort of a magic dance with his topwater plug, and suddenly there would be a violent splash, the lure would disappear, and Bill would be fast to another spirited fish.

He was almost apologetic about his success.

"Slow up and try it again," he told me in a soft voice. "You fish too fast."

I've never forgotten those sagacious words: *You fish too fast.* In fact, I must mentally remind myself of Bill Moore's wisdom practically every time I go fishing. For, admit it or not, I make the mistake that most fishermen make. I do indeed fish too fast.

Perhaps it is the hectic urban pace I live, running here and there, always on the go. I've geared myself to rapid living. When I get on the water I go at my fishing in the same frenetic way, despite what better judgement tells me to the contrary. It is difficult to go from one extreme to another.

If there is a hallmark of the excellent fisherman, it is infinite patience. When you go after fish, you play the game their way, on their terms. This is the charm of the sport.

Yet I'm still inclined to be what I call a "shotgun fisherman." I cover a lot of water and pour casts all over the place, figuring that if I hit enough different places the odds are in my favor that, sooner or later, a fish will be tempted by my offerings.

Nonetheless, I never will be what I consider a really good fisherman, simply because I do not have the temperament for it. I'm too impatient. I recognize the fault and try to offset it with common sense. But I have been only partially successful.

Another trademark of the successful angler is confidence. He believes in his ability. When he locates a stretch of water where he "senses" fish are present, he tries every trick imaginable to inveigle those fish to hit. He may spend an hour or more without moving more than just a few feet. This is one way he fishes slowly. Another is that he works his bait at a reduced speed, which fits neatly into his slow-down strategy. As Bill Moore told me, the idea is to tease, taunt and tantalize a fish into striking, whether it really wants to or not.

My friend Willie Esse, Jr. had to learn this the hard way. Willie was stricken with polio after he'd grown into manhood. He is paralyzed from the waist down. Yet he hasn't allowed his infliction to dampen his enthusiasm for hunting and fishing.

Willie primarily fishes stock ponds on his farm in southern Texas. He'll maneuver his wheel chair near the water and prop the spare tire from his pickup forward of the wheels to keep from rolling into the water. Then he will begin casting, fanning lures in every direction, staying in one place for more than an hour. He fishes where he *knows* there are fish, for his ponds are liberally stocked. Yet he might go for a half-hour or more without a strike, only to start catching bass.

Perhaps you've seen the same thing happen in a slightly different way. You have covered a stretch of water and caught nothing, only to see someone follow you through the same spot and catch fish. Did the fish suddenly get the urge to bite or was the other fisherman doing something differently?

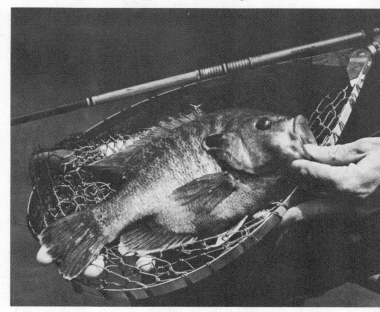

A popping bug just barely wiggled often entices large bream to hit.

Bubble-and-nymph combination fished slowly got this trout in New Mexico mountain lake.

It is important to make each cast as precise and perfect as possible.

◄A. W. McLaughlin shows results of slow-go approach with topwater bass plug.

Walleyes usually are taken deep and show preference for slow-moving bait.

Perhaps a combination of both. Fish can go on capricious feeding sprees. But there is more to it than that. How else can you explain that just a very few of the anglers catch a majority of the fish?

These fishermen know to fish the right bait at the right place at the right time. Much of this is learned through experience, trial and error. They also know how to maneuver a bait at just the proper motion to make it seem lifelike to its prey. An insect falling on the water doesn't kick frantically, if you've noticed. Instinct tells it this is sure doom. To struggle will quickly sap its strength and it will perish. Better yet is to wiggle along slowly until it regains safety. A bait thrashing on the surface often will scare more fish than it actually will attract.

A fish might, if it is hungry, pounce on a bait the instant it touches the surface. But more likely, as I've observed in clear water, the lure actually will frighten the fish for a moment. It will swim away a few feet and pause, curious as to what created the commotion. Then perhaps it will be attracted by the object struggling nearby, approach curiously closer, then with a sudden rush come up to snatch it. If the fisherman is working the lure rapidly, he probably has it beyond striking range before the fish has a chance to get interested.

I've caught more bream on a practically dead bait than I have with one that was moving. When I pitch a topwater popper into a likely spot, I let it remain still for a second or two, then barely twitch it, just enough to swirl a few concentric circles. Sometimes a definite pop of the plug will be needed to entice a strike, but not often.

Anglers after big fish are particularly mindful of the patience game. As a fish grows older, it gets more wary and lazy. It might ignore an artificial bait zipping along overhead, yet be tempted by a plastic worm that comes slowly slithering nearby. My good fishing buddy, A. W.

McLaughlin, has a philosophy that when you think you're fishing slowly enough, cut the speed of your plug about half that and you are still fishing too fast.

"Let's face it, we all fish much too fast," he said. "That's all that saves a lot of fish."

John Blanchard, a veteran Louisiana fisherman, was telling me about some prime bass lakes in his native state.

"Most of these are what we call slow-moving bait lakes," he explained. "When we think we are moving the plugs too slowly, then we slow down."

Most fishermen can cite instances when methods other than this go-slow approach produced. I have plenty of them in my own memory. But many fishermen pounce on these instances to justify their personal techniques. It gives them an excuse to fish fast. Yet question any successful fisherman and he probably will tell you that the slower you fish, the more how-I-caught-the-big-one stories you'll have to tell. This is true whether you're using natural bait, casting artificial lures or even trolling.

Consider what happened to me just the other day, for instance. I was fishing a lake near my home with A. W. McLaughlin. I'd cast a topwater plug near a shoreline rock and turned to ask Mac to reach in my tackle box and hand me a packet of matches so that I could light my pipe. As I was firing up, there was a sudden splash and my line yanked tight and I found myself battling a 5-pound, 2-ounce bass. That plug had rested there, dead on the water, for at least a minute or more. Two previous casts into the same spot hadn't produced even a half-hearted response.

Last summer Bill Browning and I were fishing the Gallatin River in southern Montana. Bill was getting trout to rise to his dry fly but he wasn't catching any. There was

When fishing for crappies with artificial bait, the slow approach is mandatory.

A deer hair bass bug barely twitched on surface duped this bass into striking.

A. W. McLaughlin likes inntertube float because he says it makes him fish slower.

one particular trout holding in a deep slick that kept coming up to flash at the fly but never would take. As Bill was making a false cast to start maybe his fourth float through the pool, I heard him mutter something.

"What did you say?" I asked.

"Ah, I'm just talking to myself," Bill admitted sheepishly. "I keep telling myself to slow down. I'm so anxious to make the next cast that I'm not getting a good float with my fly. The fish are seeing something suspicious and won't take."

Consider what Bill said and ponder the sense it makes. The one thing a fisherman has going for himself is the element of surprise. A trout, for example, is holding in a pool, watching for something to eat. An insect falls on the surface and begins floating naturally with the current. The trout, thinking the morsel might soon be washed away, rushes up to snare it.

But suppose the fly were slapped on top, picked up in a shower of spray, then put down again. The ruckus has

Red-and-white wobbling spoon bumped slowly along bottom paid off with this string of Saskatechewan lake trout.

alarmed the fish. It has become suspicious. And when a fish becomes suspicious, it *is* super-cautious, and the odds of a fish in such a state of mind taking a bait are rather remote, to put it mildly.

One precisely executed cast is much, much better than 10 haphazard and careless ones. If a fish isn't overly alarmed, it might take a bait on the fifth or even the tenth cast into a certain spot. But a frightened fish likely won't take at all, on the first or even the one-hundredth try.

This, then, is one pertinent reason for fishing slowly, to keep from alarming fish. Another is to present your bait in the most lifelike manner possible. Spend some time around a stream or lake and you'll note that fish and other aquatic creatures, which fish eat, go about their business in a leisurely and mannerly way, just as you see people strolling down a street rather than running. When you see someone dashing you associate it with caution, with alarm.

Thus it is with fish. A slow-moving bait might appear natural and they will be attracted to it. But one that is slapped down and pulled rapidly will trigger alarm rather than create the urge to pounce upon and kill or eat the fake. Remember this and you will catch more fish. Bigger fish. And you'll enjoy your fishing more, the relaxing and peaceful sport it was meant to be.

Porkrind eel is effective bass bait when slithered slowly along lake floor.

The power packed Ambassadeur 7000. An in-between baitcaster for heavy duty fresh water as well as medium bluewater action. The 7000 can be distinguished by its gleaming red and stainless finish, double locking heavy duty handle, star drag, and silent line guide.

NEW MIRACLE REELS FOR SERIOUS ANGLERS

by DICK WOLFF

MOST OF US are old enough to recall the good old days when each fisherman could enjoy his own private fishin' hole. Ah, those glorious days before spinning tackle! Then a guy could sit on the banks of a mirror-glass woodland pond; become existentially inspired by daylight's majestic purple and gold-blushed overture; and was free to curse to his heart's content while attempting to unsnarl his first cast's backlash!

In the early fifties when the spinning reel made its appearance, the fishing world was shaken by promises of no more backlashes, phenomenal casting distance, and the ability to use ¼-ounce (and even smaller!) lures. Of course a few remaining die-hards could still be seen picking away at waterlogged, silk knots, and holding to the idea that distance was no problem with ⅝-ounce split shot. Unfortunately though, even their numbers started to deteriorate as more and more fish were hauled in by the spinners.

A few short years later, the conventional bait casting reel was brought even closer to the fate of curious memorabilia with the introduction of the spin-casting reel. The spin-caster attempted to encompass all the best features of the bait reel's conventional handling, ala a line control thumb button, and combined this with the spinning reel's anti-backlash concept. The *coup de grace* for the old conventional, however, was in the fact that the spin-caster was designed to be used on bait casting rods! Refinements, including increased line capacities and the ability to handle line tests up to 20 and 25 pounds, furthered the spin-caster's popularity. Nevertheless, this instant success was destined to be short-lived.

Experience-wise anglers soon realized that although the reels had the capacity for the heavier line tests, casting distance was the price to be paid for the use of thick monofilament lines. Generally speaking, the reel's limitation was due to the line having to funnel through the spin-cast reel's nose-coned face which, unlike spinning's concept, created increased friction drag. The price was too high. So, while spinning continued to reign supreme with lighter tackle, the heavy duty chores were reassigned to the old reliable bait-caster.

Up to this point, if you've never used a standard casting reel, you're probably starting to believe that each cast predictably resulted in a string of ear scorching profanities and an hour's worth of instruction in the ancient art of knot untying. Such was not always the case with the truly dedicated sportsman—usually, with the occasional weekend worm and bobber man, yes—but not always with the every-chance-I-get-to-go meat fisherman who had mastered the technique of thumbing the spool for line control. The basic disadvantage of the early bait-caster, you see, was that once

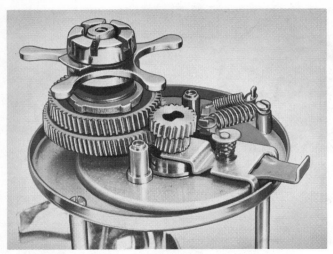

The 10,000C/9000 series automatic two-speed retrieve gearing. Timing of the shifts is controlled by the adjustment of star drag to the line weight and type of fish.

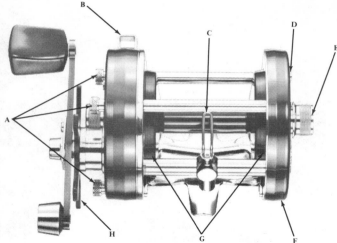

Ambassadeur features include (A) no-tool takedown screws; (B) free spool button; (C) smooth, silent level wind; (D) click button; (E) calibrated mechanical brake; (F) centrifugal brake (internal); (G) generous capacity spool; (H) adjustable star drag.

The Ambassadeur 5000 and 6000, forerunners of free-spool baitcasting and the standard of precision excellence to baitcasting perfectionists the world over.

the lure was cast, not only did the reel spool rotate, but also the gears, the level wind mechanism, and the handle as well. So, in addition to the line pulling the spool into operation, the gearing continued to push the rotation after the lure entered the water. The line had no place else to go, and the end result was an overrun. The bait-caster's classification as a heavyweight was also directly related to this machinery problem since light lures just didn't have the "oomph" to get the works rolling.

And then, as every sad story must have a happy ending, a champion of the side-lined conventional fisherman was born in 1957. With accents of Swedish craftsmanship, our hero took the country by storm with a not-so-conventional battle cry announcing the beginning of a new era in fishing —the era of the modern free-spool reel. The reel's name was Ambassadeur. Its sponsor was Garcia.

This combination produced dramatic effects in the fishing world which will continue to be apparent for some time to come. Aside from the fact that the consensus still maintains that the name is spelled incorrectly, the newcomer offered an unprecedented free spool capability, a centrifugal anti-backlash adjustment, and a star drag. A conventional style reel was finally on the market which could easily handle light mono lines, cast down to the lightest weight lures, and was simply controlled with slight thumb

pressure applied directly to the spool for light lure fishing.

The Swedes had solved the dilemma of drag and inertia in the Ambassadeur 5000 and its sister reel 6000, by including a push button which is conveniently located on the edge of the right side plate. When depressed, the connection between the pinion gear and the spool shaft is instantly severed, preventing the pinion gear, main gear, and handle mechanism from turning. Thus, the reel spool was freed from the friction of the internal heavier machinery. Never has any other reel attained such a high degree of ingenious design or engineering perfection.

The introduction of these super stars was not enough for the Garcia Corporation. Since the initial offerings, the company has gone on to bring the angling market an entire series of superb baitcasting reels, each one of which has become a standard of excellence in its own right. Take, for instance, the 5000/6000 series which includes the 5000, 5000A, 5000B, 6000, and their little brother the 1750. Each of them virtually eliminate the need for the word *backlash* (as well as a few others) from the angler's vocabulary. They all sport two sets of brakes which control the speed of spool rotation. The internal centrifugal brake, which is an exclusive feature of the Ambassadeur reel, has two brake blocks mounted on the spool shaft sliding against the brake shoe or frame of the reel. The faster the spool spins, the

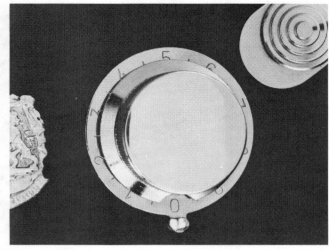

Two braking systems virtually eliminate backlash from the bait-caster's vocabulary. Left, the internal centrifugal brake; and right, the calibrated dial of Ambassadeur's mechanical brake.

Garcia's answer to the saltwater devotee with the anodized red 9000, and the luxurious black finished 10,000C. Both bear the external markings of chrome plated accents, man-sized round handle knob, and star drag.

greater the amount of pressure which is exerted against the brake shoe.

A second mechanism, the mechanical brake, applies adjustable friction directly to the spool. The control knob for this feature is located on the reel's left side plate. Pressure adjustment is as simple as you can get with a calibrated dial that serves as a memory device to the fisherman who decides to switch lines, lures, and rods in different fishing situations. By the way, if you ever get to really feeling cocky and want to test your casting proficiency, the centrifugal brake blocks are removable and the mechanical brake can be set back to full "off." As soon as I unloop the wildest backlash you've ever seen, I just may give it another shot.

Nevertheless, the goodies don't stop there. Floating bushings support the spool axle and are largely responsible for the uncanny silence of these reels. They utilize a level wind mechanism, and all, excluding the ultra-light 1750, have powerful star drags that allow for a wide range of drag adjustments. The feature is especially helpful to the "Joe Pro" type who'd rather try landing fish with light-test line. The variations on the reels in this series range from large capacity line spools as compared to the standard spool (which, by the way, holds up to 130 yards of 15-pound monofilament). We are also given the choice of a double grip handle or the counter-weighted heavy duty handle which is

available on the 5000B, and 6000 models. Believe me when I tell you that making a decision as to which of these gleaming red beauties is the best comes down to a matter of splitting hairs.

As if the choice weren't hard enough already, the same basic reels are also available in lustrous metallic black versions designated as the Ambassadeur 5000C, 6000C, and the new left-handed 5001C. The essential advantages of this series, however, is that stainless steel ball bearings are fitted on the spool axles which allow for the ultimate in smoothness, strength, and casting distance.

Also included in this series is Garcia's *piece de resistance* of the Ambassadeur line—the 5000DL. Black finish, gold plated trim, a handsome teak presentation case, and a lifetime guarantee to the original owner makes the DL a distinctive addition to any angler's collection of tackle.

To make you feel even more like a drippy-nosed kid let loose in a candy store with a nickel locked in his fist, a new combination of bait reels has recently been added to an already impressive list of models. The 5500C and 6500C are lightning-quick retrieve versions of the 5000C and 6000C. A 5:1 retrieve ratio and stainless steel ball bearings make these reels the answer to a bass buster's prayers for that extra speed to skitter a plug along the surface or just to make every minute of fishing count. And don't kid yourself

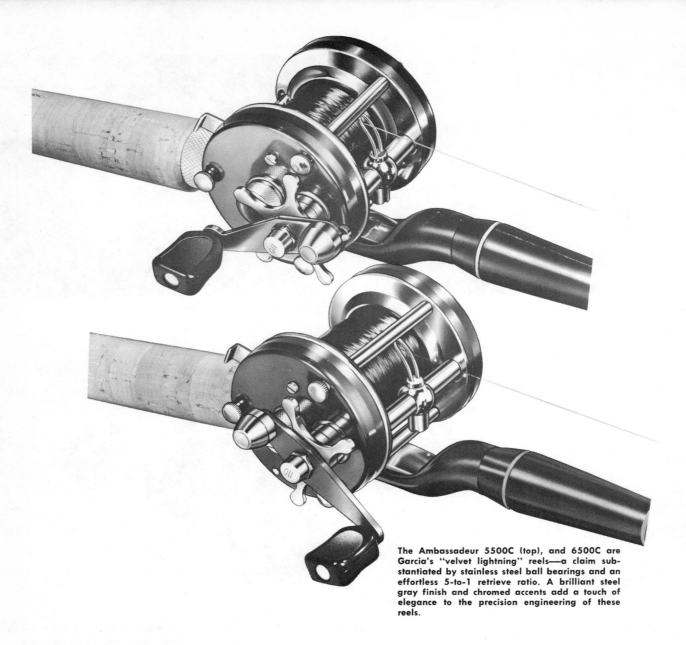

The Ambassadeur 5500C (top), and 6500C are Garcia's "velvet lightning" reels—a claim substantiated by stainless steel ball bearings and an effortless 5-to-1 retrieve ratio. A brilliant steel gray finish and chromed accents add a touch of elegance to the precision engineering of these reels.

about their rugged durability! I've taken them out to some of Long Island's busiest blue fish holes to satisfy the sadist in me. To report on their performance in a word—outstanding!

To be honest with you, I think the folks at that factory in Sweden must stay up nights just trying to figure ways of cornering the entire baitcasting market. They're aware that there does exist a shadowy creature of the deep water tides commonly known as the saltwater fisherman. In fact, they are so aware of his strange nocturnal (as well as broad daylight) habits that the result is a group of reels named the 10,000C, the 9000, and even a DL model in the 9000 class. Besides their large capacity, heavy duty construction (including ball bearings in the DL and 10,000C) these bruisers operate with a monster-taming two-speed retrieve. As soon as a fish hits, the reel automatically shifts down to a bullish 2½:1 gearing ratio for that sometimes necessary power. As soon as the beast does the inevitable and runs straight at you trying to foul up your ambitions with slack line, another automatic shift brings the power back up into a fast and furious 4¼:1 slack lapping ratio. This bit of automation may take a lot of the panic out of "bunker dunkin" which some anglers thrive on, but it sure does save a few which

may have ended up as "you should have seen the one I lost!"

In any group, there is always a kind of an oddball which can be classified as an "either/or"; the product possibly of left-over parts from everything else. Well, the Ambassadeur group is no exception with its, in this case, dynamic 7000. As well as being the perfect ammunition for muskies, steelhead, and salmon, in saltwater it's been known to subdue yellowtail, stripers, and tarpon up to 100 pounds. This little powerhouse seems to be a perfect hybrid of all the other reels mentioned earlier and has everything including a spool capacity for up to 350 yards of 25-pound mono, 4:1 retrieve, smooth operating level wind, a *four* block centrifugal brake, mechanical braking power, a full range star drag, and an explosive red and chrome finish that's bound to give you the feeling that it's just itchin' for a fight.

The Garcia/Ambassadeur team doubtless have come as close as anyone can to solving the problems of the old-style conventional reel fan. They've also made it easier for newcomers to join the ranks of the bait-caster. Of course there still remains quite a bit to be said for the art of spin fishing, but . . . well, I guess that's another story.

GOD BLESS *The* FARM POND

by DAVE BOWRING

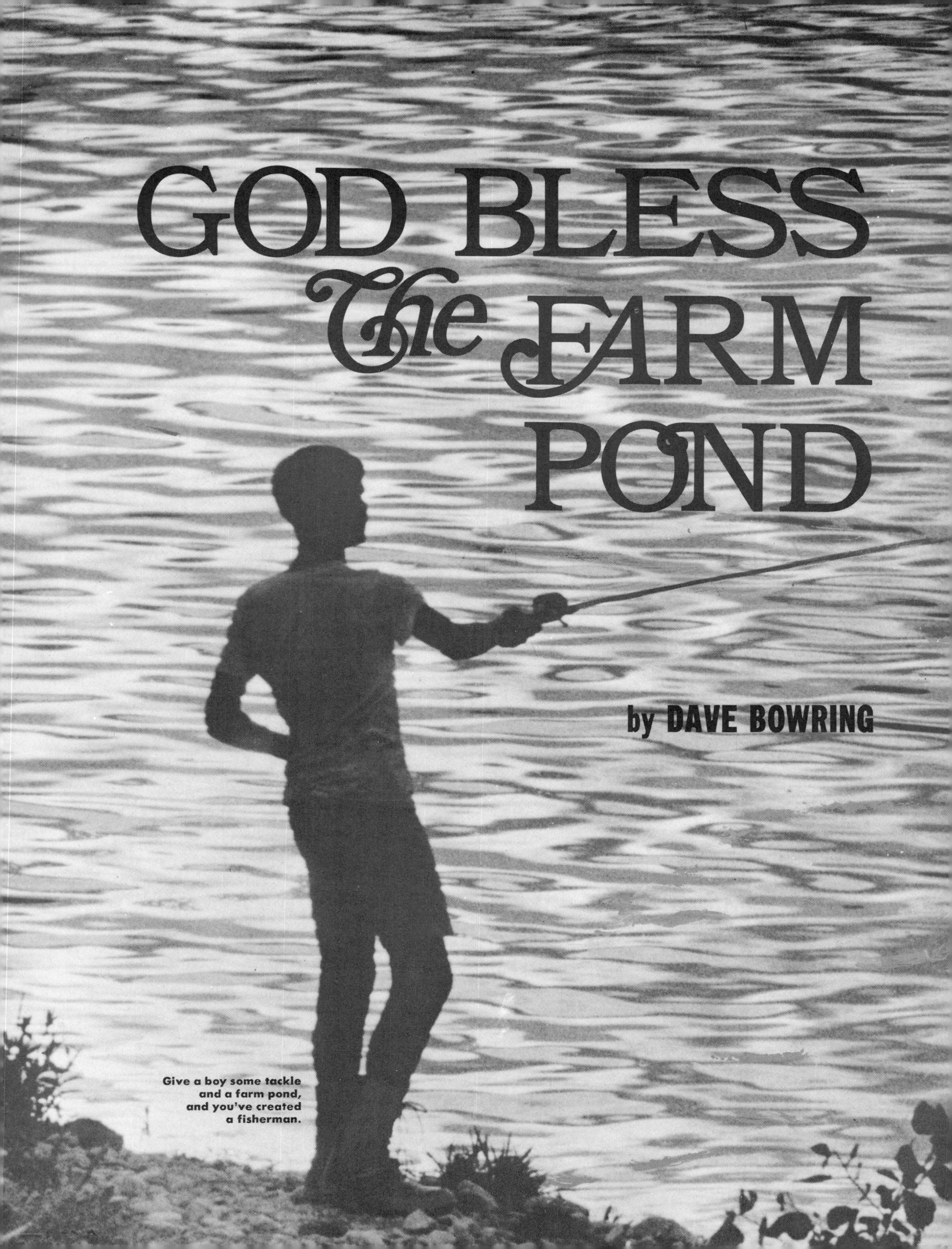

Give a boy some tackle
and a farm pond,
and you've created
a fisherman.

Light tackle plus nearby farm pond equals good sport for black bass.

Only three pound-ish, but plenty of muscle on a flyrod.

SO MANY freshwater anglers (myself included) do not live within reasonable driving distance of the hot bass lakes that, were it not for the homely but productive farm ponds, we'd be hard put to locate good largemouth and panfish territory near home.

Past and present hotspots—Lake Mead, St. Johns River, Table Rock, etc.—may be great for once-a-year trophy jaunts, but God gave the average angler enough nearby farm ponds to keep his rod dancing and his heart singing throughout the fishing year.

In my home state of Ohio, the number of fishable farm ponds has nearly doubled in the past decade. Owner-state cooperative arrangements offer free stocking of bass and panfish when new ponds are completed and filled, with the added stipulation that the owner permits public access to the water.

It's been my experience that angler friends and acquaintances can be great sources for adding new ponds to your stable of productive bass waters. Jack Shiverdecker, a fishing neighbor who regularly fishes for Old Linesides, has put me onto several good ponds. I recall one morning in particular.

Jack lives in Camden, a rural community 30 miles west of Dayton. His job releases him early in the afternoon which gives him several hours of daylight for bass fishing.

"You ought to come along tomorrow," his telephone call began. "If you can't catch bass from this pond, you'd better

◄ Jack Shiverdecker of Camden, Ohio gets cooperation from an energetic bigmouth from one of his seven "pet" ponds.

retire your rod and reel." Enough said; the next morning found us rigging our gear along the pond's edge.

The first thing I noticed about Jack's hotspot was its small size. The pond couldn't have measured more than 2 acres, and probably wasn't more than half that size. Algae rimmed its weedy shores and one end of the pond was guarded by thick willows growing right out of the water.

"My best bass from here went right at 5 pounds," Jack said, "but my son's best went 4 ounces heavier. I've hung better fish and lost them, and I'm sure there's a new state record in here."

Just think: a new state record swimming around less than 10 miles from your front door . . .

Twenty minutes of casting a minnow imitation brought four bass between 2 and 3 pounds, plus an estimated 4-pounder which jumped and split out my hook on the third try. Calling Jack's pond productive is like saying Raquel Welch has a nice figure.

Jack has collected seven ponds which he regularly fishes, all within 30 minutes driving of his house. These include an old gravel pit which holds both smallmouth and largemouth, a 50-acre pond owned by the Boy Scouts and under a public-use agreement, plus several other waters which hold bass.

If you don't happen to know anyone who can introduce you to a few miniponds, the next best bet is to take leisurely drives out in the country looking for ponds. Get off the main highways onto county and township roads, as these usually wind closer to private property and permit you to drive more slowly when scanning the country for impoundments. One fellow I know does this looking when

winter reduces foliage, saying that this gives him a much greater view of previously hidden water.

"Some of these ponds are in plain sight in winter when they would have been hidden 6 months earlier," he explains.

When prospecting for new bass water, don't pass up the miniwaters just because of their small size. Another fishing friend of mine tells of a ¼-acre puddle owned by a farmer friend. At the end of one season of fishing that pond, two sow bass weighing 7 pounds each topped the list of catches. Unlikely? Sure, but my friend's den wall has the adornment as proof.

Sometimes you won't even need a fishing friend or a Sunday drive to find new bass water. Last fall I was exercising my two beagles on a farm near my home when the landowner introduced me to a friend of his. The conversation eventually turned to bass fishing, and before I knew it I had been invited over to fish the friend's pond.

"I don't fish," he explained, "and I know I'm supposed to harvest bass from the pond, but I don't have time. You're welcome to come up anytime. There should be some dandies in there."

My best bass from that minipond so far weighed a bit under 8 pounds and fell for an unweighted sinking nightcrawler. I've also taken several bass in the 5-pound class, and countless smaller ones. The pond measures 1 acre in surface, and plunges to a depth of 26 feet in the middle. The same water supports jumbo bluegills and catfish.

A U.S. Department of Agriculture study on farm ponds shows that the little impoundments with average fertility produce 50 pounds of fish per acre every year. This means a large number of small fish, certainly, but it also means these little fish feed bigger fish, among them the largemouth black bass. Too few predatory bass can result in complete saturation by bluegills, and this can have the same negative effect as too little fishing pressure.

One study on farm ponds said that bluegills, once they reach a certain point of saturation, emit a chemical into the water which inhibits further successful bass spawning. Once this natural bluegill control is removed, the 'gills are free to inflate their population out of balance with the pond's ability to support them. No wonder many pond owners welcome fishermen to help maintain balance in their waters.

A day's bass fishing on one good pond can convert even the most dedicated stream fisherman, even my buddy Harold Barefoot. Harold manufactures and sells fiberglass canoes near Ohio's Stillwater River, and spends almost all of his efforts on Stillwater smallmouth fishing. Last summer, however, I chided him into joining me for a morning of bigmouth plugging on a pond near Cincinnati.

The 11-acre pond looked like anything but bass water. Manicured grass banks sloped to uniform shorelines, and no lily pads or sunked logs could be seen. Harold said I'd better know what I was talking about, but snapped a plug to his line and got to fishing.

By early afternoon on that June day we had boated (or canoed) 26 keepers, keeping half a dozen for the pan and releasing the rest. Our best fish went only a bit over 3 pounds, but we had plenty of fun using light light tackle. Believe me, it was a field day.

Largemouth bass are naturals for farm pond planting. The fish is tolerant of warm water in summer, yet can burrow into the warmer depths during winter. To serve as bass food, and sport fish in their own right, many owners prefer to stock redear sunfish along with their bass, reasoning the

← Fishing pressure should be given to panfish as well as bass if the pond's balance is to be maintained.

Sometimes the best way to approach a pond is to get right into →
the water with the fish.

107

sunfish have a slower rate of reproduction than do bluegills, and therefore pose less of a threat to dominate the pond. Bluegills have often, mysteriously, appeared in farm ponds where they were not stocked, so they may show up whether invited or not.

Farm ponds are great places for kids to learn to fish while making forgivable mistakes which the panfish seem ready to ignore. And there's always the chance of catching, or at least hooking, a real dandy. A lad I know of was blue-gilling near Dayton recently and ended up fighting a 13-pound channel cat for over 30 minutes before landing it. On bluegill tackle, mind you!

But for dedicated bass fishermen who think of ponds as dime-sized spots to whip the water for unsophisticated big-mouth, fishing technique can at times be even more critical than on the big-name impoundments.

The smaller the water, generally, the tougher the requirements. Far too many anglers tend to relax when fishing a farm pond, figuring whatever bass might be in the pond are too ignorant to know the difference. Don't you believe it.

Small ponds are often much clearer than larger impoundments, which means the bass react more drastically to light rays and to the reflection of a human intruder on the water. Whether casting from shore, wading, or using a small boat, fishermen should have a healthy respect for the bass' ability to sense danger.

A 1-acre pond I frequently fish holds some nice bass, and I learned the hard way to approach the shoreline as I would a gin-clear trout stream. I knew there were big bass in the pond, and it followed that these hogs would cruise the shorelines in late evening for frogs, crayfish, insects and whatever showed up for dinner. But try as I would, I could never spot a good cruising bass to cast towards.

One evening I arrived at the pond, black worm already

Ten bluegills to one bass can result from an imbalanced pond ecology.

The black worm is perhaps the farm pond's best lunker killer.

Sometimes the only really effective way to fish a farm pond is to get right into the water with the fish. Wading has several advantages over casting from shore, among them better concentration of coverage with the bait into pockets and around natural cover. Also, wading permits the lure to be started from shore and retrieved towards deeper water, the way real frogs and other food creatures route their movements. Wading, too, is best done slowly with a minimum of disturbance, because fish can "hear" you via the movements you make in the water.

Same thing for boat fishermen. If that oar lock or paddle or tackle box makes noise against the hull, silence it. Thumping the boat or splashing the anchor overboard can put your bass into determined hibernation until you leave the water.

The best bait for a particular pond depends on the natural foods available to the bass living there. In Ohio, these natural foods include frogs, snakes, worms, crayfish, minnows, small panfish, shiners, salamanders and insects. Often the same lure which takes bass will also attract large bluegills, crappies or channel catfish.

There are several sources ready to help you locate ponds and gravel pits in your home area. The county office of the Soil Conservation Service can be helpful, and many state conservation agencies offer geographic maps for a nominal charge. Local or county fishery people keep records of past bass plantings, and don't overlook your game protector or conservation officer. Taxidermists and bait shops are also good places to ask questions.

If you can't make that trip to Lake Huge Bass as often as you'd like, give the farm ponds in your area a chance to fill your stringer. Chances are, by the time you've tried the older ponds in your region, a new crop of impoundments will be waiting, and that's a deal you just can't beat.

Largemouth taken on spinning gear from Indiana farm pond.

tied on my casting rig, and walked over the final slope in time to spot a dandy bigmouth finning in one shallow corner of the pond. I immediately dropped to all fours, left all but my rod where it lay, and literally crawled behind a row of bushes paralleling the near shore. Once within range, I tossed my worm on the opposite dry bank and slithered it into the water.

The rest was anticlimactic. The bass picked up the worm, ran and nearly hooked himself, and a few minutes and several jumps later I thumbed his jaw. The bass weighed 6 pounds even, and taught me to pussyfoot when near clear bass water.

El Tarpon Tropical is not a pretentious fishing resort. It's a small, casual, and charming camp —away from it all.

An angler's wife, this gal had never fished before she accompanied her husband to El Tarpon Tropical.

Fishing: With a Latin American Beat

by Jim C. Chapralis

Whether you try the Banana Republics or trek to Argentina or Paraguay for trout or dorado, you'll find Latin America's fishing exciting and productive.

IT happens every winter.

Hundreds of American sportsmen rush to airports clasping an assortment of rods in one hand while clutching an air ticket with a Latin American destination in the other. In a matter of hours a speedy jet will whisk them to such sleepy cities as Belize or Guayaquil or cosmopolitan places like San Jose or Panama City. Or their destination might be La Paz or Mazatlan or Merida or other Latin American cities which might serve as jump-off spots to any number of small fishing resorts sprouting up annually in the tropics. For many anglers this winter trip to an exotic camp takes precedence over the usual summer fishing trip.

Why? Foremost in their minds is the quality of fishing. They have read accounts of how Ralph Brown hooked six tarpon on one cast at Parismina, or how William DuVal battled a huge black marlin to a standstill on 12-pound test line at Club Pacifico, or how Don Dobbins took a 36-pound record snook at Casa Mar. The fact remains that sport fishing in Latin America until recently was seldom practiced; hence some waters remain practically unfished, or at least so the camp folders state.

With the decline of fishing in the United States due to pollution and increased population, with the development and convenience of jet travel, and with some very attractive excursion fares (i.e., $238 round trip from Chicago to San Jose, Costa Rica), it all does make sense. Add to this that many of the anglers living in northern cities are not at all hesitant to leave snow, slush and a stubborn car battery behind, and you'll understand why some camps are filled months before the season starts.

It would be too lengthy to cover each camp in detail here, but perhaps a short description of some typical Latin American fishing resorts will give you an idea of what to expect:

CASA MAR FISHING CLUB and PARISMINA TARPON RANCHO: Perhaps these two camps have received more publicity than any other fishing resorts in the past decade. They were originated by Carlos Barrantes and both offer explosive tarpon fishing and, at times, snook fishing par excellence. They are located on the east coast of Costa Rica on rivers that pour out into the Caribbean. Costa Rica is certainly one of the most delightful little countries in Latin America, enjoying the highest literacy rate, and a place where an American is warmly received.

Dr. R. W. Koucky's first experience at Casa Mar dramatically illustrates the potential. He hooked a tarpon

Carlos M. Barrantes, developer of two Costa Rican fishing camps, is a snook fanatic. This fish weighed over 25 pounds; but his camps have produced snook of over 30 pounds.

spinning or casting gear that can handle 1- to 2-ounce lures. In other words, tackle used for hefty northern pike, muskies and lake trout can be used here, only your adversary will be a lot larger. If you are lucky enough to get a very active jumping fish, you should be able to boat him within a half-hour if you play him hard. If you take it easy and you have travelling fish, it could take you several miles from where he was hooked—and several hours! The fastest landing job I know of for a 95-pound tarpon was 12 seconds (estimated). The fish was hooked, leaped, only he did not realize the bottom of the boat was in his way on the way up. He was knocked unconscious, floated to the surface, where the guide easily removed the hook.

The seasons at both camps are mid-January to mid-May. Any time can be good (or bad if you get one of those Costa Rican downpours), but most regulars prefer March and April. Both camps offer weekly rates, Saturday to Saturday, and the tariff is $450 at Parismina and $510 at Casa Mar. This includes the round-trip charter plane flights from San Jose to camp in addition to guide, boat, motor, accommodations and all meals. Both camps employ American managers so there is no language problem . . . besides most guides speak some English. The jump-off place is San Jose, Costa Rica, which is reached easily enough from Miami, New Orleans or Los Angeles.

Fishing is done mostly in the fresh-water network of rivers, lagoons and bays from small boats equipped with 20-horsepower motors, but if you can catch the Caribbean in a tranquil mood, head out there. You may see one of the greatest sights imaginable: thousands of tarpon stacked up in tiers!

The difference between the two camps lies mostly in the accommodations. Casa Mar is the "plushier" of the two since it is the newer camp, but both provide great fishing adventure with a backdrop of tropical jungle.

CLUB PACIFICO DE PANAMA: As the name implies, this camp is located on the Pacific coast of Panama and is the newest entry in the fishing resort field. The 1972 season was more or less experimental. Bob Griffin, who had fished for pleasure at a number of Latin American camps, caught the resort business fever, semi-retired from his electrical contracting business, and went prospecting. Near David, Panama, he found Gulf de Chiriqui, a body of water dotted with many islands, fresh water rivers, bays, reefs and apparently an ideal fishing place. It had not been sport fished, and therefore had little angling history. He constructed a temporary camp with all necessary conveniences on a river and small groups began to fish these waters. The results were spectacular and convinced Bob to establish a brand new, spacious, permanent camp on the huge island of Coiba, located right in the heart of the best fishing of the Gulf of Chiriqui.

Would you believe 39 wahoo caught in six days of fishing by Mr. Charles Eberle and his son Clay? They would have done much better, they said, (!!!) if they concentrated on this species, but their log indicates that they caught 135 other fish, which included sailfish on plugs and casting gear, jacks of all kinds, dolphin, roosterfish, tuna, shark, snapper, etc. All told, they took 24 different species.

Would you believe raising 17 sailfish in one morning and close enough to cast a fly to them? Ask Ray Donnersberger or Stu Apte.

Would you believe red snapper of 50 pounds or more smacking surface lures? Ask many guests who have had this experience. Some say they cast lures to snapper running 100 pounds or more! One angler who was fly fishing sank a streamer fly into the jaw of a snapper estimated over 100 pounds. Needless to say, he got neither the fish nor the

within 10 minutes of fishing. The "silver king" made one of his spectacular leaps high in the air—and then landed right in the doctor's boat! It took more than a few minutes to subdue this 80-pound fish, but finally when all was in order and both guide and client regained their composure, they decided to hunt up the doctor's brother who was fishing nearby in another boat. When they approached brother Joe, they noticed that he had hooked a tarpon, and after a preliminary jump or two this fish also decided to leap into the boat. After it was restrained Doc Koucky exclaimed: "Two fish over 80 pounds leap into our boats in the first half-hour of fishing here. We're booked here for a week. We'll never escape this place alive!"

They survived alright—and their party of four boated a total of 66 fish and hooked over 400. They've been going back every year since.

Costa Rican tarpon average in the 60- to 80-pound class. At Casa Mar they are slightly heavier; few tarpon of under 40 pounds are taken. Casa Mar's record is over 140 pounds, while Parismina's top fish is 125 pounds. If you are looking for a world-record tarpon, this is not the place. The 60- to 80-pound class tarpon means that an angler can successfully use relatively light tackle: 15- to 20-pound test lines, and fly back. Snapper taken on the bottom with jigs or other lures can be less than exciting sport, but taken on the surface it becomes an entirely different ball game. At Club Pacifico you can often find acres and acres of water literally colored red as red snappers cruise the surface.

Panama, of course, is world-famous for its great black marlin fishing. Tropic Star Lodge, also located on the west coast of Panama, has delivered a huge quantity of black marlin. Fishing for this species in the waters of Club Pacifico has not been developed, though I will predict that in the future many big blacks will be taken here. The reason is that during the first year of the camp's operation, most clients were interested in light tackle fishing and were after variety. But more than a few blacks were seen and hooked. One angler actually cast a plastic lure at a big black shape with a light spinning outfit. It turned out to be a huge black marlin and the fight took him into complete darkness. The fish finally tired, but the rod broke, and in the confusion of darkness the marlin was lost. The feeling is that if some anglers concentrated on trolling with heavy gear and big bonito for bait, marlin of over 500 pounds could be taken. The area holds many striped marlin as well as some Pacific blue marlin.

Sailfish are also very common, and numerous clients have hooked them "accidentally" on light tackle and plugs. They average over 100 pounds and will take artificial lures readily. Sails here are often found near rocky islands or off reefs which are favored areas of other species. A 100-pound plus Pacific sail lip-hooked on an artificial lure and 20-pound spinning gear is one of the most thrilling acrobatic experiences an angler can have. Incidentally, one of the best sailfish lures here is a plastic squid.

While Club Pacifico was originally conceived to provide accommodations and facilities for fishing during the winter and early spring months, it turns out that fishing during the summer months was spectacular. Owner Bob Griffin is planning to operate his camp year-round.

"The fall months can be quite wet, but this is a great time to fish wahoo. They are so thick in our water at this time that they can be taken with casting plugs and even flies. The wahoo is one of the fastest fish that swims, and I know we have them over 100 pounds here. We've come close to taking some of the big ones," he explains.

These waters were hardly fished before the inception of Club Pacifico, simply because there were no accommodations and it would have been necessary to come by boat from Panama City or David, which is a long way off. Bookings are accepted from Saturday to Saturday, and the tab at camp is $480.00 per person, double occupancy, which includes boats, motors, guides, accommodations (air conditioned) and all meals. The camp also owns two 32-foot sportfisherman boats for marlin fishing.

EL TARPON TROPICAL: Here is a favorite Mexican fishing spa for Americans. Light tackle enthusiasts have for years fished this delightful camp located near Ciudad del Carmen, province of Campeche, Mexico. El Tarpon Tropical offers a variety of fishing including tarpon (both the grandés and the babies), snook, snapper, jacks, barracuda, an occasional permit and a dozen other species. Andy Growich has operated this camp for almost 20 years, and while the majority of anglers congregate from December to May, during the past few years some top-drawer tarpon fishing occurred during the summer months (June, July and August). The camp can be reached either via Mexico City or Merida. The expansive waters of El Tarpon Tropical contain a number of small rivers favored by those who like to cast an accurate fly or plug. Small tarpon, snook and barracuda are the likely candidates for smacking your lure in these rivers. This camp is a favored place of many anglers wives

The critical moment . . . a tarpon is gaffed. Location: El Tarpon Tropical.

because it is fairly close to home, has all the amenities, good meals, no drinking water problem, and above all there are enough smaller species available so that less arduous fishing is possible. And there are the hammocks under thatched palms where the ladies can sip a drink, read a book or just get away from it all. It tends to be a pressureless, highly relaxed camp. The daily rate is $45 per person, all inclusive.

OTHER COUNTRIES, OTHER PLACES: There are many other possibilities, and just about every Latin American country offers a fishing attraction. British Honduras has at least a half-dozen camps which feature some water sports in addition to fishing. Bill Haerr's Turneffe Island Lodge is a famous spot for bonefish and is located on the Barrier Reef. Fred Keller's Caribbean Lodge offers river fishing for tarpon and snook, but also has several houseboats whereby guests can explore distant waters without having to return to the lodge each night. Belize, British Honduras, is the jump-off spot for these camps.

Mexico's west coast, especially Cabo San Lucas, La Paz, Guaymas and Mazatlan offer excellent salt water fishing with the primary target the striped marlin. These waters have produced everything from broadbill swordfish to huge roosterfish. One camp, Rancho Buena Vista, near La Paz, offers a 5-day package (3 days of fishing) for $195 double occupancy. It's just a short flight from Los Angeles, Tucson and other western cities.

Ecuador's Carnero Inn is probably the best place to fish for striped marlin. It's a plush resort with every convenience, plus a gourmet menu. If you are there at the right time it can be an amazing experience. This writer in one day landed seven striped marlin and one Pacific sail, and if it is not a camp record, it was certainly a personal record. Carnero Inn is open year round, but most anglers favor fall, winter and early spring. A 5-day fishing package runs about $500 per person, double occupancy.

Argentina and Chile for years rightfully boasted their fine trout fishing, and while it is not as spectacular as it was 10 years ago, these countries do offer some of the world's best. The improvement of roads is one good reason why fishing has fallen off. You can get to the better streams

Barbara Erskine: "I didn't think I'd care for fishing. After this trip I love it."

Jerry Tricomi's huge tarpon taken at Costa Rica was attacked by a shark during the ensuing fight. Although the shark was scared off, the tarpon was badly injured and brought to camp. Generally tarpon are released.

Don McGuinness, head guide at Club Pacifico, strains on a huge amberjack. The line tested 14 lbs., and the fish, finally landed, was estimated to be over 75 lbs.

Author displays his 110-pound Pacific sail taken at Club Pacifico. Light gear fishing for sails is an electrifying sport.

The roosterfish is an exciting sport fish, and one of the many species offered at Club Pacifico de Panama. Average party generally takes 20 to 25 different species of fish in these waters.

faster and more conveniently, but so can many others.

Argentine fishing tends to be stream fishing via wading or casting from shore. In Chile most angling is done from boats floating down the rivers. Brown and rainbow trout are generally taken, but often one can net a good brook trout or in some areas landlocked salmon. Favorite Argentine rivers include Malleo, Collon Cura, Chimehuin, Alumine and Manso, all reached from Bariloche. The future interest may lie in the southern Patagonian regions all the way down to Tierra del Fuego. Even in these sparsely-populated countries it appears that annually one must travel farther from the beaten path.

Very much in the infancy stage is dorado fishing, best practiced in Argentina and Paraguay. The dorado, if you haven't heard by now, is generally lauded as the finest fresh water gamefish . . . and it compares favorably, if not actually surpassing, with such highly vaunted anadromous fish as Atlantic salmon and steelhead. The dorado is the best leaper of them all, and it has been this writer's privilege to receive as many as 12 jumps per dorado.

When a tarpon leaps it is necessary to bow to the fish and reduce all line tension.

George Wenckheim and Laddie Buchanan both offer trout fishing in Argentina. They are experienced guides, and the daily cost is about $55 per day (for parties of two or more fishermen); a most reasonable rate when you consider they supply ground transportation, all meals, accommodations, and are with you 24 hours a day. Trout fishing is a November to mid-April proposition in Argentina. In Chile the season starts slightly earlier. Dorado fishing is best on the Parana River (north of Buenos Aires), but unfortunately the best time here is July to mid-October, which precludes the possibility of combining dorado and trout fishing in Argentina. But the enterprising angler will discover that he can have his trout fishing during the season in Argentina or Chile and head up to neighboring Paraguay and still get a taste of dorado fishing. In this tiny country dorado fishing is best during the November to April period. Tiger Hill Safaris in Paraguay offers package deals and can provide ground transportation, boats, motors and guides, and they do speak English.

There are dozens of new fishing places planned in Latin America; some will be exciting fishing hideaways, others will fail simply because some camp owners are not cognizant of what American sportsmen require. I visited a new tropical island camp several seasons ago, and after several days of hard fishing we ended up with two small barracuda, a snapper and several other lesser fish. Although the area was extremely beautiful and the camp was very comfortable, it was obvious that this kind of fishing simply would not attract anglers.

Latin American fishing is bound to provide a feeling of excitement, especially in those seldom-fished waters. But the sportsman travelling to distant spots ought to bear in mind that a trout or a tarpon or a marlin in Latin America is controlled by the same important factors as in our waters: Weather! If conditions are against you and fish simply refuse to feed, you will have poor results.

Latin American fishing has great appeal to the angler's wife even if she has expressed little interest in previous local fishing trips. She knows that even if fishing is unappealing to her, she will be able to visit a foreign country, do some shopping and sightseeing, and practice her high school Spanish. Take her along. She'll love Latin America.

The best way to plan your fishing trip is to contact one of the several travel agencies that cater to sportsmen. They can plan the entire trip for you, including air transportation and hotel reservations, inform you of required documents, and these services cost you nothing.

THE BASS BOAT GROWS UP

by GRITS GRESHAM

FUNNY THING about genius is that, so frequently, it goes unrecognized for so long. And genius is the only adequate word to describe the happening of people, process and evolution in the Gulf South over the past decade or so which culminated in the critter called a bass boat.

What's a bass boat!

Imagine a fishing boat which will run 40 miles an hour, is shallow draft, is narrow enough for you to fish on either side, and is so stable you can run up and down one gunnel without tipping. A boat which you can operate entirely from the bow position, where the visibility is best and the fishing opportunity is greatest. And a boat which, after you have reached your favorite fishing hole, you can maneuver wherever you like without ever touching a paddle.

No such animal? Well, you're wrong, because I've been fishing from one for almost a decade. That's a bass boat, a rather unfortunate bit of terminology which has been a smokescreen for anglers who prefer other species. But genius will out, and this creation—probably the most efficient fishing platform ever built—is rapidly getting the attention of the nation.

My search for a fishing boat which would do it all began the moment I began fishing, and in that respect my experience is the same as that of most anglers throughout the country. All of us have gone through the period of leaky wooden boats, of bulky big boats, of slow boats, of tippy boats, or noisy boats, and of boats which were killers to paddle or to row.

The sad fact was that there simply weren't any boats available which were engineered with the fisherman in mind, despite the fact that many of them were called "fishing" boats. But I kept looking and hoping for something better . . . and I found it.

My favorite fishing boat was spawned in Louisiana about 15 years ago when a Shreveport friend of mine, Holmes

Author in a Terry Bass Boat — fiberglass cathedral hull, stick steering, padded swivel seats, bow-mounted electric motor.

Cathedral hull on this Terry provides enough stability that angler can walk around on the gunnel without tipping the boat.

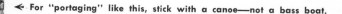

◄ For "portaging" like this, stick with a canoe—not a bass boat.

Foot control for bow-mounted electric motor frees both hands for fishing.

Thurman, designed and patented a boat which he called the "Skeeter." It has been described as being an offspring of a mixed marriage involving a pirogue, a kayak, and a Barnegat Bay duck boat. But whatever the genesis, this pointed-bowed, flat bottomed craft was a great fishing boat for the protected, cypress-studded lakes and bayous in this part of the nation.

It still is, but a dedicated corps of bass fishermen, who would settle for nothing less than the best, took the idea and nurtured it to its present state of refinement and efficiency. The beat goes on, of course, and more goodies are in store for the future, but for now let's examine what imagination and ingenuity has done to and for that original type specimen of the "bass boat."

Came the plastics, of course, and where Holmes lovingly crafted his "Skeeters" from marine plywood, the bass boats which now are popped from molds around the nation are of tough, smooth, durable, gleaming fiberglass. And the configuration has changed to make that original great idea adaptable to bigger, rougher waters, and to make the bow area more useable.

Most bass boats now have cathedral hulls which provide stability which was previously unknown in a fishing boat, and which help smooth out the bumps in a chop. They also have a rounded bow rather than a pointed one, making bow storage practical.

To find out what makes these rigs so special, join me on a fishing trip and see for yourself. It was an hour before daylight on the morning in question when I backed my Travelall up to my Terry Bass Boat in the driveway and dropped the trailer hitch over the ball. Getting ready to go was as simple as that.

My gear was already in the boat. Fishing rods were inside

their racks in locked compartments on either side of the boat. Rain gear and a warm jacket in a waterproof bag stowed in the bow compartment. So was a tool kit, including such spare parts as spark plugs and an extra prop. My fishing rig stays ready to go at all times.

I drove the 60 miles to the lake of my choice in less than an hour, with the trailer tracking effortlessly at high speed. The lake is a huge one and I elected to launch my boat in an area where there is no launching ramp. An unpaved secondary road took me near the lake's edge, and it was easy to back down until the wheels of the trailer were in the edge of the water. From there it was effortless to slide the boat off.

On that occasion it wasn't really needed, but I take comfort in having a limited slip differential in the Travelall. On the rare occasions when that positive traction can't pull boat and trailer to firm ground, an electric winch on the front of the vehicle snakes everything out.

The water at that particular point was too shallow for outboard operation, but with the controls at my disposal on the Terry it was easy to maneuver into deep water. From my bow seat position, with the touch of a button, I used the power tilt to drop the lower unit of the 50hp Johnson from its horizontal launching position down into the water, but just barely so. With the prop just beneath the surface of the water, I cranked the outboard with a turn of the key and backed slowly and easily out into water deep enough for normal operation. Another touch of the power tilt button and the outboard dropped on down into vertical position.

My rig will run better than 40 mph at full bore, and even at three-quarter throttle—which I prefer—it took less than 10 minutes to reach the first hot spot I wanted to fish. A

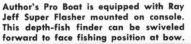

Terry Pro Bass Hunter has elevated pedestal seats front and rear, and console steering.

Author's Pro Boat is equipped with Ray Jeff Super Flasher mounted on console. This depth-fish finder can be swiveled forward to face fishing position at bow.

Checking Ray Jeff Fish Flasher and compass puts author right on structure.

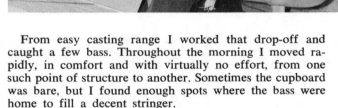

single tall tree standing alone in the open water was my marker, and I slowed to no-wake speed when I reached it.

But the exact place I wanted to fish was several hundred yards away from the tree, so the first marker was only the beginning. Finding such a small area—the critical part of this one was not more than 20 feet square—can be a formidable task for the angler who isn't properly equipped. With a boat rig like mine it is accomplished quickly. Like this: I flipped on the sonar depth finder and, watching my compass, ran a northeast course directly away from my marker tree. After a short run the bright blip on the finder rose rapidly from its 40-foot indication up to 15 and then to 10 feet. I switched off the outboard and dropped the electric motor over the bow.

Controlling the electric motor with the pressure of one foot, I swung the boat in a pattern, watching the depth finder all the while, until I found the exact point of the drop-off. Over the side went a styrofoam marker, and then I eased the boat into deeper water and gently lowered the anchors.

Dropping the anchors on a rig like this is no problem, since they are released with the turn of a button. No noise, no effort, and no loss of time. They are retrieved with the turn of a crank.

From easy casting range I worked that drop-off and caught a few bass. Throughout the morning I moved rapidly, in comfort and with virtually no effort, from one such point of structure to another. Sometimes the cupboard was bare, but I found enough spots where the bass were home to fill a decent stringer.

That electric motor, mounted on the bow, is one of the key items which takes a bass boat out of the realm of the ordinary. Called an electric "trolling" motor by many people, this great labor-saving device came of age when it was moved from the transom of a boat to the bow . . . where it pulls the boat rather than pushes it.

It took another giant step when a fellow invented a foot control with which a fisherman can stop, start and steer in any direction with just one of his size 11's, all the time keeping his lure in the water. So can my wife, or your's, with her little, bitty foot, and that epitomizes what this bass boat thing is all about.

It takes almost no effort to efficiently operate a bass boat. Electric-starting outboard, stick steering, and an electric "paddle." With that electric motor easing along the shoreline, casting is no trick at all. Even when the wind is blowing so hard it would be impossible to control the boat with a paddle, this bow-mounted accessory makes it possible to fish with ease.

Stick steering? That's just what the name implies. It's a vertical "stick" positioned near the gunnel on the left side of the bow seat with which the angler steers the boat. Push the stick forward to turn right; pull it to the rear to turn left.

Stick steering is simple and very responsive, and eliminates the steering wheel which seems to always be in the way in a small boat. It is practical for outboard power up

With electric starting outboards, stick steering, and foot-controlled electric motors, lady anglers can handle bass boats with ease.

Fishing position on Terry Bass Pro Boat is an adjustable pedestal seat on a raised bow deck. Author checks water temperature, which can be critical for many fish species.

to about 65 horses, but above that a steering wheel is preferable.

Most of the current crop of bass boats feature padded swivel seats which are as comfortable as your living room rocker. The "pro boat" configuration has a high pedestal seat on a raised bow deck and another at the stern, plus a steering console somewhere in between.

There is some doubt as to who built the first fiberglass, cathedral hull bass boat, but there is no doubt that it was the Terry Bass Boat which first got the attention of anglers. It was so dominant, in fact, that the name Terry Bass virtually became the generic name for this type of craft.

The Terry Bass boats are manufactured by the Delhi Manufacturing Corporation, a young, giant operation in Delhi, Louisiana which annually produces more than 70,000 fiberglass and aluminum boats. For this year's line, Delhi has introduced a Terry which will undoubtedly expand the versatility of this fishing machine into many new areas.

The new Terry Bass Tourney is 18 feet 2 inches in length, with a beam of 70 inches, a big boat with the stability and

"Skeeter" boat, with pointed bow and flat bottom, was forerunner of today's bass boat.

Plush, padded swivel seats, on pedestals, have replaced those early bench-type seats. Stick steering control is at left.

Tourney has three live wells, great storage areas, ice chest, and Ozite turf carpeting.

Early bass boats had bench-type seats. Angler attached his own swivel boat seats.

wave-straddling capability necessary for safe, comfortable performance in rough water on big lakes. It is B.I.A. certified for outboards up to 125 horsepower.

Not only should this new entry be a winner in inland waters, but it will bring the "bass boat" fishing efficiency to protected coastal fishing for snook, tarpon, redfish, trout, bonefish, and striped bass. Standard equipment on the Tourney includes three live wells, ice chest, several storage compartments including one which is 87 inches long (big enough for 7-foot rods without breaking them down), and built-in 18-gallon fuel tank.

Mary and I have "his and her" Terrys. One is a 15-footer with stick steering, pushed by a 50hp Johnson. The other is a 16-foot Terry Pro Bass Hunter with 100 horses on the transom. On the smaller boat I have a depth finder mounted on the port side just in front of the bow seat. On the Pro console pedestal I have a Ray Jeff Structure Flasher.

I also have a couple of other great "fishing" aids which will probably be the next "gadget" to catch fire with anglers. On the Pro I have a Ray Jeff CB-105 citizens' band radio, giving 23 channels at five watts of power. In the 15-footer we carry a portable CB.

Many of our fishing buddies now have CB in their boats, and we have a big advantage in being able to contact each other when we locate fish. Or when we have trouble of any kind.

No matter where you are in this country, there's a good chance that you can reach somebody, somewhere on a CB radio. Somebody who will telephone the marina and tell them where it is you've run out of gasoline, or lost a water pump—just at sunset—15 miles from the dock. It's a comforting feeling to have such a gadget aboard.

Terry Bass led the way, but other boat manufacturers were quick to follow. First it was others in the same general Gulf South area, with names like Tidecraft, of Minden, Louisiana; Ouachita, of Little Rock; Kingfisher, of Clarksville, Texas; and Skeeter Hawk, of Longview, Texas. Now there is a long list—Chrysler's Bass Runner; Mon-Ark; Bomber; Falcon; Cordell's Goin Jessie; Glastron's Beau Jack; Ranger, a favorite with tournament fishermen; Rebel; and more to come.

Bass boats are the hottest items in the boating field, and

18-foot Terry Bass Tourney signals the bass boat has come of age. It will open bigger inland waters, and protected coastal areas, to bass boat efficiency.

they'll get hotter before they cool off—if ever—because they simply are the best fishing platforms for *most* fishing in this country. Most fishing, not just bass fishing.

Cane pole fishing from my bass boat is so easy and effective I should be handicapped. From my bow seat, using the electric motor, I can quietly and easily slide along, probing the potential hot spots by dropping in a worm, a cricket or a shiner.

It's no canoe which can be portaged between lakes, and it is definitely not a Great Lakes "coho" boat except under the most unusual conditions, but in most waters it cannot be touched as a craft for walleye or yellow perch, muskie or trout, pike or pickerel. And that's why the bass boat boom has scarcely been scratched. Just you wait until this cajun creation gets the attention of foreigners in Michigan and Florida and New York and California. And that's just about to happen.

Bluegills which fell victim to a bass boat.

Author's bass boat stays packed, ready to roll, when he backs his tow vehicle up to the trailer.

Troy Baker snatches aboard a struggling bluefish.

I've got the gulf coast blues

by MAX HUNN

IT WAS AN amazing sight. The huge submerged rockpile extending for several hundred yards in an irregular curve was faintly outlined by the brilliant Florida sun. Six to 8 feet of water covered the dark mass as the tide flooded off Homosassa in the Gulf of Mexico.

The water's surface was churning with frightened bait fish, skipping, leaping, twisting and doing everything possible to escape a relentless horde of hungry pursuers. Savagely the feeding fish charged, charged and charged again into the bait that was unable to flee the rocks. Apparently, they were hemmed in like a wagon train attacked by Indians.

"Wow! They're still here!" exclaimed Gene Lechler, our guide, anchoring our boat within a long cast of the rockpile

rumpus. "Grab your rods, start throwing and look out!"

Gene's a guide who likes to fish with his parties. He was first into the water, flipping a long cast near the edge of the melee. He popped the three-gang hook, red and white, top water plug (South Bend Bass Oreno) twice and bang! He got a savage, jolting strike. His stiff, 6-foot casting rod bent sharply, and momentarily his tight drag yielded, even though his reel (Ambassadeur 5000) was loaded with 20-pound monofilament.

His foe suddenly erupted into aerial antics, then powered off on a line consuming run, seemingly headed for the rocks a la a sounding grouper. Busy as he was, Gene managed to holler: "Cast right behind me. There are others following!"

We saw other fish darting around Gene's foe. My cast fell 10 feet behind his rapidly moving battler. Bang! I, too, was in action. The blue hit my top water (a miniature, plastic Lucky 13) as if it were his first real meal in months. I never did start to retrieve. He connected as it landed.

Gene wasted no time in boating his chopper, but with my 10-pound line, spinning reel (Daiwa 8300) and lighter rod, I was not equipped to set a time landing record. My fish sounded, taking off on a powerful run that seemed destined to end in disaster on the rockpile, until the pressure of my reel's drag and bucking rod turned him. Then the chopper began a series of bulldog, side to side dashes, taking advantage of the incoming tide. Suddenly, he erupted in a violent jump that would have done justice to a small tarpon. He landed just as ungracefully.

Foot by foot he was slowly giving ground, and with each violent antic, tiring, but he was a stubborn brawler. As I worked him near the boat, he spooked with a spurt as sudden as a jet pilot turning on an afterburner. But this charge was short lived. Finally, I brought him alongside, and Gene swung the net.

That was a mistake with a gang hook plug. What a mess he made of the net! After subduing him with a hefty belt with my pliers, I began the chore of picking him and the gang hooks out of the netting. During landing, he viciously bit several nylon net strands. They don't stop chomping until they're dead.

Rough customers? One of the roughest. Vicious, hard fighting, brawling, even nasty are some of the suitable words for a chopper. A bluefish earns them, for there's no doubt he's a battling game fish.

Our previous acquaintance with blues has been meager, limited to a long remembered encounter with a wandering chopper in the Ten Thousand Islands. That one battled so long and hard I thought he was a 10-pound jack crevalle, only to discover he was a 3-pound blue. We've also trolled for blues off Beaufort, S.C. but there's a difference between trolling for widely scattered choppers and casting for them

where they're schooled. There's a reef near Beaufort where the blues school, and casting for them is lots of fun. Trolling isn't nearly as exciting.

Of all the methods of catching the popular, good eating bluefish, undoubtedly the most exciting is casting with top water lures—generally fresh water bass types—into a surface feeding school. The action is pandemonium, and expensive plug wise. Don't use hollow, plastic lures. We learned the hard way the sharp teeth of the bluefish will ruin such plugs in one or two encounters. Wood plugs or metal spoons are definitely the best and most durable— at least as durable as you can get. And woe unto the plugs with fragile hooks. A savage chopper mangles them in the first round. My first blue twisted my plug's hooks as if they'd been bent with pliers. You need a good supply of lures—preferably old ones—when plugging for blues.

This fantastic fishing trip started the night before when Gene excitedly telephoned, wanting to know if I wanted to go fishing. Now, when a guide sounds excited, my interest boils, although it doesn't take much to arouse it when fishing's concerned.

But Gene's news was startling. He and Bob Hadley, another fishing friend, and an avid angler when he can get away from his Evinrude dealership in Homosassa, had boated 100 bluefish 2 days before while drifting between rockpiles south of the mouth of the Homosassa river.

As Gene described it, there were blues everywhere, typical choppers on the prowl for meals or attacking out of mean disposition. Gene and Bob had been in a fantastic fishing brawl. When the blues stripped the tails off their bucktail jigs, they just kept casting with lead heads and still the choppers hit. But that was 2 days before. Prior to committing myself to a possible boat ride, I hedged a bit with Gene.

"Sounds really fantastic, but will they be there tomorrow?"

"Sure," replied Gene. "If I can find a certain rockpile. They mill around this set of rocks for a couple of weeks, or until the bait's cleaned out. Some of them are around all summer, but they tend to be scattered. Now's the time to get 'em schooling."

However, despite Gene's confidence I was a little dubious when we met that morning at the Yardarm Docks at Riverside Villas in Homosassa. Here he keeps his 24-foot, I-O powered, open Ski Barge guide boat.

My reservations stemmed from several things. For one thing, in 48 hours the bluefish could well have moved miles. Second, this was late spring. While the blues make semi-annual appearances along the Florida west coast, all reports indicate the best fishing normally is in the fall. There are some around all summer, but they're usually scattered. Still, a hundred blues in the boat didn't sound like poor fishing. Also, the run along the Florida west coast never has been as highly publicized as the traditional movements on the Atlantic seaboard.

I knew the blues started virulent fishing fever from Maine to Florida, and that fantastic catches were possible during the fat period of the bluefish cycle. But I knew little —and could find nothing in angling literature—concerning the bluefish along the Gulf coast. Maybe it's because surf fishing (a very popular method on the Atlantic coast) isn't practiced much on the Gulf coast. Perhaps the run is smaller (although a hundred in a boat would be hard for two men to beat!), or maybe the blues miss the publicity spotlight because they appear at the same time as do the kingfish and Spanish mackerel. Your hear far more reports of big catches of kings and Spanish than you do of blues along the west coast. Anyway, as far as I could see, the bluefish appearance isn't widely ballyhooed along the middle Florida Gulf coast. However, I wasn't interested in how publicized the fishing was. I just wanted some assurance it was half as good as Gene said.

We were fortunate to find the rocks without any major problems. In clear water, the rocks in the shallows aren't too hard to find. But if the water is murky, the situation is very different. Our water had a slight tinge, but it hadn't bothered us unduly; and the tide was right—incoming.

After our first netting foulup, it was obvious a net was no answer with gang hook plugs. Not only did the fish cut the net, but untangling the gang hooks wasted valuable fishing time. Gene, of course, with his heavier line had no problem in snatching aboard the 1- to 3-pounders. Our 10-pound spinners presented more of a problem, however. My wife, Kit, and I solved it by using extra long shock leaders of 20-pound mono plus the essential short wire leader.

The action was frantic. Every blue fought hard, the length and ferocity of the struggle depending upon the angle of hooking and, naturally, his size. A regular mouth hooking provided standard wild action, but when they foul hooked themselves, which was a frequent occurrence, the resulting fight was terrific. They were tigers to whip, because they could use their jack-shaped bodies to maximum effectiveness. Also the tide was on their side. It was like trying to weigh a fouled anchor and having it suddenly take to the air.

Although they strike wildly, we probably had more misses than hits. In the frantic action, it was impossible to tell exactly what was happening. We'd cast near the rockpile, pop our lures a couple of times and then begin a medium-fast retrieve. A pass followed almost inevitably, but not always a solid connection. However, by pausing, another return pass or an attack by another chopper developed. The blues, like many other fish, are jealous of each other. When one blue connected solidly, others always followed as if trying to take the lure away from the first one. Almost always a cast behind a hooked fish caught another.

Blues are dangerous in the boat, particularly with gang

Standing by to help, Gene Lechler watches Kit Hunn boat another fighting bluefish.

Gene lands a fighting chopper.

Gene plays a leaping bluefish. They not only fight hard underwater, but they use aerial antics, too.

Some fishermen prefer to use single hook lures. These are safer and have the added advantage of being easier to unhook. There's less time lost in getting back into action, particularly when trolling spoons.

The action slowed as the tide reached its peak (the best time is the last 2 to 2½ hours of the flood) and a pending line squall forced us to heave anchor and make for shore like a scalded cat.

Back at the Yardarm Docks we tallied our catch. It consisted of 40 bluefish running from 1½ pounds to 3 pounds, plus three grouper, and a pair of speckled sea trout. Gene bagged 20 of the choppers, Kit got five, and I boated 15 during the hectic action. How many we lost, we'll never know.

Perhaps the most interesting part was the fantastic variety of lures the choppers hit. We caught them on red and white, South Bend Bass Orenos; red and white and yellow spotted, plastic Lucky 13s; red and gold, 32-M-28 Mirrolures; a yellow Zara Spook; a silver flash Dalton Special with a propeller; red and white, orange, and silver Daredevle spoons; a silver Banana; and an Eppinger school striper plug.

Neither the lure nor its color seemed of any importance so long as it made a rumpus similar to a fleeing baitfish. With enough noise you were guaranteed a bluefish pass. Probably 50 percent connected solidly enough to be landed.

Obviously, we acquired a bad case of bluefish fever. Kit and I were ready to return to the rockpile almost immediately, but Gene was booked the next day. We were set for the day after.

Forty-eight hours later we were again shoving off for the Bluefish Battlefield. This time the good fairy must have been busy elsewhere. We finally located the rocks in murky water by the luckless accident of running directly over them. We went right through the massed fish to do it, too. Our chances didn't seem promising.

Some of the choppers spooked, but after anchoring, we could still see some little mild baitfish action. We began casting. This time the blues weren't feeding as wildly, but they were there, and we began boating them regularly. However, it became apparent that this was a different school, possibly a smaller one, for these choppers were all running bigger than those of the previous trip. None went under 2 pounds and several nudged the scales at 4. Since bluefish travel in schools of approximately the same size (and apparently the same age group), we were certain a different group had moved in during the intervening time.

Later in the summer, the blues are still present off Homosassa, but they don't seem to school as much. You never can tell when you'll encounter them, but, either as singles or in packs, they're great sport.

One August day we were fishing with Troy Baker. We didn't care what we caught so long as we had action. This time we were north of the mouth of the Homosassa on the "Bomber Range," so named in World War II days when it was used for target practice by military pilots. It's another fish loaded area, and suddenly we encountered a school of ladyfish. The bouncing ladies are always fun with their aerial acrobatics. Then abruptly, on the incoming tide, we began encountering our old pals, the blues. Troy nailed the first pair and immediately we were into another typical chopper brawl, although this one was over quickly as the school sped away. This time the blues hit fast moving jigs and were much easier to unhook.

After these few sessions with the wild blues, Kit and I have a bad cronic case of "blue blood." Look out when we head for the docks when we hear they are in. We might run over you. The Florida west coast blues will make any angler happy.

hook plugs. Gene was unfortunate enough to have a wild blue sink a gang hook into his finger. The hook went in below the barb, and I had to cut it off at the plug, then push the hook on through his finger. You can't be too careful in handling those wild ones.

Our safest method was to use a big rag—we had an old towel—to get a firm grip on the fish, and then remove the plug hooks with long nose pliers, being extremely careful not to get within range of the thrashing fish.

Ramps, pungent and strong-tasting relatives of wild onions, are favored by many springtime anglers in the Tennessee Smoky Mountains.

Wild Edibles For the Fisherman

by Charles Nansen

SEARCHING parties recently located a fisherman who had been missing for six days in Florida's Big Cypress Swamp. They reached him a little too late, for he was dead—of starvation.

It seems strange that any sportsman should perish of starvation. In every section of our land the waterways are virtually lined with nutritious edibles. Some of these are especially delicious—like morel mushrooms or watercress or hazelnuts which bring high prices when you find them on grocer's shelves.

Fortunately, few fishermen will ever be lost long enough to depend on wild foods for survival. But most fishermen *do* cook outdoors occasionally, and they depend to a good

extent on the foods they find around them, at least to supplement their menus. Others will return home with more than just a heavy creel of trout.

Many times when fishing was slow, I have turned from fishing to hunting mushrooms or berries—or to collecting a mess of spring greens. Fact is, the latter has become a ritual that must be repeated time and again before the arrival of springtime is official. The same is true in September when the first beechnuts ripen and fall like autumn rain.

Except in winter, there's always a good variety of wild food available—usually without need for traveling too far from the water. All those described here can be found—or are usually found—near lakes and streams.

Most common and widespread of all berries is the blackberry.

A great variety of spring greens exist everywhere in the U.S. Some can be used for salads, others cooked as vegetables. All are great with fish.

Heart of the cabbage palm is excellent with bass or catfish and hushpuppies.

AMERICAN LOTUS: A giant water plant that grows in lakes, ponds, and sluggish streams as far west as Texas, the lotus is distinguished by leaves as large as two feet in diameter attached to stems in the middle. Some leaves float; others grow some distance above the water. In summer, large (6″ to 10″ diameter) yellow flowers are followed by flat-topped, receptacle-like fruits. Seeds are imbedded in 20 to 24 pits in the hardened, ripe receptacle. When fully ripe in fall, these dark brown seeds are edible raw—after a hard shell is removed. Before they're ripe, crack the shell and roast or boil them.

BEECHNUTS: Some years in the fall it seems that every handsome, gray-barked beech tree will be heavy with brown, prickly burs. Other years there will be none. But as soon as the burs ripen, they open and fall to the ground, each one giving up a pair of triangular seeds about half an inch long. They're extremely sweet and delicious, fine for roasting around a campfire or eating raw as a snack.

BLACK WALNUTS: While other streamside trees are in full autumn color, you can always spot the black walnuts. The foliage falls and leaves them bare early in the fall. Inside a tough, yellow-green husk and a hard, rough shell you'll find a four-celled kernel with a sweet, fairly strong taste. The meat makes a tasty snack and is fine in breads and pastries. Walnuts held over for one season are considered the most delicious.

BLACKBERRIES: One species or another is found over most of the eastern United States. Perhaps they are our most valuable wild fruit, since they are so abundant in some regions. If you find whole hillsides of white blossoms in June, return in July to harvest the delicious, blue-black berries for dessert in camp or for pies at home. In a pinch, you might even try them as bait for carp, channel catfish, or suckers.

BLUEBERRIES: Few fishermen of long standing have failed to enjoy blueberries—by any of their many local names—in one way or another. They are found all across the north and central United States and southern Canada. Blue and from ¼″ to ½″ in diameter, they are also known as huckleberries. Sweet and juicy, they are delicious in muffins, pies, or plain with cream. Indians used them, when thoroughly dried, as seasoning for wild meats in pemmican.

BUTTERNUTS: Except in small, local regions, butternut trees are scarce nowadays. They're most numerous along waterways across the central United States to Kansas. The nut is hard and furrowed, covered by a pungent smelling husk. Separating easily, the kernel is sweet and oily. Once Confederate uniforms were dyed "butternut" from the husks—and today, fly-tiers occasionally use that treatment to give flies a streamside color-change.

DANDELIONS: Now spread over most of the civilized world, dandelions are among our most common plants. They are among the most nutritious, too. Gather the leaves when they are young and tender. Boil with a lump of butter and small amount of vinegar—but not too long. Change water during boiling to reduce the somewhat bitter taste. Dandelions can be cooked with salt pork, too. The dried roots can be used as a surprisingly good substitute for coffee.

All across the country, many wild plants can be gathered to make "mixed greens" or to cook with dandelions in camp or at home. Some of the most delicious and common are: dock, the tender tops of horseradish and mustard, lamb's quarter, and young poke *shoots*. Be certain to avoid poke roots, because they are poisonous.

GOOSEBERRIES: Late in July, along moist fence rows, ravines, and brooks, the brown-purple gooseberries begin to ripen over most of their range. Sometimes the berries are prickly, and in some soils exceedingly tart. But this sub-acid quality is fine for quenching thirst, a ready convenience if the nearby waters you are fishing contain pollution. Gooseberries are excellent for jellies, pies, or preserves. Native from Maine to Alabama and west to Missouri and Manitoba, they are probably most numerous in Pennsylvania and West Virginia.

HAZELNUTS: All through the summer watch for thicket-type shrubs on which many green, leafy-like husks are hanging. Then in August, as soon as the husks turn brown, collect them—or else squirrels and chipmunks will beat you to the delicious, brown, filbert-like nuts inside. They're best roasted over an open fire or in a waterfowl dressing.

HICKORY NUTS: Hickories are native all over the country in at least one species or another. All are edible, and only the pignut hickory cannot be classed as tasty. Many species grow in the lowlands, along rivers, where they are quite available to fishermen. The husks are smooth, thin, and in four sections. The kernels are sweet and aromatic. Hickory nut production seems to be cyclic; there are years of great abundance followed by seasons of scarcity.

MOREL MUSHROOMS: There are many edible mushrooms, but none rivals the morels in taste and in ease of identification. In many areas, they're called sponge mushrooms, and that's exactly what they look like. You'll find them in moist shady places, in thickets, and often not too far from water in the eastern United States. They emerge from the earth for only a short time in early spring—so keep posted. Wash them, dip in a favorite batter, and fry them. You'll never be able to get enough—or to wait until next April.

PALMETTO: Abundant along rivers and lake shores in the deep South, palmettos may grow as high as 40 feet. The large terminal bud resembles a head of cabbage in size, shape, and appearance—so it's commonly called "cabbage palm." This bud is superb fare, either raw or boiled. Try it with salt pork or corned beef. Removing the bud kills the tree, though, so it may be a good idea to use discretion in cutting it.

PAWPAW: Travel along streambanks, especially in the Ohio or Mississippi valleys late in summer, and you'll find places where stubby, banana-like fruits are ripening from greenish-yellow to brown or black. The bushes on which you find them are often close and dense enough to form heavy thickets and the fruits are most succulent where they grow in shade. The pulp is quite sweet and rich, as in tropical fruits, for the pawpaw is actually a fugitive from the tropics. Its range covers most of the eastern United States to Texas.

PECANS: This excellent nut is a resident of the lower Mississippi valley. Olive-shaped and thin-husked, the shell is smooth and brittle. The seeds it contains are probably the most delicious of nuts. They ripen in the fall, as do all American nuts. It's popular southern sport to mix squirrel hunting in the pecans with a fall fishing trip.

PERSIMMONS: When fishing in autumn, keep a weather eye peeled for trees heavy with orange fruits about one or one and a half inches in diameter. If you've had a heavy frost (this isn't an infallible rule), try them. If not, wait a little longer, for persimmons are astringent and unpleasant until they're fully ripe. Raccoons, 'possums, foxes, and birds will give plenty of competition for the matured fruit. Early settlers used them extensively in persimmon bread; if you have a pioneer spirit, try mixing the pulp with your bread or biscuit dough. Range: west to Texas, abundant in Oklahoma and mid-South.

WATERCRESS: This interesting plant has many uses around a fishing camp. It floats in clear, cold (the year around) water that usually comes from a limestone source. The small leaves have from three to nine segments; the terminal leaf is always the largest. The tangy bite of watercress is perfect in salads, boiled greens, or as a garnish. You may find it anywhere, even close to centers of populations, so be careful about gathering it from polluted waters.

Look for hazelnuts early in the fall before they are harvested by squirrels.

Morel mushrooms, found widely in woodlands across America, are among the most delicious of all wild edibles. They go well with fresh fried fish.

Even the roots of the cattails foreground, on this Ohio farm pond are edible and nutritious when cooked.

The shaggy mane mushroom of early fall can be found by anglers in the East.

WILD PLUMS: You can find at least one of a dozen varieties of wild plums in every corner of the land. Often, when heavily interwoven, they are the trees that make travel along creek banks so difficult. Only a few trees bear fruit, however. On these, yellow or red pulpy fruits with tough skins grow thick and ripen late in summer. They're grand when stewed for your breakfast in camp. Otherwise, they are tart and not too tasty.

WILD RASPBERRIES: Two varieties—red and black—are found over much of the land east of the Continental Divide. Blacks ripen in July or August, while the reds, which tend to thrive farther north, are ready for picking a month later. They are especially plentiful in cut or burned-over areas.

Fine for jams and jellies, they make a splendid camp dessert with sugar and cream.

WILD RICE: If you are lucky nowadays, you can buy wild rice on the market for as little as three or four dollars a pound. In the wild, it's a coarse grass that may grow as high as eight feet. The fruit panicles may be more than a foot long and the grains, usually dark brown or black, fall when ripe. Steamed, boiled, buttered, or in dressing, this rice is one of the most delicious, desired wild foods. It grows in swamps, marshes, and along water borders in Minnesota, Wisconsin, Michigan, and southern Canada. Indians collect the grain in canoes—by bending the stalks over the gunwale and shaking them hard. Even today, no better, more economical method has been devised.

WILD STRAWBERRIES: These are the rarest delicacies in the wild. Once a naturalist wrote, "Doubtless God could have made a better berry, but doubtless God never did." The sweet, red, pulpy berries ripen in June or July, depending on the latitude. They prosper in moist areas along streams and frequently around the margins of swamps. Range: New Brunswick to Saskatchewan, south to Florida, west to Texas and most numerous in the Midwest.

ELK THISTLE: This huge thistle is common in the Rocky Mountains and may grow as tall as two feet. Both the inner green stem and the large tap root are edible, either raw or cooked. Chopped up, the root can take the place of potatoes or carrots in a stew or fish chowder. Most other thistles also are edible, although not as tasty or the elk thistle.

Elk thistle is found not far from many western trout streams. Both the inner green stem and large tap root are edible.

Good king taken on light tackle near Bell Island Hot Springs, also in southeastern Alaska.

ON A rainy morning toward the tag end of July, John Moxley and I caught Alaska Airlines daily flight from Anchorage to Juneau with stops at Cordova, Yakutat and Sitka. On a better day we would have been able to see some of the world's most magnificent scenery en route. But outside the aircraft's windows was only a gray void.

"Our lucky streak may have ended," John commented.

This was the last lap of a month-long fishing junket through the 49th State and during the first three weeks of it, we'd enjoyed nothing but good luck. I recalled the week we

SALMON of ALASKA'S PANHANDLE

by Ken S. Bourbon

John Moxley, left, and Phil Baker unhook large king salmon hooked in vicinity of Douglas Island.

spent near Mt. Katmai on the Battle and Kulik rivers and particularly the scarlet-finned, river-running lakers we found at Battle. John pointed out that we had taken eight species of fish — lakers, rainbows, Arctic char, Dolly Vardens, northern pike, grayling, sheefish and king salmon — all from Bob Curtis's camp at Tikchik Narrows. I guess we couldn't complain if we never caught another fish.

It was raining even harder in Juneau than in Anchorage. And Eric McDowell who met us at the airport wasn't very optimistic about a change in the weather. Eric was the young deputy director of the Alaska Travel Division, which is any visitor's best friend when in need of travel information there. He drove us to the Baranof Hotel, explaining en route, that he had arranged for us to go salmon fishing the next day with charter captain Phil Baker. And that was a lucky circumstance as I will explain.

The following morning was a carbon copy of the day before — dreary and rain pelting down — but Phil Baker brought the good news that the weather should soon break. After breakfast we drove northward with him the 14 miles from Juneau to Auke Bay where he moored his boat, a 22-foot cabin cruiser especially equipped for coastal salmon fishing. Although there are ample docking facilities right in downtown Juneau, Phil explained that Auke Bay was closer to his favorite salmon areas and that he could save a good deal of running time for fishing by keeping his boat at this spot.

The great tidal fluctuations in southeastern Alaska also limit the number of places at which boats can be moored. The anchorage must be very deep and the docks must be designed to compensate for the extremes of high and low. We arrived at Auke Bay to find the tide at mid-point and falling. The skies also appeared to be clearing—at least improving —in the west.

No matter which way you cruise out of Auke Bay, it is into breath-taking scenery. Mendenhall Glacier is usually in view and mountainous Admiralty and Chichagof Islands combine to protect the Lynn Canal and Icy Strait from the heavy water of the Pacific Ocean. Seabirds, sometimes even thousands of them, are always in sight and once during this trip I counted 14 bald eagles within binocular range at one

The 49-pounder, foreground, is a king salmon of a lifetime, even in southeastern Alaska waters.

time. That is particularly thrilling since Old Baldy is very, very rare elsewhere nowadays.

Our guide, Phil, had long been a government meteorologist with a passion for the outdoors and particularly for fishing. A few years ago he decided to chuck the whole works and start a new life. In other words he resigned his secure job and bought a boat to go fishing professionally. Now when customers are available, he charters and very successfully. When they are not, he goes fishing alone and can catch enough fish on hook and line to make a go of it commercially. At only 43, he's already a sort of salmon fishing legend around Auke Bay.

From the dock, Phil set a westward course, keeping the north tip of Admiralty to the port side, until his depth finder revealed an underwater reef running away from a pair of rock piles whitened by gulls and known as Horse and Colt Islands. When the depth finder revealed waters exactly 11 fathoms deep, the guide cut the motor and dropped anchor.

"We'll give it a whirl here," Phil said, "at least until low tide."

Soon it was evident why Phil is the top fisherman in these parts; he's a perfectionist and that includes the smallest details of rigging and tackle and baiting up. Instead of relying on frozen bait as most fishermen do thereabouts, Phil had set out herring nets during the night and so had two buckets of fresh fish ready to go in the morning.

"The freshness makes all the difference in the world," he assured us. "Big salmon hit them two to one better than frozen baits."

The actual hooking of the herring is also very important. The hook must be passed through one eye, worked around toward the tail and impaled in the body to give just the right fluttering action with the pull of the tide. According to Phil, a herring without such action is no good and a bait which rotates completely is almost as bad.

We did not have a long wait to prove these theories. John's bait had been in the water only 5 minutes, "swimming" in the tide race, when there came a thumping on the rod tip and line melted from the reel. John just held on because there was nothing else to do.

I have reached a point in my angling career where I would almost as soon watch or film a fellow angler dueling a good fish as I would play it myself. Since John is thoroughly skilled and experienced, this contest was especially exciting to watch. I climbed up onto a gunwale with camera in one hand, while clinging to a cabin strut with the other. There I had a perfect perch to follow the action.

After the initial run, the salmon rose slowly to the surface where we could see its curving wake about 35 or 40 yards astern. John pumped to try to regain line and that made the king jump. But it was too heavy to make one of the wild, lunging leaps which are characteristic of smaller fish. When that failed to dislodge the hook, the fish sounded and for John it became the pure hard work of pumping it back on top. After too much suspense and a wet flurry of action near the boat, John led his fish into a long-handled net and Phil muscled it aboard.

Phil produced scales and these showed 35 pounds. That made it the largest fish of our month-long trip—and the largest Pacific salmon I had ever seen alive. John was surely the happiest angler in Alaska and I believe the size of the fish even surprised our guide.

Unaccountably, that was the only salmon we hooked near the Horse and Colt reefs. Experimentally dropping the baits deeper only resulted in catching a multitude of such bottom species as halibut (up to 18 pounds), sole, starry flounders, an arrowhead flounder, rockfish, whiting, cod and Irish Lords. I have fished southeastern Alaska water on previous occasions and each time have been amazed at the incredible numbers of bottom species which exist here—and how easy they are to catch. It is surprising to me that more sportsmen do not especially fish for these, especially for the halibut which in places run to 200 or 300 pounds. But perhaps the salmon fishing is much too attractive to waste time on anything else. At least that's the way Phil felt.

"Let's forget about the trash," he said finally, "and try another place. We ought to get a fresh charge of salmon with the changing tide."

It was a 30 minute run into Young Bay, which is on the West side of Douglas Island, and then we cruised toward a gravelly spit which is designated as Inner Point on some navigation charts.

Phil used great care in anchoring the boat off of a very steep shoreline. His aim was to anchor the boat directly over an underwater drop-off which fell away sharply from 7 to 16 fathoms. From past experience he knew that this was a gathering point for bait fish and that salmon were certain to find them there. He had to make several attempts at anchoring the boat in the new strong incoming tide before he had it exactly right. Then quickly we had three baited lines overboard.

Although we could see the occasional faint blips on the depth finder which indicated bait fish, we had only one missed strike during the next hour or so. But suddenly, as if somebody flipped a switch, all hell broke loose and there were solid strikes on two lines at one time. I grabbed one rod and promptly burned a thumb as line peeled from the reel beneath it. John grabbed the second rod and Phil rapidly retrieved the line on the third to give us room for action.

These salmon were slightly more lively than the first one; at least they performed closer to the surface. Luckily they ran in opposite directions or we might have had a hopeless tangle from the beginning. John's fish jumped once, mine didn't clear the water at all and Phil netted both. They were a perfectly matched pair of kings weighing 19 and 20 pounds, bright silvery in color and very fat.

Quickly in the next half hour there were three more strikes and we connected with two of them. These fish weighed 24 and 27 pounds. But after boating them, action slowed down to nothing. Phil broke out a couple of beers and lunch.

All day the weather had gradually improved and now only a thin overcast filtered the sun above the Young Bay area. I slipped out of a foul weather jacket and lounged on the deck while watching the sea bird show and munching on a sandwich. The cold beer tasted good.

Small flocks of herring gulls flew past and there were many pigeon guillemots and phalaropes to see out on the open water. The gulls would dive down after any discarded herring bait which Phil would toss overboard. Once an eagle tried to rob a gull of its meal, but the gull swallowed the 7-inch bait fish whole. A moment later there was a strike on John's line and he dropped his sandwich in a hurry. But the striker was a 10-pound halibut rather than a salmon and so was quickly hauled aboard, unhooked and released.

The next hour or so proved dull—if you consider catching halibut and other bottom fish dull. Phil grumbled about having to rebait the hooks so often and said we ought to try another place where the bottom wasn't paved with bait stealers.

"One of those bait stealers," I commented, "just *could* turn out to be a big king."

The words were barely out of my mouth when John's reel whined and line played off of the spool. "Probably another rockfish," Phil replied.

But this time the line didn't stop running out and John quickly had to re-adjust the drag. He had just managed to slow the run when far out astern the fish came up and rolled just under the surface, making a huge boil. It was obviously

Starry flounder here is one of countless species of bottom fish found offshore in Alaska.

A day's fishing out of Auke Bay can produce catches like this one.

a brute of a fish. My first thought was "shark!" and that's what I said out loud.

The fish didn't move with great speed, but it did make a series of powerful lunges followed by surges toward deeper water. And it made the longest run of all after John had pumped it fairly close to the boat. At that point all of us had a good look and saw that it was a very big king.

"My God, play it carefully," Phil advised, "it's a 50-pounder."

I don't know if John had the buck fever, but I did, even though I was busy filming.

From this point it was just a matter of time—of playing out the big fish—while worrying about weak points in the tackle or the hook pulling out. Eventually the fish was close enough to use the net, but it broke just as Phil was swinging the lunker aboard. Then the fish started to fight all over again back and forth across the rear deck until John tapped it on the head with a coke bottle. Then all of us sat down to unwind.

Phil's guess about the salmon's weight wasn't quite right, but at 49 pounds John still had the largest king he is ever likely to land, even if he spends the rest of his summers trying. It was the salmon of a lifetime.

We spent a few more days fishing in the Juneau-Auke Bay area, in small streams for sea-run cutthroats and Dollies as well as offshore for salmon. And we racked up a pretty good score. But as far as I am concerned, that 49-pounder was the climax—the best possible climax—for our remarkable Alaskan adventure.

In fact it just may have been my greatest freshwater fishing trip to date.

Probably I should add some random thoughts and advice here for other anglers who also are contemplating trips to fish the Great Land. To begin, it is especially wise to plan the venture well ahead. Because of the state's great size and few transportation facilities, locating a good spot to fish can be bewildering if attempted on the spur of the moment—or if you wait until actually arriving in Alaska. It is very important also to make reservations well ahead if you plan to travel via car ferry and the inland passageway. During the peak of the travel seasons recently, the ferries have been running full and have left long waiting lines at the docks.

Fishing in the most remote areas via charter flights is understandably expensive. But small groups traveling together can split costs so that the individual's budget isn't too badly battered. Probably the best bargain in Alaskan fishing is for salmon and bottom fish in southeastern coastal waters. Charter captains such as Phil Baker get $100 or $125 for a long day on the water for up to three or four anglers. That isn't bad at all. If you happen to be towing your own boat, you won't necessarily need a guide at all. A number of moderately priced fishing resorts operate in the southeast and a good example is that one operated by Alaska Airlines at Bell Island near Ketchikan. The salmon fishing is productive here all summer long.

Another fishing bargain is to rent one of the U.S. Forest Service cabin shelters erected in the Tongass National Forest at $2 per day. You fly into these at charter rates from $50 to $150 per trip, depending on distance, and fish the wilderness waters in the mountains nearby. For more information on these write the U.S.F.S. supervisor in Juneau.

One popular misconception which needs correcting is that you can travel along any of Alaska's highways (including the Alcan) and find good sport in the numerous waters close to the pavement. It simply isn't so. There are a few places, as at the Tangle Lakes along the Denali Highway where grayling can be caught—and scattered places elsewhere that certain of the salmon spawning runs occur near roads. But mostly, as elsewhere, you have to get off the beaten tracks to enjoy the best angling.

Alaska's fishing requires no exotic or special tackle which the typical fisherman doesn't already own. But a number of items which will be worth their weight in gold on any trip are a foul weather suit, a good supply of insect repellent and waders (or hipboots). The three of these can make the difference between a glorious adventure and an unpleasant experience—and there is no reason for the latter.

It is a good idea to contact both the Fish and Game Department and the Travel Division in Juneau before beginning the long trip to the 49th State. Check also the current ads in *Sports Afield, Outdoor Life* or *Field and Stream* travel sections; these may just provide the information you need for the most memorable fishing expedition of your life.

TOUGH GUY of the Shallows

Landing a permit on light spinning tackle is one of the ultimate angling achievements. This beauty is being hauled from the waters near Key West, Florida after a rough battle.

MARK SOSIN

YOUR chance of having someone detail the location of buried pirate treasure is greater than finding a competent angler who is willing to share his knowledge of permit fishing with you. The elusive permit—perhaps the greatest gladiator of the shallow, tropical Atlantic—has remained shrouded in a mystique and secrecy since the time when men first started stalking the flats in search of sport. The majority of fishermen don't even know that the permit exists, and among those who do, most have never seen one.

Compared to a permit, the popular bonefish comes out a poor second and tarpon fishing is a breeze by comparison. There's little doubt that the permit offers the greatest challenge the light tackle angler will ever face. If you feel I'm taking poetic license in describing this gamefish, catch one before you pass judgement. When you do, you'll unquestionably agree that there are no small permit; some are only bigger than others.

Permit are a deep-bodied fish resembling the jack crevalle

Permit feed heavily on crabs and other crustacea, often rooting in the bottom to ferret out food. Sometimes, their tails protrude above the surface—a situation known as "tailing." The black, sickle-shaped tail is the easiest way to tell a permit.

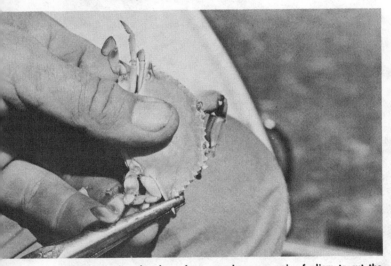

After removing the claws from a crab, use a pair of pliers to cut the spine on either side of the shell.

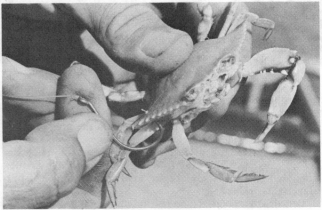

and range in weight from a few pounds to over 40 pounds. The world record on any tackle is slightly over 50 pounds and there have been unconfirmed reports of even bigger permit.

When a permit is hooked in shallow water, he'll streak for the depths like a rocket leaving the launch pad and even if you're successful in stopping him, you can count on several more strong runs. When the runs finally stop, the permit turns into the toughest jack crevalle you ever fought, turning broadside and tenaciously gripping the water with unbeatable determination. On any permit larger than 20 pounds, you can bet you'll have to follow the fish with the boat before you land it.

Still, permit fishing is more than simply a tough battle when the fish is hooked. Seeing a permit and getting a bait or lure in front of the fish are equally challenging. The permit is basically a deep water fish that prowls the edges of shallow flats in search of crustacea and small baitfish. Permit also live over sunken wrecks, but a permit in deep water does not offer the excitement that he will over a shallow flat.

Because they are deep bodied, permit require more water than tarpon or the smaller bonefish. This means that they seldom invade the flats until the tide has been flooding for a considerable period. They prefer 3 to 5 feet of water and often scatter over deeper flats on the top of the tide.

If you've had any experience trying to spot bonefish or tarpon in the shallows using polarized sunglasses, you know how difficult it can be. Permit can be three times as hard to spot as either bonefish or tarpon. Their silver coloration blends in with the bottom and they can glide silently up to your skiff before you ever see them.

Unlike the tarpon that will probe a flat slowly and cautiously or the bonefish that will work an area of shallows thoroughly, the permit seems to be a nervous individual. Whether alone or in schools, permit tend to flit across a flat hesitating for a second here and there to dip down and root out a crab that tried to take refuge in the bottom. Because they move so quickly, it takes great skill to get a lure or bait in front of them.

Although permit are not seen with the degree of regularity that bonefish and tarpon are spotted, there are probably more permit around than most people suspect. Permit fishing is generally opportunity fishing. That is, you're usually fishing for something else when a permit happens along. Only a few top-rated anglers make a practice of fishing specifically for permit. Since it is opportunity fishing and because the permit move so quickly, you generally have to cast whatever lure or bait you have on the rod in your hand. Because of that, most permit taken are by accident rather than by design.

The tough guy of the shallows is really a sucker for a live crab, providing it is presented properly. Even if you're probing the flats for bonefish, tarpon, or barracuda, it pays to have one rod rigged with a live crab and ready at all times. If permit do come along, you have an excellent chance of tangling with one.

To a permit, a crab measuring about 2 or 3 inches across the back is a steak and roast beef all rolled into one. The crab must be alive and it should be healthy. That means that you must keep the crab in a live well or in the water at all times. Crabs die very quickly if they are taken out of water.

Preparing a crab is easy, but there is a definite procedure. The first thing you must do is de-claw the critter. There's an art to that. Instead of grabbing the claws with

◄ The point of a 2/0 hook is inserted in one corner of the crab as indicated. Note that the point enters the soft underside and comes out through the hard top of the shell.

pliers and pulling, grip the end of the claw with the jaws of the pliers and squeeze. The crab will throw the entire claw (they can regenerate them) and will not be injured. After removing both claws, use the cutting edge of the pliers to trim the sharp points on either side of the hard shell. Clip off about ⅟₁₆″ from each spine so that you can handle the crab easily. Now insert a 2/0 Eagle Claw style hook in one corner of the shell, pushing the point of the hook through the soft bottom of the crab first and then through the hard shell. The hook is actually imbedded right behind one of the spines that you trimmed.

No weight of any kind is used to cast the crab and the hook is attached directly to the monofilament line. Most veterans prefer to double the mono for a foot or so using a Bimini Twist and then tying directly to the hook. Whether you use spinning or plug casting tackle, the rods are generally 7 feet long with a soft enough tip to lob the crab, but with enough beef in the taper of the rod to put maximum pressure on a fish once a hookup is achieved. Some specialists have permit rods designed to cast a crab, but most progressive taper rods will work.

Most permit fishing is done from a skiff that draws very little water. One man handles the push pole and poles the boat silently over the shallows, while the other angler stands ready—rod in hand—looking for permit. In particularly shallow water, permit create a surface disturbance when a school moves by. We like to refer to this as nervous water because the water actually seems to tremble like Jello that hasn't hardened. You'll find this condition on a falling tide when permit are pouring off the flats and working their way toward deeper water. You might also see a permit "tail." As the fish dips down to root on the bottom, the black-edged, sickle-shaped tail will puncture the surface. And, on exceptionally calm days, you will occasionally see permit finning on the surface. This doesn't happen very often, but when it does, you'll see the black-edged fins poking above the water like small sticks.

Presenting a crab to a permit is easy if you understand

Thirty-three pounds of permit are a nice catch in any league. Bot Stearns lifts Tony Souza's first permit from the waters off Key West.

This husky permit fell victim to a well-placed crab. Most permit fishermen release their fish unharmed unless the angler wants to have his quarry mounted for the wall.

This 3-inch crab is rigged for permit. The claws have been removed, spines cut, and hook inserted in one corner. Crabs will die quickly if not kept in the water.

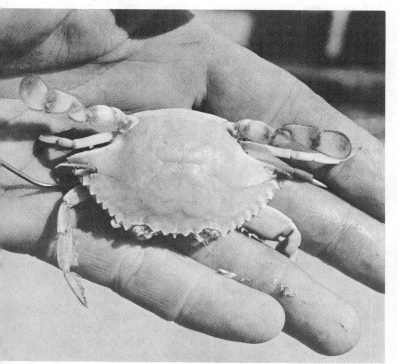

The deep silver body and black edged fins of a permit camouflage him perfectly as he prowls the rim of the flats in search of food. Even with polarized sunglasses, permit can be difficult to spot in the water.

Most permit are taken on live crabs and the first cast must be on target or you might not get a second chance. The look of determination shows on this angler's face as he casts to a permit, while his guide strains on the push pole to jockey the boat into better position.

a few basic principles. Crabs swim sideways across the top of the water and that's exactly what you're trying to duplicate. You hooked the crab in one corner of the shell so that it will move sideways when you retrieve. While you're scouting the water—both above and below—for permit, you must stand ready with the bail of the reel open and the line on your finger ready to cast or the reel in free spool (plug tackle) and your thumb on the spool. If you do see a fish, you may not have much time to make a cast.

How close you can cast to a permit without spooking it depends on the depth of the water, how many fish are in the school, the size of the crab, and the delicacy with which you can plop the crab on the surface. It makes sense to overlead a fish rather than have a cast fall short. For this reason, I like to recommend that an angler get the crab about 15 or 20 feet in front of the lead permit in the school and about 6 feet beyond the school. You may only have one cast, so it has to be right on the money.

As the crab hits the water, hold the rod high and start to retrieve very slowly, swimming the crab across the surface. There's a good chance that the permit will spot the crab and rush it. You'll see the water boil and possibly feel something grab the crab. When you see the first indication that the permit has rushed the crab, drop your rod tip instantly and open the bail or put the reel in free spool. This is important. The crab will dive for the bottom the instant you stop retrieving and the permit can't resist an escaping meal. If you hold the loose line, you can feel the permit pick the crab up and move off with it.

When you set the hook can be critical. The permit will throw the crab back in its mouth against a set of crushers. If you strike too soon, you'll probably pull the crab out of the fish's mouth. Too late and you'll come away with a bare hook. Wait until the fish has moved off about 15 or 20 feet. Engage the reel and point the rod at the line. When the line comes tight, set the hook with a series of short, sharp, upward jerks and hang on. If the hook penetrated, the permit is off on the fastest and most determined run you've ever experienced.

It goes without saying that the drag on your reel must be smooth and it should only be set tight enough to drive the hook home. You want a light drag because you know the permit is going to make a long run and the drag isn't about to stop him. As the fish starts to run (and this holds with any fish taken on a shallow flat), push the rod over your head and hold it as high as you can. This will keep

most of the line out of the water and help to eliminate the possibility of it cutting on coral, sea fans, or some other outcropping.

Ten-pound test monofilament is an ideal line size for permit. It might be a little light for some anglers, but you'll have the fight of your life with it. If it's your first fish, you may want to go to 12-pound test or possibly 15. Regardless of the line size, you should have a reel that holds a minimum of 250 yards.

You can bet that the fish is going to head for deep water. Whether you follow the fish immediately or try to work him back toward you depends on the size of the fish and the type of flat you're fishing. If there is a gradual dropoff, you don't have a problem, but if the dropoff is pronounced and there is a sharp edge around the flat, you have to chase the fish right away. If you don't the fish will reach deeper water, head for the bottom, and cut your line on the lip of the flat. Permit are frequently found along a series of flats that have deeper channels running through them. In this case, you'll also have to get on top of the fish quickly.

A live shrimp also works for permit. In rigging the shrimp, remove the tail and thread the hook part way from the point where you cut off the fan-shaped tail forward. Shrimp swim backward and you want yours to do the same. In casting the shrimp, you can make a closer presentation because the shrimp is smaller than the crab and lands more gently. Work the shrimp slowly, swimming it back to you. With a shrimp, don't hesitate as long in setting the hook.

Permit are also taken on artificial lures. Veterans prefer a brown or white bucktail with grizzly wings, but most permit taken on artificials succumb to a bonefish bucktail of some type. The reason is that a permit happens along when you're bonefishing and that's all you have to throw. There are several theories on how to work a bucktail for permit. Some anglers like to bounce the bucktail along the bottom and when they see the permit go for it, they merely "kick" the bucktail in place as if it were a small crab trying to burrow in the sand. Others believe in a relatively fast retrieve and hope to bring out the jack crevalle in the critter.

You'll have to experiment to find the right retrieve for the fish in front of you. With permit, you can't always tell. I was fishing for barracuda not long ago, whipping a tube lure across the surface as fast as I could retrieve it. I could see a shadow stalking the lure, so I moved it as rapidly as possible. Right at the boat, the fish made a pass and turned away. When it did, I could see that it was a permit of about 20 pounds instead of a sabre-toothed bonefish.

If permit are tough to entice on spinning or plug casting gear, they are next to impossible on fly tackle. As of this writing, fewer than 50 have been taken on regulation fly tackle on the shallow flats. They are not hard to hook in deep water, but on the shallows, they are a flyrodder's nemesis. You can cast to thousands of them before you find one willing to grab a fly. We've studied those fly patterns that were successful and most of them were sparsely dressed about 3 inches long. Favorite colors were white and grizzly or sand-colored patterns. Perhaps some day flyrodders will figure out a formula, but up to this point, a permit on fly on the flats is an admirable achievement.

In the United States, permit are found from Biscayne Bay adjacent to Miami through the Florida Keys. They are also found in the Bahamas and in recent years there's been a good fishery for them along Mexico's Yucatan Penin-sula and on the outside flats of British Honduras. If I were determined to catch a permit, however, I would work the flats out of Key West, Florida with a competent guide.

The best time of year in Key West is during the summer and early fall. In June the fish move out to spawn, but after that, they are back on the flats in force. You'll find them there all year around, but there are more fish in the summer. During the winter when cold snaps move across the Gulf of Mexico and the flats chill down, permit generally move into deeper water.

There's not much doubt in my mind that permit fishing can be the ultimate light tackle challenge in either fresh water or salt. It's tough to get a bait in front of them, not always easy to make them strike, and they'll put up a fight you'll never forget. Before you say that the tough guy of the shallows is just another fish story, give permit fishing a try. But I warn you. Once you catch one, you'll probably become addicted to it.

Once a permit is hooked, the trick is to keep the rod high so that the line won't be cut by underwater obstructions such as coral, sea fans, or other items on the bottom.

After the first thirty seconds, the most critical part of the fight comes when you think you've finally beaten a permit. This is no time to relax. Note how carefully this experienced angler is attempting to work the tired fish toward him, yet he remains constantly on the alert for a sudden run.

DEATHBEDS
for Rivers

By John Madson

THE OBION RIVER loafs peacefully through western Tennessee, meandering down a broad floodplain through bottomland forest. It's only a torn fragment of what it was, but it's still some of the best country in west Tennessee—and it is easy to see why the Obion Bottoms once offered fishing and duck gunning that surpassed even the fabled green timber reservoirs of eastern Arkansas.

The Alcovey River in northern Georgia is a lovely, unpolluted flowage through one of the finest remaining river swamps in the Southeast. Its headwaters, within 25 miles of downtown Atlanta, is a brooding wilderness of tupelo gum, home of bass, panfish, catfish, great swamp deer, ducks, and the big "canecutter" swamp rabbits that are twice as large as cottontails.

Far away, in northeastern North Dakota, is a region of prairie marshes, potholes and lakes called the "Starkweather Watershed." This watershed, and its adjacent country, holds over 50,000 acres of the finest prairie wetlands and waterfowl habitat left in North America.

All different places, and far apart, but with one thing in common: these good places are either dying, or being sentenced to die.

The Obion is a barren shadow of what it was; much of the river is a sterile ditch, and its broad bottomland forests are vanishing. The Alcovey hangs "in limbo," and may be pasture.

Judge, jury and executioners in all three cases are either the Soil Conservation Service of the U.S. Department of Agriculture, or the U.S. Army Corps of Engineers. Method of execution: an engineering process of "channel improvement" which entails straightening, deepening and clearing a natural waterway to hasten drainage. Done in the name of flood control, it creates new farmland at the cost of natural, free-flowing streams and wetlands.

The Obion, Alcovey and Starkweather are only three examples of this deepening evil. It's happening everywhere. Since 1954 the SCS has "improved" over 3,000 miles of stream channels—and about 300 projects involving over

8,000 miles of channelization are now under way. The SCS is planning future projects affecting another 12,000 miles of our waterways. Some of these are repair jobs of old channelized projects. But many involve natural drainages that have never been channelized.

State and Federal game and fish agencies bitterly oppose most of this channelization, but lack the political clout to stop it. And there is abundant evidence of the terrible impact that channelization has on fish and wildlife resources.

North Carolina, and other states, have found that game fishes in a channelized stream may decline by 90 per cent or disappear altogether!

In the threatened Cache River Basin of northeastern Arkansas—considered the only part of eastern Arkansas with any important remaining game cover—it is estimated that a proposed Corps of Engineers channelization would cause a loss of 75 per cent of all small game in the basin, 79 per cent of the big game, and 60 per cent of the furbearers.

In the famed Atchafalaya Basin of southern Louisiana a Corps of Engineers drainage project is cutting the heart out of 1,300 square miles of prime hunting and fishing country. Larger than the Okefenokee Swamp of Georgia, the Atchafalaya is a southern wilderness surpassed only by the Florida Everglades.

In channelizing, the natural waterway is deepened, straightened and diked, hastening runoff and lowering the water table. It is then possible for landowners to dig lateral canals and drain adjacent lowlands. In a prairie region such as the Starkweather, a new main drainage canal can permit wetlands drainage from over a mile away on either side.

In the South, this means drainage of lowland forests and wholesale cutting. In western Tennessee, channelization has helped wipe out 75 per cent of the floodplain forests. Louisiana loses about 111,000 acres of bottomland forests each year. In Arkansas, 150,000 acres of bottomland timber and wetlands are destroyed annually by some type of channelization; about 90 per cent of that cleared land goes into soybeans which thrive in deep, moist alluvial soils. Of the original 10 million acres of bottomland hardwoods in eastern Arkansas, less than 2 million acres remain.

To hunters, such resource-wrecking is of supreme concern, for in much American farm country the best available hunting is in streamside cover, in timbered or flooded bottomlands, and in native marshes. To the boater, camper, fisherman and canoeist, free-flowing streams with timbered banks offer a priceless measure of wildness and freedom.

Yet, the SCS has told Congress that "channel improvement" has "very little adverse impact" on recreation within a watershed, and stated that stream channelization can actually benefit fishing, hunting, boating and canoeing. The belief that such sports could possibly be enhanced by converting a free-flowing natural stream into a straight, featureless, high-banked, barren drainage ditch is a miracle of bureaucratic imagination.

The issue is very complex and involved; last year's congressional hearings on channelization run to four thick volumes.

But it adds up to this: countless rivers, creeks, marshes and hardwood forests are dead, dying or doomed— sacrificed to the almighty dollar and blind economics. ⌐≡≡≡≡⌐

Destruction like this to beautiful rivers follows in the wake of U.S. Soil Conservation Service shovels and draglines. These scenes are of the once fishable Little Auglaize River in Ohio. Now it is dead.

So You Think There's

by BILL RICE

REMEMBER THOSE DAYS of random plugging for bass along shoreline areas of your favorite fishing hole with your best floating or diving plugs? Well, that's a thing of the past. Certainly such methods still work occasionally, but there's a whole new breed of anglers playing the fishing game today. Today's giant, man-made reservoirs have added new complications and dimensions to the great sport of large-mouth bass fishing.

Any haphazard or time-consuming methods of searching out a few bass may be productive for very small lakes or ponds, but when you're fishing a lake with a hundred miles of shoreline, you have to turn to scientific methods which were unheard of just a few years ago.

The past decade has seen a greater change in fishing techniques, perhaps, than in all previous sport fishing history. Today it's the "scientific fisherman" who gets those big catches you see at the docks all across the nation. Fishing the big, new reservoirs requires much of the same skill and persistence that has been producing good strings of bass for years, but nowadays the use of electronics is making the difference.

A certain amount of random casting is still in use, but always with a well-defined purpose to today's new breed of fisherman. That purpose is to locate bass and establish the pattern of their regular feeding habits. Once this pattern is established, the same conditions will probably produce good action in several areas of the same lake, and possibly at other lakes, too.

One of the masters of what can be called pattern or structure fishing is an astute former fishing guide, Roland Martin. This South Carolina bass pro was a living legend at his home lake, huge Santee-Cooper, where his strings of lunker bass were always a familiar sight at the docks.

From South Carolina, Martin progressed to the tournament trail, fishing in the Bass Anglers Sportsman Society events staged throughout the south. In Martin's very first year on the trail, he finished only 7 ounces behind the reigning master, Bill Dance of Memphis, Tenn., but the future was evident. Martin would be the man to bet on from then on.

And that's the way it has been as Martin continues to lead tourney fishermen in wins and at FISHERMEN'S DIGEST's press time he was doing the same. Martin is a master at fishing the large, deep water lakes where these tournaments are being staged because he developed an almost surefire system for those unseen depths where the lunkers lurk.

Deep water fishing should not be pursued by the casual Sunday afternoon fisherman because to find these deep water hangouts for bass requires time, effort and perseverance. But it can be done.

"The first and by far most important item is for the angler to use and understand a sonar depth finder such as the Lowrance Fish Lo-K-Tor," says Martin. "With that he can observe depth, cover and structure of the lake—three of the four most important ingredients to a deep water pattern fisherman.

"The second requirement is the use of a Lowrance Fish-N-Temp, a water thermometer. This enables the angler to observe the final main ingredient to a deep water pattern—the correct temperature zone and oxygen zone, often connected to the temperature zone."

Martin's third requirement is general knowledge of the lake, either by use of a topographical contour map, which shows all the depths and structure combinations or by good information gleaned from local marina operators, experienced fishermen or professional guides. The fourth requirement involves time, plenty of perseverance and confidence to systematically pick apart and eliminate all of the pattern possibilities.

Sounds like a lot of work, doesn't it? Well of course it is, but consider the rewards and it will be well worth it. The name of the game in deep water is to locate the bass: after that the catching is easy.

"The progressive depth method is the most productive way to locate a concentration of bass in deep water," notes Martin.

First he checks the water temperature with the Fish-N-Temp, looking for either a depth zone of rapid temperature change or the preferred temperature zone for that species of bass, which for the largemouth is between 72 and 75 degrees. At that depth, the angler should now start to systematically look for the most productive pattern.

"If the ideal 72 to 75 degrees temperature is indicated at 20 feet," says Martin, "then start your fishing at about that depth, fishing all the typical structures that you can find on the Fish Lo-K-Tor. Look for such things as hills, creek bends, deep points, dropoffs, brush piles or any other feature of the bottom that is irregular with the surrounding area."

As Martin and others have often discovered, and you will, too, a lone brush pile surrounded by a constant water depth for a good distance, can be a bass bonanza. Even a small hump or dip on a flat bottom can attract and hold some bass. Most fishermen have a misconception that a dropoff must be present for good bass fishing. But dropoffs, like the brushpile, are good only when they are the most irregular underwater feature in the area.

After trying out a dozen or so such areas as you spot them on the Lo-K-Tor, and you still have no results, switch to 15- or 25-foot depths and seek out other structures. This is how the "honey holes," the real big bass bonanzas, are found claims Martin.

Now let's say you catch a half-dozen or more fish in rapid succession from this 15-foot deep spot. You probably have established a pattern and before you leave the spot, check it out very carefully. Check the exact water temperature, the exact depth, all cover in the area and the precise structural features. The trick now is to duplicate this spot. But remember that one slight deviation, such as

Nothing New Outdoors...
Well, Try Structure Fishing

At Sam Rayburn Reservoir in Texas, Roland proved his structure methods in taking this stringer of fish in less than 2 hours.

water color or angle of the sunlight, could knock it off the pattern.

"Upon approaching a new potential fishing spot," says Martin, "zig zag or circle the area. I drop a Fish-N-Float marker buoy along the structural line to mark it. Then I either troll, drift or anchor on the spot. But if I don't get a strike after 10 minutes or ten good casts, then I figure I haven't found the fish. If a big school of bass is present, there are always a couple of fish aggressive enough to strike the first few casts."

If you do catch some fish in such a spot, you've definitely established the pattern. Both spots you've worked were

15-foot deep creek bends, with brush and 72-degree water. You may find dozens of similar situations in the huge lake, and the chances are that all will produce the same results, possibly for several days running. But, because water and weather conditions will change, so will the pattern. And when it does, you are going to have to start over with the systematic elimination process again.

Always remember that the water temperature of a lake is one of the first and most important keys to setting a pattern for any day's fishing. Many lakes stratify into three distinct layers during the summer, and this is especially true of today's huge impoundments. The top layer, called the epilimnion, is made up of the warm surface water. In the middle layer, or thermocline, the water temperature drops rapidly with increasing depth to the cold bottom layer, or hypolimnion.

The thermocline is the area of main interest to the angler because this is where the fish's preferred water temperatures will be. A typical example would be for a lake to have a 75-degree zone at the surface, dropping to 70 degrees at 5 feet, 69 degrees at 10 feet, 68 degrees at 15 feet and 67 degrees at 20 feet; in other words only an 8-degree drop in 20 feet. But in the *next* 10 feet, in the thermocline, it might go from 67 down to 50 degrees. This indicates that the hypolimnion, below the thermocline, is about 30 feet, thus pointing out to you no fish will be taken from depths greater than 30 feet since there is such a lack of oxygen that fish cannot survive. So right off, you've eliminated quite a bit of unfishable water. And with the aid of electronics you've just become a "Scientific Fisherman."

One final step to any deep water fishing is to be able to mark a hot fishing spot for future reference. Remember that this spot might be a mile from the closest point of land or any good reference points and many hours could

be spent trying to find it again on the Fish Lo-K-Tor. Looking for a spot that may be only 10 feet by 10 feet in size may be next to impossible at times.

The best and most accurate method of marking this fishing spot is to cross-triangulate. To cross-triangulate, line up two objects on the same shore, such as a dead tree with the tallest hilltop, and then write it down in a notebook. Don't trust it to memory.

Looking approximately 90 degrees from this line, you now try to line up two other conspicuous landmarks, both on the same shore, and again write it down. It's also a good idea to write down all the pattern features of this spot because next week, next month or next year, the water level could change.

Taking notes at many areas of the lake is also a good idea. With the use of the Fish Lo-K-Tor you can actually chart a lot of the lake as you move from spot to spot. Just leave the depth finder running as you go and mark the depths on a map or notebook all the while, indicating the promising spots in relation to landmarks on shore.

As you go about your survey, the Lo-K-Tor will also tell you the *kind* of bottom in addition to the depth and

Roland Martin, definitely a believer in electronic aids, has marked the "structure" with the Fish-N-Float and is now taking the water temperature with the Fish-N-Temp.

The Fish-N-Temp is an invaluable aid to every serious angler.

Roland Martin, tournament angler, shows that big fish definitely come from some form of structure.

structures. Bright, strong signals will indicate rock bottoms, while dull, weak signals will show over mud bottoms. It will also reveal fish, perhaps a school of fish suspended over deep water. Sometimes just searching for structures in the middle of a lake will reveal schools and the fishing is usually spectacular when they are found.

Fishing shallow water on the big, new lakes is also a matter of systematic elimination of areas, as it is with deep water structure fishing. Just as bass have certain preferences for deep water structures, so they will show distinct preferences in the shallows. Don't make the mistake of saying to yourself, "It looks so bassy here that I *have* to catch one, so I'm going to plug it until I do."

There just aren't enough bass in any lake to be on every good-looking spot. The bass will probably be only in certain areas any day, leaving maybe 75 percent of the shallow water relatively empty.

The key is to move to several different areas. If a dozen or so good, accurate casts to that bassy cover do not produce any strikes, then move to another area. Try several different lures at each spot, also—like surface lures, diving lures and plastic worms. One of these should produce. If not, move on.

Learn to look at shallow water areas and separate different types of cover into different pattern possibilities.

Take one at a time and fish about six different locations with this same type of cover until you either start regularly catching bass or eliminate a cover type as a productive pattern. If you do eliminate it, then forget it entirely and seek out a completely new shallow pattern—that is, a different type of cover, different depth and different location.

The type of cover available in shallow water can vary considerably. You might spend some time fishing the tall, reedy areas with no success, but then switch to an area filled with stumps and find it productive. A moss-filled channel may produce, but a clear water area with just a few stick-ups of brush may not be productive. But the main point to remember is the pattern. If you do catch some fish in tall grasses and waters 5 to 10 feet deep, you might be able to catch more fish in the same type of cover 2 miles or more down the lake.

Anyway, keep up the systematic process of elimination whether the bass are deep or shallow, and eventually you'll find them. Generally, the knowledgeable anglers will try to set a shallow water pattern early in the day, then look for a deep water pattern about mid-morning. If, however, you don't set a shallow water pattern quickly, go right away to the deep water pattern of eliminating structures.

That's the way Roland Martin does it and he's always a winner.

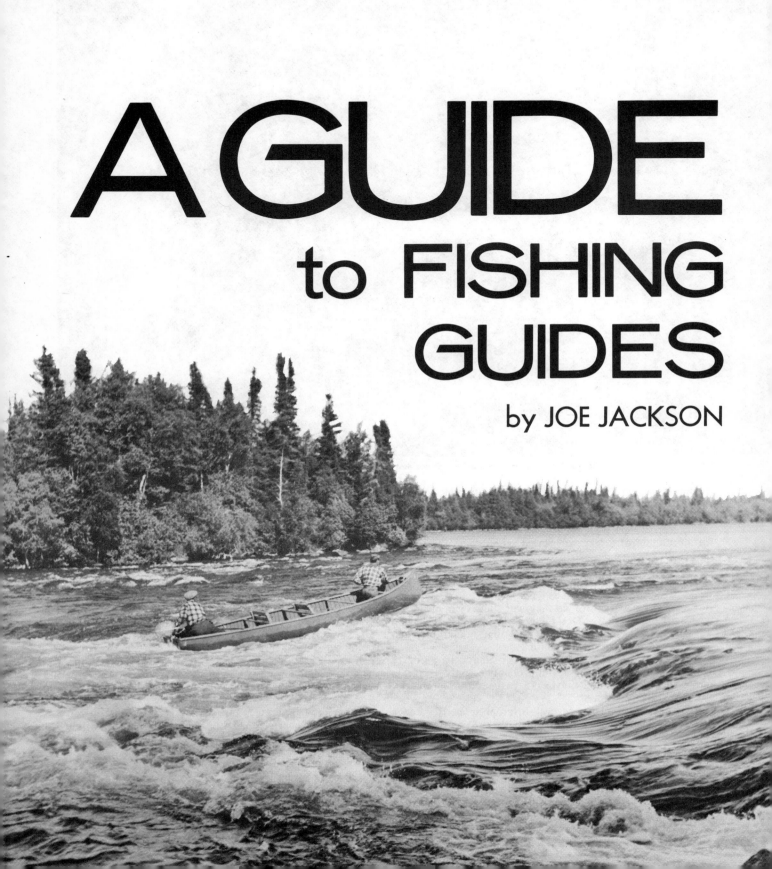

A GUIDE
to FISHING
GUIDES

by JOE JACKSON

IT WAS one of those ominously dead days at Reelfoot Lake in western Tennessee. Not a breath stirred the surface of the swamp. No birds were singing. Even the egrets in the Cranetown rookery nearby were silent in the heat. No fish rose to the lures we had offered for the past two hours.

I was ready to toss in the sponge and take a nap. But Bill Elman cranked up the motor and asked, "You'd rather sleep than fish?"

"No."

"All right, we'll catch some fish then." The ancient kicker sputtered, caught, and we threaded a course eastward toward open water.

Bill cut the motor in a vast, fairly open section of the lake. Scattered here and there were cypress stumps, some submerged and some emerging a few inches from the water.

"They're hollow," Bill said. "Put a split shot ahead of that spider and let it sink into the tree.

It sounded like a gag, but from the first cast to the last, an hour later, I hooked big bream until it became a mite monotonous. All the while, Bill quietly maneuvered the boat. Even though the stumps weren't grouped too closely together, I was always in perfect casting position to reach one. When a cast or two didn't produce, there was another. Splendid was the word for Bill's boat handling. He turned a listless morning into a memorable fishing session.

On shore, Bill dug out a skillet and a small package of ingredients. Soon, our section of the swamp was filled with the savory odor of frying bluegills and hushpuppies. And soon I was eating more than anyone should eat on such a hot and humid midday.

Bill Elman doesn't guide anymore. He has other irons in the fire. But I'll always remember him as one of the very best, a capable outdoorsman worthy of the name. He knew the water and the fishing around him. He was an excellent, discreet companion. And he was no mean hand around a campfire; in short, he was a splendid guide.

Really good guides are not truly abundant nowadays. Wherever there is any outdoor activity, you can find plenty of excellent boatmen, good fishermen, and accomplished tellers of tall tales. All these pass for guides, but all too often, in my experience, the resemblance ends right there. Here's what happened, for instance, on a two-day float trip on a well-known Michigan river.

The first day our guide was a lad we'll call Max. He was genial, willing, and a pleasant person with whom to share the outdoors. And he was a superb boatman. With his long pushpole, he deftly eased the long boat around bends in the river, and with a true touch of a veteran he piloted the craft through stretches of fast water. The only trouble was he didn't know anything about fish, fishing, and places to fish —even in his home river. As a result, we hurried past beautiful holes and stopped in places that were unproductive. The catch that day was not one to mention to friends.

The next day it was all reversed. We'll call this character Ed. He knew as much about trout fishing, perhaps, as all but a few anglers I've known. When the boat drifted down near a good spot, he would pitch out the anchor, hit the water in his waders, and begin casting downstream. There was no fooling about this lad; he could lay out a beautiful line, and his manner of drifting and retrieving was something to copy.

When the water was too deep to wade, Ed maneuvered the boat carefully so that he would be able to fish it. Except for answering a question now and then, he forgot about everything—including me—but his fishing. Which was all right . . . except that I was paying him $20 to take me fishing.

Let's go back and add up everything so far. First, a guide should know his water and the fishing. Second, he should be a skillful and safe boatman. And third, unless you request otherwise, he should not fish. Too many times, in too many places in the past, I've seen fishing guides become so intent on their fishing that guiding was secondary or forgotten altogether. That shouldn't happen if the man is professionally engaged to take you fishing.

Guides have headaches, possibly more than any sportsman can imagine. Often these trials and tribulations piled up through the years cause him to behave in a manner that may seem irregular or even surly. The guide who fishes, for instance, may have sweated through hundreds of clients who couldn't catch fish, no matter what he did. He fished, then, in self defense—to show that his waters had fish in them and that they could be caught. Perhaps this also explains the guide who constantly talks about other days and other occasions when the fish hit like crazy and everyone around winds up with a limit stringer.

A good guide must be a psychologist as well as an outdoorsman. He must interpret a sportsman's attitudes and moods consistently. He must select the proper time to tell about big catches others have made. He must know the proper times to initiate conversation and when to be reticent. I've seen both extremes, plus many in between.

It was in the Timagami region that Dan Marsh and I crossed paths with Joe Paul, Jr. Joe was a short and sturdy

Edgar
Readhead

← Cree Indian guide Edgar Redhead of Red Sucker Rapids on Gods River safely takes canoe upstream through strong rapids.

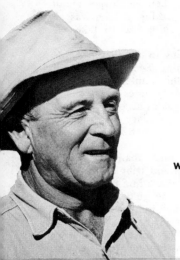

Wisconsin guide Arne Juul of Hayward is among the best known of muskie guides.

Landing fish is also responsibility of guide. Here Johnny Cass hefts big barracuda for Dick Kotis.

Good guide familiar with the region makes all the difference when walleye fishing in the far north.

In wild wilderness waters as here on Gods River, Manitoba, guide must be a skilled boatman to negotiate rapids safely.

Indian who worked harder than any guide we had ever seen. He volunteered for all sorts of extra work, paddled day and night if we suggested it, and was, in general, a redskinned dynamo. He knew fishing around him, too. But Joe had very little to say. He answered questions; nothing more.

One evening in camp on Obabika Lake, we had ample evidence of how quiet our guide really was. Another canoe party guided by one Al Cat camped near us, and we joined forces for a bull session around the fire. Almost from the moment the introductions were over until everyone retired to his sack, Al carried on a monologue. We heard about the rich bootlegger and the blonde from Gary he once guided, and we heard about fish that surpassed any ever to hit the record books. We heard a rather clever tale about the "ooman and the oolves on the ice." The man was definitely in the wrong business; he should have been a stand-up comic. For a while, Joe said nothing. Finally, when the fire had died somewhat, I noticed him slip away. Next morning I asked him about it.

"Cat got big wind," he said. "Wind don't catch fish."

Later in the day, we caught up to Cat's party again. We'd covered quite a few miles but had stopped here and there long enough to catch enough northerns and walleyes to fill the canoe. The others, however, were having trouble getting

enough for dinner.

Evidently, even little Joe had a bit of ham in him. On a reef just offshore from where they were building camp, he said, "Troll daredevil here."

I doubt if more than 30 feet had slipped through the guides when I had a jolting strike followed, seconds later, by a large northern shaking clear of the water. Then Dan hooked one, too.

For ten minutes, or so, Joe played the game for all it was worth. We never trolled far enough from the shore so that Cat's customers couldn't have a spectator's view. Joe didn't say a word—didn't even betray a slight smile. He did concede to a slightly exaggerated display of boating and releasing each fish. When we finally pushed on, he said again, "Wind don't catch fish."

Come to think about it, he was right.

You can't spend many days fishing, even during summer's most predictable periods, without encountering bad weather occasionally. And sometimes you'll run into extended periods of rain and cold. It's then that guides face an acid test. A cheerful one can salvage a trip no matter what the weather. A moody, disconsolate guide can make you give up fishing for keeps.

Cleanliness is another essential quality in a capable guide.

When fishing the flats of the Florida Keys, a guide skilful in poling a boat and with keen eyes is very important.

That does not mean he should wear an outfit fresh from Abercrombie and Fitch or keep his hair neatly combed all the time. It does mean that his sanitary habits while handling food should be perfect, and he should keep reasonably well shaven. One large resort owner I know requires absolute neatness in his guides at all times. He believes that an orderly and well-groomed guide inspires greater confidence in the sportsmen in his care.

Some years ago, a very good friend made a trip into the Everglades to try fishing some remote and isolated waters. The guide stopped to set up camp one evening on a small hammock. He suggested that Charlie take the boat and cast some of the open water nearby while he made camp and fried the bass they had taken on the way in. He said he'd call when dinner was ready.

Charlie became absorbed in the fishing. The bigmouths were hitting a black fly-rod popper with a regularity that doesn't happen too often to most anglers. Pretty soon it was dusk and he began to wonder why the guide hadn't called. He returned to the camp and found out. The guide was sleeping soundly, an empty gin bottle by his side.

Perhaps the next day's fishing cured him of doing that again, for it was hot and sultry almost beyond description.

Suntanned face is trademark of all guides who spend much time on waters.

He sweated and suffered all day in the sun without suggesting for a second that they quit or even stop to rest. He certainly wasn't lacking in intestinal fortitude, but it's fortunate an emergency didn't occur during that period when he was dead to the world.

One more qualification, then—a guide should be 100 per cent reliable. Serious accidents—and even fatalities—have been caused by only temporary lapses. More often than not where guides are employed, the country is relatively wild and without communication. In other words, a sportsman is contracting for security as well as for sport when he takes a guide.

One of the finest guides I've known, curiously enough, was a broth of a lad still in high school. But he was keen and sharp—the outdoors was his cookie. Young Fred guided muskie fishermen mostly, but he knew the whereabouts of local walleyes and bass just as well. He carried canoes and packs through swamps and bogs that were difficult for a man unencumbered—just for a few hours' casting on a back-country pothole he had worked extra hours to find. And once, although I didn't know it then, he gave me the last dose of mosquito dope remaining in his bottle. He spent the afternoon paddling me around between futile slaps at the mosquitoes which swarmed about him.

One day we drifted down the West Fork of Wisconsin's Chippewa. About halfway to the pickup point, we ran into a cloudburst. For an hour the rain lasted, and we huddled under our overturned canoe. It was a cold and miserable experience.

Even though the ground, the underbrush, and everything we carried along was drenched, Fred scraped together a few materials from a tiny waterproof container and soon had a small fire going. Quickly, under the circumstances, he nurtured it into a blaze that made the incident a lot more bearable. As if that wasn't enough, he produced a small package of tea which soon was boiled in an aluminum canteen cup.

Almost as if a reward for the fine impromptu job of sitting out the rain, we hadn't resumed the drift farther than a hundred yards downstream before an 18-pound muskie nailed my bucktail, and, consequently, left his happy home. And a clever job of boat maneuvering and handling of the nearly spent fish was responsible for the contest ending the way it did. Fred was a splendid guide.

But best of all, when the time came to leave, he talked me into staying another week.

Mexican tarpon guide Fiasco Guzman checks out large surface plug.

On longer trips, it's essential that guide be a good cook. This one is Jeep Lateral of northern Minnesota.

Guide Wayne Lindsay of Rockport, Texas, helped account for this catch of channel bass and spotted weakfish by executive editor Peggy Peters.

151

How to Select Plug Casting Tackle

by DICK KOTIS

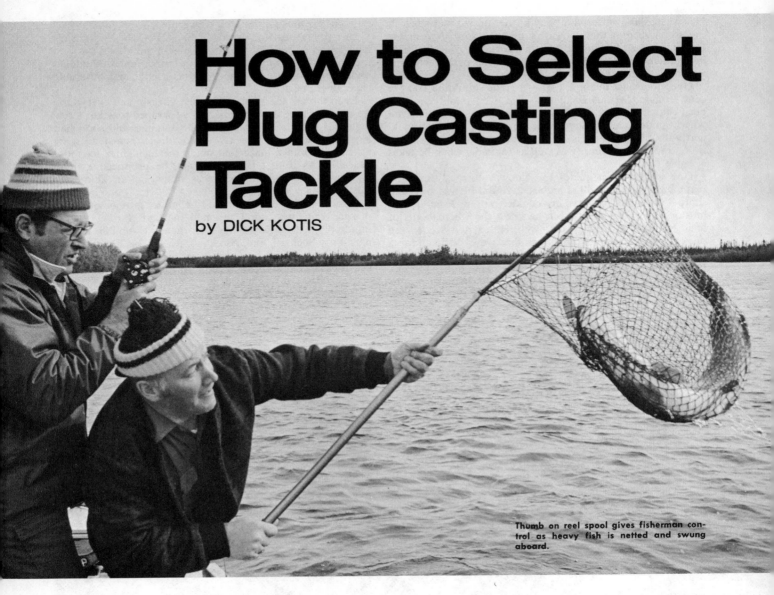

Thumb on reel spool gives fisherman control as heavy fish is netted and swung aboard.

COUNTLESS times every year I am asked how to select a good plug or bait casting tackle. I usually reply by asking the type of fishing to be done and the species of fish.

I personally prefer to use a bait casting rod and reel (as opposed to spinning or spin-casting) for most fishing. One reason is that I am more accurate with it. I also can control my lure retrieve and enjoy casting even when the catching is slow. Like most bait casting enthusiasts I stretch the limits of this equipment, perhaps much more than I should. Let me give you an example: I select the same reel for tarpon and similar big fish that I employ when using 8-pound monofilament in clear cold water for smallmouth bass. Of course I use much heavier line for the tarpon. Let me share with you some of my ideas on selecting the rods, reels and lines I prefer and why.

When choosing a casting reel from many available in a sporting goods shop, some of the features to look for are as follows. Is it a free spool reel (so you can cast light lures)? Are the reel handles large enough to be comfortable and made of a material that will not be slippery when wet? I like large, easy-to-grip handles. Can the drag be adjusted quickly and easily? Is the drag smooth; after a long, fast pull, does it have a tendency to be jerky when tight? How much does the reel weigh (you are going to be casting for

long periods of time)? Is the reel comfortable in your hands (palming a reel that has rough edges or sharp screws can be annoying and even affect your casting efficiency)? Among the reels that fit the above specifications best are the Ambassadeur 5000 C and the Supreme 510-511.

One of the most difficult items for one fisherman to recommend to another by the printed word is a fishing rod. But again there are some basic guidelines that must be considered. How heavy (in weight) is it? What material is the handle made of (I prefer cork)? Are there enough line guides to handle strain when playing a fish and the rod is bent? Are the guides made of material which monofilament or dacron line will not cut? Before buying a rod, it's a good idea to mount a reel on it and to do some practice casting.

For many years the professional fishermen preferred one-piece rods and they did have better action. However, with the advent of glass ferrules, it is almost impossible to feel any difference between a one- and two-piece model with the same stick. Therefore I now prefer the two-piece rods (for ease of shipping and when travelling) over the one-piece.

Specifically, the rod I generally use is a 6-foot, two-piece heavy action with carbaloy or speed guides, cork handle with a very positive screw type reel seat. A seat which does

Bobby Murray, a leading money winner in professional bass fishing tournaments, uses plug casting tackle to catch a hefty largemouth bass.

not hold the reel firmly can be a terrible nuisance. I also carry a medium action and a light action rod when I have to use ¼- or ⅜-ounce lures with lighter line. Generally when fishing aquatic cover, vegetation, obstructions or deep structures, I prefer the heavy action rods. My own rods are (1) Heddon—6905 Power plus action, (2) Fenwick PLC 60 and (3) Browning #312900. But there are others equally efficient.

Many of my fishing buddies still prefer to use braided line when casting, but I prefer monofilament. The small diameter, the translucency and tremendous wearability make it far superior in my mind. However I do like to use braided line when fishing surface lures because I feel I can control the action of the lure a little better.

The same plug casting reel used to handle this northern pike could be used for freshwater bass or saltwater tarpon.

THE TEXAS COAST

Saltwater Economy

Package
by Byron W. Dalrymple

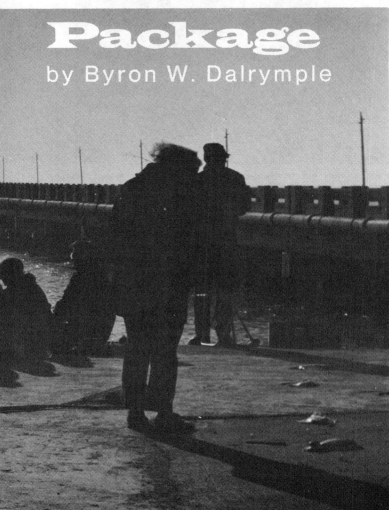

Speckled weakfish, or sea trout, caught near mouth of high river running into salt water bay. New water, and less salinity attracted them.

MY FRIEND Tom Hennessey is a wild-eyed, all-out angler hypnotized by saltwater. He is also sort of snug with a buck. "I moved to Texas," Tom once told me, "because there are hundreds of miles of coastline, practically all of it available free—and even a guy without a boat can catch more fish than he can drag up the beach!"

Tom was right. On one of my first coastal trips after we came to Texas to live, Tom and I took a couple of camp mattresses, a few staples of grub, plentiful ice in a chest, a wire cooking grill, a gas lantern, a jug of fresh water and another of amber elixir, to mix with it. We had surf rods and medium weight spin rods, a throw net for catching mullet and other bait, and old sneakers for wading surf or flats. Sort of a jack-knife bare-bones outfit. But who needed more?

We got on the beach late in the afternoon. Kiddingly Tom said, "What would you like for dinner—redfish steak, or flounder?"

"A big red," I replied. "You go catch it while I ferret

out some firewood from drift. I may even run up a coquina stew if I can find the blighters."

Now, of course reds, as they're called on the Texas coast —channel bass to easterners—can be caught on lures. But one of the best ways to entice a big one in the surf is with a live mullet about six or eight inches long. There was a small tidal overflow pool in a depression up from the surf line. In it Tom spied several trapped mullet. Easy pickin's. He ran 'em up to one end and hurled the net. A few minutes later he was belly deep in the surf and a mullet hooked slightly aft of the middle was struggling out there at line's end.

Coquinas, for those who may not know this tiny bivalve mollusk, look like miniature wedge-shaped clams, the shells in varying hues. The half-inch long delicacies are found just at surfline in certain beach strips. I located an ample concentration, pawed wet sand swarming with them onto the wire grill and sifted them out. In half an hour I had half a gallon, which I presently had barely covered with water and set to boil over a quickly built beach fire. Strained through a clean handkerchief, the broth, with a bit of onion, celery and butter added, would present a superb course to go with Tom's proposed red.

And sure enough, by the time the pot started to boil, Tom shouted, "Here he is!"

The rod was well bent. This argued well for a sizeable specimen with big slab fillets just right for broiling. But the fish wasn't on the beach yet and it was taking line in a sizzle and forcing Tom to move down the surf as it ran. After bulling around with it anxiously for some minutes, he finally was backing out and leading it into the low breakers. Then as its head came up on a wave Tom ran backward, and the wave skidded the brute up onto the wet sand. It looked like a good eight pounds. Dinner was assured.

Obviously, as any fisherman knows, it is not always that easy, anywhere. But we had hit a good period. The next day we waded the flats of a shallow bay just a quick hike across the sand dunes from the open Gulf beach, and we dragged a husky stringer of trout—speckled weakfish—and flounder in with us, to clean and put on the ice. Hundreds of anglers do this same thing day after day, all year round on the Texas coast, just wading the flats or fishing the surf. Others fish from the numerous piers, many of them free. Of course there are also thousands more who use their boats, or rent boats. And even in a small boat there is hardly a day of the year that one cannot find a quiet channel or bayou in which to fish safely, and economically.

Perhaps more important even than the ease of access, which makes the Texas coast a kind of "Everyman's" southwest fishing hole, is the fantastic amount of inside and beachside waters. An arc drawn along this coast from Port Arthur on the north to the Mexican border would cover roughly 400 miles. But those are bird-flight miles. Behind the coastal barrier islands such as Matagorda, St. Joseph, Mustang and Padre, the latter stretching for some 115 miles, there are vast expanses and checkerboards of bays, indentations and flats covering some thousands of square miles. These are breeding, rearing and living grounds for many of the coastal species, and they are also the home of untold tons of game-fish forage. All told, coastal Texas is one of the most important reservoirs of saltwater coastal game fish on U.S. shores.

Happily, as I've indicated, the major share of the beaches and shorelines are available to the boatless public, and of course, all of these waters are easily accessible to boatmen. So immense is the expanse that there is no crowding whatever, except occasionally in summer on fishing piers and jetties when things get hot. This is something unique in Texas particularly. For Texas, once you leave the Gulf coast, has virtually no public lands. All but a picayune part of the huge state's 266,000 square miles is in private ownership.

The long stretch from south to north along Texas beaches offers an unending variety and infinite changes of weather and seasons. Bear in mind that Texas weather isn't like, for example, Florida weather. Most of the "big weather," as it's said, originates along the Continental Divide. And there isn't much between that and the Texas Gulf Coast except a few barbed wire fences. Winter on the beaches, except the very southernmost, can be and usually is just that. You can be wading on a balmy day at Port Isabel, while others at Galveston are freezing their tails off. And, regardless of what the weather is, summer or winter, if you don't care for it, just hang around a few minutes—it'll change, often with a blistering day or a whistling norther.

Those cold snaps during winter months aren't something to weep about. They spark some of the hottest fishing. You

Anybody can find and catch weakfish. They are accessible from shore in hundreds of channels and bays along Texas coast.

shiver and like it. I've bundled up in down clothing many a time and turned my back to the bitter breeze as we boat-fished some bay, seeking the deep holes. Most of the bays and inside waters are shallow. Quick temperature drops to or below freezing have a severe effect on the fish, can even cause a heavy kill, because the shallow water temperature plummets. Every trout and red fanned over the flats moves to the deepest hole it can find, seeking bottom and warmer temperature.

Several years ago a friend and I were fishing out of Port Aransas during such a cold snap. We knew the usual haunts were useless. We started hunting the holes by checking a depth contour map of the waters of Aransas Bay. There was a dredged channel north out of Aransas Pass running up toward Rockport. This natural gut, we figured, should draw fish quickly into its deep spots. Trying one location after another, we finally found them. There was a particularly deep stretch of possibly 50 yards. When fish gang up in such a restricted location competition for food becomes severe. We cast live shrimp into the channel, using only enough lead to take them down to bottom, where we crawled the baits along. In a period of two hours we sacked up a fantastic catch. Spots like the boat basin at Rockport have long been famed for big catches like that during such times.

There is a wide variety of species in the bays and the surf. Chief targets are the reds, trout, and flounders. Sheepshead also are plentiful, and as in other places invariably underrated. A sheepshead is a fantastic battler. It is difficult to hook—this is the fish that droll oldtimers say should be struck "just before it bites." It is also an excellent table fish, particularly when broiled. But it too often gets short shrift here.

Golden croakers are tremendously abundant and during their "runs" tens of thousands are caught. Occasionally some lucky angler stumbles into a swarm of pompano in the surf, and a good many are also taken from the piers. Gafftopsail catfish gather in large schools in the bays. Big black drum cruise the channels. In the rough shoreside water, where it breaks across the ends of long jetties into the Gulf—as at the Port Aransas ship channel—at times huge gatherings of blue runners swarm. This is another underrated species that fights fabulously, is unknown to most anglers and is as delicious as any pompano. In the

"Planked" fish. A flounder cooked on beach. Driftwood fire, driftwood prop, driftwood board. Tacks and copper wire hold fish on board before fire.

Wading for trout is very popular, and very effective.

You have to hit hard to get the hook into that tough mug. But once you're fast it takes real work to unwind the stubborn fish.

same places Spanish mackerel schools slash small bait fish. Spadefish, improperly called angelfish, along this coast, are found in season, generally spring, around pier pilings.

There are abundant sand trout in many channels, plentiful sharks in the bays and, just outside the surfline, a modest number of tarpon in summer, ladyfish galore in the bays—great leapers but not table fish. Whiting are commonly caught from piers or in the surf. Offshore, of course, there are the larger game fish—kings and sails, bonito, and far out, marlin.

But this discussion is concerned primarily with inshore species that anybody can afford to catch. At one time, some years back, southern Texas waters were prime for snook, which were colloquially called pike. No one is quite sure what happened. But it's rare to catch one now. You have to go on down the coast well into Mexico to do so. The Soto La Marina is renowned as a snook river. It comes to the Gulf at La Pesca. Tarpon also were once much more abundant than they now are.

It pays to know the best times of year. Of course, as I've said, there is fair to good to fabulous fishing some days every month of the year. The old motto at Port Aransas has long been something about the town "where they bite every day." But there are peak months for each variety, and one's chances are helped substantially by paying attention to these. The speckled trout (weakfish) is, by numbers taken, the top Texas coastal game fish. One excellent period for trout begins in late April or early May, and grows better as weeks wear on. All of June and much of July are peak months as a rule.

For example, a couple of years ago in late April we found some wading spots at Port Mansfield, east of Raymondville, that were really sizzlers. It is a simple matter if you use spoons or shortbodied leadhead worms—now extremely effective on this coast for trout—and wade seeking openings in underwater vegetation. Some of these holes will be teeming with trout. You have to move very stealthily, and cast without commotion, past the fish and back across. Bait certainly works well, but it should be live

shrimp and these aren't as easy to carry. Either way, however, wading is usually very good for trout in spring and on into the summer. In late July things usually slow down a bit. But by fall they're going strong. September, right on through much of December is the second peak period of the year.

There's an interesting phenomenon to be noted here. Obviously nobody likes hurricanes. But Texas gets its share and September is "hurricane time" as a rule. Over several years in periods just before hurricanes struck, or while they were forming and on their way—even if they wound up missing the coast—we found trout fishing just tremendous. It was good also for reds and other species.

Do fish sense the oncoming turmoil? Who knows? Again, after a severe hurricane that wreaks heavy damage, as soon as waters clear a bit, the fishing for trout and reds will be furious. Probably this is because their routines have been utterly upset, they've been unable to feed much, are ravenous, and the heavy wave action and flooding have uncovered vast stores of new forage.

While the fall and early winter redfish "season" compares almost identically to the same peak for trout, there is another hot time for reds that's a bit different from that for trout. In normal years redfish catches begin to pick up in February, and through March and April some of the year's best fishing comes on. Flounders are good all summer and fall, but the real big bulge in this catching usually occurs during October and November. The big black drum move in ship channels and elsewhere generally at times about comparable to the high points for reds. Bottom fishing with a hunk of squid or cut bait is what gets them much of the time.

As in all fishing, when you get to know an area thoroughly you'll unearth special spots for a certain species that for some reason, not very logical to the angler, turn out heavy catches. For example, friends and I for some seasons fished a particular channel marker between Corpus Christi and Port Aransas, for drum. Many big ones came from here season after season.

During cold snaps, trout get into deep holes. Boat basins are often loaded with them. This is on Texas coast.

The big times for tough little golden croakers, which fight as hard as their relatives, the reds, and are excellent table fare, are in June and October. The April-May period and again in September is when most of the pompano are caught. Sheepshead are good all winter. In fact, during some of the colder weather if one fishes deep along pilings where big freighters come in, enormous catches can be made. The schools of Spanish mackerel, the blue runners in force, and the kings offshore all arrive from south of the border as waters warm in early spring, and stay during the summer. They drift back south as the water cools in fall.

Along this entire coast the ubiquitous shrimp reigns as the supreme bait. Live shrimp may be a bit difficult to handle and keep alive, but it, by all odds, outfishes any other bait or lure. Although croakers and occasionally reds, trout and flounders will accept dead shrimp, and peeled fresh tails of bull shrimp are great redfish bait when one is wading the flats; the live, kicking article is the item all these game fish find least resistible. However, this presents a problem at times along the Texas coast. When weather is bad for the bait-shrimp boats, there may be exasperating days or a week at a time when not one live shrimp is available at any dock. Then of course one uses fresh frozen shrimp, or cut bait. But it really pays for anyone to learn to fish artificials, for a man who is adept with them can

fill the shrimp gap any time, and if he's real hot at it he seldom falls back on bait.

A few years ago the short-bodied plastic worm with lead head made its debut on the Texas coast. This was the first place where it became popular and it literally murdered trout. From here it moved on to do likewise in Florida. This is one of the best of the lot with which to experiment. Cast it and let it well down, then jig it slowly along. Sometimes a faster retrieve with short jerks also hangs 'em by the dozen. The leadhead jig is another must item. For Spanish mackerel and blue runners it is indispensable, in yellow or white. If you have difficulty taking trout on these jigs, pin a hunk of shrimp onto the hook. Many times they'll home in to the jig action, pick up the scent trail and that's the clincher.

Lightweight spoons that will surface skitter are a standby when wading the flats for reds. This sport also came into its first full flower along the Texas coast, simply because there is so much easily wadable water. It is an absolute hair-raiser for drama and excitement. In shallow water reds like to feed over shell beds. They feed nose down commonly, like bonefish, and you can actually see the tail sticking out and waving. It appears bluish. Sometimes the identifying black tail spot shows.

Reds on the flats are as skittish as any bonefish. If they

On a day when we had intended to go outside for kings, we were stopped by a blow.
But it didn't inhibit the reds in the bays. They were eager for live shrimp or spoons.

If you like to catch big drum, March and April produce many all along the coast.
These were caught and kept cool at water's edge by a fisherman with no boat.

Blue runners. All were taken at the end of a jetty, where water breaks over large rocks.

see you, they're gone instantly. Wade slowly, sun quartering from behind. Wear polaroids if they don't bother your vision. Cast past a fish you have seen and retrieve slowly so the lure catches its vision. And when one hits, hang on! Many will cut you off, tearing through the shell and debris. But that first run of a big one is worth it.

One of the economy slants on fishing this coast concerns camping. Nowhere that I know of are there more excellent facilities available either right on the beaches or else close by. First of all, this is tourist country—winter people from the north, all-year people from Texas and nearby states. So, there are a myriad of small to large excellent tourist-type trailer parks. We've stayed in one KOA park in Rockport, for example, that is beautiful, loaded in winter, bereft in summer. Why, I still don't understand, but from April to October spaces are plentiful, high-class, and moderate. This is typical.

Then there are the State Parks. Two of the most unique State Parks in the U.S. tailored strictly for fishermen, are here. One is at Port Lavaca. Where an old causeway, replaced by a modern one, crosses the bay, the old one is now for fishermen—a fisherman's linear park in some excellent water. The park is at the south end, an enticing spot for those who like facilities and closeness to their work. Down the pike a little piece is Copano Bay Causeway State Park. Officially there is no camping here, but we personally have seen a few "cheaters" and they had no problems. At any rate, the old causeway here, several miles of it, with entrance from either end, is managed strictly as a kind of long-distance fishing pier. No vehicular traffic on it, just for fishermen. Trout fishing here, especially at night under causeway lights, has at times been sensational.

A few miles away is lovely Goose Island State Park, all the trimmings, and great wade or boat fishing. Farther north at Indianola State Park—one of the oldest coastal settlements in the state, once a busy port and now defunct —you can find fishing and camping, no facilities, have it wild as you like. At Port Aransas a county park takes care of RVs. There is beach camping below, but I won't recommend this. I don't believe in unsupervised camping—using the beautiful dunes as sanitary facilities—but some of the hippies do it.

At this time, and until they are regulated, many people camp on down Mustang Island anywhere along beach or bay or at bridge sites—anywhere they can find access. Again, I feel this should be regulated. Some do likewise along the causeways, such as from Corpus Christi or from Aransas Pass. At the north end of Padre Island there is a big county campground. Another is over 100 miles south, at the south end. The Padre Island National Seashore takes up the in-between slack—some 88 miles and this is becoming well regulated. You can fish to your heart's content and there is a fine campground—few facilities but all well run—at the north end in the Park.

At Port Mansfield, a great fishing spot with fishing on fee-charge piers under lights for trout, there is a public county campground with limited facilities. And there are limitless commercial campgrounds and small travel RV parks. Thus, this whole coast is an economy package. Good fishing, good camping, peace and quiet. Quite a lot of litter, incidentally, and the people to be blamed are not the few, but everybody. If you visit it, carry away what you brought in! This is one of the longest saltwater beaches available to the U.S. public, and the longest (Padre Seashore) publicly owned beach in the U.S. Treat it with respect and it will be a wonderful vacation spot for all salty anglers, at bargain rates, for years to come!

Wisteria and the new fashion frame George Laycock's catch of crappies.

Great New Fashion for Fishermen

by PEGGY PETERS

Noted anglers Bill Gressard and Dick Kotis just may catch more bass because of the way they're dressed.

Dick Kotis individualizes his avocado green suit with western neckwear and his own Arbogast fishing hat.

The new jumpsuit can be worn by ladies too, as the author shows here.

FOR FAR TOO LONG fishermen have been caricatured and characterized as slightly second-class citizens who dressed carelessly at best. Perhaps the latter is true because wading a stream or sitting in a boat all day doesn't seem to require any special fancy garb. Just so the angler is happy and comfortable . . . what else matters?

Well, all that seems to be changing. Check around any boat dock, marina, sporting goods store or tackle shop where anglers congregate and you will probably see a new look. It isn't that fishermen themselves have greatly changed; it's simply that new fashions for fishermen are making them more expert at the game and at the same time they are more comfortable than ever before. Strange as it may seem, an outdoorsman might be able to catch more fish because of the garments he wears.

Want an example? Warm, light, really waterproof pants and parka suits permit a man to stay out on the water longer in the worst kind of weather. And that happens to be exactly the time when many species of fish strike the best.

Dick Kotis shows the action pleats across the back of the jumpsuit which free the arms for pin-point casting.

But the newest fashion to capture the fancy of fresh-water fishermen is the jumpsuit. This isn't the ordinary denim jumpsuit of paratroopers or airplane pilots—although the basic design may have come from them. Rather it is a garment designed precisely for fishermen—both to make the sport more pleasant and even to put more pike on the stringer.

The Arbogast jumpsuit illustrated on these pages is a one-piece item of permanent press miracle fibers. Thanks to the action pleats across the shoulders, it fits loosely enough to allow complete ease of casting (tighter, heavy garments can be needlessly tiring to a caster's arm) and safe movement in, out of and around a boat. Pockets it has—everywhere. The two hip pockets plus the four patch pockets on the front are secured with velcro, which means quick opening and closing with one hand only. Besides these *six*, there are four more; two slash pockets of super-generous size below the waist in front plus two small ones on the sleeves. The idea is to provide plenty of

As the author demonstrates, fishing isn't the only activity suitable for the new jumpsuit. Backpacking is another prime activity.

Writer George Laycock chooses a bright blue for his jumpsuit.

Pockets the new fashion has—everywhere. Can you count eight in this view of Dick Kotis?

places to stuff tackle, flies, film, the new mini-cameras, sunglasses, cigarettes, candy bars, insect repellent, you name it—and all where it is instantly handy.

The suit has two metal loops, one at the back of the neck which might be used to hold a landing net, and one in the front, handy to hook a container of flies on.

The jumpsuit is closed by a plastic zipper which moves easily and won't rust or jam up. The belt, thanks to the wide belt loops, stays where it belongs no matter how you twist and turn or what shape your waist happens to be! Actually no matter what shape *you* are, this new fashion will fit. It comes in the usual variety of sizes and with its raglan sleeve design, elasticized back waist and adjustable belt you will look well-tailored and comfortable.

Any angler's wife will appreciate the ease with which it can be laundered. Dirt and stains come out easily and there's no ironing! In fact, she might even want one of these new suits for herself! Ladies wear them too, for fishing or any activity (even backpacking) that calls for an easy-wear, easy-care outfit.

The Arbogast jumpsuit sells for about $24.95 and is available in better sporting goods stores. The attractive and flattering colors are: red, blue, green and yellow.

Maybe the time has finally come to bid farewell to that miserable old felt hat, the torn flannel shirt and those Army surplus pants that smell like you've already been fishing when you're just starting out! Geronimo! Jump into a jumpsuit!

The BUCKEYE BRONZEBACK

by Dave Bowring

"LET'S wait here long enough so I can spin that log," Harold said, as our canoe drifted upstream ahead of a gentle August breeze. I obediently plunged half the length of my paddle into the water, anchoring us to the spot.

Harold's wrist snapped, and the silver spinner arched over the surface of the Stillwater River and plunked down less than 3 inches from the fallen beech trunk lying at angles to the shore. Harold paused to let the bait settle a foot or so, then began a retrieve that brought the lure so close to the trunk that the trebles must have scraped bark.

"Oop, there he is!" Harold muttered, as the retrieve stopped and the top half of his spincast rod bent. "He ain't all that big, if I can get 'im out from under that log."

The task, while pleasant, wasn't all that easy. The smallmouth had made a lair of the cover provided by the beech trunk, and seemed to know his best escape was to stay there. Harold tried to horse the fish, but only succeeded in getting hung up on a submerged branch, losing the bass and the spinner.

"The sonuvagun unbit 'n div," Harold grinned while he tied on a spinner to replace the bait that smallmouth was now wearing in its jaw. "Well, let's move on up a bit. I know of a few more logs and such that should hold a bass or two." A stroke of the cedarwood moved us upstream.

Harold Barefoot and I were after Ohio smallmouth, and there was and is nothing unique about the pleasure. The Buckeye State can boast of not only introducing much of eastern North America to *Micropterus dolomieu,* but offering some of the most challenging modern-day smallmouth fishing found anywhere in the contiguous 48 states.

Dr. J. A. Henshall, in his *Book of the Black Bass* written in the 19th century, relates many instances when smallmouth bass (called green bass, among other misnomers in those days) were captured from Ohio Valley waters and transported to likely waters along the nation's eastern seaboard. Some fish were transported in makeshift tanks and assorted containers, whatever was at hand. Henshall's book even records a transplant made by a U.S. Army colonel where three-dozen smallmouth were moved from Wheeling, West Virginia to Maryland in the boiler of an oldtime railroad engine. "The little bass survived the trip," Henshall recalled, "save three which died in transport. The remaining 33 were stocked in a small pound near Baltimore and were doing quite well the following spring."

This is the life story of the Buckeye bronzeback. Discovered to be both sporting and abundant in the clean, rocky rivers and streams of Ohio, the smallmouth was netted, transported, and stocked all over the Midwest. Heretofore, barren streams containing only rough fish now had thriving populations of Buckeye-bred bass, and the word spread.

In 1870, fisheries people in Pennsylvania netted a large number of smallmouth from the Potomac River and deposited them in their home state's Delaware River. A fisheries biologist and two companions caught enough smallmouth from one Canadian lake to stock the Black River with its first lot of breeding-sized smallmouth. The word was out, and the fishing public loved it.

They still do. Ohio, parent for so much of the bass fishing in North America, continues to offer attractive smallmouth fishing in her lakes, reservoirs, rivers and streams.

For proof of Ohio's exuberance for the bronzebacked fighter, look no further than the Senecaville National Fish Hatchery in the state's southeastern corner. Since 1935, when its construction became a WPA project, the Senecaville hatchery has annually produced about 200,000 small-

Smallmouth is mostly a fish of running, moving waters, but some lakes do contain the species.

Harold Barefoot lands smallmouth by grasping its lower jaw.

mouth bass for stocking on Ohio waters. John Hawkinson, hatchery manager, is enthusiastic about the hatchery's record.

"We annually provide most of the smallmouth bass stocked in the state," he said. "In 1969 we began experimenting with an Ohio breed of smallmouth bass, a subspecies that would do best in the waters we have in Ohio. We were successful, and now produce fish with a special depth, coloration and growth rate best suited for Ohio's water conditions."

Of course, the program had its problems. Smallmouth, says Hawkinson, are among the most difficult of species to raise under hatchery conditions. Eggs must be checked shortly after laying, while still on the nest in the spawning pond. Once hatched, the fry must be captured while still clustered over the nest, and moved to a rearing pond. After 30 days, the fry have grown to fingerlings from 1½ to 2 inches long, and they are ready for stocking. Besides smallmouth, the Senecaville installation raises 3 million walleye, 1 million channel catfish, and approximately 50,000 striped bass a year. The majority of these youngsters find their way into Ohio's waters.

While smallmouth angling is fairly good statewide, it stands to reason that some waters would be better than others, and this is the case. Each section of Ohio has its own best waters for the pugnacious fighter. Here are the best of these "top waters."

In the state's northeastern section, try the Upper Cuyahoga River from the town of Burton downstream to Lake Rockwell north of Kent. There is a fair run of big small-mouth—4-pounders have been taken with regularity here —from mid-April to mid-May. Fish averaging 2 pounds or so can be taken here all summer, with the size increasing again in autumn.

The best live baits here are lively helgrammites (larva stage of the Dobson fly), and small crayfish, either hard or soft-shelled. Productive lures would have to include wobbling spoons and spinners, and bright streamers on fly tackle do well after the various minnow fry appear in July and August.

The Upper Cuyahoga runs clear over gravel and rock bedding, and is a pleasure to wade.

Live bait is the best bet on the Chagrin River, also in Ohio's northeast region. Soft-shell crayfish and helgrammites take most of the bass, and the average size runs from 1 to 2 pounds. The Chagrin is a small stream and much of it runs through private land, so access should be preceded by landowner permission. Tip: Use extremely light tackle and fine leaders during the hot months, because this water is low and clear from June through September.

The West Branch of the Mahoning River, and West Branch Reservoir, have been known to yield 4-pounders, especially in the reservoir proper. These are stream-bred fish which migrated to the reservoir after its filling about 5 years ago.

A final "better" water in northeastern Ohio is the Grand River which mouths into Lake Erie at Paynesville. Good smallmouth are taken along the river's entire length.

In the flatland of central Ohio, Big Darby Creek, from Logan County southeast to Circleville, is perhaps the area's top stream. This 80-mile stretch flows over clean gravel and is unencumbered by dams or large communities.

Nightcrawlers and black plastic worms are best, but chromed spinners take their toll of bass too. The Big Darby is especially suited to canoe floats in late summer when the current is steady but slow and the bass must be approached with some caution. Good squirrel hunting exists along this waterway, too.

Two other popular bass streams in central Ohio are Big Walnut Creek and the Olentangy River. These are smaller streams, so light tackle and presentation are the bywords for success.

When you talk about smallmouth in northern and western Ohio, Lake Erie wins hands down. Kelley, all of the Bass and Pelee islands are tops locally. Example: A Dayton couple caught 17 smallmouth *averaging* 4 pounds apiece from the bars off Kelley island while fishing with small minnows for ring perch.

The best method however, is to drift the island's lee sides with soft crayfish or big shiner minnows. Lake Erie emerald shiners are a good second choice.

A second choice of methods would be casting bright spinners, spoons or lively plugs, again in the shallow waters near islands. Drifting, however, usually covers more good territory in a day's time.

The main problem with fishing Lake Erie is being able to get on the water with any regularity. Weather can blow up dangerously high seas in very little time, and you'll need at least a 19-foot boat if leaving the mainland area. Boat rentals are available on South Bass and Pelee islands.

The Huron River is another hotspot in Ohio's northwestern region. Try hitting that stretch downstream from Milan in the spring, drifting 'crawlers, crayfish or hellgrammites. Weekends are usually crowded here with local anglers, but weekdays often see 4-pounders taken when they enter the river to spawn from Lake Erie.

One negative note must be added concerning smallmouth found in, or native to, Lake Erie. For some unknown reason, the smallmouth bass appears to absorb and retain more methyl mercury pollution in its fatty tissues than even the white bass, on which Ohio officials have placed a commercial fishing ban. This condition, of course, does not affect the bass' sportfishing capabilities, but tread carefully if you plan to eat bass from the big lake.

Southwestern Ohio, near my bailiwick of Dayton, is literally riddled with small to medium limestone streams offering bassing at least as good as any other inland network.

Beginning on the Ohio River southeast of Cincinnati, two of the better bass streams are Straight and Whiteoak creeks

Bronzeback is a great jumper wherever it's found. This maneuver often gets rid of the hook.

Typical smallmouth bass float trip stream. Floating is an excellent way to see beautiful country and cover much suitable water.

in the Brown County area. Both of these streams are bedded in sedimentary rock, as are most of the watercourses in the region, and usually flow clear and in pool during the summer.

Moving west, the Little Miami River and its three main feeders, East Fork, Todds Fork and Caesar creeks, are examples of prime smallmouth water. Almost anyplace on these waters hold good bass, with the usual spinning hardware and livebait choices collecting the bulk of the catch.

It should be mentioned that both East Fork and Caesar creeks are now being impounded by Army Corps of Engineers dams and reservoirs. If completed, these deplorable projects will slow flow above the dams and increase siltation downstream. Both projects, however, are presently being reviewed in Washington, so it's not impossible one or both could be stopped and therefore the lovely feeder streams might be saved for smallmouth fans.

A bit further west, the Great Miami River system is excellent for smallmouth from Dayton north. The Stillwater River, from just north of Dayton well into Darke County, is perfect for anglers who like to wade and/or canoe for their quarry. Best portion of the Stillwater is from the community of West Milton north to the headwaters.

The Mad River, better known locally for its annual stockings of hatchery-raised rainbow trout, still offers spotty although good bronzeback fishing. Much of the better bass water flows through hard-access private lands, however, and although most of the Mad is covered by state-arranged public fishing easements, ask locally for the best bass spots and who owns what. The Mad drops 8½ feet per mile,

is swift over a good gravel base, so bassing here is well nigh idyllic.

The Whitewater River and its two main branches, although largely lying within eastern Indiana, does mouth on the Ohio River within Ohio boundaries, so I will include it here because it is such a clean and productive stream.

The Whitewater's gravel beds, some of which run to 150 feet in depth, act like a natural filtering system, combing the water clean of silt and other debris. A favored local method of hitting the river's top spots with a minimum of work is to float individual stretches, using either a canoe or sturdy johnboat. Two floats I favor require 8 and 12 hours respectively, including plenty of time to stop the float and wade a particularly bassy pool or riffle.

Smallmouth is king in the Whitewater, but enough keeper largemouth are around to make plastic worms and large plugs welcome among your collection of spinners, spoons, porkrinds and the like.

Try floating the stretch of the river around Brookville. A canoe livery rents canoes there, and you can set your own pace and float length. There is, however, another Army dam (damn?) about to be completed on the river's main branch just north of Brookville, and this will have similar effects as those on the two Ohio streams. What did the smallmouth ever do to the Army, anyway?

Smallmouth in Ohio are fair sized, fairly plentiful in unpolluted places and about the fightingest fish in the state. Like Harold Barefoot said, there's a place just around the bend where one or two lunker bass hang out. I'll see you around that bend.

171

HOW TO ORGANIZE an ANGLER'S CLUB

by Erwin A. Bauer

Clubs should cooperate with state conservation officers to teach young people sportsmanship and to respect our natural environment.

ANGLERS in every American community need a club that is vigorous, powerful and respected. Diminishing fish populations, increased pollution of our waterways, grabs for public land, encroachment on National Parks and scenic wonders with high-level dams, and the use of a wildlife resource as a political football are a few of the factors that make it imperative for outdoorsmen to band together. They should have a club active locally in conservation work and constantly in touch with nationwide affairs. The membership should include every man who enjoys the outdoors and wants to preserve it for the future.

What makes an active fishing club? Generally, just two things: good leadership and a worth-while continuing program to achieve a goal. These elements determine the success or failure of any club.

Suppose you want to organize an angler's club in your community. Or maybe you just want to revitalize a club that shows signs of folding. Here's a blueprint on how to handle it:

Bring a group of sportsmen together. They should be the most active men you can assemble. Try to select those with

a great appreciation of the outdoors and an interest in conservation, not necessarily the inveterate anglers and hunters. Generally you will want men who have always shown an interest in other community or service activities. Sit down with them and explain the need for an outdoor group in your town, using the reasons given here, plus all the local reasons you can think of. The next step is to select leaders and call a public meeting. Remember to pick out aggressive, responsible men—not just good fellows. Try to include an influential politician or two. You need hard workers at the top to set a good example. Have these men ready for action at the public meeting.

Invite every outdoorsman and conservationist in the region to this first public gathering. Work on it through the local newspapers, radio and television. Call on influential people and enlist the help of sporting goods dealers. If they're clever businessmen, they'll cooperate wholeheartedly. And make an effort to obtain someone well known in outdoor circles to give a kick-off speech and to draw a crowd.

Quickly and without harangue, present your case for an

angler's club. Have the speaker present his case. Then ask for prospective members. If it looks as though you've attracted an enthusiastic group, sign them up right there, have an election (for which your choices of the first meeting should be nominated) and hope for the best.

Elect seven trustees with instructions to call their own meeting very soon to select a president, vice-president, secretary and treasurer from among them. This method of election has become more popular with conservation groups than that of electing all executive officers in open meeting. It's perfectly sound business, however, either way.

One of the first official acts of a new club should be incorporation. This is a matter of prestige, and puts the group on a sounder basis.

Next, start aiming for a clubhouse or club grounds right away. If delayed, this may never be accomplished. There are many ways to begin, perhaps the best being by public subscription. Many government agencies are available to help with such a project—the county surveyor, the county engineer, or local farm agents. The high intentions of many a club have invited gifts of land. In the case of other successful groups, members have pitched in and completely built clubhouses with their own tools, time and skills.

Always remember this in planning your own installation: aim high. Don't settle for a clubhouse that is something less than the type of place you look forward to visiting. Select the site carefully. Get away from town—if possible, where you can impound water for fishing and where you can landscape the grounds for wildlife. Look forward when you design the clubhouse. Do it with banquets and large gatherings in mind. Have family participation in mind too.

Your program should be broad, long range but flexible, intelligently planned, and designed for the participation of every member. That may seem like a difficult matter to inaugurate, but it isn't. Always keep your goals in mind and aim for them. These goals should be better fishing in your neighborhood, plus a greater understanding and appreciation of our natural resources.

Here's an example of the type of project your program should include. If yours is a typical community where farmer-sportsman relations have deteriorated, encourage farmers to join your club. You might have printed "Fishing With Permission Only" signs for free distribution to any farmer who will use them. This often forestalls the posting of large tracts of land. Some clubs find it good to underwrite damage by sportsmen to farms that are registered with the club as open.

The program should provide for active support and assistance to state conservation agencies. That means planting trees and encouraging good soil and forest management practices. It means stream improvement work and pollution abatement projects wherever possible. It does not mean tormenting the state to stock fish where experts know it's unwise and wasteful. Nor does it mean involvement in such antiquated activities as importing fish for release.

No program nowadays can be complete without a wide range of youth activities. The future of our wildlife resources and of plentiful outdoor opportunities rests with the coming generation. This has been repeated so often that it's a tired cliché, but it's undeniably true.

Encourage youth groups to visit and use your facilities. Enlist their aid in your spring planting projects and perhaps offer prizes for the best jobs of wildlife management they do on their own. This is a splendid kind of competition to sponsor among 4-H and Future Farmers chapters. It gets wildlife food and cover planted in big quantities as no other undertaking can do. It's a good idea annually to sponsor courses in deportment in the field and sportsmanship. Recruit instructors from the membership.

Put everyone on a committee. Work, or lack of it, by committees can make or break your organization. Naming responsible, energetic chairmen is one way to insure committee work. The following committees should be organized in every club: Legislative, Entertainment, Farmer Cooperation, Finance, Grounds, Audit, Conservation, Membership, Public Relations. Other committees can be added to suit your particular needs. Insist that reports be submitted in writing; insert reports in the club record.

The Legislative Committee is perhaps the most vital of all. It should include an attorney as well as other members who have a nose for news. This group keeps close tab on what transpires in legislative chambers and maintains close contact with legislators. It makes known the wishes of the club on conservation matters. When new laws are needed, this committee works tirelessly and vigorously on elected officials.

Many clubs disintegrate from lack of interest at meetings. It's the job of the Entertainment Committee to prevent this. With the competition of TV, dull, uninteresting programs will not be tolerated. Charge this committee with obtaining the very best speakers available. Recruit them from newspapermen, local outdoor writers, conservation officials and legislators. Most states have fine libraries of outdoor movies. Many advertisers offer good outdoor films for club showings.

The functions of the Farmer Cooperation Committee are as vital as the problem of lands posted to public hunting. This group should keep in touch with the situation and constantly recommend ways to get along with farmers. Cooperation with granges, farm bureaus and similar organizations is good business.

The Finance Committee has the responsibility of financing an active program. Here a number of means to consider: see if your state allows clubs to act as agents for selling licenses (this is a grand source of income); provide for associate membership to merchants, well-wishers and others; sponsor annual or semiannual field days.

The responsibilities of the Grounds Committee do not end when the clubhouse is erected. It has the problem of upkeep, improvements and maintenance. And it should consider additions, such as a casting pond, playground facilities, picnic tables and development of the land for wildlife. This group might also consider the possibility of renting the clubhouse to other organizations for meetings and parties. It's a good way to help finance your own activities, and might even pay for a caretaker.

The Audit Committee should, at least once each year, carefully examine the records of the club secretary and treasurer.

Misunderstanding between state conservation agencies and organized sportsmen often causes the good work done by both groups to be wasted. There should be complete cooperation between the two, so a Conservation Committee is an effective method of liaison. It's the duty of this group to keep a finger on state policy and state activities, and advise the membership of this progress. At least one member of the committee should report regularly on this subject.

The Membership Committee has an important role too. It's up to them to keep old-timers in harness and to encourage a steady increase among younger sportsmen. Naturally, the club depends on them for securing revenue through recruitment. Good attendance at meetings should also be the goal of this group.

The success of any program sometimes depends on the publicity it receives. So an alert Public Relations Committee should use all means of communication to tell the story of the club and its activities. Committeemen should see that members doing an outstanding job get proper recognition.

It helps morale and encourages them to further effort.

Business meetings should ordinarily be short and to the point. Officers should study pertinent matters on the agenda before the meeting and should move swiftly through them. Members should vote on all major projects and on expenditures.

Much of the interest in an angler's club centers on the social activities. A member may be encouraged or discouraged by his wife, according to her own interest. A wise club holds at least one banquet for the distaff side annually. One Ohio club has a liars' contest in which the prize-winning liar is given only a token prize, whereas his wife receives something special for tolerating such a liar in the home. It's a terrific promotion.

The atmosphere around the club grounds should be congenial for family groups, especially on weekends. A member feels more free to participate in club activities if he does not have to leave his family too often to do so. If they can enjoy a visit to the club grounds too, he can be more at ease while engaged in some activity there.

Casting tournaments are regularly scheduled events for most successful clubs. To make them more important on a broad scale, all should be registered with the national organizations. If local merchants can be induced to sponsor them, more of the profits go into club coffers. Plan these events carefully, however, so that they go off smoothly and honestly.

The annual banquet should be a gala affair, an event that is eagerly anticipated. Invite public officials. Don't settle for a crude game dinner or a hastily prepared fish fry—save those for other stag occasions. Be lavish with rewards and commendations for jobs well done by members through the year. Try to schedule a really outstanding program.

Make your club and its activities a part of community affairs. Cooperate with other clubs, and when a vital issue—pollution, for example—comes up you can rely on their backing. Donate your club facilities for such drives as the Red Cross and the cancer fund. It increases the stature of your club in the community, and the citizens will look more favorably on your efforts.

Here are some activities or functions that clubs can employ or adopt:

1. Improve stream banks by planting willows. Other stream improvement, such as building small weirs, dams and deflectors, pays off in better fishing. Encourage landowners not to strip vegetation from stream banks.

2. Buy barbed wire for farmers who will use it to fence wood lots. This increases rainfall absorbency of woods and encourages underbrush. Better fishing begins back in the hills.

3. Sponsor conservation scholarships for teachers or outstanding students. Many state colleges have summer conservation courses. Send a local teacher to one of these, all expenses, or at least tuition, paid.

4. Purchase the best current books on conservation for school libraries and receive a subscription to *Field & Stream* or *Outdoor Life*. Many of the official state outdoor publications are also very informative on local conservation and outdoor subjects.

5. Wage a constant campaign against erosion, no matter where it occurs—on poorly farmed hillsides or along the fills of newly constructed highways. One Ohio club seeded every foot of a power-line cut through the entire county in grass and legumes. This provided good wildlife cover and at the same time prevented a serious erosion and silting problem in local streams.

6. Watch your conservation officials closely, but don't harass them. If they spend a lot of money for research and fact-finding, that's good. But if employees' jobs and conservation programs depend on political considerations rather than on sound reasoning, it's time to get busy.

7. Sponsor a "Farmer of the Year" award for the farmer who has done the most for wildlife conservation. Give him a worth-while memento of the occasion, plus all the publicity you can arrange.

8. Never relax in pollution-abatement efforts. Constantly besiege elected officials for proper legislation. Report pollution offenses to the proper state agency as quickly as they happen; take water samples and shoot photos of dead fish for evidence in case of court action.

Here is the framework for a constitution and bylaws. It can, of course, be altered to suit any locale or situation.

Constitution and By-Laws

ARTICLE I—NAME

SECTION 1. The name of this organization shall be _____ Angler's Club.

ARTICLE II—OBJECT

SECTION 1. This non-profit organization is formed in the interest of better hunting and fishing and for a better appreciation of the outdoors and our natural resources (a) by actively cooperating in protection of forests, soils, waters and natural habitat for fish and game; (b) by maintaining an interest in the passage and enforcement of adequate wildlife laws; (c) by educating the general public as to the importance to our economy, health and welfare of conservation and restoration work.

SECTION 2. This organization shall further express to the Conservation Department of _____ its interest in wildlife and aid in all its endeavors.

SECTION 3. This organization shall at all times work to prevent destruction of property by hunters and fishermen and shall cooperate with landowners in order to promote a better feeling between them and the sportsmen.

SECTION 4. This organization is empowered to purchase, lease, hold and own, supervise and control real estate or chattels as directed by the Board of Trustees and approved by its members as hereinafter provided.

ARTICLE III—ORGANIZATON

SECTION 1. This organization shall be controlled by a Board of Trustees numbering seven, elected annually. Within two weeks following the annual election the Board shall meet and choose from its own number club officers as follows: President, Vice-President, Secretary and Treasurer. The Board shall have the right at any time to remove any officer upon a vote of a majority of the board members at any meeting at which not less than five board members shall be present. Officers shall serve from the date of their election by the Board until the next Board shall have organized and elected. Five members shall constitute a quorum.

SECTION 2. Various committees, as established by the Board, shall be appointed by the President. Committee choice shall be subject to approval of the membership in open meeting.

SECTION 3. No officer or member shall be empowered to commit the club to any expenditure without first securing written permission of the Board of Trustees, except in such case where the Board shall decide in advance to approve a budget for operating expenses. All expenditures, after approval by the Board, shall be submitted to the entire membership in open meeting.

ARTICLE IV—DUTIES OF OFFICERS

SECTION 1. PRESIDENT. It shall be the duty of the President to preside at all meetings of the club and of the

Board of Trustees. He shall appoint all committees and make an annual report to the club. He shall sign, with the Treasurer, all vouchers in payment of expenditures incurred, after such expenditures have been approved by the Board of Trustees.

SECTION 2. VICE-PRESIDENT. The Vice-President shall perform all the duties of the President in case of his absence or disability. In the event of the absence or disability of both President and Vice-President, the Board of Trustees shall appoint a president pro tem.

SECTION 3. SECRETARY. The Secretary shall keep a complete record of the proceedings of the club and of the proceedings of the Board of Trustees, and issue all notices of meetings and conduct all correspondence. He shall keep and have custody of the list of members.

SECTION 4. TREASURER. The treasurer shall have charge of all funds and securities of the club and shall keep an accurate account thereof, subject at all times to inspection by the Board of Trustees. He shall submit at each regular meeting of the Board of Trustees a statement of the financial condition of the club, showing an itemized statement of all receipts and disbursements during the preceding period. He shall receive all moneys collected by the Secretary and give his receipt therefor, and deposit same in such bank as may be selected by the Board of Trustees. He shall give a bond in such sum as may be determined by the Board of Trustees, the premium to be paid by the club.

ARTICLE V—BOARD OF TRUSTEES

SECTION 1. The Board of Trustees shall have charge of the business affairs of the club, pass on all bills or expenditures and, if approved, submit to the membership before ordering payment by the Treasurer. Said Board of Trustees may adopt such bylaws for their own government as are not inconsistent with the Constitution and Bylaws.

ARTICLE VI—MEMBERSHIP

SECTION 1. Any person of good character, in accord with the principles and objects of this club, may become a member upon paying the annual dues hereinafter designated.

SECTION 2. Honorary members may only be elected by a unanimous vote of the Board of Trustees at any regular meeting. They shall be exempt from the payment of dues.

SECTION 3. Life members may be elected to membership in this club upon the payment of $50, such payment entitling them to membership for life without the payment of dues.

SECTION 4. The Board of Trustees shall have the power to forfeit or suspend the membership of any member for conduct endangering the welfare, interests or character of the club, provided, however, such member may appear before the Board of Trustees and be permitted to present his defense.

ARTICLE VII—DUES

SECTION 1. The annual dues shall be $5 payable in advance.

SECTION 2. Delinquents in arrears in dues may be dropped from the rolls at the discretion of the Board of Trustees.

ARTICLE VIII—MEETINGS

SECTION 1. The Annual Meeting of the club shall be held between January 1 and March 31 of each calendar year, at the discretion of the Board of Trustees, at which meeting the officers shall make their annual report and the election of the Trustees for the ensuing year take place.

SECTION 2. Special meetings of the club may be held at the call of the President at any time.

SECTION 3. Forty percent of members in good standing at any meeting shall constitute a quorum.

SECTION 4. Notices of any annual or special meeting of the club must be sent to all members in good standing at least five days before such meeting.

SECTION 5. Regular monthly meetings shall be held on the first Wednesday of each calendar month.

ARTCLE IX—ELECTIONS

SECTION 1. Seven members shall be elected to the Board of Trustees at the annual meeting of the club, and such Board of Trustees, at its annual meeting, shall elect the officers of the club from its members, to hold office for the ensuing year or until their successors are elected and qualified.

SECTION 2. All elections shall be by secret ballot.

SECTION 3. Vacancies on the Board of Trustees shall be filled by the Board, and such Trustees shall hold office until their successors are duly elected.

SECTION 4. The President shall, at a time sufficiently in advance of the annual meeting of the club, appoint three members as a Nominating Committee, who will submit two lists of seven members each as candidates for the Board of Trustees. One list shall constitute the "Green" ticket, the other the "Blue." These names are to be submitted at the annual meeting. Additional nominations, but not to exceed seven, may be made from the floor. The seven members receiving the highest number of votes shall be considered elected as members of the Board of Trustees for the ensuing year. In the event of a tie vote the tellers shall cast lots and certify as elected the person on whom the selection falls.

ARTICLE X—AMENDMENTS

SECTION 1. This Constitution may be modified, altered, amended or repealed at any annual or special meeting of this club by a three-fourths vote of the members present at such meeting, provided, however, a written notice of the proposed modification, alteration, amendment or repeal be mailed to the members at least ten days previous to the meeting at which such modification, alteration, amendment or repeal is to be acted upon.

SECTION 2. The annual meeting of the Board of Trustees shall be held as soon after the annual meeting of the club as may be deemed advisable by the Trustees. At this meeting the President shall have charge until all new officers are elected, and the Secretary shall hold his office until this meeting is completed, except that if the Secretary be not present the chair shall appoint a secretary pro tem to serve for the entire meeting. After this election the new officers shall assume their positions, with the exception of the Secretary, who will finish out the meeting in the record of proceedings. The procedure at this meeting shall be as follows:

Reading of Minutes
Reports of Committees and Officers
Report of Trustees
Old Business
New Business
Adjournment

SECTION 3. A special meeting of the Board of Trustees may be held at any time upon call of the President, and must be held by him upon the request of two members of the Board. The order of business at all regular meetings of the Board of Trustees shall be:

Reading of Minutes
Reports of Committees
Old Business
New Business
Adjournment

I'M A REALLY HAPPY ANGLER

Sal Muley (developer of the Garcia Handigear), Dave Krennick and Ken Doyle, demonstrate how a handicapped person is able to fish with skill.

by NORTON SANDERS

I WAS PROMPTED to write this article after losing the use of my left arm and leg from a stroke in 1962, at age 44. Fishing in lakes, ponds and streams always fascinated me, but prior to the stroke I wouldn't take time from a business career to earnestly fish.

While still an in-patient with lots of time to think, read and ponder, it was apparent that recovery would be a long, slow, tedious process, if I recovered at all. I had been told by doctors that it was doubtful if I'd ever be able to walk again or regain use of the left hand. Consequently my whole world had collapsed. But one thing was in my favor; my mind was clear.

One day a friend brought copies of *Outdoor Life* and *Sports Afield* to the hospital and one contained the picture of a very old man with overalls, fishing from an old rowboat. That impressed me. I would somehow learn to fish and get out in the sun and fresh air. But it would take some doing, planning and help. An editorial by Dr. Norman Vincent Peale stayed with me; it's theme was "don't be an *if* thinker; but be a *how* thinker." I never forgot it and couldn't wait to be released from the hospital to work out a system to go fishing.

I was further motivated while an out-patient at the Institute of Physical Medicine and Rehabilitation in New York, where, under my friend Dr. Howard Rusk, I saw people without arms and legs being successfully taught to do things far more complicated than fishing. I certainly knew what type of equipment I wanted, but to have it custom-made after expending all my funds for medical and hospital care was out of the question. So I decided if I were to get the job done it would have to be with existing equipment that I could practice with and could adapt to my particular needs.

To accomplish casting I started by getting a flag pole holder from a regalia supply company. With help from a saddle shop, I had it modified to my size and needs. After several visits there, I ended up with a harness affair, featuring a strap across the shoulders and slightly higher than my waist, which passed through what I called a buggy whip holder. This I found would perfectly handle a conventional casting rod and closed face reel. From a wheelchair and with a brace on the left leg I spent many happy hours in the yard with harness, rod and reel throwing casting weights at targets, which in my imagination were stickups, overhangs, weed beds, etc., on lakes, ponds and streams— exactly like those in the magazines I'd been poring over for months.

By practicing long hours I became accustomed to the feel of the equipment. Soon my timing and pin-pointing became effortless and I was ready for "the real McCoy." I was elated and ready now to put it to the test. One mid-May day I managed to join a group which had planned a one day float trip on an Ozark stream.

We loaded my harness and tackle in the car and headed for Kings River in Arkansas. I had also acquired a folding canvas back chair which afforded maximum comfort and stability on my patio. But would it work on a float trip? I would soon know. I wasn't the healthiest guy on that trip but by far the *happiest*, and most anxious. I was fully aware that if I was too much trouble and didn't keep up with the others, future invitations would not be forthcoming. I was determined to keep pace. But I didn't look for any sympathy or special treatment.

Arriving at the dock, my deck chair was lashed to the boat seat and we started off in a 14-foot johnboat with a guide and one other fisherman besides myself. I'd gotten this far, but could I handle it? Would I louse up the other men in the boat? Were the hours and effort spent to be in vain?

It was a beautiful spring day with dogwood blooming and I forgot about being handicapped. A yellow home-made wooden plug was tied on for me and after we had been afloat for about 30 minutes I cast toward some boulders near the bank. After five or six turns of the reel handle, I was hooked into an Ozark smallmouth bass of about 3 pounds.

This was it! My rod arched. I reeled in line, rocking my body and at the same time raising and dropping the rod tip. Then I began reeling rapidly to take up the slack. Meanwhile that bass was all over the river giving me a thrill beyond description. I was unconsciously using muscles and reflexes that had been given up for lost. My rooting section was wild; advice and encouragement filled the air. A camera clicked. I was in command and when the guide netted the bass for me, any troubles I had were all forgotten.

All at once I knew I could fish, compete, and was one of the guys. Within 30 minutes of the trip's completion I had my limit and with each fish my feel for the equipment had improved. Casting became proficient and my fishing partner was in no way hampered from his share of the superb fishing. We didn't get fouled one time.

In any boat anywhere no one was ever happier than Norton Sanders that day. I could do it, I had proven it, I found out how. The float trip made the newspapers and TV. Letters from similarly handicapped persons and those who wanted to take them fishing began pouring in asking how, about equipment used, etc.

For the record, I wore a canvas life vest powered with carbon dioxide cartridges which could be activated if needed by pulling a cord. This vest was light weight and comfortable in spite of the hot Arkansas weather.

This trip I described was just the first of many float trips to follow. Some were 1-day affairs, others of 2, 3 and 4 days, all giving me needed confidence and indescribable happiness. I had new friends—sportsmen, writers, etc. I had to share this with others wanting to get out and needing to know how.

A harness for the handicapped is now available and is called the Handigear, made by the Garcia Corporation of Teaneck, New Jersey. It sells for about $10 and is sold at cost. It's a dream outfit and the complete answer for any angler who has the use of only one hand. I have used it successfully on the St. Johns in Florida, White River in Arkansas, Bull Shoals Lake in Arkansas, Table Rock and Taneycomo in Missouri, in Canada, and even for sailfish in Acapulco. A Handigear would cost many times the price if it were custom made. It is constructed of lightweight metal and worn like a breast plate.

My real love is the fly rod plus popping bugs for bluegills on farm ponds, slough, and small lakes. To accomplish this I use a 7-foot fly rod with Retreevit fly reel made by the DeWitt Plastics Corporation of Auburn, New York.

It costs about $15. This reel is lightweight, single action and enables the angler to retrieve fish without transferring rod to the other hand. It has a lever and rewind action and brings the fish to the boat. The speed of retrieve can be controlled by how rapidly one operates the lever. I strip the line with my teeth after pulling the amount of line needed for a cast to desired spot. Then I let the line lay in boat and false cast once or twice to drop the lure with good accuracy to a desired target. When a fish strikes I set the hook by raising my wrist and rapidly operating the lever of reel until the fish is boatside. Usually my fishing partner boats and strings the fish for me.

I can't describe the satisfaction of being able to get out and take up to 50 or 60 bluegills in a day, and once over 100. This I do with a partner in a 12-foot boat, but a 14-footer would be better. I contend that fishing is the greatest therapy ever for the physically handicapped or emotionally disturbed. Fishing gets one motivated and involved, both key factors in a rehabilitation program. For fly fishing I use a swivel seat covered with naugahide and foam rubber. The molded contoured seat was customized by a marine shop and the swivel assembly unit by an auto shop.

I can comfortably fish from 8 to 10 hours a day from this seat and have caught bass up to 5 pounds while bluegilling. A compatible fishing partner is a must to handle boat and tie on bugs, etc. I maintain a group of them by running ads in the newspaper, noting days they can go and type of fishing they prefer. Untold hours that might be spent lolling in front of the TV or feeling sorry for one's self can be spent caring for rods, reels, lines, sorting and classifying bugs, poppers, etc. I am completely and happily involved in my hobby and that's why I have compiled this and will even furnish additional information if wanted. Write to me at 701 Westgate, St. Louis, Mo. 63130. Recreational Therapy Departments would do very well to recruit volunteers to take the handicapped, especially amputees, on fishing trips.

The untold inquiries I have already received as a result of the newspaper articles describing my fishing exploits confirms my belief that this is invaluable therapy. Both my doctor and therapist believe I have made good progress both in mental attitude and mobility since I've taken up fishing and its challenges. If you are handicapped try fishing —"YOU'LL LIKE IT."

How To Clean A River

FISHERMEN unhappy about the condition of their favorite streams and lakes can do something about the situation, according to veteran angler and lure maker Dick Kotis of Akron, Ohio. After fishing in every part of the country, Kotis found one of the best examples of sportsman action right in his own northeastern Ohio neighborhoods.

Flowing through northeastern Ohio is the 100-mile-long Cuyahoga River. The lower half of this famous river is so badly polluted that it is the only river on earth which has caught on fire . . . twice. But the upper half is still clean enough to support bass and other fish. Bill Gressard, an outdoor writer, a neighbor and fishing companion of Kotis, decided some years ago to spearhead a campaign to clean up more of the Cuyahoga.

For a start he and a few friends made a spring pilgrimage in canoes down the upper reaches of the river. They located trouble spots where pollution flowed from industries, villages and cabins. They pinpointed all trash dumps on the river banks. Then Gressard reported the whole thing in his weekly newspaper column in the Kent Record Courier. Said Kotis, "The next year more of us up in this section joined the Cuyahoga River watch."

Every year since, the size of the flotilla has grown. In 1972 Kotis and about 400 others went with Gressard on a one-day Cuyahoga float. Even the smallest sources of pollution were quickly spotted and reported. Local people have taken new pride in this river because the sportsmen have drawn attention to it.

"Sportsmen in every part of the country can do similar work with their local streams," Kotis adds. "Not only is it fun as a community project, but it also makes the American outdoors a more appealing place to spend those leisure hours."

New Hampshire Smallmouths

by A. I. "Pal" Alexander

H. G. Tapply's deer-hair bugs and super streamers.

IN THE SPRING of the year, I get an unmistakable green-edged postcard in my mailbox with a somewhat cryptic message such as, "Come quick—weather and business permitting—you know what on the beds. Latchstring out. Yrs, Tap."

The message, as you have probably deciphered, is notice that the smallmouth bass are on the spawning beds and the time is "now" to catch them. Anyone who has written an article of exactly 50 lines and six tips of precisely three and one third typewritten lines, once a month for 20 years, as Tap (H. G. Tapply) has for *Field & Stream*, doesn't mess around with a lot of excess words.

Tap has the good fortune to live in Alton, New Hampshire, which is in the heart of New Hampshire's Lakes Region. After a ride of only a few minutes from his house, he can be on the shores of the massive 72 square-mile Lake Winnipesaukee, or lakes Wentworth, Squam, Winnisquam, all large lakes, or any one of the numerous smaller, but no less productive, clear water, rock-strewn ponds that constitute some of New England's finest smallmouth bass water. And Tap watches the waters near him more diligently than any water keeper on an English chalkstream.

When I get Tap's card, it is usually late May or early June, and I know that the conditions are right for fly fishing for smallmouths. The right conditions are a combination of water temperature, around 60 to 70 degrees, and the bass' biological urge to spawn. Naturally, they don't all spawn the same day or week. The entire period, on a given pond or lake, may be about a month with the fishing very slow for the first and last weeks. During the middle period, however, for 10 days to 2 weeks, the fly rodder can have fishing that is nothing short of sensational. On a good day 50 fish are possible! Now, of course, the average fly fisherman will generally score well below that figure, but who is to complain about a dozen fish, weighing 2 pounds or more, on a fly rod, that are as stubborn as an old crocodile and which can jump like a grasshopper?

As the water temperature rises toward the 60-degree mark, the male smallmouth moves inshore to establish a spawning bed. He'll pick a bed of egg-sized gravel that is near the shade or security of a large boulder, an overhanging tree, or even a boat dock. It doesn't take long before the fly rodder can predict where his spawning bass will be. Using his tail as a broom, the male smallmouth sweeps away an area about twice his own length and then stands guard over the nest awaiting the female. When the water temperature reaches the mid 60's, the female comes in from the deep water to the nest where she deposits her eggs. They are fertilized by the male and then the female leaves the nest for good. The male smallmouth is stuck not only with the eggs but with the housework as well. He guards the eggs tenaciously, driving away all intruders, including popping bugs and streamers, and his fin movements keep the eggs well oxygenated and free of any debris. In 3 or 4 days the eggs hatch and the male guards his fry an additional 4 or 5 days before they go off on their own.

The entire process, under favorable conditions, takes about 2 weeks. As you can see from the foregoing cycle, chances are it is the male smallmouth that gets caught. The female spends but a very short time on the nest.

Fishing on one of the larger lakes, such as Winnipesaukee or Wentworth, Tap and I like to use a 17-foot, square-stern, aluminum canoe powered with a 4 horsepower outboard. Some of the very best bass fishing is right in around the rock-studded islands and shoals and the canoe allows us to glide right over the rocks although the motor skeg takes a few raps from time to time. In the canoe, Tap usually acts as the guide, running the motor and giving unerring advice, as we fish. I remember one of the first times I fished bass with him on Winnipesaukee and he asked, "You got on a big streamer?"

"Sure," I replied. I had on a No. 2 Mickey Finn bucktail and I thought it was plenty big.

Six fish came into the boat and were released. None of them were mine.

"Hey, let me see that big streamer of yours," I yelled back to Tap.

My No. 2 Mickey Finn looked like a pygmy next to the fly Tap was using. His was at least half again as long as mine—a good 4 inches long!

"When there is a lot of ripple on this lake, you need a big fly, a real big one," Tap advised.

With the score six for the home team and zero for the visitors, I didn't argue. I re-armed my leader with one of Tap's super streamers and I was in business almost instantly.

Since that day, I have demonstrated to myself a number of times that the big streamer is the answer for smallmouths when the wind is disturbing the surface of the water. It isn't that bass have poor eyesight. On the contrary, they have excellent vision, but I think the bigger streamer is seen sooner and farther away. I find I don't hook a fish as solidly, or as often, with the larger streamer but the additional number of strikes it brings more than makes up for it.

On the lee shores, where there are no ripples, we exchange the oversize streamer for a deer-hair bug. Now, catching a smallmouth on a streamer is great stuff, but nothing compares with the spectacular strike of a smallmouth on a bug. Tossing the deer-hair bug out into the flat, black, calm water shadowed by a dock or boulder and getting an instant response is enough to cause cardiac arrest to the most experienced bass fisherman.

Since the days of Dr. Henshall, deer-hair bugs have always been big medicine on smallmouths but, in recent years, they haven't been used as much. Probably, the main reason is the time required to tie one. Even Tap, who is pretty expert at it, takes 35 minutes to tie up one bug. Tap's bugs, incidentally, are wedge shaped and cast very well in spite of their size on an 8-foot glass rod (Fenwick FF 79) and a weight-forward fly line.

The deer-hair bug works best when it has soaked up enough water to make it ride deep enough in the water to cause a substantial commotion. The smallmouth is very sensitive to sounds or vibrations and when he is on the spawning bed and hears anything, he goes after it. Unlike bass bugging for largemouth, when it is best to pop the bug a few times and then move it slowly, it is far more effective with New England smallmouths to cast the bug out and keep it moving and chugging along back to the boat without any pauses. When the deer-hair bug gets waterlogged, as it is bound to do, it is hard to cast and it rides too deep in the water to be effective, cut it off, and tie on a fresh one. A bug soaked in silicone is too buoyant and it slides along the top of the water rather than causing the attraction-getting commotion. Admittedly, the deer-hair bugs are trouble to tie, get waterlogged, and are somewhat more difficult to cast, but they're so life-like to the bass that we usually put the pliers to the barb so that if the bug is swallowed, we can get it back without any injury to the bass.

On most of the big lakes, during the spawning period, a fisherman can usually catch fish all day long. But the best fishing by far occurs when the bright sun is off the water such as during the early morning or late afternoon. For this type of fishing, not much is required in the way of equipment. An 8- or 8½-foot glass rod lined with a weight-forward line, either a level or tapered leader of about 8 feet, about 8- to 10-pound test on the terminal end, should more than do the job. Delicacy is not a requirement of this type of bass fishing and with a heavy streamer or a deer-hair

bug, the casting technique is not very subtle.

If Tap and I do have one secret weapon, it has to be the fly line. When Scientific Anglers first put out the floating fly lines with the sinking tip, Tap found out that the tip was not heavy enough to sink the deer-hair bugs. This meant, of course, that it was no longer necessary to bring two rods or change lines to go from the streamer to the bug. With the floating line and sinking tip, it was possible to fish the windward shores of an island with a streamer and, then, on the leeward side, snip off the streamer and tie on a bug.

Much has been said of color and its importance to the bass. We know that the bass can discriminate a wide spec-

A hand full of dynamite.

Tap picks out a super streamer.

H. G. Tapply typing up a super streamer.

This fat smallmouth is what it is all about.

trum of colors but, as all fishermen know, it is what happens out on the lake that counts.

"What do you think of color, Tap?" I asked one day.

"Any color is good—as long as it is yellow," he replied facetiously.

This has been my experience, too. A good bass streamer has some yellow in it. Most of the streamers we tie are nondescripts with a considerable amount of yellow, red, white, orange, and, if any dark hair is used, it goes on the top of the wing. With the bass bugs, colors don't seem to be as important. Here it is the gurgling action that does the trick. Colors are important to the fisherman, however, and we tie most of our bass bugs in light colors because they are easier to see, particularly in dark shady areas or when it is getting late in the day. Being able to see the bug well is essential to getting a good strike response. As soon as there is an unnatural disturbance at the bug, strike! And hard. A bass has a very hard mouth, make no mistake about that, and a weak strike won't allow the hook to penetrate it.

So, for exciting springtime fishing with a fly rod, try New Hampshire's smallmouths. Remember, though, keep your streamers long and your deer-hair bugs noisy if you want to see them at their best.

MUSKIE—
top prize in inland fishing
by Hank Bradshaw

THERE ARE, I think, only two reasons why all of the 35-million fishermen in the United States do not fish for muskies. One reason is that many don't *know* about muskies. Then there's another group—much smaller—that shies away from trying because they're deathly afraid they might accidentally hook one of the scary monsters. Or so a guide once told me.

If you could collect all the rest and ask them which fish they'd rather catch than any other, the chorus swelling back would be "Muskie!"

This sullen, fierce, big predator fish (properly, muskellunge) that grimly stalks the reefs and weed beds of rivers and lakes in the north-central and northeastern parts of the United States, on into Canada, has so captured angler-fancy that the majority recognize it as the greatest prize of inland fishing. So great is "Muskie Fever" that a confirmed muskie fisherman will fish for days without a strike—and still keep right on hunting muskies.

That's right—you *hunt* them. Like a deer or elk or mountain sheep. You stalk a muskie much as he stalks his reef or bay or river hangout. Frequently, one huge muskie is king of an area, so fierce he chases off all competing fish, leaving only those on which he intends to feed. When he has eaten them all—and this may take months—he moves to another lair and muscles in. (Not always—some are travelers, as Wisconsin tests with balloons tied to the fish have shown.)

Obviously, to catch a muskie, you must first learn his haunt, and where he is likely to be in it. Then you must determine the time of day he comes up to prowl, and be there with tackle and lure that won't fail when the going gets rough. Then you lay awake that night praying that you'll have skill enough the next day to entice him to strike and that you'll be fast enough to hook him.

Muskies don't come easy. Hooking one may take several trips. Consider my experience with the Tepee Rock muskie in Whitefish Bay of Lake of the Woods, a huge body of water touching shores in Ontario, Manitoba and Minnesota. I first saw this muskie in sunny late afternoon when he came out of the diamond-studded water of a reef pocket. He appeared first as a long, dark shadow, arrowing deep beneath my surface plug. He followed it to the boat, and, magnified by the water, showed me his beady eyes, gleaming from his grotesquely pointed head.

Holding my breath, I desperately began to "figure-eight" the lure on the water surface near the boat—making a figure eight with the rod tip and a short line so the lure would follow with its usual action. Once the fish moved up to it as if to sniff. But he suddenly lost interest and, fins fanning, slowly sank away.

"He'll go 35 pounds anyway," said my guide, excitedly.

Author points out muskie wake to fishing partner Cease Richards on the Littlefork river of northern Minnesota. This river is so shallow in places you have to wade and pull your boat. But it has a lot of muskies in it. They come in during high water in the spring (out of Lake of the Woods) and are trapped in the deeper stretches. We look for their swimming wakes in shallow spots, then cast ahead.

"We'll work that guy over. He's new."

A new muskie can prove to be a muskie hunter's good luck. He has just moved on to a reef or into a bay and taken charge. So anxious is he to prove he owns the place that if you give him the right lure in the right way, he'll strike. I wanted this muskie . . . badly.

That night, the guide and I sorted over my tackle carefully. The Achilles heel of tackle in a muskie battle is the terminal tackle. If anything breaks, chances are it will be the knots, the leader, or the snaps and swivels.

If you're inexperienced, don't wonder at this. Once you get a muskie on, you'll realize the awe-inspiring power of the brute. Have you ever tried to wrestle with a weight-lifter? Then you'll know what I mean.

We made sure that my snaps and swivels were big and strong and working. We selected stout braided wire leaders that wouldn't kink (they may break at a kink). A muskie's sharp teeth wouldn't damage this wire. Then we tied it to my 15-pound test monofilament line by doubling the line for the double clinch knot. If the son-of-a-gun broke *that* combination, I'd use a rope hawser next time.

I rigged two lines like this, on two Ambassadeur reels—

Cease Richards sacking a muskie (22-pounds) we had to keep on the Littlefork River of Minnesota. He was hooked too badly to release. So we had a feast the next night—muskie meat is tasty if properly prepared.

a 5000 and a 6000. Expensive reels, it is true, but for a muskie you need the best. Their clutch and drag action permit use of a 15- or 20-pound test line. Before I began to use an Ambassadeur, I used 30- and 40-pound test linen lines. Of course, there are now other reels on the market that fill the same service an Ambassadeur does. The only reason I now use 15-pound test instead of 20 is that it casts much easier, and I never get in a hurry when I have a fish on. That's a habit with me. Maybe it won't be with you, so the 20-pound might be better.

For rods, I have both a 6½-foot and a 7-foot Heddon that I use for muskies and Arctic char and other big, strong fish. The rods have plenty of backbone, yet are flexible and have good tip action. Since I prefer to cast for muskies, I use a rod that does the job well, but others are comparable.

If I were trolling, I wouldn't use these rods, but would use a shorter, stouter rod. Several other companies—Shakespeare, Garcia, Johnson, Berkeley, True Temper and others make rods similar to mine and also the stout ones. I have other rods for other purposes made by some of these companies.

For lures, I have a conglomeration of muskie lures to fit every purpose, since I love to fish for these characters (and that's the right word—every muskie has a character all his own). And we usually name them according to a special characteristic, like "Laughing Muskie," a fish in Whitefish Bay that sticks its head out of the water, mouth open, when it chases a lure. Its head moves from side-to-side much as if it were derisively laughing at us. The fish never strikes, just follows. Someday I hope to fool him.

I use several large surface lures, mainly because I like to fish on the surface with plugs, adding a handicap since muskies hit more often down in the water, and are more securely hooked on spoons that slide through teeth. With a plug, they tend to clamp it so hard in their teeth an angler has a tough job yanking the hooks into flesh. Usually, the fish can spit out the lure before the hooks can be set. But I use plugs anyway. I like the surface action.

Pflueger makes the Globe bait plug, Arbogast makes a muskie-size Jitterbug and Sputterfuss, Suick makes the Muskie Thriller, South Bend makes the Surforeno, Shakespeare makes a Mouse, all of which I use. Just under the surface, I like the Creek Chub stiff Pikie Minnow best because of the way it darts but I also use the jointed Pikie. Another top-notcher is the big Rapala, and its Finnish hooks bite in very well. If I want to go deeper, Arbogast's Arbo-

Reef fishing is more fun than any other kind of muskie fishing, but also harder work. Cast, cast, cast, all day as I am doing here. The fish lie close to the rocks, or in surrounding weed beds in shallow water (a reef is no good unless it has an adjoining weed bed), rising to surface plugs like huge tanks, following frequently, striking seldom. But when you least expect it, they hit like a charge of dynamite.

Some of author's muskie lures as he shows them to Clarence Fadden, his guide on Lake of the Woods. Pflueger's Yel-Gold Globe bait in his hand, Suick, Johnson Silver Minnow, Daredevil, Pike Minnow, Rapala, Black Bucktail, Red-eye Wiggler, Tan Bucktail with red strip of flannel, red-and-white Globe, rubber minnow. Author is using an Ambassadeur reel, Clarence a Pflueger Supreme. Good equipment is a must when muskie fishing.

gaster is a good actor. And black bucktails with big spinners are excellent. One is the Muskie Hound. I've caught them on the big Mepps spinner with squirrel tail and the Paul Bunyan 66.

For spoons, Eppinger's Daredevils are impossible to beat and I usually use them as big as they come. K. B. makes some good ones on which I've caught muskies. The Red-eye Wiggler is a killer. So is the Johnson Silver Minnow with pork rind, the Doctor Spoon, the Half-Wave, and several others.

All of these lures are in my muskie tackle box, outfitting me to give the Tepee Rock muskie anything he wanted. If I didn't think the hooks strong enough, I took them off and substituted strong Swedish-made hooks I knew *were* strong enough not to straighten out under a muskie's enormous strength.

The following day back at the rock, the muskie struck at the gold Pflueger, but missed the plug. The next afternoon, I gave it to him slow. The water was calm, permitting the fish longer and greater visibility, so I cast long, and

bobbed and dabbled and twitched the lure, "conning" the fish. When he finally hit, he came all the way out of the water in a great upward smash, carrying the lure along. I jerked him off-balance and his head began shaking like a paint mixer even before he splashed down. He dived with such power, I felt as if I'd been slugged in the arms with a wrench.

The diving was another break. Usually, a muskie will swim toward the boat, get slack and spit out the lure before you can swear. This Tepee Rock giant plunged to the bottom, giving me the opportunity to slam in the hooks again. Then we fought it out until I was sweating and darkness was closing in. My hands were growing numb when the muskie turned on his side, beaten, but still defiant. My guide slipped the gaff hook through his gill and quickly lifted him into the boat, grabbed the "headache stick"—a club he had handy for the purpose—and whacked the evil one across the noggin just as he started to flounce. That stunned the fish. Three or four more whacks and he was ready for the taxidermist.

Clarence screws the hooks tightly into his yellow surface plug. He uses big, Swedish-made hooks that won't bend, replacing the flimsy hooks that usually come on plugs. There is nothing a strong-jawed muskie likes better than a flimsy hook it can straighten out with one chomp.

Clarence Fadden, who guides no longer, plays a comparatively small muskie until it turns on its side and gives up. But first, Clarence had a battle on his hands. Even small muskies are tough.

Author's wife, Vera, one of his constant fishing and writing companions, eats lunch with Guide Clarence Fadden on a reef in Whitefish Bay, Lake of the Woods, one of the world's greatest muskie lakes.

◄ In the air, the gaff through its gill, Clarence dexterously releases hooks of the big Pike Minnow plug from the fish so he can turn it back. It weighed 15 pounds, small for a Lake of the Woods Muskie, but larger than the 10-pound average of muskies caught everywhere. However, a 15-pound muskie will put up more fight than most fish of other species twice that size.

I never kill a muskie unless he is going to be mounted. No matter how large they are, I release them. These fighters are much too scarce to take out of the water promiscuously, and they afford the thrills of a lifetime, so I recommend putting them back to fight another day.

To catch fish like the Tepee Rock muskie, I don't believe calm, still days such as the one on which I succeeded, are best. The fish can see too far, and hear any little noise in the boat. Wary creatures, they spook easily. A little riffle on a dark day is, I think, by far the best. They'll come alive in rough water, too, but this is lousy for casting. One is almost forced to troll, and I can go to sleep easier trolling than any way I know. It holds no interest for me. So I fish in water and under weather conditions when casting is good. This means, among other things, not too much wind.

One of my favorite guides was Clarence Fadden of Sioux Narrows, Ontario, and he refused to fish for muskies in a wind or rough water because he, like I, wanted to catch them casting or not at all. He and I have been caught out in some bad blows on stormy Lake of the Woods, but when we went out, we did so in fairly calm water. I've been black-and-blue from the boat rides back to camp, though.

My favorite way to fish for muskies I learned from Clarence. We covered about 35 miles of water a day, moving from reef to reef according to the muskie time schedule on each, arriving during the most active hour for that particular fish. We kept a log. Maybe we'd raise as many as 13 fish a day, some of them real whoppers. But we

Phil Johnson, son of the former World's Record Holder, Cal, catching a muskie on a shallow running plug. This Wisconsin Muskie jumped in porpoise-like leaps, out of the water and back in, a half dozen times before he settled down to bulldogging. Also, catching a muskie on a plug is much more difficult than a spoon. When a muskie hits a plug, he clamps down on it. The angler must move that plug in the Muskie's jaws in order to set the hooks. This takes a terrific yank, frequently more than one. If the plug does not move, the muskie invariably will swim toward the boat, jump, and throw the plug on the slack line he achieves by his speed-swimming. A spoon, on the other hand, slips easily in the muskie's jaws and it is no trick to set a hook.

were lucky if we could coax a strike from one of the old timers. New muskies? That's different. They usually struck with all the fury of a tornado.

In addition to Lake of the Woods, many other good muskie waters are scattered through this section of Ontario and Manitoba. The Manitou lakes are renowned. I once caught a muskie in Sphene Lake. Eastern Ontario has a lot of muskies, too, as does the St. Lawrence River where the World's Record—69 pounds, 15 ounces—was caught in 1957. Upper New York State lakes are good, such as Lake Chautauqua. Wisconsin is known as the best muskie state in the United States, largely because of the restocking program of the state fisheries department. I'm going to fish Grindstone Lake this fall for the first time—it has a great reputation. According to Eleanor Williams of Williams Grindstone Lake Lodge, huge muskies come in along her beach in the spring during spawning season, moseying around in the water as if unaware they are on exhibition.

I've had good muskie fishing in the Chippewa Flowage and I understand the Flambeau is equally good. Teal Lake and the adjoining group of lakes (including Ghost, Lost Land and Spider) produce. Some big ones came out of Teal during one fall I spent at Ross' Teal Lake Lodge. I've caught them, too, in Bone Lake, farther south, near Luck.

Over east, the lakes around Manitowish Waters are excellent. So are those in the Boulder Junction vicinity. Most northern Wisconsin rivers have muskies.

Lake St. Clair in Michigan is a famous muskie water.

In Minnesota, the Mississippi above the Twin Cities is good muskie water. Same with the Little Fork and Big Fork rivers up by Big Falls. Leech Lake has had a real history of muskies and so have the Man Trap lakes. Muskie fishing is on a rapid rise in Minnesota, largely due to an organization called "Muskies, Inc." that is leading a stocking program. It's fishermen also are supposed to release any fish they catch less than 30 pounds.

Iowa will some day come into its own with muskies. The state began stocking a few years ago and last year a 23-pounder came out of Clear Lake. They've been planted in deep West Okoboji and in new Rathbun Reservoir.

Ohio and Kentucky have had muskie programs a long time, with some good fish resulting, especially in Ohio's Muskingum lakes.

When is the best time of year and day to catch muskies? In Lake of the Woods, the warm months of July and August are best when muskies come out of the depths into the 15-foot shallows of the rock reefs with weed beds near by. When September's cold storms hit, they go back deep again, and you must use "hardware" to get them. In Wisconsin, however, fall is best. You can catch small muskies as early as June, and once in a while a lunker, but for consistent sizeable muskies, late September and October get the nod, after frost has colored the trees and water is chilling.

Time of day? When the warm sun is out. Not much use fishing before 9 or 10 in the morning or after sundown, the muskie is a fish ready-made for vacationers who like to sleep late. As with every fishing rule, though, there are variations: in the St. Lawrence River, some muskies feed in the wee hours of the night.

The longer I think and talk about muskies, the more excited I get. And right now, I'm in that fix, but good. I had a letter the other day from my guide who was with me when I caught the Tepee Rock muskie.

"There's a new muskie on Tepee Rock now," he wrote. "He has broken three lines already. He is no patsy. How about you coming up and giving him a try?"

You can see why I have Muskie Fever again. It's so gnawing that I can barely sleep nights. Let's see, I can be in Sioux Narrows day after tomorrow . . .

Hayward, Wisconsin, taxidermist showing off a 30-pound muskie caught by Phil Johnson, son of Cal Johnson who once held the World's Record with a 67-pound-plus muskie caught in Wisconsin's Lac Court Oreilles. Phil then lived on Teal Lake, now in Arizona.

Net Gains and Losses

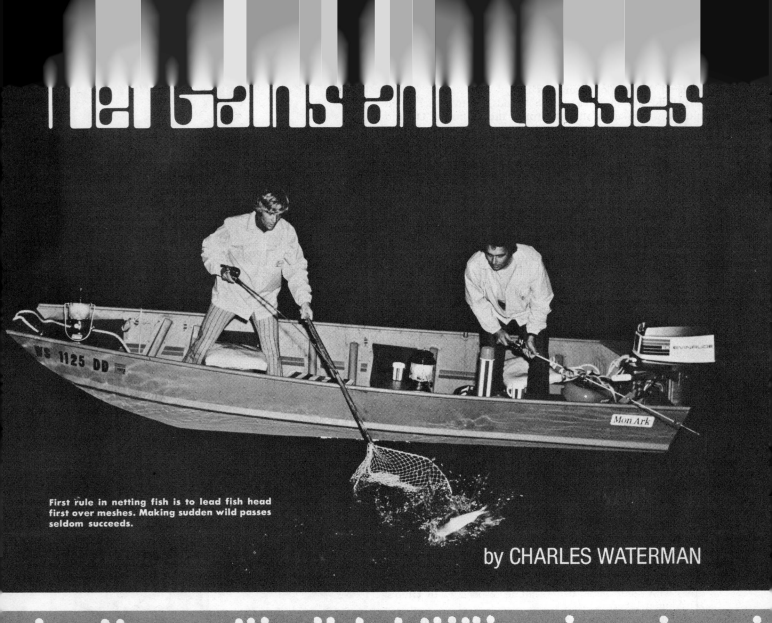

First rule in netting fish is to lead fish head first over meshes. Making sudden wild passes seldom succeeds.

by CHARLES WATERMAN

KNOWING HOW to net a fish is perhaps the most

SOME of the longest and coldest silences ever endured in a fishing boat have resulted from misuse of a landing net, for misguided swats send many a lunker back to his loved ones.

It's hard to understand how a fellow fills a tackle box with expensive equipment, prides himself on his hard-learned fishing prowess, and then neglects to learn a simple little stunt like ladeling up a seafood dinner with a landing net.

Friendship is probably insured by the simple rule that each angler nets his own fish, but he's apt to have hands so full that he yells for help when the big moment arrives. Help is usually quick in coming, and often would provide high comedy if the end results weren't so tragic

In the first place, three out of four fish are landed "green." For most anglers, "playing a fish" means dragging it toward the stringer as fast as tackle and strength permit.

I once saw three men catching pike in a 12-foot boat. Their method was so startling I sat and watched. When A had a strike, he would shriek, "Get the net!" B and C would wrestle briefly over it, and the winner—generally B—would rush to A's side, extend his arms as far toward the fish as possible, and start making powerful swipes with a landing

net of generous proportions. A would crank in the fish, thrashing and splashing (it must have been very heavy line). As the victim approached the boat, B would chase in hot pursuit as the fish circled. C always managed to be in the way while he shouted advice and encouragement. On about the tenth or twelfth try, the fish would be netted.

The first rule of netting a fish is to have the fish ready to net. He should be pretty well played out before the net puts in an appearance. Some species make last-minute rallies. If this happens when the net is already in the water, it's wise to recall it and let him make another run. Bring the fish to the net instead of chasing him with it. If he can't be brought to it, it isn't time to use it.

A net should never be moved quickly unless the fish is actually going into it. Many a quick swish has caused the final tug that broke the leader or pulled out the hook.

But have the net handy. Don't jack a big one's head out of the water while you hunt for the net or dig it from under your tackle box. If your fish is a jumping type, this is an invitation to disaster. The fish has no place to go but up, and a floundering jump on a snubbed-up line strains

186

Teamwork paid off here. One angler nets walleye for buddy.

◄ John Moxley has his prize in the net. But now he has ticklish problem of extricating the toothy barracuda from the meshes.

things aplenty.

If you're fishing from a boat, net the fish away from the boat if possible. If you make a pass at him when he's between boat and net, he might get under your craft, and it's an uncomfortable feeling to have a prize catch sawing your line on the keel or gaily wrapping himself around a propellor or anchor rope.

When the battle nears an end, put the net quietly into the water and lead the fish to it. If he's big enough to really require a net, always lead him in head first, for several reasons. First, if his tail is in and head is out, he's in an excellent spot for jumping all the way out. Second, if you sneak up on him from the stern, you're apt to get the hook or hooks near the net rim. Then if he flops his tail out of the net, you can neither land him nor let him run. He's hung up solid enough to get a good twist, and the worst can happen. Third, a fish can't back up very fast. If the net's in front of him he has to turn to escape it. If it's behind him, all he has to do is take off, and you're left holding the net—empty.

It takes cooperation if you net your friend's fish. Unless he gives his quarry slack line as its head enters the net, the net rim tends to pull the fish out. The rim hits the line and maybe catches on a hook. You pick up the net smoothly, but the fish slides off.

Most new nets are made of treated cotton or linen for the sake of manufacturing economy, although nylon seems to be a very nearly ideal material. Cotton nets will rot away before their time if they are stored wet, the deterioration hastened by the presence of fish slime. All nets need frequent washing and, if they don't get it, they acquire a hair-raising aroma. It's the aroma, by the way, which attracts and invites mice to nibble on the mesh.

Some "persnickity" anglers think it worth-while to camouflage netting by dyeing it a neutral color. They object to white netting because it scares the fish.

Mesh varies from fine netting in trout nets to about 1½ or 2 inches in boat nets. Big mesh is an advantage when multi-hooked lures are used; it reduces tangling. The chief disadvantage of large mesh is the possibility of a powerful fish getting part of his anatomy outside the net and then biting or tearing the mesh.

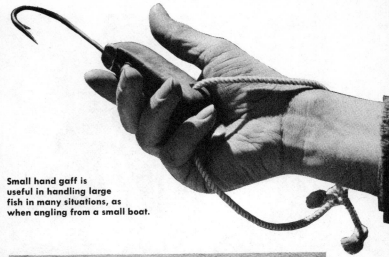

Small hand gaff is useful in handling large fish in many situations, as when angling from a small boat.

Long-handled net ready for use here is ideal for most small boat fishing.

← Dick Kotis and George Fennen almost didn't land this trophy pike. Notice the busted net rim.

performed of all the arts of fishing.

About a 3-foot opening is maximum for a boat net; trout nets sometimes have a diameter as small as 8 inches. Nets for boat use often have jointed or telescopic handles which boost the price but are convenient. Net depths run up to around 3½ feet.

Usually, the bigger the net the better, but, in an emergency you can do the job with only net enough for the front two-thirds of the fish. If he's in head first, he's at least immobilized, even if you don't want to try lifting him aboard or ashore with net alone.

Most wading fly-fishermen are limited to a small net. Their fish usually run a little on the small side, and they sometimes form the habit of netting the catch any old way at all. Then when the prize of a lifetime turns over on his side with his tail wagging feebly, the chance is muffed with a misdirected swipe.

Gaffs are the thing for whoppers, but for small fish, the gaff may cause serious injury if carelessly used—a big factor if the fish is to be released. Gaffs should not be fastened to the wrist if fish are big. A fish gaffed in the jaw is seldom hurt and can be easily released as soon as

the lure is removed, but he can do a lot of flopping once he is in the boat. If he's in a net, you can keep him out of the lunch and tackle box.

Net handles must be strong. Although aluminum is a highly satisfactory frame material, some of the lighter handles will quietly droop with a 10-pound fish. Generally, the weakest point in a net frame is the fastening that holds the "hoop" to the handle. If there is doubt about a net's strength, bring the fish alongside and support the hoop with one hand before lifting him aboard.

Floating nets are an advantage, although more expensive. The wooden floaters used by wading and canoeing fishermen are sturdy with one slight disadvantage—they appear bulky in the water, and a fish sometimes takes extra pains to avoid them.

Frantic use of landing nets has resulted in tragedy. Boats and canoes have been overturned; fishermen have stepped just an inch too far into swift currents; and eager dippers have tumbled from bridges and boulders risking life and limb.

Another thing: Where *is* the net?

THE CASE OF THE BRIGHT STRING

by FRANK WOOLNER

Fluorescent yellow or orange lines definitely aid surf casters who must contend with wind, wave action and current.

Surprisingly, at least to anglers who try it for the first time, the brilliant mono's do not spook striped bass and blues.

ROLLING along on a deep green sea 20 miles south of Little Compton, Rhode Island, I'd reached a drowsy state of suspended animation that, for me at least, seems to guarantee a strike on offshore grounds. Sprawled in a fighting chair, supremely comfortable and warm in hot summer sunlight, I watched the baits skip nimbly—two plastic eels and a pair of pseudo-squid. We were right on the eastern extension of Coxes Ledge—the right place and, supposedly, the right time.

But my eyes were involuntarily closing. I hardly heard the radio chatter and the cockpit conversation between Kib Bramhall, Nancy Wilder and our mate, Chris Cornell. As usual, I was dropping off, mesmerized by the somnolent roll of a big sea, the winking diamond flashes of light from cresting wave tops, the steady purr of *Surfmaster III's* powerful engines.

Captain Bud Phillips, up on the flying bridge, remained wide awake. He was streaming four lines, two of them brilliant fluorescent yellow monofilament, and the others dun-colored Dacron braid. One of those incongruous yellow strings billowed from an outrigger to starboard, while another was flat-lined over the transom. Still nodding, I thought that no respectable white marlin would ever be fooled by one of those neon-lighted monstrosities. Then, of course, a furious little skillagalee stormed into the wake.

There are people who always describe this moment aboard a charter boat as a "Chinese fire drill." Certainly there is action and a lot of noise. I heard Bud yell "Marlin!" and Chris came down the ladder so fast that he missed every other rung. Nancy and Kib had lunged for rods, and I snapped wide awake. That sort of thing is better than an alarm clock!

This gladiator had come up blind, right behind a rubber squid on a flat line. He was all feeding color, obviously fighting mad, and he looked tremendous in the clean water. Swiftly he switched from squid to eel—disappeared for a moment, and then struck his bill out right behind the eel

that happened to be attached to a rod I was holding. The line was bright yellow.

There was no drop-back. My marlin simply engulfed that eel, turned—and I felt raw power as the hook went home. A split second later the brute came soaring out. Then he ran hard, to jump again in the distance. I began to wonder whether this one was too tough for 30-pound test.

He wasn't, of course—few of them are—but he was a grand and acrobatic battler, finally coming to boat. We stuck a tag alongside the marlin's dorsal and let him go. Phillips guessed 75 pounds, but I think he was being kind.

The important thing is that this wild little skillagalee had taken an artificial bait trolled on a brilliant fluorescent yellow line and had scorned lures dragged on more prosaic braids. Nancy promptly got another, also on bright string. I hate to admit it, but she handled her fish far more professionally than I had mine. I can only alibi by stating that Nancy Wilder is one of the finest offshore anglers on our Atlantic Coast, and she doesn't need Women's Lib as a crutch.

Initially, skippers like Captain Bud Phillips experimented with fluorescent lines for one overriding reason—they are easy to see. Where more than two baits are skipped in the wake of any boat, and even where there are no more than two, it is essential to keep them separated. The reason is obvious: tangles can usurp fishing time and destroy tackle.

While it is all very well to seek an edge—in this case greater visibility—all of the professionals wondered whether the brilliant lines might also possess a built-in disadvantage. Mightn't they also spook wary gamesters right over the horizon?

Now, after several seasons of hard use, this question seems to have been answered. Brilliant yellow lines are vivid against sea and sky, yet there is no evidence to suggest that they either frighten or attract game fish. There is a possibility, curiously enough, that such lines may even afford a greater degree of camouflage than any of the solid braids or translucent mono's. More on this later.

A way down on Virginia's Eastern Shore, Claude Rogers was one of the first to experiment with, and then applaud the new yellow string. Claude is the Director of the Virginia Sport Fishing Institute, and his headquarters is the beach and open ocean—often those grounds currently producing huge red drum.

Rogers fishes the surf, often with bait. Since he is an outdoor personality and therefore a guide for visiting firemen, it is often necessary for him to line up a half-dozen rods on sand spikes. He needs to know the location of each bait and it is necessary for him to determine whether current and wash moves these tempters out of prime areas. Visibility is tremendously important—and the yellow fluorescent line is highly visible.

I'd rank Claude among the best channel bass fishermen in the world, and he is firmly convinced that yellow fluorescent monofilament is better than any other fishing string for surf work. If the bright line scares red drum, Rogers isn't aware of it, and his annual catches make headlines.

This high visibility factor is quite as important in North Atlantic areas where striped bass are tops on any surfman's list. Again, there are ground swells and combers and scouring currents to thwart a bottom fisherman. Mono is the best line to use, simply because it presents less water resistance than braid and therefore allows an angler to "hold bottom" in a prime location. When mono is also easily seen, the task is further simplified.

In 1971, *Salt Water Fisherman,* the magazine I guide when I can't con assiciate editor Spider Andresen into doing all the mule work, received several letters from marine anglers who maintained that the new fluorescent lines might be easy to see, but were also easily seen by a fish. Sharptoothed species, they claimed, would chop the string and ignore a lure. Bluefish were said to be particularly destructive, cutting bright lines whatever the color.

I'd used fluorescent blue monofilaments for a number of years and had caught a lot of striped bass, bluefish and other species on said lines without difficulty, so it seemed that the critics must be talking about this new yellow. I knew that it worked well offshore and that it was excellent in the surf where channel bass and striped bass were sought. What about blues?

Kib Bramhall, our magazine's advertising manager and—like everyone else on the staff a first class fishing nut—instituted controlled tests early in 1972. Kib lives on Martha's Vineyard, a Massachusetts island surrounded by blues during each summer month. He rigged two one-handed spinning rods, one with a reel jammed full of 10-pound test translucent mist-grey mono, and the other packed with yellow fluorescent. Then he and a companion, equally proficient, spent a week catching big blues. The action was fast and they paused only long enough to make notes.

Kib found that there wasn't a bit of difference in the incidence of strikes on colorless and fluorescent. The real shocker was a discovery that there were more bite-offs on the colorless than on the yellow!

Blues are called "choppers" for good reason: their jaws are forever chomping, and anything soft that gets in the way has to give. Plug casters who use monofilament line without steel leaders often get cut off. It's an occupational hazard—because sometimes the cussed blues won't hit a lure presented on wire.

Kib almost apologized as he offered his findings. It didn't seem possible, but during that week of controlled testing there were eight times as many bite-offs on the colorless mono as on the brilliant fluorescent yellow!

Why? It's anybody's guess and a scientist would certainly wrinkle his brow to come up with two hypotheses. One: the blue can *see* yellow line, so he doesn't hit it. Two: he *can't see* yellow very well, so it offers a form of camouflage.

What about the few fishermen who reported cut-offs on fluorescent line? They are honest, working anglers and they stated a case as they saw it. Is it possible that they were using polished swivels—always strike-inducing? Might they have been fishing in weedy waters where a spot of gunk on any line is likely to draw a strike from a murder-bent bluefish? How is it possible for a brilliant yellow fluorescent strand to score fewer bite-offs than the apparently translucent grey-mist line? It happened.

There are explanations. One is the remarkable idea that most of our shallow water fishes possess color vision, but "see as through a yellow filter". This is not a new departure: it has been suggested by reputable scientists in Europe and America, And it makes sense!

Evolution provides the tools for all creatures. Fishes live in an environment dominated by blue and green shades of the spectrum. Yellow is a contrast shade, so it tends to overpower blue. Human beings can test this by wearing light yellow glasses on a dark day. There is much blue light on such an occasion and therefore the yellow lens sharpens objects and makes them seem bright. The sun appears to shine!

This contrast factor is, of course, the reason why practically all skeet and trap sharks wear yellow shooting glasses. A flying clay, regardless of background, is more sharply defined and more easily picked up by a gunner swinging his piece to overtake, lead and fire.

If a fish actually sees "as through a yellow filter," prey

Kib Bramhall caught this 17-pound bluefish on a yellow fluorescent line. In a week of testing, Kib found that there were fewer "bite-offs" on yellow than on translucent grey mono.

Claude Rogers of Virginia Beach, Virginia, one of the world's foremost channel bass fishermen, swears by yellow monofilament for work in the surf.

Captain Bud Phillips bills a white marlin caught by Nancy Wilder. Off-shore trollers are increasingly going to the bright lines.

species may be more sharply outlined against the omnipresent blues and greens of water, while yellow shades might fade into insignificance, or almost disappear. Scientists are still a mite cloudy about specific values altered by subsurface refraction, reflected light and the changes which occur with depth.

It is popular to declare that activated colors are manmade, "unlike anything in nature." That's an over-simiplification, because nature was fooling around with fluorescent hues before man came down out of his tree. There are hosts of deep-down sea creatures blessed with fluorescent light, and lots of forage species use it to a certain extent. If a striped marlin, glowing like a neon sign as it attacks a trolled bait, is not truly fluorescent—we need another word.

Certainly nothing in nature apporaches the present highly activated paints and dyes produced by mankind, yet all of these are engineered for use above water and for detection by the human eye. If research technicians are right—and current experiments at least prove them to be on a right and

straight track—some of the highly visible fluorescent lines may be most easily seen by men, and least likely to be spotted by a fish. This is a delightful state of affairs, if true, and the hypothesis may change an entire concept of camouflage in lines. Instead of the translucent, the mottled or the shadowy, we may see a revolutionary shift to the fluorescents which take advantage of a fish's view of its environment.

There are three basic fluorescent colors now employed in monofilament, all of them pioneered by E.I. DuPont de Nemours in Wilmington, Delaware. Initially there was, and is, blue fluorescent. It is a good line and I have used it to catch all sorts of fishes in fresh water and salt. However, there are lots of good mono's produced by a host of reputable firms: they come in translucent greys, greens, blues, pale gold, pink—even black—and all are efficient. I cannot declare that blue fluorescent has any appreciable edge, other than a measure of visibility above water. That shade certainly helps an angler to keep track of his string while trolling, casting or bottom fishing, yet the degree of improvement is slight because sharp contrast is lacking. Even when glowing with activated pigments, blue against blue tends to lose itself.

DuPont's busy technicians thought it over, and then created monofilaments in bright yellow and orange. Both glare like streaks of neon light, so they are highly visible to a human eye. Both have been approved by a host of advanced anglers who, often to their surprise, discovered that the brilliant strands seemed to produce as well as any translucent and, because of the contrast colors, were easier to manage.

Obviously, one major hurdle to clear has been public acceptance of something new and startlingly different. The average fisherman believes his eyes, conveniently forgetting that values change under water where sunlight is filtered and the spectrum is subtly warped by water that is variously grey, green, blue, and finally shades into the darkness of the depths.

And, no doubt about it, the orange and yellow fluorescents are shocking to a human eye which has become conditioned to accept old theories of camouflage. The activated lines look far larger in diameter than they really are. Miked, all equal or are finer than translucents of comparable pound test. Against cobalt offshore seas, the bright string flames. They are quite as evident inshore or on the flats, becoming almost errie in the blue light of dawn or dusk.

There have been complaints, duly noted, about bluefish striking line instead of lure, but it is interesting to note that critics seem few on America's long seaboard. If fluorescents were possessed of any massive foreign devils there'd be a ground swell of condemnation. No angry mass protest has developed.

Indeed, reaction has been just the opposite. Comments from master anglers range from: "I wouldn't have believed it" to an amazed "The stuff really works!"

So far yellow fluorescent is most universally accepted, with orange enjoying a flush of popularity on Florida's bonefish flats. It is instructive to remember that South Florida boasts the finest light tackle anglers in the world, and that they work in an arena where water clarity is superb.

American sportfishermen are rapidly moving into an age in which monofilament lines will dominate. These extrusions will be better with each succeeding year: they'll be finer in diameter commensurate with pound test rating, and stretch will be controlled. Finally, color will play a major part in the old game of camouflage, and there is a distinct possibility that these brand new bright lines will challenge existing thought and pioneer an entirely new concept in the delightful business of catching game fish.

KENTUCKY

THE FERTILE FISHING GROUND

by KARL MASLOWSKI

IF THE Indians came back to Kentucky today they would have second thoughts about whether it should still be called the Happy Hunting Ground. The bear, the elk, the bison, the passenger pigeon, and some of the other creatures which once helped feed and clothe the redmen are now gone forever. However, after taking a closer look at their old stomping grounds, the Indians might soon decide that today Kentucky is the Fertile Fishing Ground. Many modern day anglers are making or have already made that discovery.

Kentucky has so many streams that if a fellow fished just 1 mile a day he could look forward to 35 years of pleasure! And he still would only have rippled the surface of the angling potential for there are at least 100,000 farm ponds up to 30 acres in size; there are about 30 modest-sized lakes containing 100 to 1000 acres; and there are almost 2 dozen big lakes that range from 1,000 to 150,000 acres in size.

(Above photo) Fisherman Bob Hart joyously sees his fish, a Kentucky muskie, netted. Large muskies like this are not uncommon in this area.

All these impoundments have been created within the past century or so. Anyone who aspires to fish all of Kentucky's waters will have to at least equal Methuselah's longevity record of 969 years.

All told, there are about 170 species of fish native to the Blue Grass State, and of these about two dozen are sought by hook and line fishermen. In addition, within recent years two other species highly regarded by sport fishermen have been stocked successfully, namely the rockfish (or striped bass) and the rainbow trout.

Fishermen may angle under a wide variety of pleasant environments. In the far west where the Ohio and Mississippi Rivers join near Monkey's Eyebrow there are cypress sloughs that exude a semi-tropical flavor and produce bragging-sized largemouth bass, bluegills, and crappie. By contrast, there are turbulent little streams over in the eastern mountains cold enough to support rainbow trout. Between these two extremes are the dogwood and redbud-lined lime-

Author Maslowski, jig fishing at Lake Cumberland, Kentucky, with catch.

stone streams of the Bluegrass Region. The smallmouth bass fishing in these streams proved to be the mother that required the invention of multiplying reels (which were invented in Kentucky) such as the famous Meek Bluegrass. Just to the west of the Bluegrass section is the Pennyrile Region. Through it flow such streams, as the Green River, from which muskellunge of almost 40 pounds have been caught.

The very names of some Kentucky streams are enough to suggest that an angler's physical stamina, as well as his fishing skill, will be tested—Difficulty, Troublesome, Bloodyshins, Rough and Dogslaughter among others.

Kentuckians are noted for having devised some novel ways of catching fish—methods suitable to specific situations. One is called "jigging." The best practitioners of this exist around Lake Cumberland, which incidentally, has produced a 21½-pound walleye and a 72-pound spoonbill, or paddlefish. Here in late winter and early spring, when the waters are just beginning to clear along the edges of the precipitous banks, really big bass are taken with fairly simple tackle.

To jig, the angler uses a long bamboo or fiberglass pole to which is attached about 8 feet of 40-pound test line. A treble hook is affixed to a heavy leader tied to this line and above it rests a slip-sinker. Depending on the turbulence of the water, a plain round adjustable cork is positioned 1½ to 4 feet above the hook. The hook itself is baited with a gob of either live or artifical night crawlers and strips of pork rind.

Thus equipped, the fisherman then either very quietly sculls his boat with a short paddle or maneuvers it with an electric trolling motor about 15 feet off shore. The baited hook is cautiously dropped down in submerged brush, around roots or logs, or near other favorite fish hiding places, jigged up and down several times, and the cork permitted to rest momentarily on the surface.

If the cork vanishes, the cane pole is derricked into the air and all in one smooth motion the fish jerked out of the water and plopped into the boat. Jig fishermen will tell you that the only time to watch a bass play is in the live well. This may not sound very sporting but I have never known a fellow to turn down an invitation to go "jigging" once he has tried it. Moreover, conventional methods just will not produce fish when the lake is still high and murky.

Within the past decade, thanks largely to practical research done by fellows like Vard Curtis and Carl Hamilton, people have learned that crappie fishing is a wonderful wintertime activity on Kentucky Lake and Lake Barkley which have a combined shoreline of 3,500 miles. Even though ice forms in the harbors, these men, dressed in insulated jump-suits, will cruise about with their eyes glued to Lowrance Fish Lo-K-tors. Once they locate a drop-off where the water is perhaps 25 to 35 feet deep, they will begin fishing with live minnows and invariably end up with a legal limit of 60 crappies, all being over 12 inches long. Some will weigh as much as 3 pounds! These two men have learned that in wintertime crappies seek out a specific temperature which occurs at drop-offs of the aforementioned depths.

Perhaps the single greatest fishing hole in the entire state is the tail-water just below Kentucky Lake Dam. The variety of fish one may catch here is almost bewildering. One day last summer I checked a woman angler's stringer that contained channel and blue catfish, white and black crappie, largemouth bass, white perch, and sauger! Try to match that almost anywhere in fresh water.

The sauger is a close relative of the walleye. Jim Boone specializes in fishing for this species with unusual tackle in the racing Tennessee River tail-waters below Kentucky

Hope Carlton, Jr., displays a long-nosed gar caught at Harrington Lake, Kentucky, where they sport-fish for these heavy, hard fighters.

The Dix River, near Danville, Kentucky, is a productive spot for catching white bass in the early spring.

Early spring finds Carl Thomas jig fishing for largemouths at Lake Cumberland, Kentucky. He demonstrates that his method is a successful one.

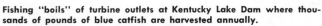

Fishing "boils" of turbine outlets at Kentucky Lake Dam where thousands of pounds of blue catfish are harvested annually.

An average sized crappie taken from Kentucky Lake.

Here you see the world record smallmouth bass caught at Dale Hollow Lake, Kentucky. It weighed 11 lb., 15 oz.

Rock Creek, Kentucky, was the former home of these rainbow trout here displayed on a shiny bed of magnolia leaves.

Dam (see FISHERMEN'S DIGEST, 8th edition, page 124.) He fastens a large automatic fly reel loaded with nylon-coated wire line to a seat in his outboard boat. To the end of the line is tied a 1-pound sinker in the form of a lead-filled 8-inch-long section of small diameter copper tubing.

Floating gold and black Rapala surface lures are attached to two dropper lines, one 5 feet and the other 15 feet long. The lead sinker bumps along the bottom as he trolls at slow speed, but the floating lures swim safely just above the numerous tackle-traps that line the river floor. And apparently the lures are at just the right depth for lurking sauger, because it is not unusual for Jim to get his limit of ten within 90 minutes. Other fishermen using conventional tackle rarely catch a sauger and are constantly losing gear that hangs up on underwater obstructions.

Incidentally, these same tail-waters below Kentucky Lake Dam have produced the world's record blue catfish—a monster weighing 100 pounds.

As one might expect in a state with 12,000 miles of streams (that is more than found in any of the other states, except Alaska), there are countless opportunities for float fishing. Such trips can be made through Kentucky's most scenic grandeur. Take the Rockcastle, a brawling stream that tumbles through Laurel County near London. Once you put in at the bridge on State Route 80, a 17-mile journey to Bee Rock Camp will take you past high cliffs, fern-studded boulders, and a forest-clad shoreline populated by pileated woodpeckers, Kentucky warblers, and wood thrushes. There will be quiet pools, lots of fast whitewater in the narrow gorges, and a satisfying number of black and rock bass will try to run off with your lures. This float makes a fine two-day angling outing. Like Dan Boone and the first pioneers, *you* can decide where you want to camp at night because much of the eastern shore is part of the Daniel Boone National Forest.

Other fine float fishing streams are the Red, Cumberland, Green, Licking, Barren, and the South Fork of the Kentucky Rivers. Some should not be attempted by novices because of the fast whitewater between pools where the drop is as much as 6 feet.

No matter how you like to angle, be you a purist who will perform only with flyrod and dry flies or an opportunist who will fish with any kind of tackle including jugs and trotlines baited with aged cheese and chicken entrails, you will find a place in Kentucky waters where you can practice your special skills.

It may not be out of line to add that the hospitable people of Kentucky have gone out of their way to insure that visiting fishermen may find suitable accommodations wherever they try their angling skills. If you like to camp, campsites ranging from the most primitive to the most modern abound throughout the state. Every camper will be pleased with Kentucky's unrivaled park system. On the other hand, if you prefer a bit more comfort, motels and lodges may be found within easy driving distance of most of the state's best fishing waters. The state-operated lodges, in particular, are among the finest accommodations to be found anywhere in the Union.

It is rather significant, I think, that to this date only one Kentucky born individual, Abraham Lincoln, has made it to the White House. I suspect the reasons have been swimming somewhere beneath all those miles of streams and acres of ponds and lakes. Kentuckians have simply wasted too much of their happy youth fishing to ever find the time to study to become President. They find it simply too difficult to waste time resisting the temptation to go angling in the original Fertile Fishing Ground.

The Bluegrass state may be far better known for its bonded bourbon, its blondes and race horses, but that is only because the natives want to keep it a secret. Now the secret is out and for more detailed information, write to the Kentucky Department of Fish & Wildlife Resources, Frankfort, Kentucky 40601.

Pugsy Bursell baits up for jig fishing at Lake Cumberland, Kentucky.

My Top Dozen Tips

Largemouth bass is a wary species with excellent vision and sense of smell. A wise angler keeps these points in mind.

By DICK KOTIS

for All Bass Fishermen

EVERY YEAR more fishermen in America ask me more questions about how to catch black bass than any other fish. Here are my dozen top tips and why I think all are important:

1. I believe all fish have a very keen sense of vision. Therefore, when fishing relatively open water or clear water, I use natural colored clothing and a natural colored boat as I feel that bright colors tend to put fish down and particularly the older, larger largemouth bass.

2. I think that you must use an "active" lure—that is— I believe that every successful fisherman fishing for big bass imparts a life-like action to his lures. This can be done by jigging the rod tip, by varying the pace of retrieve or by popping a surface lure.

3. Proper presentation of a lure is important. A great many fishermen spend too much time on the retrieve of the lure rather than on the original presentation. I always fish the shady side of a log, the down-current side of a stump or the area of a fallen tree that is protected from the wind first. At the critical moment the lure hits the water, if it's a spinner, I immediately get the spinner blade going by jerking the rod; if it's a popping-type lure or surface lure, I try to cast a foot above the water so that it settles to the water as gently as possible; and if it's a noisy, fast-swimming or spinning lure, I start to retrieve immediately. If the lure were a jig or a worm, I would take my thumb off the cylinder or casting spool, or if a spinning reel, take my index finger off the spool allowing the lure to sink where it hit rather than having it sink in a sloping direction because of the line pull.

4. If a bass fisherman is extremely serious about trying to catch a trophy bass, he must set up a definite fishing pattern with the following factors in mind: What does the fish normally feed on? What are the normal feeding habits? What particular lake or stream conditions am I confronted with? Are they abnormal or normal? How do I adjust my fishing techniques to them?

5. I believe that fish have a very acute sense of hearing through vibrations. When fishing out of a metal boat or one that is not a double-hold boat, the chances of catching fish are greatly reduced when you drop objects in the bottom of the boat, scrape the oars against the side or cause other sharp vibrations.

6. Fish probably have a keen sense of smell. With that in mind, I am always very careful about handling any fishing lure after I have handled gasoline or oil or any highly aromatic material. This is particularly true of a petroleum product and a surface lure such as a Popper. I suggest fishing a Popper very slowly for big bass and if the fish does have a keen sense of smell and vision, any oily or petroleum product would surely discourage him from picking up a surface lure.

7. One of the most important things all fishermen must realize when trying to catch a trophy fish is to keep fishing. Often the biggest single factor in why one bass fisherman catches more fish than another is that he does not quit.

8. Another technique that I like to pass on to trophy bass fishermen is I always have two identical, complete casting outfits in the boat with me. Here's why. If I were to overcast a very good spot or get hung up in what looks like an ideal hiding place for fish, I just put my rod down, pick up the other one and cast with accuracy to that same spot. This way you do not have to go in and frighten out good fish while trying to retrieve your lure. As a result it increases your chances of catching a good fish.

9. Take your time. You just can't catch a big fish by fishing in a haphazard fast way. The fisherman who carefully selects a good area because of its protection or food habitat or structure (See Structure Fishing elsewhere in this book) is much better off than one who fishes an entire lake in a day.

10. Make the weather conditions work for you. I personally like to fish storm fronts or rising water. Fish seem to go on a feeding spree during these conditions and as a result become reckless and quite often the cautious lunker bass will gobble everything in sight because of slightly

Author Kotis with string of really fine largemouth bass from typical southern reservoir. Kotis believes in the power of thinking positively when bass fishing.

Success with bass also depends on accurate casting in tree-filled, stump-filled lakes like this one in central Florida.

Kotis sits in bow of bass boat (see article elsewhere by Grits Gresham on bass boats) with extra casting outfits set up and ready to use. Notice also the Lowrance Lo-k-tor set up for ready reference.

muddy water condition. Otherwise it might be extremely cautious and difficult to catch.

11. People are not the only ones that live in split-level homes. Any successful angler can tell you that fish have been practicing this mode of living all along. What's more, the fisherman who understands this and what to do about each situation is certain to catch more fish than are the anglers who believe fish occupy a one-floor plan. There are three major levels at which fish may be found: surface, mid-depths, and bottom.

Here are the top pointers for fishing surface lures. First, present the lure carefully, placing it on the water with as little commotion as possible. Fish around the stumps, rocks, and weedbeds which offer the fish hiding places. Fish most surface lures slowly, but vary the retrieve to find out what works best. Use darker lures for nights and dark days, tie the line directly to the lure, keep the line free of the water as much as possible, and hang on.

When this doesn't work, switch to mid-depths, offering such lures as the Hawaiian Wiggler and fish with special attention to weedbeds and obstructions. Work out an area methodically by fishing the nearest obstructions. Vary the pace of the retrieve, and use a variety of lures until you get the winning combination.

Then there are times when the big fish are right on the bottom, and there are fishing lures such as the Arbogaster designed to cruise down where they live. There are times when they may strike fast-moving lures best, and others when they want them moving slowly.

The big point to remember is that fish move up and down in the water depending on temperatures, light, and food conditions. By carrying a selection of lures designed to work at these various levels, you can cast for the fish where they're living at the moment.

12. Every year more bass are taken by trolling than anyone suspects. Most serious fishermen prefer to cast because accurate casting itself is a fascinating sport. But there are times and places where trolling pays off with heavier stringers. For one thing you need open water—water without vegetation. And trolling is most effective when the bass are in deep water, such as very early or very late in the year.

The best trolling lures are those which run deep, such as the Arbogaster, behind a slowly moving boat. It is important that the lure brush the bottom occasionally and that it always "rides" in an upright position to avoid twisting the line.

Selection of weedless lures suitable for mid-depths when split level fishing described by Kotis.

Some of the typical old reliable bass lures which will score in bass waters almost anywhere.

Thermometer which measures water temperature at any depths is also a valuable accessory for every serious bass fisherman.

Surface lures are effective as well as exciting to use when largemouth bass are in shallow water.

Trolling is also a good way to learn about any lake. Start by setting a course parallel to the shoreline and then by moving farther and farther out until you locate the bass. Troll around off-shore islands and never pass up points of land, underwater bars or reefs. An electronic Fish Lo-k-tor can help you locate these hotspots and is a valuable accessory, in fact, for every troller. Casting for largemouth bass is the greatest sport on earth but there are situations when trolling can be more productive. I never hesitate to try it when casting the shallows is too slow.

Think positively. It is absolutely amazing the number of individuals who do not believe they can catch fish and as a result never put all of these tips to work for them on each and every cast. I like to think that every cast, every shadow, every tree stump and every rock has a fish behind it and that it is a matter of my accurately and properly presenting a lure in a life-like manner to catch the fish that's hidden there. Often enough I get amazing results.

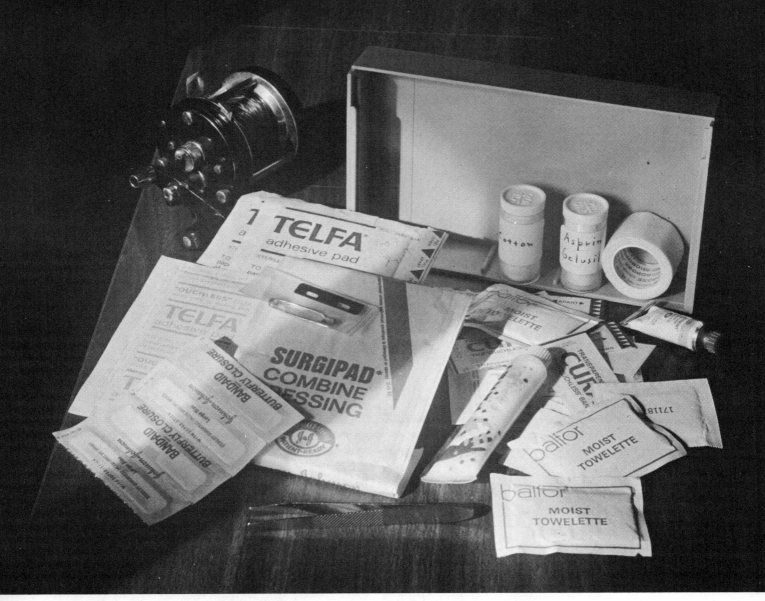

First Aid Kit For the Tackle Box

by C. Joseph Cross, M.D.

THE AVERAGE tackle box demonstrates a concentration of a variety of gadgets in a limited space that would do credit to the packers for the space probes at NASA. It has an additional advantage of always having room for one more object. A most important accessory that should be included in this grab-bag is a first aid kit. Because of the nature of the activities involved, there are some special requirements that make this different from a first aid kit for a car, a boat, or the home medicine cabinet. Here are my suggestions:

1. The container:

The one thing that most tackle boxes are not noted for is neatness. There is a tendency for reel oil to leak, for plastic worms to melt, for water to splash and for beer to spill. There is also a need to keep first aid materials as clean and sterile as possible. This adds up to the necessity of having a container tight enough to prevent these contaminants from coming into contact with its contents and strong enough to hold together under the knocks and bounces that every tackle box will absorb. Many solid plastic boxes will work very well for this, including some of the commercial first aid kits which should be repacked. Certain metal boxes, particularly the kind that contain imported candies are equally satisfactory.

2. The contents:

Surgipad Combined Dressing (1), (or other pressure dressing).
Gauze bandage—1" (1)
Adhesive tape—½" (1)
Sterile pads: 3" x 4" (3); 2" x 3" (3)
Band Aids—Assorted sizes
Butterfly closures
Liquid soap
Absorbent cotton
Sealed disposable moist towelettes
Sealed disposable alcohol sponges

Burn ointment or cream
Razor blades
Safety pins
Medicines—Aspirin and Gelusil

Surgipad Combined Dressing (1)

This is a large sterile absorbent pad to be used as a pressure dressing in the unlikely event of a large laceration which would involve excessive bleeding. It should be placed directly over the wound and firm external pressure applied, initially by hand and later maintained with the gauze bandages and adhesive tape, until the victim can reach a physician's office or a hospital.

External pressure is the preferred method for controlling bleeding, both arterial and venous, and should always be used in preference to a tourniquet. It is safe to say that over the years more harm than good has come from the injudicious use of tourniquets and that this apparatus has no place in anyone's first aid kit.

Gauze Bandages 1" (1)
Adhesive Tape ½" (1)

These items are so obviously necessary that little need be said about them. The 1" size bandage is the most useful for all purpose bandaging, being small enough for fingers yet adequate for larger areas. The ½" adhesive tape is satisfactory for taping sprains and strains, as well as for anchoring bandages. The heavy protective metal container in which adhesive tape is usually dispensed is totally unnecessary and occupies far too much space. A simple roll of surgical tape is perfectly adequate.

Sterile Packs

3" x 4" (3)
2" x 3" (3)

These are sterile and self-contained pads which are placed over the cleansed wound for protection and prevention of further contamination, held in place by the bandaging. I prefer the use of Telfa Pads, commercial products which consist of a thin layer of sterile cellophane on either side of an absorbent pad, perforated to permit oozing from the wound. These are individually packed, easy to handle, absolutely sterile and are considerably easier to remove from the wound when the time comes as they do not stick.

Band Aids (6, assorted sizes)

These are perhaps the most useful first aid devices ever invented, beautifully designed, easy to use, compact and easy to store. Several sizes should be included, each one individually sealed, and they should be replaced each year as the adhesive has a tendency to deteriorate.

Butterfly Closures (4)

These are used instead of sutures to close gaps between wound edges in any relatively large laceration. The cut edges of skin should be approximated and space left between the closures so adequate drainage can occur. Care must be taken not to touch and thus contaminate the sticky edge of the strips.

Liquid Soap
Absorbent Cotton
Sealed Disposable Moist Towelettes
Sealed Disposable Alcohol Sponges

This may appear to be a sizable list for the sole purpose of cleaning up a burn or wound area, but except for stopping a dangerous bleeding episode, this is the most important step in proper first aid. Cleanliness is the cardinal principle in wound care, whether in the field or in a hospital operating room. The injury and the surrounding area must be cleansed of all external dirt and debris: a clean wound will heal, a dirty one will not—it's as simple as that.

Soap and water remain the most effective cleansing agent, just as in grandma's time. Using cotton pledgets and liquid soap the area can be thoroughly cleansed and flushed without damage to the skin.

For several years now I have carried several of the moistened, sealed cleansing packets in my kit for use on the areas around the injury and also to clean up my own hands before getting to work. They are effective, easy to handle and easy to pack.

After the area is adequately cleansed with soap and water, a more antiseptic application of alcohol will put on the finishing touches. This is most easily done with disposable alcohol sponges in similarly constructed sealed packets.

Ointment

This is a popular item in first aid kits, but perhaps the least useful of all. A mild anesthetic ointment—there are many on the market—is helpful in alleviating the discomfort of insect bites, minor burns and other very minor trauma, but its use must never supercede the other basics of wound care.

Tools

Razor blade
Safety pin
Tweezers

Mechanical objects are kept at a minimum but the above items have many different uses, and have the added advantage of occupying very little space in the packet.

The razor blade may be used instead of scissors to cut tape or bandage material or to cut clothing for more easy access to wounds.

The safety pin has multiple uses. It can help secure a bulky bandage; the point, when adequately sterilized, can puncture blisters or aid in removing splinters or insect stings.

Tweezers are delicate extensions of the fingers which can be useful in assisting in the removal of splinters, in the proper placement or removal of the protecting pads over wounds and in handling dressings or removing cotton for wound cleansing.

Aspirin
Gelusil

These are the only two specific medications included in the kit, since my tackle box is not included in any prolonged wilderness trip and more sophisticated medical needs are usually available in a fairly short time. I put them both in the same small, tightly stoppered bottle.

Aspirin is a multipurpose pill, a safe and effective pain killer useful in a multitude of situations, from assuaging the pangs of the previous night's indulgence to relieving the muscle aches stemming from rowing, poling or pulling in a giant tuna.

Gelusil (or any other antacid tablet, they all do about the same) is often a great help in relieving an upset stomach that could easily spoil a day on the water. Indigestion can be the result of excitement, overeating of camp foods that don't match home cooking or simply changes in water or habits. Antacids have no harmful side-effects and act fairly promptly.

The contents of this kit are adequate for most on-the-spot emergencies, and will suffice for the day or so required to get back to more adequate medical facilities. All of the items can be purchased over the counter in any drug store, and do not require a doctor's prescription. It is obviously not designed for long term care and hopefully will never have to be opened.

by A. I. "Pal" Alexander

THE LANDLOCKED SALMON is the wildest, toughest, highest jumping, sky-rocketing resident you'll ever find in New England waters. He is fussy, too, demanding water temperatures between 65 and 70 degrees for optimum growing conditions and seldom will you ever find him in other than a clear, cold, free-flowing river or a deep lake less than 300 acres in size.

Originally, the landlocked's range was restricted to the lakes of four different river basins of Maine; the St. Croix River drainage in Washington County, including West Grand Lake; Union River drainage in Hancock County, including Green Lake; Piscataquis River sub-drainage of the Penobscot River system in Penobscot County, including Sebago Lake where the record landlocked salmon of 22 pounds, 8 ounces was caught on rod and reel in 1907.

Since the 1800's, landlocked salmon have been transplanted to some 22 states, most unsuccessfully, and to numerous foreign countries as far away as New Zealand and Australia. Its U.S. home, however, is New England and, particularly, Maine where it has been introduced into well over 100 lakes. Maine's sister state, New Hampshire, with many large, deep, cold lakes similar to Maine's, also boasts substantial salmon fisheries. In recent years, even Massachusetts, which is highly industrialized and has limited salmon water, has made startling progress with the intro-

duction of landlocked salmon into the massive 25,000 acre Quabbin Reservoir. Salmon smolts of 6 to 9 inches from Maine were stocked in 1965. From this stocking, a record fish of 9 pounds, 5 ounces was caught in 1971.

The key to the success of any salmon fishery in New England is the smelt population. To catch landlocked salmon successfully, you need to know something about the smelt because it is his principle diet. The smelt (Osmerus mordax) is a small, olive-backed, silver sided bait fish that lives in the same type of water as the salmon and where you find them, you'll usually find salmon.

In Maine and New Hampshire, the opening day of the season falls on April 1st, but usually on that date and for some weeks to come, all the major lakes are locked under ice. Strangely enough, however, they are fishable, if you know how to do it.

The ice, in the springtime, opens up first near bridges, pilings, docks, and places where there is some current, especially near an inlet or outlet. Oftentimes, while the natives are sitting around and spitting on the stove, trying to guess when the ice will go out, my fishing partner and I will be slowly winding our way around one or the other of the big lakes, looking for some open water, with a canoe mounted on top of the Bronco. Admittedly, some days can be hopeless, particularly with a cold wind whipping a sheet of snow across the wide expanse of the lake. We would be more likely to see Nannook of the North sledding across the bay than any open water. But, once in a while, Lady

SLAMMIN'

Merrymeeting River, New Hampshire, on opening day. The target: salmon.

Luck does smile and we find an open patch of water we can fish. We don't need much. An opening the size of a baseball diamond, or even smaller, is enough to warrant putting the canoe in.

At this time of year there is usually deep snow on the ground so sliding a canoe or car top to the water isn't very difficult. Once out on the water, we cast a big streamer, a No. 2 or 4, along the edge of the ice, using a sinking fly line. A fast stripping or hand-wrist retrieve works best; salmon like a fly that is really moving. If there is enough room in the opening to troll, we troll close to the edge of the ice and at a good rate of speed.

When the ice finally does go out, or "sinks to the bottom" as the old Mainer used to say, you'll find salmon on the surface for about a month or so, until the surface water gets too warm and drives them down. Early morning and the few hours before dark are the most productive times. Again, a big streamer trolled behind the boat will do the trick. During the day, when it is bright or warm, you may need to use lead-core line on your fly reel with about 20 feet of 6-pound test leader.

Now, even though the ice has gone out, don't ever neglect inlets or outlets where there is current. This is a favorite place for landlocked salmon and they love to hang there in the moving water. A number of times, after trolling fishless all over the lake, I have come inshore, in 10 or 12 feet of water, and anchored near the current of a river or brook and caught salmon after salmon by casting into it. While the salmon like the feel of the current, in the early spring they have another reason for being there. Our friend the smelt spawns in the spring during and shortly after ice-out in the lake tributaries and along the shoreline. The salmon are right there after them.

Many of the best streamer patterns for salmon closely resemble the smelt. The famous Gray Ghost, the Black Ghost, Green Ghost, and Nine-Three are of this variety but the landlocked salmon, being the contrary cuss he is, frequently will go bananas over an attractor such as a Col. Bates, Mickey Finn, a Red-and-White, Maynard's Marvel, or a Yellow Marabou. It pays to try both types. I always prefer my flies for salmon tied on single long shank hooks in sizes No. 2 through No. 8. Seldom do I use the tandem-tied streamers anymore although some expert salmon fishermen still swear by them.

When the season opens on April 1st there is another alternative to looking for potholes in the lake and this is to fish one of the rivers. The Winnipesaukee River and Merry-meeting River in New Hampshire, with ready access to major highways, are two of the most popular ones. The fish are there in the river, particularly in the dark water of the deep bends, but you have to be prepared to fish at a rod's length from your neighbor and put up with a carnival-like atmosphere. The road along the Merrymeeting on opening day, for example, is made into a one-way road and the cars, trucks, and campers parked along it resemble a D-Day marshalling area. All night long the lights flick on and off

SALMON!

New England's greatest challenge—the landlocked salmon.

Fishing partner, Roger Aziz, with early ice-out salmon.

and at daybreak a thundering herd charges for the river. On this opening day, anywhere from 100 to 300 fish are caught in the Merrymeeting River, mostly on small streamers, No. 6s and 8s. But, personally, as much as I enjoy river fishing, I would rather fish one of the lakes where there isn't so much commotion.

After ice-out, salmon fishing holds up pretty well until the first real hot spell. Windy days with a good "salmon chop" on the water are best. Salmon like rough water and seem to be invigorated when the lake acts up. A small boat or canoe can be easily driven off most of the large lakes and when the wind comes up extreme caution is necessary. When a salmon lake is mill-pond flat, go home and tie up some flies; you won't catch any salmon.

The day to watch for is one that is dark and overcast, with or without a slight drizzle, late in the spring or early summer. I remember one such day when my partner and I had been fly fishing for smallmouth bass all day with great success and on our way back, almost as an afterthought, I said, "Hey, put on a streamer and we can troll going back over the deep water." My partner put on a Gray Ghost and I tied on a Mickey Finn. We were both fishing two colors of lead line and a measured leader of 20 feet. We couldn't keep the fish off. It was bang and a salmon was flying through the air every time we let out a decent length of line. It was like that all the way back across the lake to the dock and until dark. With all those willing salmon out there, we scarcely saw another boat and no one else was fishing. On many other dark days I have had exceptionally good fishing for salmon too, so I always think I can smell salmon when I see those dark clouds.

The warm days of June drive the salmon down to depths where it requires very heavy tackle to get them, although you may still find an occasional early morning or early evening when you can get them on top. For the most part, the fly fisherman is done. To get down to them requires cow bells and sash weights and even the magnificent salmon can't do much with that kind of handicap.

The fall is something else. When the water cools and the leaves begin to turn, the landlocked salmon comes back to shallow water. It is different this time, though. There are no smelt spawning and, basically, the salmon is inshore in a response to his own urge to spawn. Frequently they will be found off the mouth of a river, or where a brook comes

in, rolling on the surface in the evening. Unlike the springtime however, when the salmon was mauling everything that resembled a smelt, you'll find him now more like his sea-run brother, the Atlantic, in that he is difficult to catch. He can be taken, but he has other things on his mind.

In the rivers things go a little better in the fall. My two favorites are the Moose River in Rockwood, Maine, and the West Branch of the Penobscot in Piscataquis County. In the Moose River the fish run smaller, averaging about 2 pounds, than in the West Branch. The Moose River, which flows from Brassua Lake to the huge Moosehead Lake, also has some excellent brook trout moving through it. Here, most fishermen like small streamers and fairly large wet flies. A Red-and-White bucktail has always worked well on the Moose and patterns resembling a small yellow perch are popular with the local fishermen.

The charm of the West Branch, I think, lies in its dry-fly fishing. I have spent endless hours during the daylight hours flailing the water with a streamer, swearing nothing was in the river, only to see it come alive in the evening just before dark. The massive hulks gulped in caddis flies with the delicacy of a Labrador retriever going after a downed duck. If your heart can stand it, there is no better fishing than this in New England. For flies, I like an Adams, a Light Cahill, Wulffs, the March Brown, Caddis, and especially the Badger Spider. The Badger Spider is tied on a short shank spider hook and the rest are tied on regular wire hooks in size No. 12 and 14. I avoid fine wire hooks for salmon flies and I like a little heavier tackle than usual to keep the fly up on the rough water. If you have a trout fisherman's reflexes, you'll have to re-educate yourself or you won't catch these salmon on a dry fly. They're very slow takers and frequently cause a substantial bulge before they even get to the fly. You have to wait.

The landlocked salmon doesn't have the caution of a trout, nor the predictability of a smallmouth bass, but, to most New England fly fishermen—he is king.

A. I. "Pal" Alexander with a quartet of fly-caught salmon.

These Rivers...

Eleven Point River, Missouri,
has its famous landmark,
the arched tree.

Wild and Free

by DOUG JEFFERSON

JON WADED halfway across the submerged sandbar and began casting his minnow imitation into the willow-lined pool bordering the current. Before I had beached our canoe his rod was arching and a smallmouth was jumping into the afternoon sunlight.

Jon subdued the fish and held it up for my admiration, still dripping and bronzed from the clean limestone river. He filled the last remaining snap on our stringer.

Jon Yates, a hunting and fishing instructor for the Ohio Division of Wildlife, had joined me for a float on the Little Miami River in southwestern Ohio. We had heard that the stream was presently under study for scenic and recrea-

tional river status, and had decided to combine a casual inspection tour with some of the fine bass fishing this river has to offer. We ate a relaxed shore lunch and moved on down the river.

Afternoons like ours are being enjoyed all over the country these days, thanks to forward-looking conservation measures on both state and federal levels. It all started back in October 1968 when Public Law 90-542, the national Wild and Scenic Rivers Act, was passed by the U.S. Congress.

The need for such legislation was plain, and becoming more so all the time as industry, the U.S. Army Corps of

207

Engineers, and various highway departments consumed the few truly primitive rivers remaining in the country. A statement by Stewart L. Udall, then-secretary of the Interior, summed the situation well:

"Alternative uses are rapidly preempting our remaining wild rivers. Their numbers diminish as the recreational need for them grows. It takes but one harness to change a river's character forever. Future generations are entitled to know the wild river heritage that has been so significant in the development of this nation and its character. If they are to know that heritage, we must now make provision, federal and state, to keep some of our rivers, or portions of them, wild and free, protected from uses that destroy their natural beauty and recreational desirability."

With this concept as a guide, the Interior Department and its Bureau of Outdoor Recreation began a study to determine which rivers across the country were to be included in the initial designation when the act was passed into law.

On October 2, 1968, when PL 90-542 was made law, the following eight rivers were included in the national system:

Clearwater River (Middle Fork), Idaho, from the town of Kooskia upstream to the town of Lowell; the Lochia River from its junction with the Selway at Lowell forming the Middle Fork, upstream to the Powell Ranger Station; and the Selway River from Lowell upstream to its origin.

Eleven Point River, Missouri, from Thomasville downstream to Missouri highway 142.

Feather River, California, the entire Middle Fork.

Rio Grande, New Mexico, from the Colorado state line downstream to Highway 96 crossing, and the lower 4 miles of the Red River.

Rogue River, Oregon, from the Applegate River confluence downstream to the Lobster Creek bridge.

St. Croix, Minnesota and Wisconsin, between the dam near Taylors Falls, Minn. and the dam near Gordon, Wis., and its tributary, the Namekagon, from Lake Namekagon downstream to its confluence with the St. Croix.

Salmon River (Middle Fork), Idaho, from its headwaters to its joining with the main Salmon River.

Wolf River, Wisconsin, from the Langlade-Menominee County line downstream to Keshena Falls.

The act required that by the fourth quarter of 1969, boundaries be established along the designated sections of each river, giving the federal government free title to lands not to exceed an average of 320 acres on both sides of the river. This was done to assure public access to the rivers and to preserve, among other things, the best fishing.

All that remained for initial designation was the matter of classification. The act provides three categories into which individual rivers can be placed: Wild, scenic and recreational. The difference lies in the streams and their immediate surroundings.

A wild river, as defined by the act, is free of impoundments and generally inaccessable except by trail, with watersheds or shorelines essentially primitive and with its waters unpolluted.

A fine example of a truly wild river is found in northern New Mexico. The Rio Grande, from the Colorado line south to the Taos Junction bridge, runs its 50-mile course free, clear and cold. Ardent fly fishermen with a bit of mountain goat blood can scramble down the rocky cliffs and catch rainbow trout for the casting.

A scenic river's requirements are essentially the same as those for the wild river, but small changes in the official definition allow for designation if the river and its surroundings are somewhat less pristine. The shorelines, however, must remain "largely primitive and . . . undeveloped."

Cincinnati outdoor writer Karl Maslowski with Stillwater River smallmouth, one of several Ohio streams being considered for state scenic status.

Public access is easier along a scenic river, where roads may approach the water more closely than in the highest designation.

Missouri's Eleven Point River, a scenic stream, nestles in the Ozarks in the state's southern section. Due to the more relaxed classification, the two managing agencies (the U.S. Forest Service and its parent Agriculture Dept.) can actively manage the area to accommodate heavy use drawn by state development in the region. Plans have been made for as many as 10 man-made lakes in the vicinity, and in the Ozarks that usually means smallmouth black bass.

A recreational river, the act's most flexible classification, may have some development along its shorelines, is readily accessible by road or rail, and may have undergone some diversion or impoundment in the past. Such a stream is the lowest 11 miles of the Little Miami where Jon Yates and I floated that afternoon. The southern-most

A nice rainbow comes to net in Wisconsin's Wolf River.

portion of this river flows through a fertile flood plain before mouthing with the Ohio River at Cincinnati. U.S. 50 and Ohio 126 parallel this portion of the river, allowing very easy access anywhere along its length.

Recreational river status serves a very important function in the overall system. Without it, portions of streams might be named wild or scenic rivers, providing state and federal protection to only those particular sections. This could result in industry and other encroaching agencies slamming the door forever on future improvement of the waterway.

It is difficult to say whether aesthetic appeal or public recreational needs brought about the Wild and Scenic Rivers Act of 1968. But like the chicken or the egg, it makes little difference. Each of the country's fishermen find their own special relaxation on clean, free water, and the act seeks to provide this opportunity.

As of this writing, some 27 additional rivers are undergoing study for possible inclusion in the federal system. They offer many sportfish, from the smallmouth bass of Tennessee's Buffalo to the trout of several rivers in the upper Midwest.

The last of these 27 studies is expected to result in a decision no later than December 1973. Findings will then be forwarded to the President and Congress for final consideration.

While it is true that the final say belongs to the federal government, local groups can do a great deal on state and local levels to preserve worthy rivers.

One such group, Little Miami, Inc. (LMI) of Lebanon, Ohio, can point with pride to its accomplishments. In 1965 three men took it upon themselves to rally support for the little river. This support took the form of a delegation to Washington to present a case for the river's preservation.

Dave Bowring, outdoor writer for the Dayton Daily News, with a trio of Ohio smallmouth.

Some wild rivers offer both trout and bass. This angler scored on both.

The Buffalo of the Tennessee River, Tennessee. This is a fine bass stream.

While the trip was successful, the group didn't stop there. Through the efforts of this and other groups, an Ohio Scenic Rivers program came into being, utilizing many of the same criteria and guidelines as were then proposed for the federal system.

The first stretch of the Little Miami to be given state protection was its headwaters in Clark County, where the water is small and primitive. As the years passed, however, more and more of the stream was included until, at this writing, all of the river enjoys state protection. Federal studies were favorable enough to await only state-federal cooperation before scenic river status can be bestowed.

Needless to say, such local action as that by LMI goes far in advancing the chances of federal protection. More information about ground-level efforts may be had by writing to Director, Little Miami, Inc., P.O. Box 303, Lebanon, Ohio 45036.

There is something of America in these free and wild rivers, something above pollution, beyond dams, running cold and silver to the sea. All the moods of a nation are here: Roaring down a no-man canyon in Oregon, hushed to a quiet murmur beside an Iowa cornfield, or moving silent through a Maine pinewoods. They are, in a sense, the lifeblood of a nation, and we must see that they remain intact.

Small lures, especially spinners are effective in ponds. A full day's supply can be carried in small box. The beaver's craving for food and protection creates good fishing.

HOW TO FISH BEAVER PONDS

by Charles J. Farmer

Profile low, I approach likely beaver pond. Casting accuracy is a must in pond-full of snags. Notice beaver-chewed limbs.

Here's a string of good producing ponds in Wyoming. Aspens and willow growth, plus stream add to beaver-built ponds like these.

ANY outdoorsman who is adept at stalking whitetail deer in scrub oak thickets, has the credentials to become a top beaver pond fisherman. The qualifications are rigid and patience is the main ingredient. But the rewards are justly satisfying.

Wherever the beaver thrives in the United States and Canada, anglers find a brand of fishing with its own rules for success. The industrious beavers seem to have a naturally devised system of quality angling in the ponds they created because it takes an angler with finesse to master the ponds and the fish within them. The fly caster must lay an artificial on the water in the same manner as a snowflake comes to a landing. The spin fisherman plays a game of inches, not feet, when zeroing in on pond fish. Hard landings and bad casts are extremely unnatural to the normal, delicate movements in and on the water of a beaver haunt.

The fisherman who does not like to walk; does not like to blaze new trails through stream and pond quagmire; and who shudders at the idea of fighting tangles, unhooking back casts and swatting mosquitoes, is better off back at the civilized pond in the city park.

For me at least, the rewards of challenging beaver pond obstacles far outweigh any efforts an angler makes. Fish grow fast in ponds due to an abundance of natural food. In areas of heavy fishing pressure on well-known lakes and streams, the beaver ponds offer best chances of success. Most anglers pass up the tangles of willow, and refuse to set foot in the myriad of birch and aspen downfall that typically surrounds a beaver pond. Yet the same anglers, fortunately, will stand elbow to elbow with other anglers in a well used fishing hole. So there is a feeling of privacy —wilderness isolation if you like, on a string of ponds.

Fish variety is another good reason for hitting beaver holes. In the West, trout reign supreme in the ponds. Brook trout are usually the predominant species, but some ponds also contain rainbows, browns and cutthroats. Trout abound in beaver ponds in other parts of the country and in Canada. But warm water species are evident also. Bass, pike and panfish find the deep, cover-laden ponds to their liking. Trout will be the main concern here and the techniques for fishing them will apply to other species.

Beavers create good fishing. They can turn a mere trickle of a stream into a deep pool filled with scrappy brook trout. Where a narrow, brush-lined creek may have been impossible to fish with lure or fly, the beaver's log dam means a tempting pool. Man has destroyed millions of acres of prime beaver habitat in the guise of progress, but there is still enough left to support vigorous populations of dam builders. Where the beaver is controlled by selective trapping, but not over-harvested, there results a reasonable balance of nature. In turn, anglers fortunate enough to live near beaver country are treated to an ever-changing variety of fishing holes. In the beaver's quest to store a sufficient amount of water for protection in summer and winter, top fishing usually results.

Pond Prospecting

Few beaver ponds are ever marked on maps . . . another reason why good fishing often goes untapped. Many ponds are found along state and county roads and naturally receive the most pressure. But ponds *off* the beaten track usually yield the biggest surprises. State game and fish department personnel give fishermen tips where likely ponds are located since most of them were stocked at one time or another.

In areas where beaver are active, an angler can discover his own ponds by following streams. Topographic maps are handy in pond prospecting. They pinpoint well known drainages as well as those little known streams that often yield good fishing. Areas along the stream course where such softwoods as aspen, birch or willows predominate are likely dam locations for beavers. These species provide food and building materials. Lowland spots on the topo map are usually areas of dense vegetation and beaver activity. Stream valleys in the west are highly favored by the flat-tails.

Not all the ponds an angler discovers will contain fish.

Some are too shallow to support fish throughout winter's freezeup. Some ponds that "winter kill" are stocked each spring and produce good fishing. Ponds that may have been good producers one season, may be dry the next. Natural leaks and dam breaks occur in ponds causing fish kills. And government trappers and game wardens may purposely dynamite beaver dams when water flow is severely restricted. An angler can be assured, however, that a new dam site will be secured, or the old dam repaired. As new ponds are built and old ponds abandoned by beavers, the fishing varies according to the population of fish in the stream, the depth of the pond and availability of natural food.

Old ponds are marked by dry, weathered cuttings of trees and shrubs in the area. If the dam is holding water to the pond's full capacity and there is a beaver house nearby, chances are that beavers are still using it. Most likely, the pond will be a good producer since it has endured several seasons.

A new pond on the other hand will usually be bordered by fresh cuttings of aspen or birch. The water is often more turbid looking than the "settled" water of the older pond. The dam itself is a wall of freshly packed mud. At such a dam, it is common to see beavers in the process of construction. Sit still for 20 minutes and watch the creatures that make good fishing possible. They provide an entertaining bonus to pond fishing. Beavers have poor eyesight and extremely keen hearing.

Since beavers are working full force in new ponds and the water is murky, fishing usually is not as good as it is in the settled ponds. But, try a few casts to be sure. If nothing happens mark the pond in your memory for future use. Next season, it could be a winner.

Judging a beaver pond's productivity is an important technique in this type of fishing. Some anglers linger too long at ponds where there are no fish, few fish, or stunted fish. It takes only a few minutes to evaluate a pond in most cases. As opposed to lake or big river fishing, the first two or three casts usually tell the story. Only in rare cases have I stuck with a pond and caught fish after the first ten casts. Repeated casts, especially with flies or lures, only tend to spook fish that may be in the pond. It is best to move on to another pond. And if the situation presents itself, try the same pond an hour or two later.

With live bait such as worms or minnows, it is possible to wait out beaver pond fish. Still fishing has some advantages over fly and lure fishing in ponds well used by anglers.

Pick ponds carefully and concentrate efforts on the ones that look good. Those containing submerged logs seem to produce well. A more valuable sign is evidence of running water. Some ponds seem almost stagnant. But there is usually water running into the good ones at some point. Water action at this point has probably produced a deep hole in the soft bottom. The movement of water also carried food with it or kicks up tempting morsels from the bottom. This is the spot in the pond favored by fish. And usually the biggest fish in the pond claims the choice area. Look for this spot first in every pond and make the first cast there. Sometimes the sound of gurgling water will draw your attention to it if you can't see it.

The Stalk

There is some genuine belly-to-ground, light-footed Indian or infantry stalking involved in all pond fishing. And perhaps it is this skill which separates the fish-catchers from the fish-spookers. The spookers greatly outnumber the catchers, leaving plenty of fish in the pond.

The reason for the fish-catchers being in the minority is simple. Not that many anglers want to belly-up to a pond.

Stay back from the bank—keep low and gently present bait.

Few are willing to cover a pond via duck walk. And too many anglers want to see what is going on. The methods described for an attack on a beaver pond may seem somewhat severe and the actions somewhat awkward, but there is method in the madness.

The main reason for the stealthy approach to a beaver pond, as described, is presenting a low silhouette. This one technique can make the difference in catching fish. There are several reasons why. A beaver pond is never a big body of water. Fish often hide in the shallows, under shrubs or branches—so they can see you coming and will spook to deep water. When this happens, all the fish in the pond may end up spooked. All the casting in the world won't bring any to the bait. You might as well move on.

Walk with light feet. Maybe you have walked around beaver ponds and discovered a muskeg-like springiness to the banks. Many ponds have undercut banks, Some banks are built on a sponge-like foundation. Fish will often hide under the banks as far as 2 feet back from where you see the edge of the water. It doesn't take too much to spook them by walking. Just the sound and vibrations of walking on the bank will spook fish out of biting. This is the reason for bellying up to the pond and keeping a low profile. You can do this by casting from a prone position, or by casting from behind the beaver dam itself or in back of available cover.

Casting accuracy may suffer on the first few tries, but fish catching success will result. Make it a rule to stay at least 5 feet back from the water's edge. And by crouching or kneeling you won't spook too many fish. I have caught several trout from one pond on numerous occasions and surprisingly enough, other trout in the pond were not spooked until I stood up. The lesson is that fish in a beaver pond can be spooked from quite a distance away; so plan a careful approach from 50 feet out, using available cover and terrain to your advantage.

The Delicate Way

If you have made a good, quiet stalk on a pond full of brookies, you can almost count on a mouth-watering fish dinner. The rest is simple. Start with light tackle—ultra-light spinning outfits are tops for beaver ponds. Five-foot rods work best in the tangles. Small lures can be cast easily with mono lines in the 4- to 6-pound class. Small, light spinners can be as effective as worms when tossed gently into the water. Size 0 to 1 spinners have the right weight

Overall view of the stalk or attack of a pond. Use dams or vegetation to break outline. Cast along dam in deeper water or where water enters pond.

and action for ponds. Choice of color is up to the individual angler, but a red and white combination has taken a good share of fish for me. Silver or brass blades also work well. And many times a small "Colorado spinner" threaded with a worm, has saved the day.

Worms are probably the most sure-fire bait for pond fishing. For spinning, a split shot or two a foot ahead of a worm on a number 12 hook, is deadly. A small piece of worm cast with a fly outfit has fooled many lure-wary trout.

There are times when fly fishing is the most effective method of taking beaver pond fish. Ponds are busy breeding areas for insects. During the summer, in the evening, the surface of a pond may be alive with ripples of feeding fish. Almost any good dry fly, size 14 or smaller will take fish. Gray, brown and black seem to work best. Beaver ponds have a tendency to become crowded with surface vegetation during mid-summer. Often, it is impossible to fish spinners and worms in the moss and therefore a dry fly is the only answer.

Basic Gear

Common sense dictates the use of various equipment for fishing beaver ponds. Hip waders are good and chest waders even better. They will keep you drier. It is a good idea to make use of wader knee harnesses when navigating beaver pond terrain.

Landing nets are fine for open streams and ponds, but they are a nuisance in fishing the tangles. So unless you want the net with its elastic carrying strap popping you in the back on occasion, it's better left at home. Since most of the landing of fish is done in the low profile position, netting is awkward anyhow.

Mosquitoes can be a menace in pond marshes, especially when there is no wind. Recommending ways to keep them from biting is like prescribing a cure for the common cold. A long-sleeve shirt, hat and plenty of repellent will help. A creel of some sort is handy because stringers get in the way. The canvas, over-the-shoulder creel is fine as is the standard wicker basket.

A stripping basket for fly roders, considered a gimmick by some, is especially handy for beaver pond conditions. It prevents the line from snagging on tangles.

The rest of the gear is a matter of choice. As is standard with most fishing, the best hours are in early morning and late afternoon until darkness. But the art of beaver pond fishing is studied by many and mastered by few.

Good beaver pond techniques put brookies in the pan. Here my wife, Kathy fixes our catch.

PUT THE FUN BACK IN SAILFISHING

Fighting a sailfish with heavy tackle from a fighting chair deprives the fish of its ability to put on a good show. The fish should be fought from a standing position with the rod hand-held as the author demonstrates.

by MARK SOSIN

THE majority of people who land sailfish don't know what they missed. Sounds cockeyed? Well, read on.

Typically, the angler relaxes in the cockpit of a charter boat, listening to the monotonous drone of the engines while watching four baits skip along the surface astern. The standard tackle is 50- or 80-pound test line and four heavy rods sprout from four rod holders along the gunwales of the boat. In the middle of the cockpit, there's a vacant fighting chair with a gimbal mounted in front, ready to accept the butt of one of the heavy rods. That's the picture.

But, suddenly, the skipper or his mate yell "sailfish" and all eyes focus on the wake. The slender bill and unmistakable dorsal of the sailfish rises above the water behind one of the baits. Instantly, the mate grabs the rod in question, while the angler watches the proceedings.

The sailfish is baited by the mate and after the angler is finally settled down in the fighting chair, the rod is handed to him. After that, it's pump and reel until the fish is alongside the boat. Then the mate grabs the leader and a shimmering mass of blue, gold and silver is rolled over the gunwale and onto the deck. While everyone pats the successful angler on the back, the skipper suggests that the fish should be mounted and hung on the den or office wall of the intrepid angler. Next a round of cold drinks. That, basically, is sailfishing as most people discover it. And ever so sadly.

The sailfish is truly one of the greatest gladiators the sea has every produced. Given half a chance, the spindle-beak is one of the fastest fish in the ocean and has the ability to put on a dazzling display of aerial acrobatics. It's a tremendous game species. But you can't expect any fish to perform when it is hopelessly outgunned by the tackle. That magnificent denizen of deep water knows he doesn't have a prayer against heavy lines and he reflects these feelings in the fight.

There's another subtlety that newcomers to billfishing tend to overlook. Perhaps the most exciting part of the whole adventure is the skill required to hook the fish in the first place. There are many veterans who are delighted to merely have the opportunity to bait billfish and they'll gladly hand the rod over to anyone after the intial moments. Unless you bait and hook your own fish, you've taken part of the fun out of sailfishing.

Sailfish are relatively abundant throughout the warm, tropical seas of the world. The Atlantic variety is smaller than its Pacific cousin, averaging about 50 pounds. Pacific sails usually weigh about 100 pounds. Regardless of which ocean you fish, you don't need very heavy tackle to land a sailfish.

As a basic rule, you should never use anything heavier than regulation 30-pound class trolling tackle. With a 30-pound outfit—that is 30-pound test line and a rod and reel

On tackle balanced to the size of the fish, a sailfish will put on a dazzling display of aerial acrobatics. Nothing is more exciting than fighting a sail on the surface.

Sailfish are famous for tailwalking. When a sail jumps, the angler must push the rod at the fish, creating controlled slack line. When the fish re-enters the water, move the rod to normal fighting position.

to match—you don't have to sit in a fighting chair. The tackle is light enough so that you can hand hold it, using a gimbal belt around your waist to keep the rod butt from pressing against your skin. When you're on your feet, bellying up to the gunwale, you'll gain a new perspective of sailfishing and increase your admiration for this gamester.

When your personal skill in handling this tackle increases, you may want to drop down to 20-pound test line or even 12-pound test. In fact, it's really no great trick to take a sailfish on spinning tackle, plug casting gear, or even a flyrod. The lighter the line, the better a sailfish seems to perform. Yet, they have the physical ability to dive deep and hang on the bottom, and a few seconds later, they may skyrocket through the surface.

Almost all sailfish are taken by trolling. The standard setup is to drag skip baits behind the boat and you would normally have three or four lines depending on the size of the boat. If the boat has outriggers, two lines would be fished long and one or two lines would be fished short. The short lines are called flat lines because they are not attached to pins in the outriggers. Although distances vary with skippers, a good average is to fish the outrigger lines between 100 and 125 feet astern and the flat lines 50 to 60 feet astern.

The reels are left in free spool with the click mechanism engaged and the line running through a clothespin device on the outrigger. Flat lines can also be rigged through a clothes-pin tied to the stern cleats. How fast you troll depends on sea conditions, but as a general rule, you should adjust boat speed so that the skip baits are working at the slowest possible speed. During the course of the day, you can vary the speed until you find the right combination.

The price of a sailfish is eternal vigilance; you should be watching those trolled baits constantly. Actually, you scan the water area right behind the baits and look for the bill or dorsal of a sailfish. Occasionally, you'll get a blind strike and you won't see a thing, but in most cases, the fish will show behind the bait and follow it for a short while.

Baiting a sailfish isn't difficult, but you *do* have to stay alert. When the fish shows behind the bait, grab the rod and get ready. On some fish the bait will be knocked out of the outrigger pin (or flat line pin) when the sail strikes the bait with its bill. Remember that the reel is in free spool with the click engaged. Most veterans prefer to remove the click the instant they have the rod in their hands. When the click is disengaged, you must keep your thumb on the reel spool to keep it from overrunning.

There are two basic schools of thought on how to bait a sailfish. The older method advocates a dropback. That is, you're going to free spool the bait back to the fish once he strikes. The basis for this theory is that a sailfish normally strikes its food with its bill and then circles to pick up the stunned baitfish. That's the situation you're trying to duplicate.

When the fish strikes the skip bait, drop the rod tip and point it directly at the fish. Use your thumb to keep the line from overrunning, but allow the line to flow off the reel smoothly. You don't want the fish to sense any resistance or he may think the bait isn't natural. Some anglers advocate counting to ten, others suggest allowing a reasonable period of time. Usually, you can feel the fish ingest the bait and then move off again.

The skipper will probably coach you through the entire affair. That can be helpful or not, depending on the skipper. When you feel the fish has had the bait long enough, throw the reel into gear, *wait until the line comes tight,* and then set the hook with a series of short, sharp, upward jerks in rapid succession. If you're aboard your own boat, remember to throw the gears in neutral (on the boat) while you're dropping back. Otherwise, you will increase the distance between you and the fish to such an extent that it will be difficult to set the hook.

Supposing you strike the fish and nothing happens. In that case, you must react quickly. Hold the rod tip as high as you can and reel rapidly to bring the bait back on the surface. The boat should start moving again and there's a good chance the fish will come back for a second try. When you feel the sail strike the bait (and it feels like a gentle thump), drop the rod tip, throw the reel in free spool, and drop back again.

The second school of thought in baiting a sail advocates teasing the fish by repeatedly pulling the bait away from the fish after he has it in his mouth. The fish will eventually get excited and really ingest the bait. At that point, you merely drop your rod tip with the reel still in gear and then set the hook. Both methods work, but for a beginner it's easier to use the dropback method.

In some areas, artificial baits are used for billfish instead of rigging natural baits. When fishing an artificial, a drop back doesn't make much sense, because the fish will know he's not getting the genuine article. That's when the teasing procedure really works well. Drop the rod tip and set the hook. If you missed, try it again and again.

If you are in the process of dropping back to a sailfish and you suddenly see the fish jump, you have had your play and must act. The fish knows something is wrong, so your

In the Pacific, sails are often spotted cruising on the surface with just their tails showing. Most billfish travel in the same direction as the seas.

A lightweight harness can be used to hold the rod when you are standing up to fight a fish. In combination with a gimbal belt, you have every advantage and can enjoy sailfishing.

only alternative is to reel as fast as you can until the line comes tight. Then set the hook. A knowledgeable skipper will ram the gears forward and push the throttles to the stops to get the boat moving and help you take up the slack line.

Playing a sailfish on light tackle is superb fun. There are only a few rules you must keep in mind. Since you'll be on your feet, it's no problem to face the fish at all times. You may have to have the skipper chase the fish with the boat and the best procedure is to shorten the distance between you and the fish as soon as possible. When the fish jumps, you should push your rod directly at the fish to minimize the pressure on the light gear. As the fish re-enters the water, go back to the normal fighting angle with the rod. Otherwise, the fish could land on a tight line and break it.

Sometimes, even on light tackle, a sailfish will sound. When he's deep there are two procedures to follow. The first is to get the boat right over the top of the fish and try to pump him toward the surface. If that doesn't work after a fair try, have the skipper move the boat off a little until the line scribes the water at a 45 degree angle. Try working the fish from this position and you may be able to plane the fish back to the surface. Normally, however, when a fish comes topside after sounding, he's going to explode in one of the most spectacular jumps you've ever seen.

Old guard sailfishermen still prefer wire leaders or even cable because the bill could cut through anything else. Yet, the new theory is to use monofilament leaders for sailfish testing between 100 and 150 pounds. The mono will bring many more strikes and it is much easier to handle, especially if you're fishing from a small boat. Baits are still rigged with wire, but a loop is placed in the wire right in front of the bait and the mono is attached to this loop with a swivel or snap.

Handling a sailfish alongside the boat is easy if you know how. Unless you want to keep the fish for mounting, most sportsmen release their sailfish to provide sport for someone else. If you're going to keep the fish, you could use a gaff to land it. Yet, most veterans "bill" their fish—that is, they grasp the bill and hold it. If you're going to "bill" a fish, you must be wearing cotton gloves. The bill of a sail is coarse, like heavy sandpaper, and it could shred your hand.

In grabbing a bill, you have to make a quick and positive move. The fish should be alongside the boat. Grab the leader and pull the fish closer, leaving his head just underwater. Reach down and simply grab the bill. Cut the leader as close to the mouth as you can and turn the fish loose.

If the fish is exhausted, you might give it artificial respiration by holding the fish alongside the boat and having some-

This sailfish crashed two baits at the same time and engulfed both of them. Sails will readily take a variety of offerings.

Sailfish are easy to take on saltwater spinning tackle as the author demonstrates here. The trick is to tease the fish first and then cast when the fish is "turned on."

Small, fast, center console boats are being used for offshore fishing in many areas of the country. This one is equipped for sailfishing in southern waters.

The critical part of the fight occurs when the sailfish is near the boat. He could explode at any second, either jumping for the sky or surging for open water.

Immediately after striking a bait, sailfish sometimes greyhound across the surface in a superb effort to put distance between fish and angler. It's exciting to watch and even more exciting to be on the end of the rod.

Sailfish are eager eaters and will strike a variety of skip baits. Mullet and balao are among the better baits for sails.

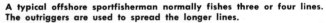

A typical offshore sportfisherman normally fishes three or four lines. The outriggers are used to spread the longer lines.

one run the boat slowly. Water will be forced through the gills of the sail and the fish will revive. Let him swim right out of your hands.

Off the coast of Southern Florida, anglers often catch sailfish while kite fishing. They stream a kite off one side of the boat and use live blue runners or other small fish for bait. The kite holds the bait right near the surface and it's a great way to lure sailfish and other gamesters to a bait.

Another way to fish live bait for sailfish is with a piece of styrofoam. Find the top to an old ice chest and cut it into small rectangles about 2 by 3 inches. Put a small notch in two opposite sides and wind the leader around the styrofoam and through the notches several times. The foam will keep the bait near the surface where a sailfish could easily strike. When you go to set the hook, the leader around the foam will cut through and you'll fight your fish without any encumberances.

If you enjoy casting tackle, the sailfish makes an ideal target. Since you'll be using artificial lures or flies, the trick is to tease the sailfish first and then cast when the fish has been turned on. To do this, you must rig hookless baits that can be used as teasers. The casting tackle is kept ready and you start to troll as you normally would. When a sailfish comes up on a bait, one man has the job of teasing the fish. The best way is to let the fish grab the bait and then pull it away from him. You can actually pull the bait out of the fish's stomach and that will really turn him on. Watch the coloration on the fish. When the sides "light up" and begin to look like a neon sign, the fish is ready. Pull the teaser away and cast the artificial. He should clobber it without hesitation. If you are fly fishing, remember that the boat must be out of gear *before* you cast for the catch to be considered legal or regulation.

Taken on heavy gear designed for marlin or tuna, the sailfish is just another creature in the sea. But if you fish for him with light tackle and bait your own fish, you've really started to put the fun back in sailfishing.

Author Leon Martuch executes backcast when tarpon fishing on a Central American river.

Fly casting lines were developed to cast small, nearly weightless imitations of natural insects.

SPEAKING OF FLY LINES ...THE SHAPE'S THE THING!

by LEON MARTUCH

hair frog

SEVERAL CENTURIES AGO *in the dim and distant past, someone discovered that trout were good to eat. But he also found they were difficult to catch, at least with any of the fishing techniques then known. Luckily our ancient anonymous friend was persistent and observant. He noted that trout fed largely on small insects—and so was well on his way to solving his problem of trout for dinner.*

We can assume that this pioneer angler tried capturing some insects alive and impaling them on hooks. We're also reasonably certain that he had some success with this method. Sooner or later, though, he found he could create an imitation insect of fur and feathers—and so the first artificial fly was born. No one can be exactly sure when in history this occurred.

The preceding may be a somewhat romanticized version of how fly fishing began, but it's probably not too far off the mark. The significance lies in the fact that our early fisherman had developed an artificial lure *which had no weight.* But, the casting techniques available to him were completely inadequate, depending as they did on a bait that was heavy enough to throw. Finally, someone stumbled on the idea of a *line* that had weight in itself, and fly casting was born.

Before we examine fly line shapes as they are today, we have to describe two other factors that have a bearing on why there *are* different shapes: (1) It's sometimes necessary to cast fairly long distances, and (2) some lures, used to entice game fish other than trout, have a fair amount of built-in wind-resistance.

Let's take a look at a typical, largemouth bass fly rod lure: Tied usually from deer hair, the bass bug has practically no weight, but it is tremendously wind-resistant. The fly line shape that does the best job of casting a bass bug is much different than that used to drop a very small trout fly gently on the water!

The other factor, distance casting, has had its effect on line shape, as well as casting technique. The act of fly casting is such that it's not too difficult for the average caster to handle up to 30 or 40 feet of line in the air. Distances greater than that are more readily attained by using a technique called "shooting."

When we shoot, we use the weight of line already out of the rod to pull additional line after it. The amount of line we can shoot depends upon the amount of friction between the surface of the fly line and the rod guides.

Skipping now to the present, we arrive at the array of fly line shapes available and what your choice should be in terms of the lure and how far you have to cast it.

Although we illustrate four shapes, there are three basic fly line configurations (number 4 is a modification of number 3 and will be discussed a little later on).

Royal Wulff dry fly is one of countless patterns designed by anglers in the past century to take trout.

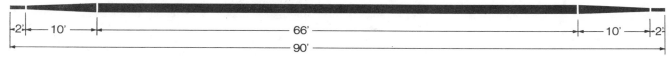

75'

1. Level

2' | 10' | 66' | 10' | 2'
90'

2. Double Taper

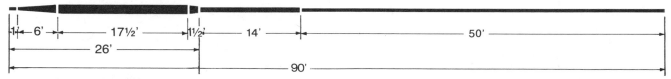

2' | 10' | 20' | 2' | 17' | 39'
34'
90'

3. Weight Forward

1' | 6' | 17½' | 1½' | 14' | 50'
26'
90'

4. Bass Bug or Saltwater taper

Number 1, the level line, is the same diameter from one end to the other, and that diameter is comparatively large. In terms of the lure, the level line is an excellent choice where wind-resistance is involved. It's a good line for the bass fisherman if he does not have to cast more than 30 or 40 feet. Due to its significantly large surface area in contact with the rod guides, the level does not shoot as readily as other line shapes. Where delicate presentation of a trout fly is concerned, the level line is not the best choice, due to its tendency to slap down comparatively hard on the surface of the water.

Within the category of tapered lines, we find those that are tapered toward the tip because of the effect on presentation and those that are reduced in diameter back toward the center of the line to facilitate shooting.

Number 2 is actually two lines in one and is called the double taper. You'll notice that it's like a level that peters out at the end. As we move toward the tip of the line, we are effectively reducing its weight, which means that this area tends to travel more slowly through the air than the rest of the line. The end result is a more gentle drop of the fly on the water. The line which has a fairly gradual taper toward its tip is the type to use for gentle presentation of a fly that has no wind resistance. Like the level, however, the double taper is not the best line to use for distances in excess of 30 or 40 feet.

Number 3, the weight-forward, is the line to use for distance casting. Note that approximately two-thirds of the weight-forward line's length is small diameter. This means that with less surface area than the level or double taper, shooting is greatly enhanced. Notice also that the standard weight-forward, as shown in figure 3, has the same length of front taper as line Number 2. In other words, a standard weight-forward and a double taper of the same weight will present the fly with equal delicacy. The weight-forward is the choice, however, for distance casting.

The weight-forward line is the one fly line shape most frequently altered for one reason or another. The reason for one very typical alteration is to allow us to cast even greater distances than we can with the standard version.

This particular alteration is called a shooting taper and, to create one, we cut off all the small diameter portion of the weight-forward line and substitute nylon monofilament. The monofilament with its smaller diameter and slicker surface shoots even better than the weight-forward fly line.

We mentioned earlier that **Number 4** was a modification of 3. You will note that it is also a weight-forward line but that the front taper is much more abrupt. By shortening this front taper, we more closely approximate the shape of the end of the level line and, if you will remember, we said that the level was highly effective at handling wind-resistant lures. This modification—often referred to as a bass bug or saltwater taper—is the best choice for casting wind-resistant lures substantial distances.

Choose your fly line shape by starting with the fish you plan to catch. The species and the type of water you find him in will usually determine the nature of the lure. Then, it's a fairly simple process, based on the information presented here, to choose whatever fly line that will do the best job for you.

For best casting results, a fly fisherman must match the proper type line to the fishing at hand.

Fly Line Broken? Nail it Together!

"IS THERE any chance that you could fix my fly line?" Almost daily, we at Scientific Anglers receive letters from distraught anglers who have broken, cut or burned a fly line. They're hoping against hope that we have some magic method of making the line whole again. Unfortunately, we do *not* have a magic method.

However, we look on these letters with sympathy, because we've had "accidents" happen to our fly lines, too. We are usually equipped with spare fly lines, so the damage or loss of a line is no tragedy. But it can easily ruin the fishing for a day or an afternoon. I can remember when I was the victim of a fly line "accident" and lost some valuable fishing time as a result.

I had made a long cast while balanced on rocks at the shore of Quebec's Whale River. As I retrieved the line, I dropped it at my feet. Usually the line will come back up from between the rocks on the next cast, but this time the line caught. I gave it a slight pull and the line parted. It had jammed between two rocks, one of which had a sharp edge. When I pulled, that sharp edge sliced through the line like a razor.

If I had known then what I know now, I wouldn't wasted the rest of that fishing day.

I learned how to nail a fly line together from Captain Cal Cochran, a fishing guide out of Marathon in the Florida Keys. I had sent some experimental lines to Cal for field testing and had wanted to fish with them myself. Cal showed me a loop he had spliced at the rear of the running line to facilitate attaching the backing. He had made the splice using ordinary nail-knots.

Cal's splice was pretty fancy. He had nail-knotted the two ends of the line together at four places before using a final nail-knot to bind the loose end to the running part of the line. Of course, when you're fishing for giant tarpon, you want every bit of strength you can get.

When I saw that splice, I suddenly realized that I had discovered a way for a fisherman to nail his line together after an accident.

The splice shown in the running line of a WF-7-F AirCel Supreme is almost as strong as the line itself, and it shoots through the guides with hardly any additional drag. It rattles a little as it goes through the guides, but it doesn't seem to slow down the cast.

It's not necessary to carry special materials to splice a broken fly line. You are almost certain to have additional leader material with you, and you can use the leader material itself to assist you in tying a nail-knot. No leader material? How about using the butt end of a knotless leader? It works perfectly well.

If you ever encounter a broken fly line, just remember to "nail it together"!

Leon Martuch

NAIL KNOT SPLICE

FLY LINE HOLLOW TUBE OR NAIL ◄ FLY LINE MONOFILAMENT

Alternate Method

◄ Pull
MONOFILAMENT LOOP

← Turn Back 3 Ends.
Trim Close.

FIRST KNOT **FINISHED SPLICE**

NAIL KNOT SPLICE . . . *for splicing together two lengths of fly line with monofilament or leader.* Overlap two ends of fly line, short length of monofilament and nail or hollow tube. Hold coils securely. (Withdraw nail or tube.) Alternately pull on opposite ends of monofilament. Pull hard to "set" the knot. Turn back short ends and trim close. Repeat with another length of leader and snug second knot against first knot.

(Alternate Method . . . using a monofilament loop instead of nail or tube.)

BIG NORTHERN

Fishing does not end with freeze-up in Manitoba. More and more people are turning to ice fishing during the winter season.

Manitoba's Master Angler Awards list gives reliable information on where a prospective angler can hope to land a beauty like this.

where they're at in MANITOBA

by Cory Kilvert

WHAT AMERICAN ANGLER hasn't had at least one "bad trip"—and we don't mean the kind you experience from a hallucinatory sugar cube. The kind of "bad trip" meant here is one that sometimes results from where-to-catch-fish advice freely offered from perhaps your TV repair man, your Aunt Amanda or that man you met on the street in the resort town last year.

Anyway, the free advice you got from one or all of these "experts" all added up to the fact that old Lake Osheespeechee had to be loaded with trophy fish just waiting to be landed. As it turned out, the old lake was loaded all right—loaded with your lost lures after you left. Apparently it contained little more than long, stringy weeds while you were there.

After one experience like that even the dullest angler begins to question the quality of fishing advice he's getting and hankers for some kind of reliable information that will give him at least a fighting chance to come home with a respectable stringer to show his friends.

In Canada's Province of Manitoba it seems there is just such a barometer—the Master Angler Awards list issued annually by provincial authorities. This handy-dandy "fish finder" is nothing more than a long list of most of the trophy size fish landed from Manitoba waters in the pre-vious fishing season. What makes the list so interesting to anglers who are looking for lunkers or just plain good fishing is the fact that it contains other valuable information besides the size of the catch that won someone an award. It also documents the date of the catch, the angler who caught it and, most important, the lake or stream from which it came.

It doesn't take a PhD in biology to figure out from this sort of information such important facts as (a) where the most lakers, northerns or walleyes are coming from and (b) where an angler would have the best chance of landing a trophy respectable enough to hang on his rumpus room wall.

Here's the sort of dope one could have gleaned from this friendly province's 1971 Master Angler list:

Although the M.A. list tallies trophy fish from more than 15 different species, the longest list of trophy catches is in the northern pike category. During that year 465 northerns, weighing 18 lbs. or better, earned bronze hat badges and certificates for lucky fishermen. Records show not all trophy size fish by any means are entered, so, anything up to about twice as many of these big ones were likely landed on hook and line from Manitoba waters in 1971.

A little simple arithmetic can show the area or lake where a dyed-in-the-wool northern fisherman may have the best

Explosive action is what keen anglers look for and have no trouble finding in the 40,000 square miles of water divided among an estimated 100,000 lakes.

Failing to connect with a great northern, this angler appears more than content with these hefty lakers; and why not?

chance of running into lively fishing action or landing that biggest-ever fish. According to the 1971 list, Gods Lake, a fly-in spot some 350 miles north of the Canada-United States border, accounted for 48 of the big northerns listed.

But, the biggest northern landed in Manitoba last year came out of the Churchill River, a fish-laden watercourse consisting mostly of a chain of large, labyrinthian lakes sprawled across the northern area. It gave up a 35-pound fish to a resident of the nearby mining town of Lynn Lake. This happened to be the sixth largest northern pike ever caught in Manitoba.

The biggest one, a 41-pound lunker caught by Ray Koecher of Chicago, Ill., came from Fishing Lake, a fly-in area approximately 150 miles northeast of Winnipeg. That was in 1969.

Next to Gods Lake in the quantity category in 1971 was beautiful Reed Lake where anglers boated 43 northerns between 18 and close to 29 pounds. Reed Lake, part of the famous Grass River chain, is an auto-accessible pike spot where going after big northerns is more than a sport. It's almost a way of life. Anyone can reach it via Highway 10 and Provincial Road 391. It's about 600 road miles from the U.S. boundary and all but the last 50 are paved.

Right in the same neck-of-the-woods lie three more big northern producing lakes next on the list—Third Cranberry, with 39 recorded trophy catches, and Athapapuskow and Cormorant Lakes, each with 21 northern trophies in 1971. Cormorant, until recently a lake accessible only by air and train, can now be reached by road as well.

Athapapuskow and Third Cranberry, both reached via Highway 10, "Main Street of the north," have both been flailed to a foam by two generations of anglers but are still very much in the running when it comes to producing the big ones.

Other northern lakes high on the list include:

Cross Lake—adjacent to the hydro settlement at Grand Rapids and reached by Highway 6 from Winnipeg. This is the last pike hole on the mighty Saskatchewan River before it swirls into the power turbine complex and spills into Lake Winnipeg.

Winnipeg River—its most productive reaches are a chain of lakes in the northern tip of Whiteshell Provincial Park. This fishing area is reached by road (Highways 44 and 11 and Provincial Road 313) and is about 70 miles from Winnipeg.

On the 1971 list these were the "big" lakes, but, Manitoba—a province boasting over 100,000 bodies of water—has many more lakes where big northerns thrive including

Guide nets a good sized pike for visiting fisherman.

This northern came from Manitoba waters to tip the scale at almost 24 pounds.

Happy angler at a fly-in spot in northern Manitoba sees his catch netted by guide.

Shore dinners are always a favorite way to end a successful fishing trip.

these fly-in spots in the north and northeast—Dogskin, South Knife, Moar, Waskaiowaka, Vandekerckhove, Molson, Sasaginnigak, Island and Kississing. And then, of course, there are plenty of lakes throughout this immense territory (251,000 square miles) that have never been seen by any angler, let alone fished. Taking into consideration that a northern will survive in just about any water situation from a wet dishrag to an ocean, there has to be a good chance that one of these untried lakes harbours "Old Fighter," that legendary northern slated to break all heavyweight records.

In the meantime, the known pike-producing lakes and streams in Manitoba have something else going for them. Almost without exception they have good-to-excellent fishing for at least one other species.

For example, the Gods Lake-Gods River area, in addition to trophy northerns, is known for trophy lake trout, brook trout and whitefish. Reed Lake and the rest of the Grass River area has first class walleye water. Third Cranberry and Lake Athapapuskow are known far and wide for trophy lakers and the Winnipeg River has good walleye and exceptional smallmouth bass.

So, even if you bomb out on your quest for a trophy northern on a Manitoba fishing trip—which is not too likely—at least you should be able to fill in with good catches of some other species.

Don't worry about what lures you should have in your tackle box to entice big northerns. Just be sure you have plenty of them. If you've had any experience as a pike hunter you'll know that a red and white spoon is a good bet. However, as you probably also know from experience, "old greedy guts" will go after just about anything you have including, some claim, your hand.

Third Cranberry and Lake Athapapuskow are well-known for their fine lake trout.

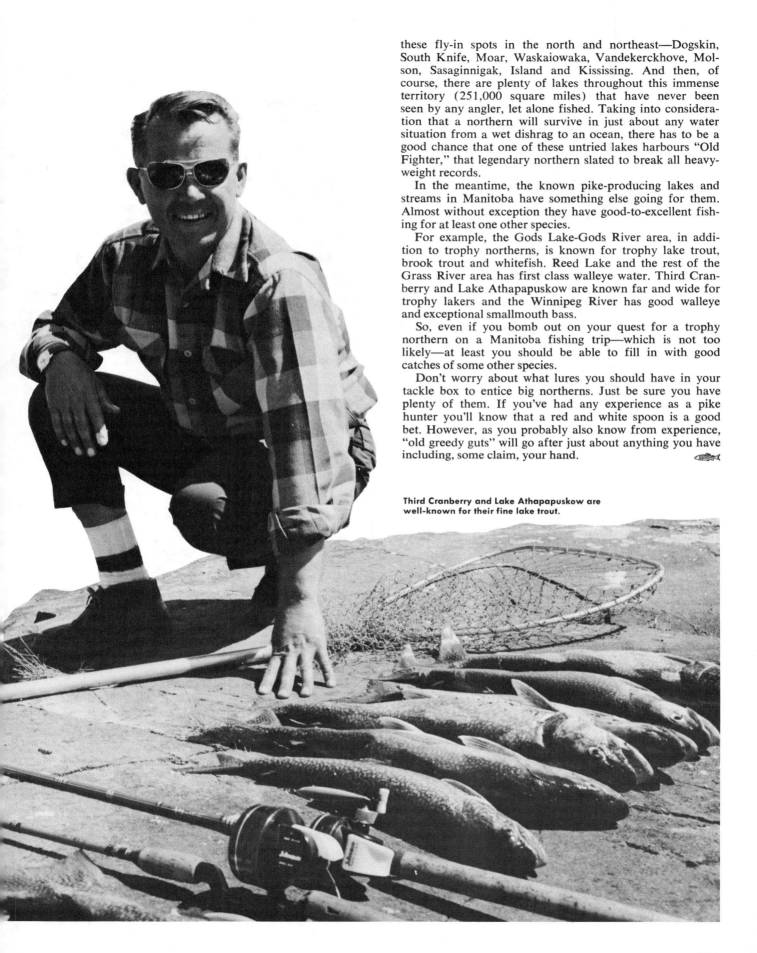

HARD TIMES IN HOG BASS HEAVEN

Steady casting and pinpoint accuracy brought this one to Pat Williams' hook.

by RICHARD MARTIN

Heavy duty gear brought him to the net.

CYPRESS trees. Small and scattered in thin lines or clumps here; dense groves of towering, Spanish moss-clad veterans there. Flat water burnished by a red rising sun; egrets and fish crows calling raucously along the hummocks. Ominous swirls among the thousands of stickups as something big swallowed something small. There wasn't any doubt that this Ohio boy was a long way from home.

I turned to my guide, Pat Williams. "Looks good," I said.

Pat continued the task of attaching a blue 10-inch plastic worm to his short, stout casting rod and without lifting his eyes answered, "It's good all right. Hook up a worm rig and try to lay it right against the bole of those cypress trees. Hog bass down here lie right among the roots and each cast has to be right on the money."

After a pause he added, "If one picks it up, hit him quick and hard. Once they get back to cover, it's all over."

Like I said, I'm an Ohio bass fisherman and I took a hard look at the unrippled water punctuated by swirls here and there as huge bluegills sucked in surface insects. "Mind if I start with a surface popper?"

"Suit yourself," was the answer.

Pat is the 31 year old director of the Santee-Cooper Country tourist bureau and he spends a lot of time fishing Lake Marion in southern South Carolina. So he knows his business. But if water was ever made for a surface lure this was it. I snapped on a frog finish Hula Popper and made a cast. The ripples had hardly widened when Pat murmered "There's one," counted three, then reared back on his stubby rod hard enough to break any fish's neck.

Several things happened almost simultaneously. The husky largemouth dove for cover, didn't make it, rose near the boat and dumped a gallon of water on one astonished Buckeye, then geared up for open water and ran smack into Pat's waiting net. "You can't afford to give them an even break in water as brushy as this," he grinned, lifting

Cypress clumps and dense stickups brought my best fishing at Santee.

a chunky 3-pounder free, "or they're long gone. Ready to change to a worm?"

"Just give me a chance, Charlie," I replied. "They'll eat the popper."

But they didn't.

These words marked the beginning of a long awaited morning and I was hoping its end would see me racing back to the campground with a 10-pound bass, a real "hog largemouth" in southern angling terms. Big bass are the Holy Grail to any serious largemouth fisherman and every year thousands of northern anglers make a crusade south in hopes of landing a real monster. Ohio has fair fishing and when I'm not teaching biology courses at Shelby's senior high school I'm roaming nearby lakes and taking some fine

Some of the bass, like this one, were fine fish. But no hogs.

ones. But a fine bass here is barely 4 pounds so I've been heading south too, to look for bigger game.

Lake Cumberland in southern Kentucky held my personal record for several years, a 7-pound, 2-ounce lunker, but most of the real hogs are further south yet, where feeding is good year around. And after reading that professional bass angler Roland Martin (no relation, unfortunately) considers Lake Marion "the best bass lake in the country" I figured I'd found my spot. A call to Pat Williams had set up the trip and the middle of June saw me pulling into Rock's Pond Campground on the shores of the big lake.

Rut Conner, the owner, was plenty happy about fishing prospects. While I waited patiently for the inevitable "You should have been here last week," he toured me through the cool sand and pine needle covered campground and waxed eloquent on fishing prospects. "They're catching some whopper brim and crappie out of those big stickups across the flats over there and some of the boys have been bringing in heavy stringers of bass and stripers. Pat called just half an hour ago and said that he'd bring his bass boat over around seven and go catch you that hog you wanted." It sounded mighty good.

Promptly at seven Pat arrived, lean and suntanned, and hauling a brand new bass rig complete with bucket seats, live well, and electric motor. With tackle and lunch aboard he said, "hang on" and we raced at high speed across the still water, through a saw grass cut, past acres of young cypress, to that aforementioned meeting with his first bass of the day. Later his fourth bass of the day managed to convince me that a popper wasn't the answer this trip and I stubbornly switched to a large spinner and jig combination.

"That works pretty well sometimes, at least early in the morning like now, but remember to lay it in close." And Pat went back to rhythmically tossing his worm toward the timber.

It took a dozen probing casts among the stickups, drowned logs, and small cypress to bring action, but when it came, it came with a vengeance. Wham! The rod, a heavy spinning stick, bucked in my hands then arched down in a straining curve, and the line sang thinly as it sliced through 30 feet of water. The bass dived for cover and darn near made it, then plunged for bottom and tried to fight his way beneath a moss covered log. I had my hands full with that one and gasped: "Get the net, I've got a lunker," but it dripped free at a mere 2 pounds of thick-bodied bass.

"They sure don't fight like that in Ohio," I commented, "what's the explanation?"

Pat cast again. "I don't know, unless it's the warm water temperature and plenty of food. The lake is full of mayflies and bait fish, and bass grow fast down here. Maybe that makes 'em more energetic than usual."

As the morning passed our good luck continued. Pat picked up bass after bass as his worm skipped unerringly among the roots. I took one more fish on the spinner, a twin to the first, then switched to a worm and ran into immediate trouble.

The light bait took some getting used to after bulleting heavy hardware into scarcely 6-inch targets, and cypress trees proved to have tough limbs and hook-grabbing needles that almost guaranteed a hangup on every miss. After my tenth pitch into a scrubby little tree, I began to reach angrily for the lure and Pat said, "Hold it for a second. Better let the resident leave first."

A 4-foot snake dripped off its limb and eased silently into the water. "Got to watch those cypress trees. They're good sunning spots for snakes and while most of them are just water snakes, you'll find a cottonmouth now and again."

Santee bass are fighters and this near hog proved no exception.

At noon we stopped for lunch and a swim. Temperatures were reaching 95 now and the smoking hot water rippled beneath a merciless sun. "Are we quitting?" I asked. "They won't bite again till evening from the looks of it."

Pat grinned, "We get some of our best fishing during the afternoon hours if you can stick it out."

"I can stick it out okay." With that Pat lifted the trolling motor and we raced down the lake toward a special little bay that he likes. It's rimmed with cypress trees in a double line, marking the shores of an old creek bed, and hog bass favor the deeper water for hot weather loafing. Our casts spun out simultaneously toward a trio of cypress, mine striking between the first two, his between the latter pair. I reeled in slowly.

The 20-pound test line sang, water blew skyward, and a bass that looked as broad as he was long forced his gaping mouth above the surface. That one weighed a disappointing 7 pounds, plenty good by my standards, but as Pat said, "He's okay, but no hog."

By 4 p.m. I'd had the course and was plenty glad to see the boat spin back toward Rock's Pond Campground. Now I was nursing a stiff shoulder from long hours of casting, a set of bruised knuckles from reel handle slaps, and a budding sunburn. On the credit side we had an impressive stringer of keepers topped by Pat's 7-pounder, and that alone was credit enough for the mishaps.

The remainder of the afternoon was to be devoted to my wife and youngsters' often repeated wish to see the magic old city of Charleston, but Pat had his own plans for the next day. "I'll meet you in Santee at the office and we'll drive over to the state park. There's some huge old cypress groves over there with black water underneath where I've taken half a dozen hogs this year. Don't be surprised if Bob Hart comes along. He's down."

The rest of that day was all a family man could ask for. We drove down long roads shaded by live oak and Spanish moss, watched bobwhite quail skitter across the dusty road, picked a fresh peach or two, and finally wandered into Charleston with Rut Conner acting as tour director.

"Lord, I love this country," said the big, burly outdoorsman. "I fish all spring and summer, hunt quail all fall, and jump shoot ducks half the winter. When are you northern boys going to wise up and come south to live?"

I had no answer for that one. Next a tour of the city with dinner at one of the charming old waterfront restaurants satisfied my family and back at the campground I whiled away the pre-sleeping hours going over some background on Lake Marion with Rut.

Lake Marion, named after famous redcoat fighter Fran-cis Marion, the Swamp Fox, is a man-made lake and a big one. It's also a lucky accident. In 1941 the Federal Power Commission dammed the Cooper River, planning to build two lakes with a channel between as part of the Santee-Cooper Reservoir plan. The first, Lake Moultrie, was cleared of trees before being flooded, but with the war getting ever hotter, there wasn't time or manpower to clear Marion. As a result the lake is cluttered with drowned forest and cypress trees, a shallow, 110,000-acre puddle of flats and hummocks, saw grass and hyacinths that makes big bass country supreme. And it's rich.

On summer days untold millions of mayflies emerge from months of larval feeding in the mud below to cover buildings, docks, and watercraft. Bass and panfish gorge like starving Hessians on this heady provender. Then there are untold hordes of small panfish, herring stocked by the Wildlife Resources Department, and tons of gizzard shad. Little wonder that Marion bass grow so fast and show such a chunky outline.

With 410 miles of wild shoreline and thousands of acres near the center that rarely see man, a bass' chances of eating a shiny metal lure are small. Their chances of dying of old age at 10 to 16 pounds are proportionately better. The lake record right now is a 16-pound, 2-ounce bass and it's a record that isn't likely to hold for long, even though in Marion the odds are with the fish. Once hooked they'll inevitably dive for the nearest brush and with their awesome strength they make it all too often. This is why locals favor short, stubby sticks, 20-pound test line or better, and heavy duty hooks tipped with razor sharp barbs. I worried a little about the stubby little casting rods, but not much. My heavy duty, 6-foot spinning rod should handle anything the lake had to offer. I hoped.

The day dawned bright and clear, already growing hot as I bundled gear into the station wagon for a short drive to Pat's office in Santee. Bob Hart was already there. Bob is a well known Ohio sportsman whose main duty is running Hart Productions which handles the Ohio Valley and Columbus sports, vacation, and travel shows. His main interest otherwise is hunting quail on his Hillsboro ranch or bass fishing anywhere in the country. Bass fishing was his aim this time and he was ready with pounds of plastic worms and a spanking new bass boat of his own. While we traded stories, Pat drove up, shook hands and said, "Let's head out. Reports are good from the state park area and those hogs won't wait forever." So we headed out.

Bob and his missus elected to fish their own craft, leaving Pat and me to handle the other and we motored swiftly through some of the best of Marion's prime bass water.

Mayflies proved extremely plentiful and they're a major food source for fish of most species in Marion.

I kept just enough for a major fish fry, but at that the stringer made heavy lifting.

"Let's work a few of these scattered clumps again for openers, then we'll move back into the big timber near an old sawmill I know about. There's hogs all through this territory."

While he shouted instructions to Bob, I rigged up with worm and slip sinker. I'd learned my lesson. Action came fast that morning, but the fish were running small around the singles and we soon headed for taller timber. Brim fishermen were scattered here and there and one boat had some impressive crappies, but few anglers were working for bass. "Most of the people around here are like that," Pat mused as he dropped the trolling motor near a bed of hyacinths. "They've got the best bass fishing going, but they stick to brim and crappies or work the channels for striped bass. It's easier fishing, I guess, and a 2-pound crappie is sure worth taking, but they don't match a 10-pound bass."

I was wondering about that 10-pound bass myself.

While Bob and his wife worked one end of a long, semi-circular stretch of cypress, Pat and I attacked the other end and fish started hitting the boat deck. Pat scored first with a 3-pound fish that gave his worm a steady tap, tap, then eased off toward home plate and I took a fat 2-pounder that followed the same tactics. An occasional whoop from our distant partners showed they were doing fine, too. As Pat strung my third fish I asked, "How do you tell the big ones from the little guys?"

"That's easy," he replied, "the small bass tap the bait then run, a big one just engulfs the lure and the first word you get is a tight line that's getting tighter in a hurry. If you get a whack from a hog, you'll know it."

Half an hour passed and finally Pat pulled the motor and swung over to hard fishing Bob Hart. "You two doing any good?"

"No, we've got some 2- to 4-pounders, but nothing big. Where's all the hogs in this lake?"

A general bull session brought the decision to head for a section near the park where Pat had hooked and lost several lunkers last week. "It's a little bay that looks just like 50 other bays and it even has a few cottages down one side, but for some reason the point and a spot about midway along turn up consistent catches of whopper bass. We'll give it a try."

The bay proved to be just as Pat had described it and Bob Hart opted for the middle while we stuck to the point. Suddenly I was getting prickles of anticipation, a touch of the tingle that all bass fishermen feel when they *know* a big hog bass is waiting just below. Call it ESP or whatever, but I hadn't felt the tingle in two days and it was racing up

Bob Hart and wife shared the last day's fishing with us.

and down my spine right now. This was it!

Our twin baits paced each other in flat arcs toward a cluster of four cypress bordered by stickups and buttonball bushes. Mine hit, sank, and I'd scarcely turned the reel twice when I felt my tight line getting tighter. "It's a hog," and I set the hook with all the rod and line would take.

The huge bass wallowed at the top showing more length than I've ever seen, then flipped his paddle-like tail and steamed for the stickups just a few feet away. The line sang like violin string, my reel handle slipped free and beat a tattoo on already sore knuckles. Such power from a bass simply took me by surprise and before I could really react the rod was parallel to the water and my fish had reached the stickups.

Now the fish rose once half out of water and shook a head that looked to my eyes like a pony keg. That's when the line snapped like a rifle shot and it was all over.

Pat was sympathetic. "They're hard to stop that close in, especially a 10-pound fish like that one." I nearly shed tears but contented myself with a few well chosen words that brought lifted eyebrows from my partner.

"There's more than one in here, so hook up another rig and start casting," he consoled.

I quickly rigged up again and flipped a cast that bounced neatly off the bole of a cypress and settled into 4 feet of water. Again a few turns brought that fast tightening of the line. "Good God, here's another one," and I drove the hook home.

It was a repeat of the first act. An 8-pound-plus bass rose almost free of his element and roared through a tumble of brush like an express train. It rose again and slammed between two cypresses with inches to spare, splashing water several feet up both trunks. Then it sounded and

sulked on the bottom, with line throbbing at each lunge, but miraculously holding. Pat dropped his rod.

"Hang on," he said. "Sometimes we can work a bass like that free if he isn't hung up too bad. Let's ease in and see if we can snake him out."

Those were well chosen words. A 3-foot snake sunning high on a limb of the cypress above picked that moment to bail out of his penthouse apartment. He missed Pat by inches causing a mad scramble for the back of the boat. I reacted with a jerk on the rod, my hook tore free as one suddenly stung bass plunged for freedom, and two sheepish anglers sat looking at each other through a chaos of scattered gear.

"That's fishing."

"Yeah," I agreed.

This idyll should have ended the story, but it didn't. Bob left the lake at noon hurrying home to another fishing trip with his growing youngsters and we continued to work the lake with varying results. Finally, heading back to the dock I said, "Let's hit the bass on the point once more for luck."

You guessed it. Another lunker hit the tantalizing worm and pulled an exact repeat of his two partners actions. "How the hell do you catch these @#$¢?*& fish anyway," I gritted.

"Come on down next year about this time and I'll show you," said an exceedingly mirthful Pat. "Man, if you could have seen the look on your face when that last fish broke loose . . ." Then he succumbed to a whooping gale of laughter. "But you'd better throw away that willow wand and pick up a real hog bass stick before you do. Marion fish don't seem to even notice that rod."

I sucked throbbing knuckles for a moment. "I'll do that, and I'll be back too."

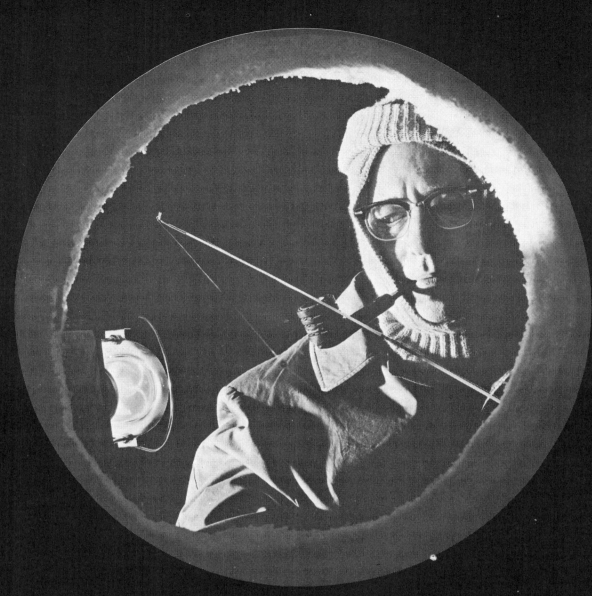

A fish's-eye view of an ice fisherman.

Angling When the Freeze Is On

by Erwin A. Bauer

DURING the past few winters a recreational survey was conducted in several northern states and it resulted in a few slightly surprising statistics. For one thing, the popularity of ice fishing has more than doubled during the past decade. But that is no wonder because another statistic shows that overall fishing success is greater in wintertime than during midsummer. In other words the time between strikes is much shorter after a safe crust of ice covers the waterways. That is especially true of such species as walleye, yellow perch, bluegill, northern pike and pickerel which comprise the bulk of the winter catch.

Not only is fishing through the ice more productive; it is also simpler than in summertime. A rank beginner has a better chance to score and a few experts do not necessarily account for all of the fish. Winter success depends entirely on finding the fish, followed by observing a few basic techniques. These basics vary for different species, but certain equipment is necessary for all.

Every ice fisherman requires the following: terminal tackle, lures or bait, something to open a hole in the ice and keep it open; a portable shelter and/or warming device, and a sled or other means to transport this equipment. Other gear is helpful and since, with experience, ice fishermen tend to become gadgeteers, they carry a good bit of it. Let's examine all the essential equipment, omitting the tackle and bait for the present.

There are a good many ways to cut holes in the ice. The simplest method is to use a large, heavy, iron chisel called a spud. With it, holes of any size or shape can be chopped out. Nowadays more and more winter sportsmen use manual ice augers or drills which bore holes 7 to 8 inches in diameter. A number of different types are available in northern sporting goods stores. Small power saws will also cut neat holes quickly in the ice, but they are bulky and heavy to carry. A small strainer or scoop is also handy to dip chips or slush out of the hole.

On sunny, windless days, warm clothing is all that any angler needs to be comfortable on a frozen lake. But these fine days occur too seldom and usually some sort of shelter is necessary. Often a windbreak will be sufficient and these can be either the roll-up or collapsible frame-and-canvas models which are light and easy to transport. Small camping tents can also double as ice fishing shelters, but most fishermen prefer shanties.

A shanty can be of any size, depending on the number of occupants, but the typical shanty seats two side-by-side on a bench. That means a square or rectangular floor space of about 35 square feet and 6 feet or so of headroom. All shanties are mounted on runners for moving and towing. Most contain a small stove or heater. Sportsmen who prefer luxury with their ice fishing have designed really elaborate shanties big enough for larger parties and equipped with cooking equipment, lounge or deck chairs, a radio and perhaps even a portable television set. It is not necessary to own a shanty because they can usually be rented at very nominal rates wherever ice fishing is popular. However there may be a great demand for the supply on weekends when the action is fast.

Heaters used by ice anglers range from the efficient, compact catalytic models to gasoline lanterns (which furnish considerable warmth as well as light) to homemade stoves using a variety of fuels. In the interests of mobility, some fishermen only use handwarmers stowed conveniently in pockets. Of course a shanty should be well ventilated when using *any* heating device and open charcoal cookers (which produce carbon monoxide) should never be used inside as heaters.

Any sled with enough room on top to carry equipment is a good enough carrier for ice fishermen. But many prefer to construct them especially for the sport, with built-in compartments, a special space for a heater and perhaps a warm seat on top of it. The December, 1969, issue of *Sports Afield* carried detailed plans ("Nifty Rig for Frostbite Fishing") for an easy-to-make fishing sled.

There are many ways to travel on the ice and which mode to use may depend upon the size of the lake or the thickness of the ice. A crust of 8 to 10 inches will safely support passenger cars. In many northern areas, however, only old jalopies or autos stripped of roofs and other excess weight are used. They are often available on a rental basis or can be hired to shuttle you to the best fishing spots. Each year more snowmobiles make the ice fishing scene, as do motor or trail bikes. But for fishermen who walk, cleats or spikes which strap or clamp onto boots make travel much easier and less precarious on the slippery surface. If there is a thick layer of snow on the ice, snowshoes are very helpful.

Everything depends on first finding the fish—or the lake bottom of the proper depth. Once this was mostly a matter of trial-and-error, but now more and more sportsmen are depending on electronics to spot fish under the ice. Such miniature sonar devices accurately spot schools of fish swimming at mid-depths and also record the exact depth of the water. It isn't even necessary to cut a hole in the ice to use the device and that can spare any fisherman plenty of wasted time. It also reduces the interval between strikes.

Now let's consider terminal tackle and bait which, unlike shelter and ice augers, depends on which species of fish is the target.

BLUEGILLS: Of all winter-caught species, this popular panfish has the widest distribution and is accessible to the most fishermen. Except possibly for the yellow perch, it is also the easiest to catch.

As soon as a lake starts to freeze in late autumn, bluegills begin to concentrate in a few spots where they remain fairly inactive until springtime. These spots normally are in shallow water rarely deeper than 20 feet and I have found them in water only 4 feet deep. Catch one bluegill anywhere and you should be able to catch a good many more. Angling pressure seems to have little effect on success and at times seems to stimulate bluegills into more action.

When starting out on an unfamiliar bluegill lake, look first for knots of other anglers and join them. Such a concentration usually means that the fish are biting there or at least that it is considered to be a good spot by the regulars. Do not worry about butting in (as good manners would dictate on a stream in summer), but instead move in close because ice fishermen are gregarious and the more the merrier. If there is no one else on the ice, you have to go prospecting. If this is a first trip, cut a hole close to shore and keep moving farther out toward deeper water until you connect.

Only a small hole, say 8 inches in diameter, is necessary if you are fishing exclusively for bluegills. When prospecting, you can dunk bait in a couple of holes at once (check the legal limit on this where you're fishing) while cutting another new hole farther away. You not only cover more territory that way, but it keeps you warm.

The main mistake most beginners make is to use tackle which is too complicated or too heavy. When water temperatures are very low, none of the warm-water species are very active; when they bite it is only a soft nibble which may be almost imperceptible on the ice far above. Some beginners miss it altogether at first.

The best bluegill outfit consists of a short, limber rod (which may actually be the tip section of a discarded spinning or fly rod) and a fixed reel which does nothing at all except hold excess line. The line should not test more than

A typical ice-fishing shanty. This one in use in the Great Lakes area.

2 pounds and 1-pound monofilament is strong enough. For bait use earthworms or any of the so-called grubs, mealworms or waxworms which are available in bait shops everywhere. These are the larvae of various kinds of insects which can be used alone on a tiny bare hook or on the tip of a small metal fly or jig. At times tiny ice jigs work well enough without the addition of bait.

Lower the bait or lure to the bottom and if bait only, affix a very small bobber to the line so that the bait will be no more than an inch or so off the bottom. Now jig the bait or lure very gently and not very far. At the faintest touch, set the hook and haul the fish out onto the ice. There is a knack to detecting very soft bites, but everyone soon gets the hang of it.

Never pass up the small lakes and ponds when ice fishing for bluegills. On larger lakes, the deserted, frozen-over areas of docks and pilings are good places to try. If daytime fishing is slow, stay out for an hour or two after dark; often the bluegills become more active then. The best fishing of all generally occurs soon after freeze-up and in the weeks just before break-up.

YELLOW PERCH: Ice fishing for perch can be a feast-or-famine game. One day you might quickly fill a gunny sack in a given spot which, a day later, appears to be empty of fish. However the good days more than make up for the bad ones and in good yellow perch water, the fish are active most of the time.

Perch fishing is not unlike bluegill fishing except that the fish may be in much deeper water (sometimes I've found them almost 35 feet down) and the tackle is a little different. This is even more of a school species in winter and after catching the first one, the odds are high you will get many more.

Because of the greater water depth, most experienced perch fishermen prefer a short stubby rod with a regular plug casting reel and fine monofilament line. There is an obvious drawback to this and all other reels with moveable parts; water soon gets into them and freezes if it is cold enough. In that case you are better off without them.

Yellow perch will strike tiny slivers of shiny metal or weighted ice flies (nymphs, really) when fluttered or jigged right on the bottom—and this is a most fascinating way to

Ice fishing is sometimes more productive when the sun has set.

catch them. But day in and day out, small live minnows about 1½ inches long are the most deadly. Use very small, light No. 10 or 12 hooks onto which the minnows are impaled through the lower jaw. Sometimes it helps to gently jig the minnows; other times it makes no difference.

Only a small hole in the ice is necessary, except when a device peculiar to perch and walleye anglers known as a spreader is used. This is a U-shaped section of spring wire with a swivel in the middle and loops on the ends. It permits fishing two baits at once by tying 12- to 18-inch dropper lines onto the outer loops.

The main fishing line is tied to the swivel and the whole works is lowered through the hole in the ice. Most experts use a small, light bobber to suspend the bait just free of the bottom. When the perch are actively striking, the spreader permits catching them at a wholesale rate.

Often when fishing for perch from a shanty, no rod and reel are used at all. The line is simply tied to the inside of the shanty roof directly over the ice hole. The fisherman then is free to jig with an idle hand, to stoke the small wood stove, eat a sandwich or even to read his latest copy of *Outdoor Life*. Many anglers also carry along simple cooking gear because yellow perch are easy to fillet and are never more delicious than when fried after only a few moments out of the cold water.

WALLEYES: The perch's heftier cousin, the walleye, is another very willing biter when the water is locked with ice. Like the perch, this species is a school fish and you seldom catch only one. It is less predictable, though, and wanders widely, which means a good deal more prospecting may be necessary before finding a bonanza.

Minnows are the best baits for walleyes and they may be as long as 2½ to 3 inches, fished singly or two on a spreader. A fisherman must always be alert, however, because even the strike of a large walleye on a large minnow can be difficult to detect.

The origin of tip-ups for ice fishing is unknown, or at least is obscure, but the clever devices (which replace rod and reel) are made to order for walleyes. These gadgets depend either on balance, leverage and/or springs to signal a biting fish and hopefully to help hook it. The simplest tip-up consists of crossed arms or bars placed over the top of a hole in the ice. When a fish bites it pulls down the end of one arm and flips up a small red flag on the other. You then handline your fish onto the ice.

NORTHERN PIKE and PICKEREL: Both of these closely related species can be taken in the same manner described for walleyes—and, in fact, a good many pike are caught by anglers when fishing for walleyes, and vice versa. But in most lakes pike and pickerel spend the winters in shallower water and that is the place to look for them. Live minnows are the best baits, but they must be hooked very

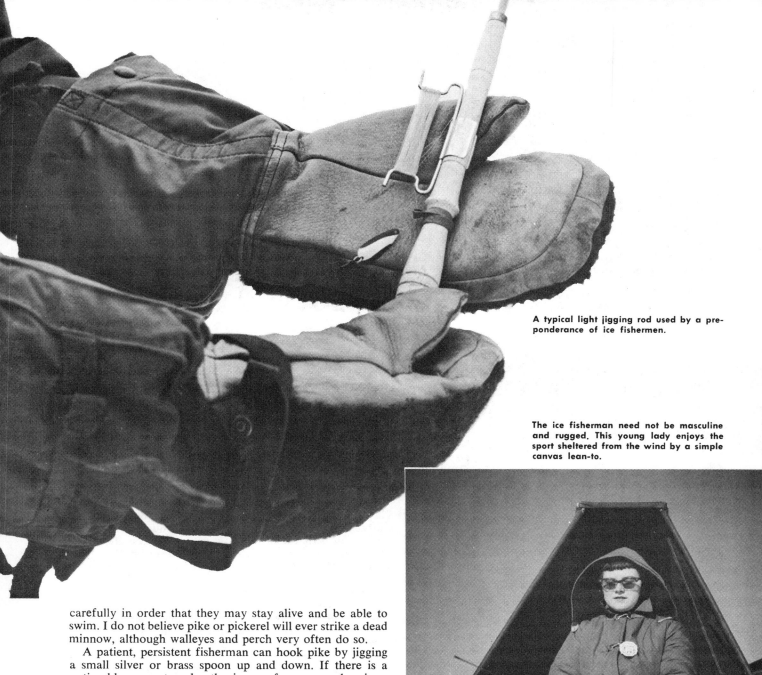

A typical light jigging rod used by a preponderance of ice fishermen.

The ice fisherman need not be masculine and rugged. This young lady enjoys the sport sheltered from the wind by a simple canvas lean-to.

carefully in order that they may stay alive and be able to swim. I do not believe pike or pickerel will ever strike a dead minnow, although walleyes and perch very often do so.

A patient, persistent fisherman can hook pike by jigging a small silver or brass spoon up and down. If there is a noticeable current under the ice, as from a nearby river, the velocity of the current itself may be enough to flash the spoon and attract pike. One technique is to offer a live minnow near such a flashing spoon.

The most successful pike fisherman I ever knew employed an unusual method to catch many fish, including some jumbos, every winter. Just before freeze-up, he would sink several bales of hay in a bay known to harbor pike. The hay gradually decomposed and formed small organisms which attracted large numbers of minnows. The feeding minnows in turn attracted pike. Often the same result can be obtained by baiting an area beneath a fishing hole with cornmeal or with finely ground grubs (the same used for bluegill baits) or meat mixed with sand for bulk.

A heavier monofilament line should be used for pike than for other species, although 4- to 6-pound test is good enough in pickerel waters. In most pike waters, 8-pound test is sufficient. Stronger line would be necessary only in places which regularly produce fish heavier than ten pounds. For pike the hole in the ice should be 15 to 18 inches in diameter and smaller than that for pickerel.

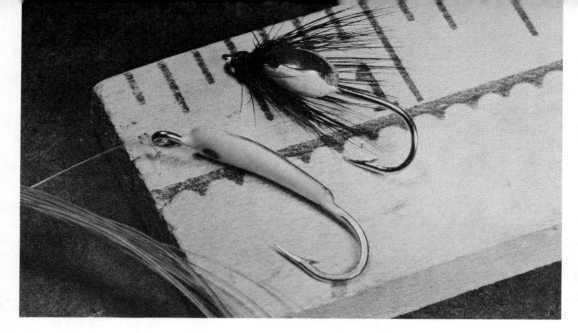

Ice jigs such as these can prove irrestible to many winter nibblers.

Many fishermen prefer aluminum shanties such as this to ward off icy blasts.

An ice sled especially equipped to carry necessary gear.

At times in scattered places, spearing pike through the ice is legal. For this the area beneath a hole is baited or a live decoy fish (sucker or perch) is allowed to swim on a free line. When a pike comes to investigate, it is impaled from above with a heavy iron gig. The spearer must wait in a darkened shanty or shelter; otherwise it is difficult to spot fish far under the surface.

OTHER SPECIES: Almost all fish can be taken at least occasionally through the ice. That even includes bass which, although very sluggish when water temperatures are near freezing, are occasionally hooked by bluegill fishermen.

Both lake trout and rainbows are willing strikers in winter when they are not in especially deep water. Fishing is generally done from shanties and by methods similar to fishing for walleyes. Live minnows account for the most trout, but perhaps only because more anglers prefer to use them than to jig with a spoon or leadhead jig. Of all fish caught under the ice, lakers are the most likely to strike artificials.

Often crappies can be taken in the same places where they are concentrated in early spring. Use very delicate tackle with 1- or 2-pound test line around brushpiles, docks, pilings and breakwaters. Small live minnows are best, but crappies also will nibble (and nibble is the correct word) on earthworms and grubs.

Because they often run very large, carp can furnish plenty of sport for the ice fishermen. A few are caught accidentally when fishing for other species. But at times they can be spotted under thin ice in shallow water and then is a good time to try doughball, cheese or marshmallow baits on very small hooks. More action still is possible by cutting a fairly large hole, say 20 to 24 inches, and waiting there to spear, snag or gaff carp as they pass. The fish can actually be driven by other anglers tromping on the ice or thumping the crust with poles.

In the Great Lakes region, lawyers or burbots can be caught with minnows fished in deep water. Smelt, which also strike minnows, range in large schools at mid-depths and these are especially easy to spot with an electronic locator. From time to time there are short spearing seasons on sturgeon particularly in Wisconsin, and this is any angler's opportunity to horse a really big fish through the ice.

Ice fishing may lack much of the high adventure and excitement of summertime angling, but it has a fascination of its own and can be the best way of all to pass an otherwise gloomy, bitterly cold winter weekend.

MINI-LURE MAGIC

by AL EASON

AS A WHOLE, most professional fishing guides are as cantankerous as mean old mothers-in-law. Not only are they martinets in the boat, demanding exact compliance of their clients, but like the comic strip character, Bull Moose, in their own opinion can do no wrong. This latter is a delusion shared by most guides—but few clients—and leads to an egotistical evaluation of the guide's own prowess at finding and catching fish.

While a certain amount of this ego is absolutely necessary to the guide's profession (what man would take fishermen out for pay if he didn't believe he was at least twice the fisherman as any client he was apt to encounter?), it also leads to a certain narrow-minded certitude which precludes use of any fishing technique suggested by the client. Ninety-nine times out of a hundred the guide has good reasons for rejecting a client's suggestions because he knows the water, fish behavior at various seasons, and the unique fishing requirements of the place where he guides. But there's always the joker . . . that *one* particular time when a client's suggestion can revolutionize fishing methods on an entire lake. Yes, it *can* happen. That's how the guides of Toledo Bend Lake in Texas learned of mini-lure fishing.

To be honest, this writer must include himself in that category of cranky old guides who over the years have developed rigid patterns for taking fish. Although it doesn't take us all day to look at a hot horseshoe if the evidence is convincing enough, old habits and old fishing methods are given up rather grudgingly. As an example, it was over 3 years after Nick Creme introduced the plastic worm before we would use it. (Any idiot should know the damned thing wouldn't catch bass!)

And so with the mini-lures. Prior to the enlightenment, tiny lures and the ultra-light gear required to throw them was "Mickey Mouse stuff" . . . interesting for children playing in small ponds, but still . . . toys. This was the attitude of professional bass guides on Toledo Bend, an impoundment noted for brushy bottoms and brawling bass.

And then came the awakening!

An inkling of the things to come made itself evident one crisp February day 2 years ago. More new ideas come in the depths of desperation than on the summit of euphoria, and certainly on this day we were desperate. Sure we knew the crappies were there, blanketing a sandbar off the end of an island, for hadn't they been tapping our plastic worms with frustrating regularity? But how to catch them? . . . that was the question. A little bitty girl named Tina innocently supplied the answer.

Tina has bouncing black curls, a slow, shy grin and a

← Crappie like this are suckers for the mini-lures.

Author with a string of Toledo bass.

Ken Sawyer, one of the many Toledo Bend guides who fell for the magic of the little lures.

mind of her own. At 12 the first stirrings of teen-age rebellion were becoming evident: she enjoyed disregarding elders. So Tina had tied a small "Tailgator" onto her line when I suggested that she and her father use plastic worms. Because action was slow and without a valid argument for using the worm, I ignored her selection. If my arm was twisted enough, I'd be forced to admit I've done a lot of smart things during the 15 or more years I've been a guide, but keeping my mouth shut on this occasion was one of the smartest.

To put it bluntly . . . little Tina tore us plumb up!

As is usual, the action came at the very nadir of any morning's fishing. Frustrated because the fish wouldn't hit, Tina in true female fashion, began tapping an ever increasing cadence on the bottom of the boat with her foot. Trying to divert her, her father called attention to a couple of ducks which came whistling over our fishing spot.

"Look, Tina," he called, "Look at the wood ducks. Aren't they pretty?"

Distracted, Tina allowed her lure to sink. She was barely turning the reel handle.

At this instant she had a strike. And at the same moment the riddle was solved because I'd been watching Tina's rod instead of the ducks, and I'd seen something . . . something which was to prove the answer to the usual lull in fishing at this time of the year.

Hastily I changed to a replica of the lure Tina was using. Shaking with anticipation and hope, I flipped the little lure far out over the submerged bar. Now, to duplicate her exact motions at the moment the fish struck . . . allow the lure to sink for a slow count of 10 . . . now, without moving the rod at all begin the retrieve in agonizingly s-l-o-w, s-l-o-w motion. Then—but the "then" never came. There was a tiny, half-felt tap on the other end of the line. I set the hook. The riddle was solved. Using the slow-reeling method (remember, the rod isn't moved at all—not even the slightest twitch) we eventually came in with a mixed string of *81 crappie and bass.*

Once the proper method of using the small lure was discovered, we made good catches well into the month of May. Later experiments showed bass and crappies would also take other small lures nearly as well as the "Tailgator." All, however, demanded the slow motion retrieve for best results.

Early the next spring, (crappies and bass begin the usual movement to shallow water spawning grounds in this section of East Texas as early as mid-February) the situation of the past year was repeated. And then came a howling cold front and the sudden change in fish location and behavior. Thanks to the guide's best "stool pigeons"—the gulls—we soon located a large concentration of bass in deep water.

Happiness is a battling bass on ultra-light.

This one fell for a little ⅛-ounce white jig.

While this concentration was immense—the fish would often break water over an area of ½-acre or more in pursuit of shad—these fish had chosen a wooded area where fishing was extremely difficult. Spoons worked along the edges of the half-submerged trees proved effective, but most of the time the greatest fish activity was in the denser brush. But on a continuous feeding binge, these fish refused a topwater lure of any kind. To throw a sub-surface lure of the type most commonly used on Toledo Bend was to risk an immediate hangup in the underwater brush. Fish by the thousands, but how to catch them?

Again the answer was mini-lures, but to the great fraternity of fishing guides on Toledo, this was far from obvious. Even when word of our success using small lures the previous spring got around, most guides still wouldn't accept it. When one particular character up the lake finally began using ultra-light equipment to throw a tiny, ⅛-ounce marabou jig, the egg really hit the fan.

"You wind up with about as many crappie as bass in the box when fishing the light stuff," another guide complained, "and I'm not about to get a reputation as a crappie guide." As if to emphasize the statement, he spat after enunciating the last two words.

"I won't use it!" another declared flatly. "I'd just as soon be found naked in a barrelhouse by my blackmailing brother-in-law as to be caught with that Mickey Mouse

A 6-pound line demands use of the net.

stuff in my boat."

Brave words, but within less than a month, both were on the phone trying to locate an ultra-light rod and reel plus a good supply of marabou jigs. Competition—especially competition that's coming in each night with a limit of fish—will do that to you.

The experience with the mini-lures the previous year had alerted me to the potential of using small lures, but use of the ultra-light rod and light line was a cat of a different color. All the lures previously mentioned in the mini-lure category were heavy enough to throw with the heavy bait casting gear which is standard on Toledo, and, by substituting 15- or 17-pound test line for the usual 20, could be cast respectable distances. Not so with the ⅛-ounce jig. Because of their extreme light weight they *demanded* use of ultra-light rods, small spinning or spin-cast reels, and line of not over 8-pound test. Considering the dense underwater brush and fighting ability of the local bass, this tackle seemed nothing less than ridiculous.

So naturally I balked at switching over. Probably not so much at the idea of using light tackle, but surely at the source of information on how well anglers were doing with the small jigs.

Then the "message" came from no other source than Mike Carmichael, ex-guide and proud owner of Carmichael's Marina, near Hemphill, Texas.

"You boys," Mike said in a fatherly tone, addressing his motley crew of guides, "had better get with it. Guides up the lake have been limiting every day with those little jigs."

Now, there are certain things even a dumb fisherman learns after spending most of his life around fishing camps and marinas. Sadly, most are learned by slow disillusionment rather than example, but once learned are never forgotten. First and foremost of these is that a marina owner is the worst possible source of fishing information. Not only does he rely entirely upon word of mouth reports from another highly unreliable source—fishermen—but he also is swayed by his own economic well-being. As a result, some marina owners have been known to prevaricate . . . outright lie, that is . . . when telling how many fish are being caught out of their particular marina. Ol' Carmichael is no exception. I've known him too long . . . and too well.

Al Eason didn't get off the last load of watermelons that came to town . . . Old Al had been in the racket too long to be taken in by "marina talk" . . . yes this boy would keep on doing exactly as he had been doing. And he did; that is he did until the next night when Cashman, another guide at Carmichael's, came in with a limit of bass and crappies.

That was the time of the second enlightenment, for this sojourner and stranger in the never-never land of ultra-light, my favorite guide Al Eason, had exactly six fish for the entire day of fishing.

To say I spent half the night digging around in my cluttered trailer trying to find an ultra-light rig some misguided soul sent me in past years, would be nothing less than simple truth. The next morning I left my pride at the door and laid my money on the counter. Giving me the victory grin I expected, Mike slid the cursed jigs across the counter. He didn't say anything. He didn't need to. But if Cashman hadn't been lying *too*, maybe it would be worth all the trouble.

The test came less than a quarter of a mile from the marina. On previous days, I'd managed to scrape up a bass or two off the points of an island using plastic worms. Hopefully, I again cast the worm, relying on my clients and their ultra-light rigs to keep me informed as to what the fish preferred.

The information wasn't long in coming. Jim's little 10-year-old, freckle-faced daughter had a fish on within sec-

Author with catch of bass made on mini-lures.

On rare occasions one of Toledo's salt water stripers are taken on the little lures.

Ultra-light and a brawling bass . . . a winning combination.

These are the big guns in the mini-lure fisherman's arsenal. The ⅛-ounce marabou jig, shown third from left, is a pure killer.

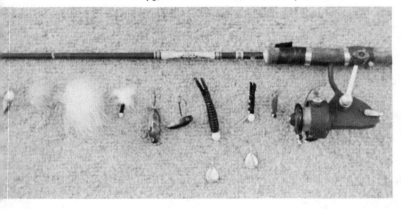

A mixed string of crappie and bass taken on the "Tailgater." Note orthodox casting rigs used to throw the little lures.

onds after we pulled onto the underwater bar. I'd no more than slipped the net under her fish, than another fish struck Jim's little black jig. And thus it went for over half an hour . . . me busy with the net and them pulling in the fish.

The catch that morning was nearly evenly matched between bass of from 1 to 2½ pounds and crappie of equal size. It seemed to make little difference whether color of the jig was black or white; required only was the simplest manipulation of the tiny lures. After getting a good catch in the live-well we experimented with all types of the larger lures commonly used for bass, but did not have a single bump. Then a return to the little jigs produced instant action.

The mini-lures seemed to have a special kind of fish-taking magic. It was unbelievable they would produce fish after fish from waters which failed to even provide a single strike on lures which usually caught fish on Toledo Bend lake, but there was no denying the results. Keeping only in the near vicinity of the island, we had a catch of 34 bass and crappies by noon.

Learning to fish with the light rigs and small lures brought first success and then confidence. To begin, a 3-pound bass was enough for excitement and shouts for the net, but a week or so later after we'd located good bass in a deep water bend of a submerged creek, we were hauling in bass up to 5 pounds without undue carrying on. The secret was in correct setting of the drag, plus patience to let the little wand of fiberglass do its work.

Sure we lost a few fish to underwater brush, but not nearly so many as had been feared. Usually, working the boat directly over a fouled fish and giving a bit of slack line was all that was needed for the fish to free itself. Snagged lures were freed by clamping a heavy clinch sinker lightly on the line and allowing it to slide down to the fouled lure. If the first bump of the sinker didn't do it, a bit of jiggling of the rod tip would. The little lures continued their deadly work well into early summer.

Although most strikes occurred when the rod was twitched with a quick, sharp movement of the wrist, and the lure allowed to sink momentarily before twitching the rod again, fish would hit the jigs on any type of retrieve. If fish were feeding well, both bass and crappie took the lure with a rather sharp tap. At other times, the only signal coming up the line would be a slight tightening of the line. Either occasion was the cue for immediate setting of the hook.

The little magic lure took fish in all types of water. Prime spots were the aforementioned bars and points, but we soon found the jigs were just as effective in deep water where fish were suspended. The ⅛-ounce jig produced untold thousands of fish from the large concentration mentioned earlier and proved to be a near perfect lure for working the dense underwater brush. Because of its slow sinking qualities, fish would take the free sinking lure *before* it hung in underwater brush.

There was a time on Toledo Bend when "ultra-light" was a dirty word and some guides refused to take out a party with such tackle. Even mention of taking good fish on such rigs elicited the same reaction one could expect from telling a Southern Baptist "God is dead", and resulted in nothing but pure pity and scornful looks. Today, the little rigs and lures have worked their magic on both fish and fisherman. During springtime no self-respecting guide would be caught *without* at least one ultra-light rig in his boat. From "Mickey Mouse" to a professional tool of recognized worth is a giant step, but the little fishing rig made it.

Such is the powerful magic of the mini-lures . . . the true light has at last come to Dixie.

Casting in Parismina River which winds through lush jungle of Costa Rica lowlands.

to COSTA RICA FOR TARPON

**FISHERMEN'S DIGEST
Interviews Globe-Trotting
Angler Dick Kotis About
His Greatest Fishing Trip**

FISHERMEN'S DIGEST: Where exactly did you go?

KOTIS: Costa Rica. The name of the camp there is the Parismina Tarpon Rancho located at the mouth of the Parismina River on the Atlantic coast. We flew to San Jose, the capital, from Miami. You can also fly there from New Orleans. Either way it makes a very easy 2½ hour trip. You fly first to Grand Cayman and then on to Costa Rica where you are picked up in Cessna 180s and flown across the mountains to land on the beach at the mouth of the Parismina River. Here is a small native fishing village and the Rancho.

F.D.: Why Costa Rica and why this remote spot?

KOTIS: We selected this particular camp because of the known abundance of tarpon. They apparently school here before migrating north when the water starts to warm up.

Editor Erwin Bauer suggested that we try this particular area because the fish come into fresh water streams which are very easy to fish. Tarpon also congregate in the ocean nearby and you do not have to go far in any direction to find action. The calm easy water is ideal for plug casting or any kind of light saltwater fishing equipment.

F.D.: Tell us about your party. What gear did you take?

KOTIS: Eight of us made the trip. Two were interested in fishing with fly rods only, one being Leon Martuch of

The wild ballet of a tarpon on the surface is one of the most ➤
exciting spectacles in the angler's world.

Kotis, left, carried plenty of tackle for the Costa Rica expedition. He needed it.

Scientific Anglers. I was interested primarily in plug casting. The others were friends of mine who live in the Kent-Akron (Ohio) area and who make frequent fishing trips with me. The type of tackle doesn't make too much difference to them.

Our equipment consisted of a variety of bait casting and heavy spinning equipment. We used Ambassadeur 6000 reels with 15- and 20-pound test monofilament line. Our spinning rods also contained 15- and 20-pound test line. Most of our plugs were on the large or heavy side—½ - to ¾ - ounce—such as the Hammerhead, Saint, Hula jig and Wiggle Diver.

We were very careful to take all of the equipment possible from home because the camp has little fishing tackle available. I personally like to use familiar light equipment because its much more challenging to catch big tarpon that way.

One other reason we selected the Tarpon Rancho is that we knew that we could do fly casting there. At that time (1970) Leon Martuch was doing experimental testing with special heavy saltwater fly lines and glass-filled rods to see whether they would hold up under extreme pressure. We found that this experiment worked very well.

F.D.: What about the fish? Were they big?

KOTIS: The tarpon in this area run anywhere from 30 to 80 or even 90 pounds. You do not find the few big, monstrous tarpon that you do in the Florida Keys, say the 130 or 180 pounders, but you do find 50- and 60-pound fish in incredible numbers. In fact I have never seen such a heavy concentration of fish and they are very easy to catch. You are fishing in relatively shallow or protected waters and the tarpon pick up lures very well. The lush background is excellent for photography because these big silver fish come up out of the water and the dark green jungle makes for great contrast. Between casts you can see an abundance of very colorful birds and bands of howler monkeys. That is unlike tarpon fishing in other areas of the world.

Our typical fishing day would be as follows: get up at 6:30 or 7:00 in the morning and fish from 7:30 until about 10 or 10:30. Then it gets very hot. Rest during the afternoon and go out again at 3:00 or 4:00 in the afternoon. Frankly, 3 or 4 hours of fishing for big tarpon is about all anyone or his equipment can stand. Use that 3 or 4 hour break during mid-day to put new line on reels, tie more leaders and do all the other repairs necessary. There are so many tarpon and the action so fast that all keep several outfits ready to go. When one breaks down, just pick up a replacement.

F.D.: Was the action all you expected?

Leon Martuch handles high-jumping tarpon on fly rod in Parismina R.
Kotis stands by with gaff.

KOTIS: You bet—and even greater. We had so many experiences where one fish would throw the lure, the lure would hit the water and another fish would pick it up. Quite often you would get four or five hits on one retrieve. Of course you only brought to the boat a fraction of the fish hooked. So it worked out very well.

And the tarpon were schooled up. I was really surprised about that. Besides the river, we managed to fish in the open ocean two different days, which is very unusual because of rough water. But the ocean was so calm that we fished out of Boston Whalers—14-foot boats with 20 horsepower motors. Out there in the Atlantic I didn't know there were that many tarpon in the world. Tremendous concentrations of them. The schools would be anywhere from ¾ to 1 mile long and maybe 250 to 300 yards across. We cast out to them and when the lure would hit the water one fish would rise to it and another would be fighting for it. This was going on constantly. As I mentioned, the big problem was trying to keep ourselves in operative equipment because the fish tore up equipment so fast and we lost so much line.

F.D.: That's hard an tackle, isn't it?

KOTIS: I took maybe 12 rods with me and split those up between two men. A number of times I had to quit fishing in the mornings because all the line was gone from the rods. In one week we ran out of all our 20-pound test line—about 2500 yards altogether. That gives you some idea of the action.

One other thing was peculiar about Costa Rican tarpon and I can't explain it. These fish seemed to be much more active than the fish I've caught in Florida. They jump more and seem to fight harder. In my estimation it's more fun to catch a 50- or 60-pound tarpon that jumps 12 times than it is to catch a 120- or 130-pounder that jumps once or twice if at all.

Kotis tied into a 60-pounder on plug casting tackle.
Tip of rod has been snapped.

A 50-pound fish was about our Costa Rica average. It was spectacular to be fishing for these tarpon the way you fish for snook or even largemouth bass in Florida rivers. In other words, you are always casting the shoreline or to rolling fish. Our biggest tarpon was an 80-pounder.

F.D.: But was the spot really as wild as you say *all* the time?

KOTIS: One of the things we discovered about the second or third day was that all these fish come into fresh water apparently at the change of the tide. You could stay at the mouth of the river, which was maybe 50 or 60 yards across, and just catch one fish after the other while they were migrating in and out of that fresh water. You couldn't believe the numbers of them that were moving in and out of there. If I had to make a rough guess I would guess that we would see anywhere from 5,000 to 10,000 fish a day coming in out of the river. It was just constant.

One thing you also see is the daisy-chaining which is so typical of tarpon and this may be a spawning ritual. They seem to swim in circles like a conga line. I don't understand it, and I don't know if icthyologists do, but I've seen tremendous schools of fish, maybe 200, daisy-chaining and just jumping out of the water in a big circle. That's mighty exciting to watch.

F.D.: Can FISHERMEN'S DIGEST readers get in on this kind of fishing in Costa Rica?

KOTIS: The camp handles only 12 people at a time, which means six boats are available. There is only one camp on the entire river, the fishable part of which is 12 to 15 miles long. So you have only limited fishing pressure. I don't remember anytime that the fishing was slow. We were there in the springtime—in April. Later they do have a very rainy season and then the action declines because of the influx of too much fresh water. The most ideal time to go

These surface plugs took tarpon consistently in the Parismina River.

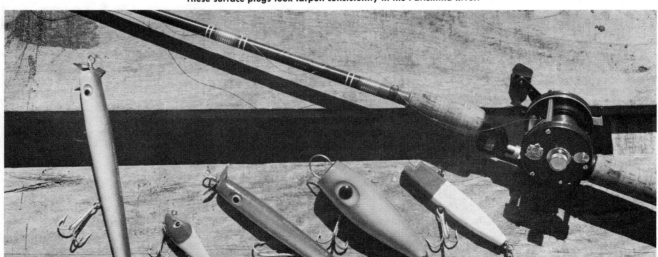

Villagers of Parismina serve as tarpon guides. They are good boat handlers.

Webb Morris of Kent, Ohio, plays leaping tarpon in ocean at mouth of Parismina River.

Kotis with typical tarpon taken near Parismina Tarpon Rancho. Few fish were killed; nearly all were released unharmed.

for tarpon would be Christmas through about April; later on is taking a chance. I understand fall is ideal for snook fishing; large snook exist in the same river.

F.D.: What about guides? Are they experienced?

KOTIS: All the guides you use are local people who live right in the little town of Parismina. They are good boatmen, familiar with tarpon habits and, by now, also with the habits of visiting anglers. English isn't well spoken.

F.D.: Can you give us more details about those central American tarpon?

KOTIS: As you know they have very hard, bony mouths. When fishing with treble hook lures, it's not unusual for them to flatten out the hooks and escape. These particular fish hit two types of lures very well. They hit surface lures and that was the most spectacular. At the other extreme they hit lures such as the 1-ounce Hula jig, that were retrieved deep and very, very slowly. Those tarpon must feed mostly on shrimp or crabs right on the bottom. A yellow or white Hula jig with a big rubber skirt (and with a single hook) was more reliable than a plug treble hook.

I mentioned that our guides were natives, young boys mostly. They are very small, not very strong but they do not have to be. All they really do is run the boat to where the fish are schooled, or near where they *think* fish are schooled, and with a skulling paddle keep you in position

to cast. They are afraid of sharks and assorted other things which amazed me. When I prepared to hand-gaff a tarpon, for example, our boatman was very concerned about wrapping the rope around my wrist. He worried about the fish pulling me overboard where sharks would be lurking. But all the time there I didn't see any sharks. Maybe over the years they have lost friends swimming and as a result are very concerned about everything. But their biggest fear is the sharks.

One day we were coming down the river and saw a herd of pigs—peccaries, really—swimming across the river. In that area red fresh meat is very scarce because of the lack of refrigeration and electricity. As a result the guide became most excited and wanted to "catch" some of them. So he simply hand-gaffed two while in the water, wrestled both into the boat, killed them, and that night a tremendous feast was enjoyed by all.

F.D.: Tarpon aren't considered edible. Did you catch anything to eat on Parismina?

KOTIS: Yes, we ate a number of different fish. One of the fish we caught was a guapote and another was a mojarra. The latter looks like a very large, colorful bluegill. Guapotes resemble a large heavy bass. Both of those were excellent eating. With the fish we enjoyed plenty of papaya, plantain and also fresh pineapple which is grown right there. I might tell you that we tried to eat tarpon one night. Even though marinated to eliminate some of the strong fish taste and then broiled, it wasn't very edible. I've heard people say they have eaten tarpon, but it's not the type of fish I want to eat if something else is available.

If you go to Florida nowadays you may catch one or two tarpon a day and, if lucky, you may have five or six hooked. In Costa Rica we had 50 to 75 on and caught 10 or 12 or 15 a day. This was pretty remarkable. All were released alive, of course, other than the one or two that we decided to try and eat. One day the guide asked us if we would catch one fish for him and his family so apparently the native people do eat the fish.

The weather in coastal Costa Rica is in the high 80s and humid during the middle of the day. That's why we fished only early and late. When you fish for tarpon here it is hard work. Once you hook a fish, it can be sweaty business for the next half-hour or so, unless you have heavy tackle.

If I were making the same trip again, I would suggest loose fitting clothing such as a fishing jump suit (See "Great New Fashion for Fishermen," elsewhere in this book) that is very thin, airy, and loose on your body. Make sure that you have enough sun tan lotion. We had absolutely no problems at all with mosquitoes, although we slept in open cabins.

All you need to enter Costa Rica is a valid passport or a tourist permit. Lacsa Airlines, which is the national carrier of Costa Rica, leaves Miami every other day early in the morning and it is a short pleasant trip.

One of the things we have always worried about in central America is water and food quality. No problems exist at the Tarpon Rancho which is owned by one Carlos Barrantes. The food is excellent; and accommodations are clean and neat. You have showers and individual bedrooms. It is by no means luxurious, but is certainly adequate for any outdoorsmen who are just interested in the greatest fishing. Summed up, this was by far the best tarpon fishing experience I have ever had, both in the number of fish and the crazy way they struck lures. We didn't have to resort to any unusual techniques. Anyone who can cast could catch—or at least hook—fish there.

Until something better comes along, it was the greatest fishing trip of all—and I've had my share of good ones.

RX for dog days—
Go after the big cats
by TROTLINE FISHING

Trotline spread across Wills Creek in eastern Ohio produces a large flathead catfish. That's the late Andy Repasky handling the oars.

by KEN BOURBON

THERE IS A RIVER—a creek, rather—where summer seems to arrive very early and then lingers long after the shore-line sycamores shed their rusty leaves. I say summer because the creek warms long before other waters in the region. Perhaps that's because, after the early spring floods, it meanders slowly, sluggishly for 50 miles or so between a maze of bottomland cornfields to a meeting with the Ohio River. It's Sunfish Creek, where fishing the way grandpa used to do it is still the best way to do it. And the best way is by trotlining.

Alvin Hawkins and I used to rush the season. We had the legal limits of trotlines strung across the river below the mouth of Elkins Creek before the dogwood blossoms had dissolved with the cold winds of a dogwood winter. We caught a few fish, too, usually buffaloes, but it was only

a token catch—as promise of what was to come. Trotlining is a pastime of summer—of dog days, really—and to rush the season is to miss the real pleasure of a kind of fishing as old as Ike Walton himself.

When summer suddenly arrived, Sunfish Creek settled well within its banks along which cane, field corn, and tobacco grew green and high. Alvin cultivated his corn once to give it equal chance with the horseweeds, gathered a vast supply of bait, and then dropped by the house to announce that the season was on. What season? I always asked.

"Trotline," he would answer. "What else is there—'cept squirrel?"

We'd move a great array of edibles and potables into a camp about half way between Waterloo and Arabia. Then we would launch Alvin's ancient johnboat, an angular,

Catches like this sometimes come to trotliners in Muskingum Lakes region of eastern Ohio. All fish here run over 40 pounds.

square-ended job, and begin prospecting. As junior member of the team, it was my job to row while my partner surveyed every likely spot. It was an interesting ritual in a way, but we usually wound up placing our lines in the same spots we'd placed them for several seasons before. After all, they were tried and true.

One line was located in the middle of a wide, sweeping bend where the water was the deepest of any place for several hundred yards either upstream or down. It was the jackpot location—the one where we caught the biggest fish, but also the smallest number. It was the place, one day, where we hooked a brute of a shovelhead cat that almost broke my arm before it straightened a No. 2/0 hook and faded back into the murky depths.

We spotted the other line just below a riffle. The water raced for 50 yards, perhaps, and then dropped abruptly into a short pool, undercutting the bank on one side. It was our camp meat line, the one that was a consistent producer, although the fish were small. On one eventful weekend, it accounted for enough channel cats, fiddlers (young channel catfish), and bullheads to feed hungry members of the local fish and game club. A greater number of more prodigious appetites never existed.

Once the lines were in—anchored firmly on both ends and labeled with a waterproof tag as Ohio law requires— we returned to put our camp in shape. Erecting the tent and camp cots came first. Then while I cut a supply of firewood, Alvin fashioned an oven from rocks gathered on the spot and a table from green willows. Next came a rack between nearby trees to hang the pots, pans and other utensils we'd carried along. Only after that would Alvin settle down to relax—and then only until dusk. It was time to bait up.

Bait could be a multitude of things, depending on season, availability, and my companion's mood. Dogmatic in some matters, he had an open mind where baiting trotlines was concerned. Crayfish were best early in the season, possibly because they were easiest to obtain at that time. During mid-summer, Alvin seemed to favor chicken entrails and such as that. Then in fall, it generally was back to crayfish again. Leeches, lampreys, minnows, carp, liver, and cut baits all came in for innings now and then. I've known trotliners who used prepared baits and blood baits with amazing results, but it was with them that Alvin drew the line. He never bothered to explain it any farther than to say, "Ain't natchrul."

A trotline, essentially, is a heavy, high-quality, white cotton line, or rope that is stretched between two points across a stream. At intervals often limited or prescribed by state law are droppers—short lengths of lighter line— tied to the main line. Hooks are tied to outer ends of the droppers. The main line should be stout, perhaps testing from 60 to 100 pounds or more, depending on the length of it and the speed of the current.

The droppers can be cut in less than 2-foot lengths from white cotton line or seine twine. Twenty-pound test will hold most fish nowadays, but more optimistic trotliners use much heavier stock; it's better to be safe than sorry, they probably figure. Ready-made trotlines are available on tackle shelves, but most fans prefer to make their own to suit local conditions.

There are several ways to attach droppers to the main line, which is much easier to store and to place in the river without droppers attached. There are snap and ring sets, for example, that can be fastened in place when the trotline is baited and which can be unsnapped when running the lines for fish. It saves time and trouble all around. But most old-timers have a better way. Many of them bait their dropper lines on shore and fasten them to the main-line with a single bow knot (sometimes called a half-bow) that is easy to open, but which will never pull free no matter how powerful a fish is hooked. Just wrap the dropper line across the main line, make a loop, and pull it back through the warp. Tighten with thumb and forefinger against the knot while you pull on the dropper. To free the dropper, merely pull out the loop.

Weights are necessary in some places to keep the line and the baits down near the bottom. Lead sinkers are available or can be made easily in home workshops for the purpose. It's also a simple trick to imbed a U-shaped wire into a plastic jug filled with fresh concrete. When the concrete hardens, break the plastic away from it and you have a weight that's hard to beat. Experience alone will reveal how much weight to use in various situations.

There are almost as many theories on hook styles and hook sizes as there are trotliners. Perhaps a consensus would agree that Viking, Kirby, Eagle Claw and O'Shaughnessy just about cover the best styles to use. O'Shaughnessy hooks are made from the heaviest stock. Long shanks are usually desirable because they make removing hooks from smaller fish a less tedious chore. The size of the hook pretty much depends on the type of water and the size of fish you'll likely find there; 1/0 and 2/0 are old standards with the river men, but larger sizes (up to 4/0) will be in use where the real jumbo cats are fairly common.

Trotlines should always be anchored at both ends to keep from ending up with a hopeless tangle, and in some regions, to comply with the state law. Trees, bridge abutments, and permanent holds make the best anchors. Lines should never

Dale Yoho, who holds Ohio record for flathead catfish and is now the state's champion catfisherman, holds a 50-pounder from Piedmont Lake.

be stretched taut; rather, the main line should have a definite bow. A bowed line will allow placement of extra droppers—and extra opportunities to hook fish. Slanting a line across stream will also give more space for droppers, but it will also encourage twisting if the slant is too great. A little experience will show just how far you can go with this.

You'll catch fish on trotlines in daylight occasionally, especially early in the season. But night, of course, is best —just as the summer months and the lazily meandering rivers are best. And among nights, those mellow, misty ones are the occasions when catfish and carp develop restless streaks and start cruising to find the baits you've carefully strung across the current.

Over in the Muskingum Lakes region of eastern Ohio, where a man is known and respected by his artistry with

Catfish expert Dale Yoho uses large live carp to bait the big shovelheads.

a trotline, activity around the boat dock becomes down-right feverish after a midsummer storm or shower brings a rise in the river, no matter how slight. Such occasions stirred old pros like the late Andy Repasky—he didn't need much stirring, though—into baiting the lines he kept on the job nearly all summer long. And Repasky knew what was best; a few years ago, in a season that most veterans rated as "slow," he collected 27 shovelheads and channel cats between 9 and 32 pounds each. He never kept any of the hundreds of smaller ones.

Repasky's top trophy was a 52-pounder, a real "bar-room-betting" fish, since Wills Creek isn't "big" water as the top-notch trotline rivers generally run.

I've never been around when a 52-pounder, or anything like it, was hauled aboard. But let me tell you about a memorable experience back on Sunfish Creek with my trotlining mentor. If you ever pass down that way and cross the creek at a slumbering crossroads called Aid, you'll be getting warm. There was a covered bridge in those days just downstream from the present steel structure, and it was a long cast or two below that where we pitched a tent and set up shop.

Dog days had descended in earnest; there was little escape from the heat and humidity until dusk, so we just picked the deepest shade we could find and strung a pair of canvas hammocks there. It was sticky and still; the only sounds were of wandering bumble bees, of the soft trickling current, and rattle of cars occasionally crossing the loose floor-boards on the covered bridge. I dozed.

When I awakened, it was dark and considerably cooler. A pale blue haze had fallen over the valley. Alvin's john-boat was gone, probably to bait the lines which were located just around a bend and not visible from camp. I collected a supply of kindling and soon a fire was crackling in a stone fireplace that another party of fishermen had built long before. Water for tea was boiling when Alvin maneu-vered his boat into the bank and tossed me a line.

"As sure as I vote straight Republican and try to pay my honest debts, this is going to be a night you'll remember," he said.

Then Alvin broke out a couple of frying chickens, anointed a large iron skillet with fat, and placed the works on the fire. Already it was a night to remember.

We ran the lines the first time just before midnight. Alvin fired up a pair of gasoline lanterns and mounted one in each end of the boat. We also stowed a long-handled net, a gaff, and a fresh supply of crayfish aboard and then pushed off downstream into the darkness.

It was remote and peaceful out on the creek. Besides the crickets which alternately chorused and were quiet on both banks, nothing disturbed the stillness except a lonely phoebe and a pair of oarlocks that needed attention. The world was completely black outside the sphere of light from our lanterns. Alvin panned a flashlight along the bank, picked up the beady eyes of a bullfrog in its beam, and just below it the aluminum tag on the first trotline. I swung the boat toward the exposed sycamore roots to which it was anchored.

Talk about tense moments outdoors; it's hard to beat running a trotline at night. This first one was jumping, alternately tightening and falling back in the gentle current. We found one of the reasons on the second hook from the bank. A channel cat of about 5 pounds had wrapped the dropper completely around the main line until he was in fair position to pull free. Alvin made a pass with the net and for a second the brute balanced on the edge of it . . . and fell into the meshes. One for the pot.

The next two or three hooks were bare and then we were really among 'em. The next three hooks had pound-size cats; fact is there were eight altogether on the remainder of the line—plus a 4-foot American eel. We got him un-hooked and in the boat, but that's where our trouble began. The critter's tail brushed across one of the hot gasoline lanterns and he went wild. Both of us were soaking wet, and I picked up a dull splinter in my wrist before we cap-tured the eel and stuffed it into the live box.

The hooks re-baited, we checked our anchor points and pushed on downstream to inspect the second line. For a few moments we had trouble finding the end of it among the debris that had collected along shore, but eventually we spotted the metal tag. The line hung limp; it looked like we had drawn a blank, but we decided to check the hooks for bait anyway.

I swung the boat around where Alvin could pick up the line. He pulled it up and checked several hooks which were undisturbed . . . then suddenly the line was jerked out of his hand.

We had to go to shore again to retrieve the line which now was taut and throbbing. I pushed the boat back to mid-stream and Alvin slowly gained line. Almost in the center of the current, he hoisted a whopping big shovelhead to the surface, caught a bucketful of water squarely in the face, and shouted, "Hand me the gaff, quick!"

I passed him the gaff, but lost an oar in the process. The experience with the eel was mild compared to what hap-pened when Alvin hooked the gaff into the big cat's lower jaw. The fish beat a tatoo on the gunwale while coming aboard and then tried to break the venerable craft apart at the seams from the inside. There was nothing to do but sit on the critter and that's exactly what Alvin did. Fact is, he was still sitting on the fish when we pulled into camp where game warden Johnny Adams was waiting.

Adams' scales were old and rusty, to be sure, so maybe that accounts for the 24 pounds they registered. But just the same he stayed with us in camp until the second check of the line—to see if lightning strikes twice.

Sometimes it does when you're trotlining.

The Arctic char fishing on the George and Korok rivers is as fast as one could expect to find anywhere in the world. But there is a great deal more than fishing in this tree-less land.

UNGAVA:
Land of Char and Eskimo

By Jim C. Chapralis

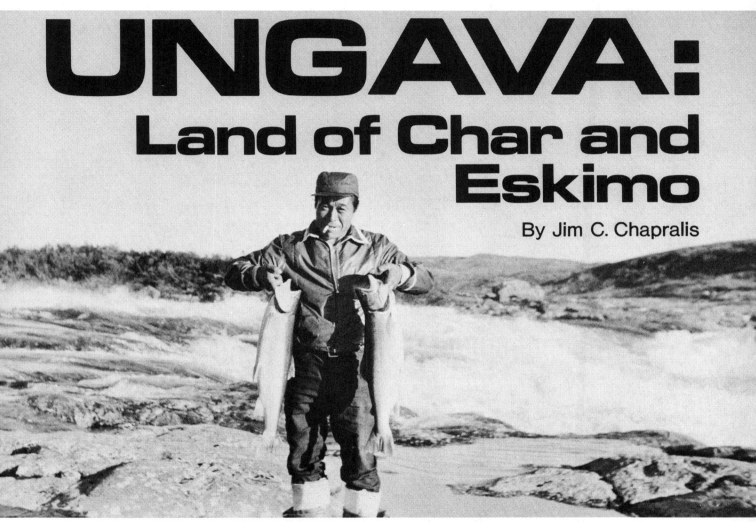

Arctic char in the Ungava Region of Quebec are not as large as some of those taken in the Northwest Territories. But then, there's nothing wrong with this pair . . . taken on light gear.

IT WAS a lonely place. It was a quiet place. I could hear Bev Dean's voice as he hooked another char somewhere downstream, and, yes, the Eskimo guides speaking in hushed tones. The occasional cry of a lonely gull swooping efficiently on some unsuspecting fingerling, and the roar of the mighty Korok River as it tumbled and crashed down the cascading falls.

There was also the constant cacophonic buzz-buzz of gnawing mosquitoes, but somehow all of this seemed to evaporate into nothingness and finally into a vacuum of stillness. At least that's the way I felt on this July morning as I swished a fly rod back and forth, hoping that my casts would methodically explore the huge pool before me and uncover that certain fish that I had seen the day before.

It was a special fish. It was special because it was a big

Arctic char, I am sure over 20 pounds, and for Northern Quebec this represents a good challenge. In this area, char simply do not seem to grow quite this big. Hence the concentration.

I could watch the yellow streamer fly swerving below the surface and finally the fish emerged from the dark deep and hypnotically followed the fly into the backwash of the current before disappearing. Much as he had done yesterday and the day before.

A few more casts over the same glide. He appeared again, this time pursuing the fly faster, and I can still see those jaws opening up, and I'd like to think that the fly was well in the char's mouth, before I quickly set the hook. But when the fly whipped past me, and I did not feel the weight of the fish, I knew I was much too premature with the

257

A switch in battle plan . . . Eskimo guide does the fishing, guest the netting. In this case, guest was tired catching fish . . . so he asked his guide to fish.

strike. I spooked him for good. Sure, I took some casts after that, but it was much too mechanical. The fish would not come up again. It was my last chance.

Now an Eskimo guide came up the trail and motioned that I should follow him. The boats were ready for the return trip to the main camp on the George River. Soon the tide would not be right so we would have to leave. And we did.

The trip to the George River was by no means unsuccessful. In fact it was very productive and certainly one of my most interesting experiences. The place has all the ingredients.

The camp, Ilkalu Lodge, for instance, is located on Ford Island near the mouth of the mammouth George River,

which empties into Ungava Bay, Quebec. You fly to Fort Chimo (by jet, mind you), and then a float plane takes you to the island camp. The George, of course, is one of the finest Atlantic salmon rivers, and several camps upstream offer top-drawer fishing. Ilkalu, however, provides primarily Arctic char fishing as this area has few holding pools for an Atlantic salmon. The salmon just rush right by. Of course it is possible to take salmon here; every week at least some Ilkalu guests are successful. But it is a char place, and I'm convinced the area has the fastest char fishing found anywhere.

But what makes this place interesting is that the camp is owned and operated by Eskimos. Willie Imudluk is the bossman and he started the whole thing with a loan from the

The big pool at the bottom of the Korok River was easy to fish; big slab of rocks formed natural casting platforms.

Canadian Government. Thoughtfully, the government assigned John MacDonald to Ilkalu. John is a very intelligent young man, born in Scotland, who not only assists in the operation but speaks Eskimo fluently. So he is the man you see if you want to find out something that would be too intricate for a round of charades.

Back to the fishing. There were a half-dozen of us fishing that week. Walter "Bev" Dean was my partner, and I remember that on the first afternoon Bev took a total of 30 char. Really it was a period of not more than 2 or 3 hours. I took a char on spinning gear and then switched to a fly rod for most of the remaining time. The first afternoon I took over a dozen char on flies. These char were not big by any means. They probably averaged 3 to 5 pounds, and my best that day was 7 or 8 pounds, but on a fly rod or light spinning gear they are a worthy adversary. Elliott Sproul, who was along on this trip, had several fish over 13 pounds —so there *are* bigger fish.

To be honest, I had never been impressed with the Arctic char, that is before I tried fishing for them on this trip. I had pre-conditioned my mind that if you are going to Eastern Canada you fish for Atlantic salmon, and if you are in the west, you fish steelhead or rainbow trout. But these char of the George can certainly hold their own. They do not always jump, but enough of them made spectacular leaps that I found myself calling them "salmon."

I remember one fish that I hooked at the Korok River which jumped twice and then headed for the bottom of a falls. That char valiantly started swimming *up* the falls, defying any laws of gravity. You have to marvel at a fish that tries the impossible.

One morning on the George we decided to beach our boats and fish from the banks. There was a high, rocky point with a flat rock on top, and from this vantage point I could observe numerous char moving in. The water was clear and not too deep, and with polaroids I could pick out the dark shapes. Casting a fly from this point was an easy matter since this area is above the treeline and one need not be concerned with planting a fly on a tree limb. The wind at times can be wicked, but this was a still morning. From high above I could watch the reactions of fish to various fly patterns, presentations and retrieves. An orange streamer proved very deadly, especially when it was cast upstream, allowed to sink and float freely. When a char showed interest, moving the fly much as though the morsel was trying to escape, nearly always resulted in a strike. Of course, I would have to climb down from my perch to the water's edge to land and release my fish, but in today's complex world you can't have everything.

I must have released a dozen fish or so, when I began using a "Portland Hitch." This is accomplished by tying a half-hitch slightly behind the eye of the fly. By retrieving with the rod tip high, the fly skitters across the surface, leaving a V-like wake behind. The advantage of all this, is that the strike takes place right on the surface. It worked well.

The other guests were primarily using spinning gear with irresistible spinners, small spoons, and the Tee-spoon. Their results were more impressive. Many times I would see four of the six fishermen fighting fish simultaneously. Sometimes all six would have char on.

As a change of pace, Bev Dean and I fished a small lake located on a hill. Our Eskimo guides told us that it contained brook trout and lakers. The first hour of fishing only produced a few small brookies, but later a hatch of mayflies appeared and fishing picked up. Slurp. Slurp. Slurp. All around us. Dry fly time.

I had several strikes right on top with dry flies, and in addition to brook trout, I was amazed to hook and land

Sometimes he would succeed . . . often he failed. This time Willie succeeds at the Steeplechase Run. John MacDonald is holding gleaming char.

lake trout, usually a very deep-water fish for which deep water trolling is usually required. Now, I am not going to say they were "Great Bear Lake" size, but then how often can you take lakers on dry flies?

Heavy brook trout began making their appearance and Bev landed several over 2 pounds on his light spinning gear. I hooked several of the bigger fish but lost them quickly. Now the hatch really was on full blast. But again the guides said it was time to leave; it turned out that the tide was going out and if we delayed we would have trouble getting to our boats. The slurps were increasing. So was the size of the fish inhaling them. Rats!

I should mention that the tides on the George River and Ungava Bay are awesome. They talk about 40-foot tides. I think we were having 20-foot tides.

But for sheer excitement I recall one afternoon on my beloved Korok River. This river is about 2 hours of boat riding from the main camp. Thoughtfully there is a small outpost camp, where one can overnight; comfortable but without frills.

Most of the guests fish at the bottom of the falls which is perfectly safe and easy fishing. Big slabs of rock make ideal casting platforms. There is a stretch where the river groans and roars angrily as white water pours down a steep cascading rapids before emptying over the falls and into the rather placid pool. The whole stretch is several hundred yards.

The one on the left appears doubtful, the one in the center skeptical, but the one on the right has been won over. These Eskimo children were watching author fly cast.

Willie, one of the guides, John MacDonald, and I were walking along these rapids when Willie spotted one, two and then a half-dozen char *under* the white water. I had polaroid glasses on and I could not see a thing. Neither could John, or Noah, another Eskimo guide. Sensing my doubts, Willie asked if he could use a spinning rod, and after studying the water intensely, he pointed out a char, announced its approximate location and cast the lure. I was convinced Willie was putting us on. Apparently he directed the lure right in front of the fish. The rod arched and I said "Bottom." But it was a char.

Willie hooked fish after fish in this white water. After the strike he had to run downstream at full speed, jumping from boulder to boulder, climbing above desk-size rocks, and in general doing a good job of imitating a goat. If everything worked out well, he ended up at the end of the rapids, at the pool, about the same time as the char would. He would land the fish and return for another try at the "steeplechase run." Grinning. Always grinning. Several fish he hooked and lost looked like 15-pounders.

Do I want to hook one on my fly rod, he asked. "Would you like a date with Racquel Welch?" I countered, cleverly I thought, until I realized the name would mean nothing to Willie. But John did his best to describe R. W. It was hilarious.

Willie directed my casts. No, further. Too, far. I was not getting the fly right. He took my fly rod, pointed to a fish and managed a short cast. Then he made another, struck and handed me the rod. The char jumped, I could see that he was at least 10 pounds, and then took off right in the throat of the current. I took off downstream as fast as I cared to go, which was not really fast enough. I came to a huge rock and somehow I did not quite negotiate it as smoothly as Willie. I tried to stop the fish. He was now right in the fast current. No hope. My fly line was well beyond the rod tip and my backing melting fast. Fifty yards . . . 100 . . . 150 yards. PINNG! He broke off the backing at the reel, taking, of course, my trailing fly line with him. Willie laughed. John laughed. So did I. Until I realized that I lost the only sinking fly line I had with me. But we laughed some more anyway.

Because of its location Ilkalu Lodge has a relatively short season, confined to July and August, though sometimes it can be fished in early September. Bookings are only accepted on a weekly basis because of the charter plane costs from Fort Chimo to camp. Ilkalu Lodge is immaculate, the meals are excellent, and the guides are extremely anxious to please the guests. Willie Imudluk, the owner, takes a good deal of pride in running a good camp. He has good motors, big motors, and there is an air of progress from his very modest beginning. The rate is $575 for a week's stay which includes the charter plane from Fort Chimo. Safari Outfitters, Inc., 8 S. Michigan Ave., Chicago, Illinois 60603 can provide you with all details and reservations.

It is a land of arctic char, of awesome tides, of loneliness, of caribou, but most of all it is the land of the Eskimo. An endangered race? Hopefully not!

The Eskimo is not void of a sense of humor nor an occasional surprise. My favorite story takes place when Willie Imudluk first opened up his camp. The departing group posed Willie for picture after picture. One of the shutter-clicking guests, took some time to explain in sign language the purpose of the camera, what it does, and assured Willie that upon his return he would eventually send him some pictures of himself.

Willie excused himself, went into his room, came out and posed the entire group. Then with his Polaroid camera, took a photo of the stunned group, and after timing the development with his Bulova watch, he produced a finished photo and handed it to the camera man.

The Eskimo is full of surprises, I tell you!

Then Willie would race downstream . . . jumping from boulder to boulder.

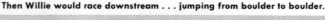

Bottom fishermen working the Chesapeake Bay are often rewarded with a mixed bag such as this, which included a flounder, seatrout, whiting and numerous spot. All were taken on small pieces of squid.

BOTTOM fishing is without question one of the most contemplative methods of fishing you'll ever try along the seacoast. While requiring a minimum of exertion or sophisticated tackle, bottom fishing does have many rewards other than just relaxation, for a wider variety of bottom feeders are available than all gamefish species combined. Making it still more attractive is the fact that bottom feeders are usually in a feeding mood and eager to take a properly presented bait.

You don't need a tremendous amount of skill or expertise to catch these fellows either. Just using basic techniques and common sense will invariably result in a good day's sport on our Atlantic, Pacific or Gulf coasts.

Over many years of traveling along our three coastlines I've caught close to a hundred different species of bottom feeder. They have ranged from ½-pound porgies to groupers that topped 50. Many of the species had remarkably similar habits, such as the starry flounder of the Pacific and the winter flounder of the Atlantic; the summer flounder of the Atlantic and the southern flounder of the Gulf; the rockfish of the Pacific and the sea bass of the Atlantic, to name but a few.

During my travels I've tried a variety of bottom rigs, baits and techniques, and I have found that there are certain basic rigs, tackle and methods of bottom fishing that will put a good catch in your ice chest regardless of where you go.

I like a simple, uncluttered rig. The less terminal hardware on the rig the better, for fish are less apt to be spooked by it. Also, the less hardware, the less likely you are to get

The Fundamentals of Bottom Fishing

by MILT ROSKO

hung on obstructions frequently found in productive spots.

I most often use one of two basic bottom rigs. My favorite consists of tying a small three-way swivel directly to the end of my line. From one eye I tie a 3- to 5-inch long dropper of line that is weaker than the fishing line. Onto this dropper loop I slip a bank or dipsey style sinker. Should the sinker foul on the bottom and the light line break, and I lose only my sinker, not the entire rig.

To the remaining eye of the swivel I tie a length of leader material ranging from 18 inches for those species that aren't leader-shy, such as sea bass, codfish, rockfish, porgies, sand bass, and red snappers, to upwards of 36 inches of leader for summer flounder, halibut, weakfish and seatrout.

To the end of the leader I tie a Claw or Beak style hook. Both of these styles are universally popular with bait fishermen, for they are made of fine diameter wire, have a curved, offset, hollow point, and a needle-sharp point that penetrates fast. The design of the hook is such that it holds a bait nicely and does not rip even small minnows, anchovies, or other delicate baits.

A variation of this rig that is also popular is the high-low rig, which is basically the same thing, except that you add a second, or high hook about 18 to 24 inches up from the bottom, or low hook, which often enables you to catch some plentiful bottom feeders two at a time!

My second favorite bottom rig is especially popular along the Gulf coast and off Florida, but I've used it most everywhere I've fished with good results. It consists of an egg-shaped sinker with a hole through the center which is slipped directly onto your line. Next comes a small barrel swivel, which holds the sinker on the line. To the remaining eye of the barrel swivel tie your leader, and finally your hook, using the same guideline offered earlier with respect to leader length. Always remember that when fishing in clear, shallow water it's always best to use a longer leader than when in deep, dark water.

Sheepshead are tough, fast-striking bottom feeders, plentiful throughout the south. June Rosko landed this beauty while fishing a shrimp bait on the bottom around mangroves in the Caloosahatchee River in Florida.

Grouper like this heavyweight are plentiful over reefs throughout tropical areas. Al Grant used a chunk of pilchard bait to hook the beauty just gaffed by Captain Lynn Yawn while fishing off Walker's Cay in the Bahamas.

Rockfish are favorites of Pacific coast anglers everywhere, with some species found all along the coast. Leon Adams hooked this one while fishing off the mouth of San Francisco Bay, while using a live anchovy fished on the bottom.

Sand bass are a popular bottom feeder with Southern California anglers. The author fished a live anchovy on the bottom off Newport Beach California, to land this chunky bass.

These two bottom rigs, and the high-low rig variation, will see you through most bottom fishing situations. On the West coast, however, many successful anglers simply tie their hook directly to the end of their monofilament line, and attach one or two small rubber-cored sinkers a couple of feet up from the hook, and let the entire rig settle to the bottom. This is by far the most basic bottom rig in use, and the success of California fishermen attests to its effectiveness.

When employing these rigs I use either a light conventional, or popping outfit with a small level wind reel for inshore fishing, or a spinning outfit of corresponding size, utilizing 10- or 12-pound test monofilament line. If I'm after fish in the 5-pound and heavier class, I then switch to a standard party boat rod, and a reel spooling a couple of hundred yards of either 20- or 30-pound test monofilament line, for bottom feeders can be stubborn, especially big codfish, pollock, groupers, snapper, rockfish and big halibut and summer flounder.

While the basic outfit you use and the bottom rig are important, perhaps the most important consideration of all is the bait. Selecting the right bait for the species you're after makes a world of difference, and care should be exercised to obtain the freshest bait possible. For while some bottom feeders are scavengers, most will respond more readily to a fresh bait than a stale piece which has been out in the sun and is deteriorating.

It's important that you present your bait in as natural a manner as possible. When using live baitfish, such as anchovies, killies, or pilchards, or the myriad other small forage species found along the coast, you should hook them so they may swim naturally while hooked. Refrain from hooking them so they spin or are dragged through the water. I usually hook live baits either through the lips, lightly through the gills or gill cover, or just beneath and ahead of the dorsal fin. Hooked in this manner a baitfish will stay

While winter flounders aren't big, they do provide fun on light baitcasting tackle. As a bonus they're a great table fish too. These were taken on sandworm baits fished on the bottom in Moriches Bay on Long Island.

Chub Cay in the Bahamas produced this big mutton snapper for the author aboard Captain George Seemann's *Mitchell II*, and using a whole pilchard as bait. Heavyweights like this are extremely strong.

The tautog, called blackfish in many areas, is an extremely plentiful bottom feeder, but it ignores open bottom, preferring to live around the rocks, wrecks or other debris. This was taken on a green crab while fishing aboard a party packet off Cape May, New Jersey.

alive for a long while, and it will swim actively, making it attractive to the fish.

Another possibility that annually accounts for great catches on all coasts are the many species of shrimp found in our coastal waters. Tiny grass shrimp along the Atlantic measure but an inch or two in length, while some Gulf coast species attain 6 inches and more. All are extremely potent baits, with live shrimp preferred when they are obtainable. Fresh dead shrimp will also bring results. When using small shrimp you may have to thread three or four of them on your hook. With large shrimp I often hook them lightly through the hard shell of their back which permits the macruran crustacean to swim actively. Oftentimes I'll take a *really* large shrimp and cut several small baits from it, particularly when I'm after small bottom feeders that wouldn't respond to a whole one.

Another fine choice found in all our coastal waters is squid. The ten-armed cephalopods are often used whole when small, but with larger squid it's best to either cut them into strips which makes an attractively fluttering bait, or into small chunks for small-mouthed bottom feeders. I've even used the head section and its arms with good results for many bottom scrappers.

Bivalves such as clams and mussels are another useful bait. Their meat should be removed from the shell. Because it is sometimes soft, I frequently soak the meat in a heavy salt solution overnight, which toughens the clam or mussel meat and makes it a superior morsel which stays on the hook well.

There are many seaworms found buried in the sand or muck of our waterways, and these too can be well-used. While seaworms do not constitute a major portion of the diet of most bottom feeders, the fact does remain that seldom will any bottom feeder pass up a seaworm draped attractively on your hook. Here, as with most bait, use a small piece of worm if after small-mouthed bottom feeders, and several worms and a larger hook if after more formidable game.

Bottom feeders most often take up residence in an area where there is a plentiful supply of food which suits their fancy. Winter flounder will look for a mud or muck bottom where it finds tiny worms, shrimp and clams plentiful. Its close cousin, the summer flounder, shuns this type of bottom preferring a smooth, sandy spot where it buries itself and awaits the unsuspecting shrimp, squid or small fish to happen by. Ditto the California halibut which feeds exten-

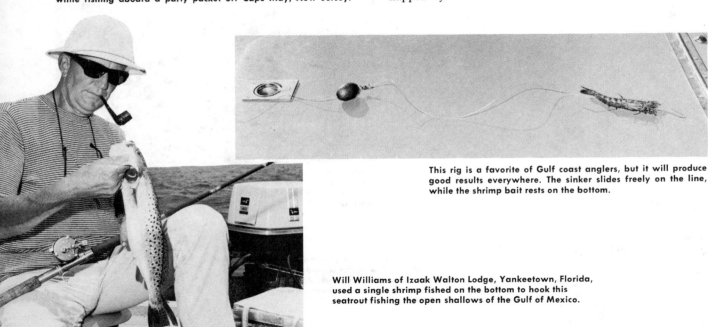

This rig is a favorite of Gulf coast anglers, but it will produce good results everywhere. The sinker slides freely on the line, while the shrimp bait rests on the bottom.

Will Williams of Izaak Walton Lodge, Yankeetown, Florida, used a single shrimp fished on the bottom to hook this seatrout fishing the open shallows of the Gulf of Mexico.

This deckhand on a party packet fishing off Ensenada, Mexico, has just unhooked this sand bass. It was hooked on an anchovy bait fished on the bottom near the kelp beds located offshore.

sively on squid and anchovies.

Some species congregate around a rocky, broken, irregular bottom; around a coral reef, or perhaps a wreck resting on the bottom of the ocean. This is particularly true with tautog, sheepshead, codfish, pollock, snappers, grouper, and Pacific rockfish. They know that crabs, small fish, mussels, shrimp, etc. will be plentiful in such a spot, and often they spend months at a time not moving more than a few feet from their food supply.

It's difficult to drift over locations such as these so most bottom fishermen, whether fishing from a private boat or aboard a party packet, anchor just off the spot and permit the current to swing their boat right over the desired area.

Once baited up and employing a sinker of sufficient weight to hold bottom, permit your rig to settle to the ocean bay floor, all the while keeping a taut line. Often you'll receive a strike the moment the bait reaches bottom and with a slack line you'll be cleaned of your bait and not even realize what has happened.

The summer flounder is a favorite of Atlantic coast bottom fishermen everywhere. Here Bob Rosko unhooks a typical flatty for his granddad, Milt, Sr. while drifting a strip of fluke belly bait along the bottom off Sandy Hook, New Jersey.

◄ Here's a typical high-low rig, with one bait fished the bottom and a second fished off the bottom, or high. Live shrimp are the bait. When bottom feeders are plentiful it's not unusual to catch them two at a time.

Bob Rosko landed this fine croaker while fishing off Pensacola, Florida, using a chunk of fresh mullet as bait.

Spot are favorites of Chesapeake Bay bottom fishermen. They'll readily take a small piece of squid or sandworm bait, and while not big, are great on the dinner table.

The porgy, or scup, is a favorite of Atlantic coast bottom fishermen. They prefer broken, irregular bottoms and will readily take a small piece of clam or sandworm bait.

With the bait on the bottom and a taut line, keep ever alert for a strike. With some species, such as sheepshead or tautog, the strike will be lightning fast and you'll have to react equally as fast by yanking back smartly to set the hook. Other species will sometimes suck on a bait as they take it, particularly the rubber-mouthed winter flounder, and here you've got to slowly lift your rod tip. At this juncture the fish usually bites down hard and you can begin reeling. Halibut and summer flounder often toy with a bait, holding it in their jaw before taking it into their mouths, so when you're after these bigger members of the flatfish clan remember it's "he who *doesn't* hesitate is lost."

Should you feel a strike, lift back to set the hook, but fail, just lower your rod tip and let the bait settle to the bottom again. There's always a chance the fish didn't rip the bait from the hook, and if so it usually will return and you may have a second chance. If, however, after a few moments you haven't received a strike it's best to reel in and check the bait. It's probably gone.

After anchoring in one spot for a half hour or so and not receiving a strike, it's wise to move on. Some bottom feeders are boat shy, and perhaps before you arrived there may have been a lot of boat activity, which may have spooked the fish and put them off their feed. A move to a new area may find a body of fish in a more receptive mood.

Keep in mind that it's important to keep moving until you find a body of fish that is in a feeding mood. Drifting is an extremely rewarding method for many species, particularly if the bottom isn't so rugged that you continually lose terminal tackle. By drifting you cover a lot of area and with species such as seatrout, weakfish, summer flounder, halibut, rockfish, sand bass and many other bottom feeders you'll often catch more fish.

While the glamor species and exotic gamefish steal most of the headlines in local rod and gun columns, it's really the bottom feeders along the seacoast that provide most anglers with the most fish on their stringer. If you're new to the shore and haven't tried bouncing a bait along the bottom, you might just give it a whirl.

Croaker are popular with Gulf coast bottom fishermen, and are taken along the Atlantic coast from Chespeake Bay as well. Captain Buck Fernandez swings an average size croaker aboard.

GENE LECHLER and I simultaneously tossed our white nylon jigs far across the shallows as we drifted off Homosassa, blind casting for speckled sea trout in the Gulf of Mexico.

After only a short retrieve, a silvery streak erupted from the water firmly attached to Gene's jig. Within seconds, another hit mine. Like jet propelled missiles, they took off in different directions cartwheeling, tail dancing, going generally berserk. In quick succession came a series of back flips, somersaults, streaking runs and violent surface wallowing. Name the antic, and they performed it. They jumped so fast so often that I thought I had two fish hooked at once.

"Oh, no!" exclaimed Gene halting another streaking run by the silver streak. "Poor man's tarpon! Goodbye trout fishing!"

A veteran guide from the Yardarm Docks, Riverside Villas at Homosassa, Gene knows the waters of the Gulf as a native New Yorker does Times Square. He's fished from Homosassa for many years. I knew what he feared —that the leaping ladyfish, widely called the poor man's tarpon, would ruin our trout fishing.

I wasn't about to argue with his prediction because I had my hands full with the silvery leaper trying to shake my jig or break my 8-pound test spinning line. I'd encountered the poor man's tarpon before and I agreed the trout would have scant chances of nailing our lures with these streamlined speedsters on a feeding spree. Obviously, we were suddenly in the middle of a frantically feeding school of ladyfish. And when they school to feed—wow! They make other saltwater fish appear to be moving in slow motion.

These bounding ladies are among the top game fish for

of a snook or tarpon, they couldn't be handled with anything less than a hawser. As it is, they're piscatorial dynamite.

However, the fighting spirit of the species and eagerness to charge have not made them highly popular with most anglers. Too often they're encountered when fishing for other species and usually with too heavy tackle. Naturally against heavy gear, the bouncing ladies can't perform properly. But tailor your tackle to their size—8-pound spinning line and a light rod are ideal—and they match the lordly silver kings in aerial acrobatics. You can also use light bait casting tackle, or a fly rod if the ladies are within casting distance. However, a spinner and ladyfish go together like old Col. Sanders and Kentucky fried chicken. The lighter the tackle, the greater the sport.

Also contributing to their lack of general popularity is the fact that ladyfish definitely aren't table fare. Although edible, the numerous fine bones put them in the don't-cook-unless-you're-starving category. But in my book, table rating shouldn't govern the popularity of any sports fish. Bonefish and tarpon aren't eaten, yet they rate at the top of the sports fishing list. But then, the bones and tarpon have better press agents. Personally I rate ladyfish as one of the top, light tackle fish in the sea.

Gene's split-second forecast of our immediate fishing future proved true. The trout never had a chance after the ladyfish school moved onto the flat. We tangled with half a dozen or more of the leapers, and then decided to seek other territory. They're fun, but they also can completely dominate a fishing area temporarily, and that time we definitely were after trout.

However, the presence of the poor man's tarpon doesn't always mean the end of good fishing. Much depends upon the circumstances. In the Ten Thousand Islands of south-

Adroit acrobatics are the trademark of the poor man's tarpon, as ladyfish are often called.

Ladies Shouldn't Leap Like That!
by MAX HUNN

their size in the sea and one of the most aggressive in charging a bait—natural or artificial. They throw caution to the wind when in the hitting mood. Also they're seldom as temperamental as other fish. And for aerial acrobatics, they're almost impossible to match. Ladies also do such stunts as vaulting across skiffs, (definitely startling unsuspecting anglers) and socking outsize plugs and appearing in strange places.

If the bouncing ladies, known as poverty tarpon, chiro, ten pounder (although seldom reaching that weight), and by the Latin moniker of *Elops saurus,* achieved the weight

west Florida, ladyfish and snook often go together. Many times I've seen the sudden appearance of the leaping ladies herald the approach or presence of snook. Cal Stone, an old fishing buddy of mine, always predicts snook success whenever he encounters the leapers. When we catch the ladies on a falling tide, he always figures snook will follow. His forecasts seldom are wrong.

The walloping wenches are caught all along the Florida coast from the Panhandle to the Keys and up the Atlantic seaboard. Basically they're a warm water fish and the farther south you go along Florida's coasts the greater are

Troy Baker unhooks one of several ladyfish hooked during a school's frantic feeding spree.

Author Max Hunn handles a leaping ladyfish that muscled in on a redfishing trip by airboat in the marshes of Chassahowitzka.

your chances of encountering the leaping ladies. They're also very common in the Bahamas and throughout the warm waters of the Caribbean.

Ladyfish are readily available to small boat anglers. They're usually encountered in large schools in shallow waters over sandy and muddy bottoms. Bays, estuaries, and the mouths of creeks and rivers are their normal hunting grounds. Also they're often caught from bridges, causeways and piers.

The ladies wander where they will, seeming to be always on the move and many an angler is surprised to encounter this aerial acrobat in unexpected places. The oddest encounter I've ever had was far back in a shallow, tiny creek draining the saltwater marshes of the Chassahowitzka National Wildlife Refuge on Florida's middle Gulf coast.

Silvery leapers—ladyfish—often called poor man's tarpon because of their antics.

Action is the middle name of a ladyfish. The wanton wenches always put on an aerial show sometime during their fight.

The water was so shallow that we went by airboat. Obviously, since she couldn't walk, this lady came in on a terrifically high tide.

Inexperienced anglers often mistake ladies for bonefish. However they are not remotely related, although both are noted for their spectacular, underwater sprints. But once your foe vaults into the air, you're certain you have no bonefish. Bones just don't jump.

Actually a ladyfish is much more slender than a bone and when the two are compared, there's scant resemblance. A chiro is slender, finely scaled and generally silver in color with a blue-green back. Too, this pseudo-tarpon seldom matches a bonefish in weight. The average lady is in the 1- to 2-pound range, although some do grow larger. In the Bahamas, 8- to 9-pounders are often caught in

Gene Lechler calmly waits for a ladyfish to abandon her aerial acrobatics before landing his prize.

the vicinity of Andros Island. Take my word that this size fish really guarantees a battle.

Boca Grande on the lower Florida west coast is another area harboring big ladyfish, but they're overshadowed by the widely publicized tarpon and lunker snook. Occasionally these ladies run in the 4- to 5-pound class, a size I'm anxious to tackle anytime anywhere with a 6- or 8-pound test line. Just imagine the action!

Unless you've witnessed it, you can't believe the ferocity with which ladyfish attack when on a feeding spree. They move like a pack of hungry wolves, striking anything that resembles a meal. Their lack of caution then makes them easy to hook, but not necessarily easy to land.

They herd their quarry of small fishes expertly. Fishing with Hank Keith, a veteran guide in the southwest Florida mangrove country, we witnessed such an attack one day off Caxambas pass. The water began churning at the mouth of the pass as the feeding ladies rounded up a school of baitfish. Then the melee sped through the relatively short pass with baitfish leaping frantically to elude their attackers. The ladyfish (what a misnomer! These were no ladies, but were greedy ruffians!) pursued the school onto the flats.

We tossed our bucktails into the confusion and immediately had simultaneous hits. But most of the leaping ladies flipped our lures. During the brief, frenzied action, we fought at least a dozen of these leapers. What great action while it lasted!

There aren't many species of fish that will provide *too much* action for an angler. The usual complaint is *lack* of action. But on more than one trip I've cried "uncle" to marauding ladies. Action can be too much of a good thing sometimes.

There's one episode I'll never forget when the ladies actually made me quit fishing. Perhaps you would have, too, if you'd hooked 36 leaping, fighting fish on 36 successive casts. I held out for 45 minutes before surrendering. Enough is enough, and those ladies were too much for me that day.

Another time Gene Lechler, Troy Baker and I were fishing off the old bombing range north of Homosassa. We got into a school of fast moving bluefish and we thought the action was tops. And it *was* until the blues moved on and a school of bouncing ladies took over. They were far more rambunctious than the wild blues. Few will dispute that ladyfish on a feeding prowl are tops for aggressiveness.

Another reason the ladies should rate high on the sports fishing list is their eagerness to clobber virtually any type of artificial. That day when I fought 36 on successive casts, I threw every lure in my tackle box, and the ladies socked them all. I even finally found a use for some of the odd-ball lures that never had even previously provoked a strike.

Still—although seeming to be unselective about lures, they do have a definite preference regarding retrieves. I've found that a slow retrieve seldom interests a bounding lady. Instead bring your lure back fast, particularly using the Florida whip retrieve. If there's a silvery speedster in the area, look out!

Whether you're using a jig, a top water plug or a shallow runner, retrieve your lure fast. During the session when the ladies wore me out, I experimented with retrieves. I started several retrieves slowly with no results, but the moment I speeded up the lure action, zowie! The ladies were present all the time but they preferred a fast meal.

Color also plays an important role. Although at times I've caught ladies on almost every imaginable color combination, including some of my homemade variations, there's little doubt but that a white or silver lure is the most productive. A white jig is excellent, retrieved fast. The silver flash coloring on many sub-surface plugs, too,

Gene Lechler and Max Hunn (right) examine the twin ladyfish, members of a school that ended a trout fishing trip off Homosassa. Like most schooling fish, ladies are of the same size in a school. Strays are the bigger ones.

Kit Hunn plays a leaping lady that seems determined to board the boat in anger.

is deadly, as are small silver spoons.

But whatever the color, don't use too large a lure. While the poor man's tarpon attack recklessly, they won't charge too large a lure. After all, they know what they can swallow and they don't have the bucket mouths of largemouth black bass. Lures in the ¼- and ½-ounce range are the most productive, and are always retrieved fast.

Another point in the ladyfish's favor as a sports fish is availability. The leapers are caught the year around. I've found them in the cold of February and in the heat of July. Admittedly, however, the odds are better during the warmer periods, particularly farther north in Florida. The hottest fishing I've had with the wild wenches has been in the period from March through October. Then sometimes they really perform like dizzy blonds. But they're dizzy blondes that any light tackle angler can love without really trying.

Womenfish aren't equipped with particularly vicious choppers, but they can brutally maul a bucktail jig. That's my main reason for using nylon instead of bucktail. The nylon seems to stand the abuse a little better, Too, the ladies can be rough on line. While they usually don't break it, they do fray it as if they were sandpapering experts. Check your line frequently or you may donate a lure unexpectedly. Some anglers use light wire leaders, I don't care for that much terminal hardware, and my insurance is using a 15-pound shock leader which I check often.

While the walloping wenches hit with abandon and their mouths are not rock hard like a tarpon's, nevertheless you have to be skillful to boat them. The main problem is keeping a tight line with a foe that is out of the water half of the time. If you don't keep your hook well set, you often get a lure tossed back with the speed of a bean ball. More than once I've had jigs sail between me and my partner when a lady left our company abruptly. That's my only complaint about ladies and lead jigs. The jigs do travel like bullets when the line is released suddenly. The ladies play violently!

Even if you do keep your hook set, the odds are great you'll lose more than you ever bring boatside. But who cares? The fun is watching the poor man's tarpon perform in the air. They put on a real show if you meet them with light tackle. You won't forget an encounter with them.

The Making of a Fisher-Woman

by Tom Gresham

First bass, slightly longer than the lure, and tangled in a wad of moss.

Nobody learns to bait cast without getting backlashes, and Linda was no exception.

Linda Evans with her first fish, a bluegill from Toledo Bend.

WHAT'S A hundred-pound gal friend like you doing trying to cross the eyes on a big bass when two months ago you didn't know a plastic worm from a live cricket?

It was just about 60 days ago when Linda Evans, a sociology graduate of Northwestern State University, and my girl friend of a couple of years, decided she would like to go fishing. That needn't have presented me with a problem except for one thing: she asked *me* to take her!

Linda has a lot of attributes, but I didn't know whether being a fishing partner was one of 'em. Home from my study of photo-journalism at the University of Missouri for the summer, I was trying to juggle a full-time job with the U.S. Forest Service establishing wildlife areas in the Kisatchie National Forest, with one of my favorite avocations: fishing. Time for the latter was at a premium, which made me think twice about using any of it to share a boat with a novice.

But, and this won't come as a surprise to many fishermen, girl friends have a gift for getting their way. After deliberating the issue at length, for about 2 minutes, I said yes.

With selfish malice aforethought—I didn't want the rest of my summer fishing trips ruined—I plotted the making of a fisherwoman with some care. The only proper course of action was to train Linda correctly, as you would a good bird dog, which doesn't happen in one session.

Beginning fishermen don't like fishing as much as they like *catching* fish. With that in mind I decided to make Linda's fishing debut a trip for bluegills, on a lake where I could guarantee (almost) catching fish. I chose Toledo Bend, 60 miles from my home in Natchitoches, Louisiana, a huge reservoir which is nationally famous for great bass fishing but not as well known for its exceptionally fine bream fishing.

As the cookie happened to crumble, we ended up with two females on the trip who had never before fished. In addition to Linda, who fished with me in one boat, there was Phyllis Spear. She and her husband, Bob, fished in a

"Ooophs! What did I do?" The author, untangling Linda's line from the electric motor prop, considers the disadvantages of teaching a beginner to fish.

272

I discovered that Linda's hand and wrist were too weak for comfortable bait casting, so switched her to a two-handed grip. With that two-handed grip she can cast with power, for hours, without tiring.

bigger boat with my parents—Grits and Mary.

We arrived at Toledo Bend in the middle of the afternoon, to avoid the midday June sun which can make conditions miserable for seasoned anglers, much less neophytes. The first rule in teaching a beginner to fish is to program that first outing so he—or she—will be as comfortable as possible.

In the remote case that I might be wrong, that the fish didn't bite, I also took along enough food and drink to take up the slack. Nibbles and soda pop will make the time pass quickly regardless of what the fish are doing.

Cane pole, hook and line are the ultimate in simplicity insofar as fishing gear is concerned, so that's what we used. But "simple" is relative, so I first explained that basic rig. We were also using live crickets for bait, and teaching Linda to impale one of these critters on a hook took a bit of doing. So did getting her to stick her hand down into a box full of live crickets.

My tactic for taking bluegills in numbers at this time of year was to ease along through the flooded timber, fishing as we moved, until a concentration of the fish was located. When a "bed" of bream is found it isn't unusual to fill an ice chest from that one spot.

Depth is frequently critical where bream beds are concerned, and on Toledo Bend at the time of our trip the magic numbers were 10 to 15 feet. After a short run from Pendleton Bridge, we cut the throttle back to stump-bumping speed and moved from the channel out into the flooded forest. It took only minutes for Dad, using the depth finder in his boat, to put us on a 12-foot ridge surrounded by deep water.

A depth finder is invaluable, as Linda learned not long after we began fishing. We didn't have a flasher in our boat, and as Dad went past he said, "By the way' you're fishing in 43 feet of water." We had drifted off the ridge and over the old river channel.

Almost as soon as I moved our Terry Bass boat back

She discovered the plastic worm, and learned to fish it well.

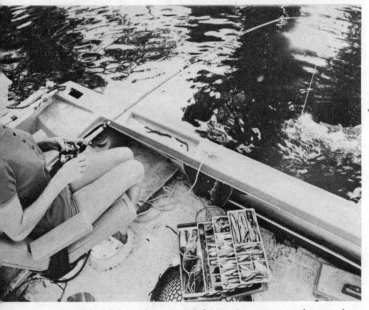

to the ridge I heard a squeal from the stern, and turned to see Linda fighting a fish which had her cane pole bent almost double. When she finally managed to get the big bull bluegill out of the brush it came flying into the boat. It was her first fish, and she was shaking with excitement.

Linda watched closely as I showed her how to remove the bream from the hook. Then, before I could drop the fish into the basket that hung alongside the boat and turn back around, she had already baited her hook and had it back in the water.

In seconds she had another fish on, and two more crickets produced another pair. Figuring that this must be the place—I had been too busy unhooking Linda's fish to get my own line overboard—I gave a yell to the other boat.

With the two boats side by side, tied to the brush, we fished that spot for a couple of hours. Phyllis quickly learned the technique of setting the hook and wrestling the little fighters from the flooded thickets, and she and Linda vied with each other to see who could whoop and squeal louder with each new fish.

My mother is a veteran, accomplished angler with the enthusiasm of a beginner, and her voice completed the trio

which must have carried a long way across the lake. At least a half-dozen other boats moved in close to see what all the shouting was about.

Back at Pendleton Harbor Marina manager Charles Byerly greeted us with, "I hear y'all really caught 'em!"

Charles told us that a couple of fishermen had come in a half-hour earlier and told him, "We caught a good bunch of fish, but you should have seen those two gold Terry boats. Must have been a dozen people in them and every-time we looked they had half a dozen fish on. Bet they caught a thousand bream!"

All of which goes to show what advertising—squealing and whooping—will do. The six of us did catch something over 150 big bluegills, and Linda had the best day of all. She landed almost a third of them. It's understandable that from then on she has been just a bit crazy about fishing.

The next week, in a moment of weakness, I asked Linda if she'd like to try bass fishing. You'd have thought I offered her the mother lode!

For her first bass outing, as with the bream, I chose the cool, late afternoon hours. It was even more important this time since bass are far more unpredictable, far harder to catch with regularity, than are bluegills. If a beginner is not going to catch anything, let her do it under comfortable conditions.

Friends, fathers and husbands, too frequently, make the mistake of expecting their fishing pupil to endure the hard-ships they take for granted. But beginners will become discouraged quickly if they are too hot, or too cold, or too thirsty, or too hungry.

Or . . . if they're given equipment to use which an expert couldn't handle! Don't handicap a beginner with cheap or worn-out rods and reels.

There are two theories about how to teach a beginner to cast. One is to do it on the lawn with a practice plug, without the distractions of boat, water and hooks. But a backyard session on practice casting can be pretty dry without any direct incentive, so I decided to teach Linda to cast while we were fishing . . . where she had a chance of catching a fish immediately.

Spinning, spincasting or casting? The spincast reel is the easiest to use, so I rigged such an outfit for Linda. "Push the button before you cast," I handed the rig to her once we were afloat, "and release it on the forward part of the cast."

She pushed the button and immediately released it, and the lure fell to the water beside the boat. I decided that

Linda braces her feet and sets the hook on a bass down deep. She doesn't always cross their eyes with the strike, but always gets their attention.

Linda has learned to use all kinds of lures, and uses women's intuition in her selections.

demonstration was better than oral instruction, so made a couple of casts while she watched.

She cranked back and let a cast fly, and looked around bewildered when she didn't see the lure. In a moment or two it splashed down 20 feet from the boat after its infield-fly trajectory.

"You released the button too soon. Try it again."

Her casting improved as I eased the boat down the shoreline with the bow-mounted electric motor, although much of that first half-hour was spent getting her lure unhung from underwater brush and streamside tree limbs.

I decided to move to another spot about a mile down the shore, and got a quick reminder that I shouldn't take anything for granted in this fishing lesson. As the boat reached planing speed I discovered that Linda had accidentally pushed the release button and the line was peeling from her reel. After an abrupt "whoa" we reeled the 100 yards or so of line back in, and this time stashed the rod in its rack before proceeding.

At the next fishing stretch I cured the problem of Linda's lure—a spinner bait—hanging on underwater brush. I tied on a topwater lure.

To show her how to work that surface Bang-a-Lure I made a cast with her rod. "After the plug hits the water," I demonstrated, "let it lie still until all the ripples fade away. Then give it just a slight twitch with the rod tip."

My demonstration was interrupted when a good bass smashed into the lure. He put on a good show for Linda, jumping a couple of times, and as I lifted him aboard Linda moaned, "You caught my fish, with my rod. If I had just cast there I'd have caught him. And I've never caught a bass."

My explanation that it was simply superior skill that caused the bass to strike didn't keep her from being upset, but the incident did perk her interest up considerably. Before I had the bass on the stringer she had reclaimed her rod and had made a cast.

Guiding the boat through some moss beds I suggested, "Cast into the openings in the moss and just reel the lure back in. You're having a little trouble working it as a top-water, and it has good action on a straight retrieve."

Both of us snagged a handful of the lettuce now and then, and it was while I was bringing in a double handful that Linda yelled, "I've got one! I've got a fish on!"

"Well, I thought I had one on," she continued as I whirled around in my swivel seat. "But I guess it was just moss."

"Reel it on in. The fish may have just swam into the moss," I hit the foot pedal to swing the boat away from the moss bed.

That's what had happened, and Linda hauled aboard a large pile of weeds with a very small bass tangled somewhere in the middle.

"Look! It *is* a fish," she was bouncing up and down in her seat. And then, more slowly, "I guess we'll have to put him back?"

After extracting it from the moss, she could see that the

Linda has also learned how to fillet bass, but prefers just to eat the ones I fry.

bass wasn't much longer than the 6-inch plug. She knew it was much too small to keep but still hated to throw back the first bass she ever caught.

As she watched the fish swim away she looked as if she'd lost a close friend.

"Now let's catch his papa." I turned the boat down the shoreline again.

In just two months Linda Evans has progressed from never having fished to an avid, competent angler.

We caught more and bigger bass that afternoon and in the following weeks, and I guided Linda from the spincast outfit to the more efficient open-faced spinning rig. She particularly liked the faster retrieve ratio of spinning, which enabled her to move a lure faster with less work.

When she began using plastic worms she fell in love. As is frequently true with women, her sensitive sense of feel soon let her know as soon as a bass picked up the worm. After that it wasn't unusual for her stringer to be heavier than mine at the end of the day.

Casting, working the various kinds of lures, setting the hook, playing and landing fish: in the month following that first bluegill trip Linda got to be a pretty fair hand at all of them. Even at filleting bass, with an electric knife, but after learning how she immediately lost interest in that phase of fishing.

But the ultimate tool for bass fishing in our part of the country, albeit the most difficult to master, is the revolving spool bait casting reel. Spincast is great for openers, and spinning is a good intermediate step.

Bait casting it had to be for Linda, since she had zeroed in on bass fishing as the kind she liked best. I finally decided to teach her to use the best tackle for the job.

Since there was no longer any possibility of her losing interest in fishing, I decided on dry land instruction for the bait casting reel. One afternoon, before she could say, "Why aren't we fishing?" I had her in the backyard with a 5½-foot casting rod and an Ambassadeur 5000 reel in her hand.

I quickly discovered that she doesn't have enough strength in one hand and wrist to handle a casting outfit comfortably for long periods, so suggested that she try a two-handed grip. With that technique she gets far more power into the cast and can fish for hours without tiring.

Many hours and many backlashes later my girl friend is still no "pro" with the short stick and the 5000, but she is good enough to get the job done . . . and improving. Linda has progressed, in only 2 months, from "never fished" to using the kind of bass tackle I use.

When a bass takes her plastic worm 20 feet deep and down in the brush, her strike may not cross his eyes every time . . . but one thing is a sure bet. She'll get his attention!

The Dearborn River, near Wolf Creek, Montana.

You May Like Off-Beat Trout Waters Best

by BILL BROWNING

Big Spring Creek Lewistown, Montana, has supplied record brown trout and is a favorite of knowing anglers.

The Smith River, near White Sulphur Springs, Montana, has been ranked as one of the state's top trout waters.

SO RENOWNED have Montana's top trout fishing waters become that many knowledgeable anglers make their annual treks to fish the state's big six blue ribbon trout streams —the Missouri, Yellowstone, Madison, Big Hole, Jefferson and Rock Creek.

Unfortunately, some visiting anglers blow their fishing vacations fighting the problems of fishing waters too big, of trying vainly to read the new areas, and finding trout wary and wild, stung by too many hooks, or nervous from river traffic and activity.

For those anglers interested in lesser known, yet challenging trout waters, scaled down in size and with fewer traffic problems, I'd suggest the off-beat streams. These are larger in number and are spread over a greater area, and may well be better suited to vacation plans. Also, they are only a shade less important in the national fishing picture. They just haven't been publicized as much.

Take for example a friend of mine who prefers fishing smaller tributaries to the popular blue ribbon streams. Jerry Hutch is a Pennsylvania newcomer to Montana who discovered and stayed with these streams because they were much like his home streams of some 15 to 50 feet wide.

Jerry is not the classic fly fisherman but loves his spinning sport. He fishes the first couple or 3 miles of tributaries upstream from the famous waters, finding superb trout passed up by hustling anglers.

One day I followed Jerry to a favorite branch of the Missouri River near Helena (I promised not to divulge its name). We hit the stream at dawn and as the leaden sky turned to pink a big brown trout flashed out from under a fallen aspen quartering into the stream to take a #2 French spinner. The fight was on; Jerry carefully but nervously led the brown into faster water, letting him slide into a deep still pool where he could manage it better with his 4-pound mono and light rod.

As carefully and delicately as any flyrodder, Jerry played the brown to an exciting finish, beaching a 19½-inch vermillion-speckled trophy worthy of any angler's praise.

Glancing back to the spot of the strike I saw a narrow, fast riffle. It was only a foot or so deep, sliding under the half-submerged tree trunk where Jerry's trout had flashed from safety. The stream was fly-fishing water for sure, but Jerry adapted his technique to shorter casts, putting the spinner in familiar holding spots. He ended that day with a string of five trout of from 16 to 20 inches, and returned an equal number for seed.

Jerry reasons that the trout in the lower tribs migrate upriver from the big popular rivers to spawn. Many find holes and feeding stations to their liking under grassy cutbanks, spreading tree roots, fallen trunks, or brushy meanders. Here, finding little traffic, they remain.

Also, these streams tend to slow up somewhat toward their mouths creating more meanders, more bank protection, and deeper holes on wider stretches. Here, too, are both browns and rainbows with some tribs also supporting cutthroats. Most hold smaller brook trout in their upper reaches.

During spring rainbow spawn and fall brown trout runs, some of these streams have trout traffic you wouldn't believe. A careful angler can spot the redds and mating trout. Holding stations behind rocks, around submerged logs, under brush, etc., are easier to spot here than they are on the larger open stream.

I was fascinated with the waters in which Jerry Hutch fished his spin lures, getting into holds under brush, and in pockets that I couldn't manage with a fly. In such clear water and short runs you have to stand far back in order not to spook the trout. This he did with much finesse and savvy, although with some loss of lures to brush.

Not all off-beat streams are small, though. Generally, sizeable headwaters make up the popular trout streams and some of these rival the blue ribbon sections. There are also some spectacular trout waters which flow past populated areas.

Take the Missoula area, with a population of some 40,000 people. Upstream to the south is the fairly large Bitterroot River, made up of snow waters from the Bitterroot-Selway Wilderness area. Here is a red ribbon river only slightly lower in quality from the nearby famous blue ribbon Rock Creek. There are good browns and 'bows especially in the lower reaches, where 5- to 6-pound and larger trout are taken annually. It's a temperamental river, however.

The Bitterroot headwaters are made up of East and West Forks, both small, yet fine fly-size streams. Lower, the pools are deeper and suitable to floats, yet wadable too. It offers good spin and fly waters before emptying into the Clark Fork of the Columbia.

Missoula or Hamilton would make good headquarters for the fisherman with their fine accommodations. Camp spots are few on the river but there are two fishing access parks in the Florence area. Short side trips up Forest Service roads will bring you to some fine mountain camping: some spots raw and some developed.

West of Missoula in the Alberton area lies some really grand trout fishing in the Clark Fork. This is bigger water but the chances of bigger fish are here also. Some anglers use a raft or boat to float the river, flyfishing or spinning along the interesting pockets and holes. Bank access is easily found especially by asking rancher's permission. This is true along most of Montana's streams.

Some of the more popular holes below Missoula are Tank Creek, Cooper's Island, Big Pool, Log Pile, and Petty Creek, to name a few. Several islands break up the area offering many pools, riffles and choice fly or spin fishing. It's not a classic water, but has very heavy fish and it's a top state offering, regardless of its classification. It rivals any blue ribbon water.

Upriver from Missoula at Bonner, the Big Blackfoot enters the Clark Fork River. This is another fine stream, a little smaller, faster, and quite scenic, which at times produces some great fishing. From Bonner on upriver on the Big Blackfoot to Lincoln, there are many fine pools and runs, and most of them fairly accessible to State Highway 200.

Here again, the popular rainbow and browns predominate, but Dolly Varden do migrate up this stream into Monture Creek. Several good floats are possible and guides are available. One top guide I have fished with is Paul Roos of Lincoln, Montana. He can float you on the Big Blackfoot, or the classic Clearwater, a delightful tributary. Hit these in late June or in July. The salmon fly hatch insures superb fishing.

Accommodations are nearby at Lincoln, Missoula, and Seeley Lake, with state park camps, and fishing access camps available throughout the area.

The main Clark Fork from above Missoula to above the city of Drummond is also a good bet for excellent browns. Most of this area is within walking distance from I-90 and its frontage roads.

Emptying into the Upper Clark Fork at Garrison is an almost secret fly stream, the Little Blackfoot. From here to its headwaters, some 40 miles distant is one of the finest small streams you will find anywhere. Challenging browns are a specialty. This is a top *evening* trout stream. Gray dry flies are recommended for heavy action. You'll take a surprising number of 1- to 2-pounders from this water with small flies and lots of skill. It, too, follows a primary

highway, U.S. 12, but be sure to secure rancher permission for access. It's very wadable and clear, so sneak up on the trout—or get beaten. Fine brooks and cutthroats are taken in its upper waters.

Camp spots are few but a short run up to McDonald Pass on the Continental Divide will bring you to two well-developed Forest Service campgrounds. If the family is along, drop them off at nearby Frontier Town, a replica of a pioneer village where they can see bears, dine, and visit the curio shop. Helena, the capital, is an interesting place for the family. It boasts deluxe accommodations and is also within a reasonable distance of the river. Incidentally, Helena's original name was Last Chance Gulch!

Let's try another fishing hub around the tiny agricultural town of Twin Bridges. You have a choice of the blue ribbon Big Hole, or the sleepers: Jefferson, Ruby and Beaverhead Rivers. Any one of these will keep you busy matching wits with wild trout up to 4 to 5 or more pounds. Rainbows and browns are the most sought after, with both fly and spincasting popular.

The Beaverhead is usually clear and a top contender from below the Clark Canyon Dam downstream to about Dillon. The stream is a long flycast wide, slides past lots of brushy banks, follows I-15, and offers very heavy trout. Lower down in it can be off-color due to irrigation, but generally tremendous trout have been taken under ideal conditions. Would you believe up to a record 18 pounds? Willows along the banks *do* present two obstacles: one of back casting, and the other of mosquitoes. Boats can float here and a short Muddler or Missoulian Spook will turn up many hits.

The Ruby, east of town, is wadable and brushy. One school teacher I know fishes here religiously after school, turning up some surprising rainbows. I once saw a friend take a 4-pound brown from a heavy riffle, above which a beaver was felling the tall aspens. Several miles of the Ruby, right up to the Ruby Reservoir, make a fine, easily read, smaller stream for the fly fisherman. It's wadable with fair access.

The Jefferson River, a Missouri River headwater, west of town is a fine bet for big fish and heavy action. The waters here as in the Beaverhead, may be off-color at times, but hit it when it's clearing and you can take some real lunkers with well-placed flies of any type, or spin lures. I like the Muddler or Spruce Fly here for streamers, and Wulff and Adams flies for dries. For many miles these waters run through scenic ranchland and canyons near the Lewis and Clark Caverns State Park. The waters are accessible even to floating. Browns and 'bows again are the main targets, with good whitefishing on smaller flies. Do be careful of snakes in the lower, dry, rocky areas, however.

There are some camps and motels in the area as at Twin Bridges or Dillon. Check Frank Rose at Frank's Sports Shop, Twin Bridges, for best fishing and current best lures. Or Sneed's Sports shop at Dillon for the upper Beaverhead.

Nearby, famous Virginia and Nevada City will take care of the faimly both day and night, with early-day gold mining and ghost town atmosphere. This is the cradle of Montana history.

At the Lewis and Clark Cavern State Park you can find excellent new camp quarters including a dump station. Besides, you can treat your family to one of the nation's top limestone caves, billed by some as the world's most varied and colorful. It's open during the summer.

So you want to get away to some secret fishing spot with little competition from other anglers, yet good fishing potentials? It can be done in literally scores of offbeat

← The Swan River, in northwestern Montana, offers fly- or spinfishing and is suitable for wading or floating.

trout streams on both the east and west sides of the Continental Divide. Try, for example, the Yaak River in extreme northwest Montana.

This river runs through a narrow, scenic, wilderness-type valley. With a short hike you can reach remote spots such as the high-walled canyon in the lower end. Here you have the river to yourself. The fish aren't big but action is fast and chances for a 2- to 3-pound 'bow are good. Cutts and some brookies also take the flies well. The setting is dramatic and soul-satisfying with canyon walls which soar 500 feet above the river.

Another wild river just out of sight of the well-travelled state route 209 is the Swan. Here are some exciting bows up to several pounds, together with cutts and brookies. Also running the Swan in early July are the large Dolly Vardens. It's a fly or spin river, and suitable for wading or floating. This Swan River area is worth several days of exploring. Camps in the area provide beautiful, natural settings. It's also an area of shining lakes for side trips.

A special favorite of mine is the raw, wild South Fork of the Flathead River just at the south end of Hungry Horse Reservoir. You can reach it by gravelled road. Try for some especially fine native cutts to 2- to 3-pounds and really heavy Dolly Vardens in the fall. Camp spots are easy to find, or you can hike or pack in with KNL guest ranch outfitters to fish the true wilderness area. One close friend said he never saw such fishing in his life as in the upper stretches. It also has great scenic float potential.

Not long ago the Smith River, near White Sulphur Springs, was reported in a major outdoor magazine to be one of the state's top trout waters. The writer of the article, George Laycock, and I made a two-day float here taking some spectacular browns and 'bows. Certainly the scenery was equally spectacular. It's a remote and primitive forest area. The best time to be here is in July before the waters recede too far to float. There is a good Fish and Game access site for launching. See your official Montana map for the exact spot.

Several spring creeks in the state are choice waters for the purist expert. The classic example is Armstrong's Spring Creek south of Livingston. Some far-sighted organizations and tackle companies have bought the fishing rights to keep this short stream open to anglers. Here is the top level of sophisticated dry fly fishing to very wary but superb trout. It supports an unbelievable number of both anglers and fish.

Another spring creek is the Big Spring Creek near Lewistown with its enormous 'bows but particularly browns, called Lockeys locally. Almost every season sees an 8- to 10-pound trout caught, and a brown of about 18 pounds is on record here. Good accommodations are another feature. Tie this one in for a fall run on brown trout and excellent bird hunting in the area.

Montana has about 3500 miles and over 125 rivers whose waters are classified red or yellow ribbon. The majority of these would fully satisfy most anglers. Some are sections of larger blue ribbon rivers, but most are of lesser known, off-beat rivers, from small to large. Compare this to only 452 miles of blue ribbon waters in the Six Rivers.

In the off-beat streams an angler probably can find more comfortable fishing than he could in the larger blue ribbon streams. I believe his success ratio would be higher, too. Casts can be shorter, feeding fish can be more easily spotted and wading is safer and more comfortable. Yet there are many in this group that would rival the larger rivers in every respect. Many can be floated. Most will take the same flies and lures. To frost the cake, many are more remote and less populated with anglers. I have taken a slice of only a few areas, but these reflect accurately what you

Big Spring Creek, near Lewistown, Montana, offers large rainbow and brown trout.

Author Browning takes a grayling from the upper Big Hole River, Montana.

can find in many areas of Montana.

Flies recommended are the usual menu of western flies and other favorites. (See "The Ten Top Western Trout Flies" elsewhere in this book.) The old reliables, wet or dry, will take trout here as they will in other places.

For lures, the Mepps type of spinners are hard to beat. A big variety of spoons will take big fish with red and white, and brass colors favored. I don't worry much about size, and generally spin with medium to large. I believe

that casting expertise is more important and prefer to fish upstream, keeping the lure just off the bottom. I once saw an angler who had this technique mastered, taking a 5-pound brown in the small East Gallatin River near Bozeman. On the other hand, Jerry Hutch fishes down, across, and upstream, depending on the trout lie and obstacles. He's successful, too, so take your pick.

The best seasons are the first couple of weeks following the opening of the season in May; again during the June salmon fly hatch on many rivers; then following run-off water, generally about the last three weeks of July. August can be slow on some waters. However the trout appear to be gathering strength for the fall season through October, which I personally like the very best. For the biggest fish, but slower fishing, the nod must go to November when the largest average trophies are taken.

For rods you don't have to go too heavy. Simply match your rod to the weight and type lures you use. Of more importance might be to fish the smallest mono you can handle to secure more hits. These trout are wild and wary, and getting more so. Of course, if you float and fish brushy banks you can go to heavier tippets, preventing the loss of too many lures.

If you are a newcomer to fishing, practice casting in your yard, local park or waters. Then read all you can about logical trout holding and feeding stations. You'll find this knowledge very helpful in many Montana situations.

Trout are spooky, so poor casting, noisy approaches, or flashy clothing can easily flush them. If this happens, try resting them a bit and improve your presentation. No side-drag on flies, please. The natural float or drift is everything in flycasting.

I like to catch trophy fish as well as the next angler, but it took me a long time to understand the big, famous waters where larger trout are supposedly found. Fishing the smaller off-beat streams gave me the confidence and skills I needed. As a bonus, more of these streams traverse scenic, wild country than do those which are very well known. I like the intimate wilderness aspects of these waters, and fish them for a fulfilling trouting experience second to none.

Write to the Montana Chamber of Commerce, Box 1730, Helena, for more data.

BEST BETS FOR BLUEGILLS

by Stan Fagerstrom

Here they are, a stringer full of the scrappiest little panfish you'll find anywhere. Three different fly patterns take them best.

MY fly rod was in hand and I was heading for my boat when my wife called from the front door. "Stan," she said, "aren't you forgetting something? Where's your fishing vest or tackle box? You haven't got either one."

I reached into a shirt pocket and pulled out a small plastic container I'd swiped from the family medicine cabinet once the pills were gone. "Thanks," I replied, "but this is all the tackle box I'll need tonight. I'm going fly fishing for bluegills. If I can't get 'em on one of the three patterns I've got here, it's not likely they're going to hit anything."

More than 30 years of fishing and writing about it have been enough to convince me that a fellow is on thin ice whenever he believes that this one lure or that one bait will get fish under any and all circumstances. And I'm not about to claim any such distinction for my three favorite bluegill flies. But, I do know that although I spend by far the most of my fishing time busting bass or searching for steelhead, I've still managed to put an awful dent in the bluegill population. And I stick mainly to three basic fly patterns which have proven their effectiveness over and over again.

What are those three patterns? They are an imitation bee, a black ant and a sponge-bodied spider. A variety of circumstances will dictate which of the three I'll employ on any given trip. Those circumstances might involve the season, the area of the lake to be fished, the manner in which the fish are feeding, the time of day or perhaps a combination of all of them.

The sponge spider, while one of the best for big 'gills, is the most limited in its use. This bluegill killer is limited because it is strictly a surface lure and there are times, quite a few of them, when these hard-fighting, good eating little panfish just aren't interested in taking anything off the top.

I find myself using the spiders mostly in the spring when the males begin to congregate in water from 2 to 4 feet deep to prepare the spawning beds. Water temperature always plays an important role in the movements of the bluegill clan. I'll find the 'gills moving into the shallows in late April when the water temperature starts hitting 60 degrees or more. Some of my favorite fishing spots in the spring of the year are the little open pockets one finds in the lily pads in lakes all over the country. It is in little pockets and openings like those in the pad fields that the sponge-bodied spider can be tremendously effective.

A lightweight fly rod and three productive fly patterns add up to a nice catch of bluegill. I've used sponge spiders, an imitation bee and black ants to take hundreds of bluegill like this.

This metal basket is one of the best of all methods of handling bluegill. The fish will stay alive and in better shape than on a stringer when the basket is employed. My dog, Chub, is interested in the catch I've just made.

I buy or build my own spiders on number 10 hooks. Use anything bigger than a number 10 and even the larger bluegills are going to have trouble getting themselves hooked although they try ever so hard. Use anything smaller and you'll be forever taking the little tiny fellows that you don't really want to bother with. I stick to a number 10 hook size for each of my three favorite patterns.

My choice of colors on the sponge spider is white or black. There may be in-between shades that would work as well, but whenever I've been able to take bluegills off the top at all, I've had no problem getting them on either the white or the black spiders. The bodies of the spiders I use aren't very big; again that's my preference because of the small mouth of the fish. I prefer a slender spider style with dangling legs of fine, lightweight rubber strands.

Never be in a big hurry when you are fly fishing for bluegills. Haste is one of the most common mistakes the newcomer to bluegill fly rodding usually makes. It applies if one is using the sponge-bodied spider and is even more important when the lure is the bee or ant pattern.

Your eyesight and a careful approach are every bit as important as casting ability when you are after bluegills in the shallows. That's why I emphasize taking time. Chances are excellent, if the water is clear, you'll be able to spot the fish if you are quiet and careful. They'll give themselves away as they feed in and around the pad pockets, especially in the spring and early summer.

There's a similarity in taking bass consistently and in being able to bring in a bag full of bluegills just about every time you go out. Knowledge of water is the answer. One of the primary secrets of any successful bass man is the constant pounding of those areas of a lake which he knows hold fish. He'll probably have a dozen or more spots on any lake he knows well that he'll hit again and again every time he's on the water. They won't all produce fish every trip but one or another of them will almost always provide something to put on the stringer.

That's how it is with bluegill. Once you've located spawning beds, especially in May, June and July in northern sections of the country, you can go back year after year, season after season and still stand an excellent chance of taking fish in the identical spots you scored the last time around. As with the bass, not all of the spots will produce all of the time. But once you've pinned down a half-dozen bedding areas, you're almost a cinch to find the fish active on one or another.

As I've mentioned, bluegills won't always hit on top. They do, however, keep an eye on the surface often enough to justify using the sponge spider any time out. I employ the spider first because it's so darn much fun to use. The spider attracts more than its share of big, husky 'gills and there are times when they will smack into it like you wouldn't believe.

My most consistent bluegill producer, whatever the season or the area of the lake I'm working, is that imitation of the bee. I suppose one could call it a sort of bastard version of the McGinty, except that I tie it without any wings. My bee has a red tail, alternate bands of brown and yellow yarn for the body and sparse brown hackle up front. The fly is designed to sink, slowly, and I think it is this gentle descent from the surface of the water which makes it the efficient little fish catcher it is.

I fish the lake I live on almost every day from April through October. A fellow can do that when he beds down every night only 60 feet or so from his boats. I was getting ready to head for my dock one evening early this season when I heard a fisherman cussing up a storm just a short distance away along the edge of the pad fields. He was fly fishing and I knew he was over water which had a

This is a bluegill spawning bed. Fish will frequent areas like this from April on through July in much of the northern United States. I cast to the area beyond the big log . . . then raise my rod tip high to keep the bluegill which has grabbed my imitation bee out of the heavy cover.

sizeable bluegill population. I eased my boat up behind him to see if I could help out.

"What's your problem, Pete?" I called out to him.

"Aw, hell, I can't get those cussed bluegills to hit. I know they're in here because I can see 'em feeding. But you think I can hook any of 'em. Hell, no!" He answered his own question and it was obviously an effort for him even to be friendly.

I watched for a couple of minutes and it didn't take long to see why he was having trouble. He would cast, then start yanking the fly back in with big pulls on his line before it ever had a chance to settle in the water.

"Mind if I make a suggestion?"

"Absolutely not. I sure couldn't do any worse than I am."

"This time when you cast, leave the fly alone. Let it settle in the water, maybe even sink 3 or 4 inches and then just barely twitch it with little jerks of the line in your left hand."

He made a false cast or two and the fly curved out into a little clearing 30 feet away in the pad fields. The fly lit softly, settled then gradually disappeared in the surface film.

"Now twitch it but don't move it more than a couple of inches."

There was a swirling of the water where the fly had disappeared, Pete jerked up his rod tip and then it was dipping and throbbing as a dandy bluegill flashed about in those circular dashes so characteristic of the way the little scrappers battle for their freedom. I hung around long enough to see him boat three fish and miss that many more before I fired up my own kicker and moved off. When I left he was wearing a smile that helped brighten my own evening.

I've already mentioned the necessity for taking it slow and easy when fly fishing for bluegill. Pete was making the mistake ever so many newcomers to bluegill fly fishing commit. He was beginning his retrieve before the fly had a chance to settle and sink and there are many, many times when you just can't buy a hit with that kind of approach.

Learn to leave your fly alone when you are after bluegills. Make the cast, then let the fly settle to different depths before you make even one little twitch with the line hand. Oftentimes a bluegill will rise slowly in the water to a position just below and behind your fly. One little twitch or two and . . . bingo! He'll move in and hit going away in one blur of motion hard for the eye to follow.

Usually I'll do best with the bee pattern where the fish

Note the plastic bag I have attached to my belt. It's another handy method for carrying fish when you are wading for bluegill.

I always work over those areas carefully where I've taken fish before. That's one of the key secrets of taking fish consistently. Concentrate on areas where you know the bluegill hang out and sooner or later you'll find fish.

Bluegill hardly ever break water, but this one didn't know that. My wife, Anita snapped this picture as he came up and out.

A basket full of bluegill. Fish will live for a couple of days in a basket like this if the water isn't unduly warm.

Here's the way I use the metal basket on my boat. Just depress the top and the fish is safely inside. Push up on the bottom and the fish drop free for cleaning. It's much faster and less bother than a stringer.

The bluegill is everybody's favorite. It's one of the best of all fish for the beginner with the fly rod. They might not weigh 10 pounds apiece but this happy youngster doesn't care. The bluegill is a great little scrapper and he'll thrill both novice and expert with his go-for-broke battle tactics.

Yes, that's a big bluegill making all that fuss. These popular panfish are among the games of the warm water species.

are in water no more than 4 feet deep. The fly sinks so slowly that using it on water any deeper makes fishing a terribly slow process. The bee is an all around pattern. It will take 'gills off the top just about as well as the spider when they happen to be working on the surface and it has taken hundreds of them for me at the mid-depths.

When bluegills are deep, and some of the bigger fish almost always are, I'm often able to make my best catches on the faster sinking black ant. The ant is a simple fly to construct. I simply tie an ant shaped hump at the rear of the hook, a little dab of black hackle in the center and another hump up front. I like to give those humps a couple of good coatings of head cement to provide a slick, shiny surface.

The retrieve I employ with this imitation ant is very similar to that used with the bee except I let it get down deeper. It's easier to use where the fish are farther down because it doesn't take all day long to reach them. Once the ant is down where I think the fish are I start moving it back easily and gently with those same little twitches of the line held in my left hand.

It's tougher to hook fish when they are well below the surface. Moving the fly with the left hand tugging the line

helps. Because the bluegill hits as the fly darts away, you'll oftentimes set the hook with the same tug you use to move the ant. Keep an eye on your fly line where it enters the water. If there is a straightening of the line or movement of any kind, hit him! The best way to do that is by pulling back sharply with the line hand at the same time you raise the rod tip.

Sometimes in fairly deep water I've fished two ants on one leader. I tie one on the end of the leader and put the other a couple of feet back up on a dropper. Hang two sizeable bluegills on the same cast as I've done a time or two and you'll have a real hassle on your hands.

There are a couple of things a fellow can do to greatly simplify the handling of bluegills whether he is wading or fishing from a boat. I prefer to wade if possible. I can get closer to the fish and disturb them less when wading.

Forget about using a stringer and get one of those mesh metal baskets or the plastic type of bag which can be attached to the belt. Of the two, I like the metal baskets best. They are available with a round chunk of styrofoam that does double duty as a lid and as a device which keeps the basket afloat and within easy reach. I tie a short length of cord to the top of the basket and attach the other end

Here are the best bets for bluegill. From left they are an imitation bee, the black ant and a sponge bodied spider.

Here's about all I need to take bluegill from the waters I fish most. Those flies at the top are sponge bodied spiders. Imitation bees are in the middle row. The bottom pair are black ants. All have taken hundreds of bluegill for me.

to my belt or waders. Then I just set it in the water and it floats there beside me. It's no trouble at all to handle fish because I have both hands free to unhook them and pop them in the basket.

That basket also comes in handy if you want to keep the fish alive for one reason or another prior to cleaning. If I come in after dark I just tie one end of the cord to my dock and the fish are free to swim around safely inside until I have a chance to get at them next day. One can hang such a basket over the side of the boat and use it in much the same fashion. Either way, the basket is twice as easy to handle as a stringer, keeps the fish alive and in better shape and is much easier to employ when you want to get the fish separated for cleaning. Baskets like the one I'm talking about have a second opening at the bottom. Just push up on the bottom and the fish will drop free.

Stick a pair of long nosed pliers in your pocket or tackle box when you go fly fishing for bluegills. If you really get into the fish (something that will happen frequently if you are on good bluegill water and learn the hot spots) you can use them to pinch the barb of the hook back. That way it will be much easier to free the fish you don't want to keep. Those pliers are going to be useful if you are keeping fish too because every now and then a bluegill will zap a fly so hard the hook gets embedded deeply in the tough gristle and flesh around the mouth and will be almost impossible to free by hand.

I haven't gone into rods, lines or leaders—use what you like best. I do most of my bluegilling with a little 7-foot lightweight fly rod which really lets me enjoy the sport. My 3- or 4-pound test tapered leaders are light enough to take fish and still of sufficient strength to pull free of quite a few of the snags and obstructions the fish will often be around.

Bluegills are great little warriors. If they had just a little more muscle and meat on their bones they'd kick hell out of every bass in any pond! Give my trio of favorite flies a try. I've got a big hunch you'll wind up agreeing they really are the best bets for bluegill.

The Top Ten Western Trout Flies

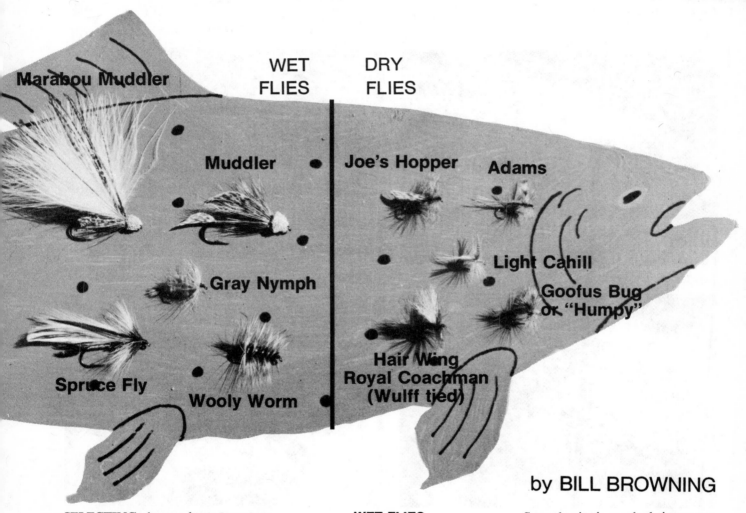

WET FLIES — DRY FLIES

Marabou Muddler

Muddler

Gray Nymph

Spruce Fly

Wooly Worm

Joe's Hopper

Adams

Light Cahill

Goofus Bug or "Humpy"

Hair Wing Royal Coachman (Wulff tied)

by BILL BROWNING

SELECTING the ten hottest western flies would be a formidable task to a lesser experienced person than Dan Bailey of Livingston, Montana, a renowned angler and fly shop owner who deals in massive fly sales to both dealers and hundreds of anglers.

Dan and his associates, and a select group of very knowledgeable anglers I've checked, agree almost without exception, that any angler with the following ten most popular flies in his vest could fish confidently and well anywhere in the west and beyond:

WET FLIES

Muddler (original)	#4
White marabou	#4
Spruce fly	#4
Black wooly worm	#6
Gray nymph	#8

DRY FLIES

Light Cahill	#12
Adams	#12
Royal Wulff	#10
Goofus (humpy)	#10
Joe's hopper	#8

Several criteria mark their success, according to Dan Bailey. They suggest insects ranging from mayflies and hoppers to swimming fry. They don't necessarily represent single insects but groups of insects. The way they float and the way they attract is the ultimate test of success.

The muddler was developed by Don Gapen to represent a sculpin, but it also imitates a hopper when fished dry. The white marabou was developed in Dan's shop from a plain streamer until they made a muddler out of it.

Dan Bailey, Livingston, Mont.

wet flies

Muddler

Marabou Muddler

Spruce Fly

Wooly Worm

Gray Nymph

The spruce fly was a standard wet fly in Oregon and Washington turned into a streamer.

The gray nymph is a general pattern of muskrat fur with blue-gray hackle and badger hair tail. It looks very buggy. Joe's hopper was developed from the original Michigan hopper, while the black wooly worm was first tied by Don Martinez of West Yellow-stone. The Cahill and Adams are standards.

Dan and Lee Wulff developed the Wulff tied flies, with the royal Wulff one of the best offshoots. The goofus was called Horner's Deer Hair until Pat Barnes of West Yellowstone coined the name "goofus." Others call it the "humpy."

Dan will admit that the fly isn't everything, however. He doesn't be-lieve it's necessary to match the hatch-ing insect exactly, but to come reasonably close in color and size, with size being perhaps the more critical. He does feel the most important thing is the presentation and float to the fish. Dan feels, too, that a skilled angler with ten other flies of his own selec-tion would do better than an unskilled

Dan Bailey, with Joe's Hopper

dry flies

Light Cahill

Adams

Royal Coachman (Wulff tied)

Goofus Bug or "Humpy"

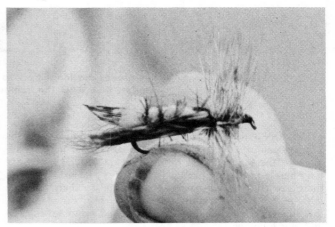

Joe's Hopper

angler with the ten best flies named here.

The flies here will work fine on trout across the country, but western seasons and weather are more unpredictable than in the east. Generally streamers and wets are best spring and fall. Dries come off early then taper out by fall. However, warm days can change this pattern. Our most predictable Montana hatch is the June and early July salmon fly hatch on certain rivers. Then the sofa pillow fly reigns supreme.

To sum up, Dan advises this basic group of flies, then add to it other favorites. "Just so it looks alive, and good to eat" he says. Success in fly fishing lies with the angler's skills and he should stay with flies his own ex-perience proves best. "These ten flies will do the trick," he says, "but when trout are ready to eat, they aren't so choosy. We don't have all the answers yet, and that's a good thing, too. We'll have more fun checking out the tricky trout."

"SQUIRREL HUNTING" IN SNOOK COUNTRY

by JIM MARTENHOFF

Mangroves Make Casting A Challenge!

Everglades National Park is snaggy, fish-filled paradise.
Anglers here work the mangrove shoreline of a tiny island.

LOOK ON almost any map and the southernmost tip of the Florida peninsula seems to be reasonably solid land. Actually, it's the tattered hem of the Florida skirt. There's dry land here and there, but mostly it's soggy and marshy. And there are zillions of mangroves standing on their multiple legs in the shallow water. Seen on the horizon as a thin, low line, they seem like a finely stitched seam sewing sea and sky together.

Hundreds of channels and creeks lead back into the mangrove wilderness of the Everglades National Park. There are wide rivers, too; and the intertwining waterways create so many islets a portion of the coast is known as the Ten Thousand Islands. The count is modest.

This is snook country, spawning ground for that rampaging gamester who starts moving in during May and June. It is also home to redfish, jack, the southern spotted weakfish or trout. You'll find tarpon, too; and barracuda, and the ubiquitous black tip shark which will smack a top-water plug as readily as any gamefish.

You can fish the open water areas, or the flats offshore, but since snook especially like to lurk under the overhang-ing mangroves the more popular form of angling is casting to the snaggy shorelines. Twisted remnants of dead buttonwood, pockets of water beneath the bushes, tiny, overgrown coves, the narrow mouths of little creeks, all make tempting targets and the plug-caster lives in hope throughout the day. Never have you seen so many spots likely to conceal husky fish.

The catch is, of course, that you have to be fairly skilled with plug gear, or your lure winds up in the branches with irritating frequency. Some of the local fishermen who have experienced the exasperation of retrieving plugs from the mangroves call it "squirrel hunting." The guy who is all thumbs will spend all his time squirrel hunting; but for the caster who has some talent—or who seeks to develop it—this is a casting heaven.

It would be a disservice to assert there are fish under every tree or snag. It simply isn't so. But there is a special fascination in slowly cruising the mangrove edges and casting to likely targets. It's reward enough to watch your plug drop into a selected spot, in a perfect bullseye. If you can make repeated casts with the same or similar success, there is even a sense of achievement; of fulfillment. It's the place to hone your casting skills to a fine edge, even if you don't catch a fish. Many South Florida fishermen have even mastered a specialized bounce cast, whipping the plug with a sidearm motion, keeping it low, so it will ricochet off the water and bounce 4 or 5 feet back into a hole under low-lying mangrove branches. It's almost awe-inspiring to watch a really good caster working the mangroves.

You never really tire of it, and there is always the moment you waited for—a moment when the water explodes in an eruption of spray, with a sharp, popping noise, and a snook slams into your plug. That's when you go to work, for you've got to work him away from the mangroves before he wraps your line around a root and breaks you off. Snook are nasty that way, and seem to know exactly how to make a fool of a fisherman. They can root down in the mud and tear you off, speed around a mangrove stub growing upward from the bottom and pop the line. Redfish (channel bass) depend on sheer, brute strength; tarpon like to jump and spit the plug in your general direction; jack turn sideways in the water to get leverage with their broad, flat bodies and swim around the boat trying to tire *you* out. But the snook releases you, then swims back to his buddies to brag about the one that got away.

Squirrel hunting is an utterly fascinating form of angling with its own rewards. You are rarely skunked, usually catch a satisfying bag, go home with the pleasant memories of a few bruisers that broke off; sometimes make your limit with ease. Fish are just as persnickety here as they are anywhere else. Sometimes they'll slowly follow your plug, stare at it in disdain, and you'll get the distinct feeling that if they had a thumb it would be at their nose, pointing in your direction. And sometimes the calm morning is a series of explosions as fish strike regularly. You never know what will happen. I've seen tarpon, hooked underneath the overhanging mangroves by a bounce-caster, leap straight up into the branches. There's a wild racket as the tarpon thrashes in the greenery, a mighty splash as he dives back into the water—leaving your plug dangling from the tree.

Squirrel hunting country is big country—and boat country. The "inside" waters are fairly sheltered; it can get bumpy outside when the wind's up. Since fish make the decisions for the fisherman, local anglers often try both—and may run 60, 80 miles in a day. Flamingo is the headquarters area in the Everglades National Park with docks, launching ramp, marina, lodge, restaurant and all the facilities. "Out front" is Florida Bay, dotted with islands. You reach the inside waters via the Buttonwood Canal which connects with Coot Bay. From here it's a short run to Whitewater Bay. The main channel leading all the way to remote Shark River, some 20 miles from Flamingo, is well-marked. A stranger who wanders too far off the beaten path can get lost very easily—unless he buys a chart at Flamingo, refers to it regularly, combines it with a good marine compass on his boat to keep himself oriented.

There are rental skiffs at Flamingo, although their size and engine horsepower limit distances. Tourists can bring their own trailer craft—no problem these days when you have interstate highways reducing travel time.

One of the best possible boats for the Flamingo backcountry, oddly enough, is still not too popular locally. It's the bass boat, at its best here in about 16 feet of length with a 40- or 50-horsepower outboard and an electric trolling motor. A few of them are seen, and they'll probably grow in popularity. The electric trolling motor, used in bursts, propels you silently along the mangrove shorelines. Without it, you must either pole the boat or use the outboard to move from one section to another. Once in awhile you find a patch of shore with a paralleling breeze and you drift gently from one cast to the next.

Novice squirrel hunters can always explore in easy stages. The first, logical step is to visit Coot Bay, perhaps a 10-minute run in the average outboard. You can't get lost, and there are miles of snag-filled shoreline to explore. Plenty of snook have been taken from Coot Bay pockets. Occasionally you may see an alligator examining your lure. Don't let him get it. Alligators have a low boiling point. Keep an eye out for what seem to be low, waterlogged, bumpy logs. If it moves, it ain't no log. It's a 'gator.

Next step would be Whitewater Bay, reached via Tarpon

Casting toward the shore, shortly after sunrise.

Creek. When you leave the creek a vast expanse of island-dotted water stretches before you. A marked channel leads straight across it. You can explore the shoreline to the right first—and you should get action before going a mile.

Total boating tyros shouldn't explore too far without first acquiring some background. A midwestern angler, for example, who'd like to try squirrel hunting would profit from first taking a U.S. Power Squadron or Coast Guard Auxiliary boating course. Pay special attention during the lessons on charts and compass.

With that kind of know-how you can make the grand tour, halting to fish where the mood strikes you. It's about 4 miles from Flamingo to Whitewater Bay. From here you can follow the markers to Cormorant Pass and Little Shark River and run down to the open Gulf of Mexico. Swing eastward along the shoreline, and within 2 miles you'll come to Big Sable Creek where, if the fish are in the mood, you can have a ball on a falling tide. Ditto for Little Sable Creek a little further on down the coast. Middle Cape Canal can provide plenty of action, especially at its upper end in Lake Ingraham on the ebb. And you can finish your voyage running down the coast to Flamingo. Stay fairly well offshore to avoid the occasional bars and shoals; follow the markers when they appear.

If you don't vary much from your course it amounts to about 45 nautical miles; with some exploration of side areas along the way, and maybe occasional back-tracking, it can mount up easily to 50 or 60 miles. Every inch of the way is virgin mangrove wilderness. The only sign of civilization is the channel marker and an occasional boat you pass.

Veteran local anglers, armed with specialized knowledge and familiar with favorite holes, may work just one area all day. If the fish are in a lazy mood, they may make the entire run knowing they will find action somewhere along the way.

They'll keep an eye on the weather, however; for the Cape Sable area can be downright nasty for small boats when the wind's up. It's safer, on those occasions, to stay inside.

Tackle is pretty well standardized for the veteran plug casters who fish the mangrove country. Most anglers carry two rods—both with revolving spool reels. One will be equipped with a topwater plug; the other with either a jig or a shallow-running plug. It gives the fisherman a chance to make a fast switch when necessary. So far they're fairly typical bass outfits, but there are these differences: line is usually monofilament, around 10, 12 or at most 15 pounds in test. A 3- or 4-foot section of 20-pound mono is tied on for leader, the plug tied directly to that. No hardware, no snaps, no swivels. Spinning gear is not too popular with the local casters; you have better control, they feel, with revolving spool reels equipped with an adjustable drag. You need every break you can get when you hook a snook under a bush or next to a snag. This kind of squirrel hunting calls for fairly heavy artillery, or the fish will just make a monkey out of you.

Casting ability is important. Distances are usually short, perhaps averaging 50 feet or so, rarely much farther. If you can consistently drop a practice plug in a peach basket at 50 feet—regardless of windage—you can squirrel hunt in snook country. If you can sidearm with that accuracy, you can master the bounce cast—which can produce fish when all else fails.

Flamingo is about 80 miles south and west of Miami. It is some 50 miles from Homestead, nearly all of it empty wilderness within the National Park. Accommodations are plentiful in Homestead, but a visitor is better off if he can stay at Flamingo itself. Lodgings are excellent, the restaurant will even cook your catch for you. The mosquitoes,

Vic Dunaway holds up nice redfish (channel bass) captured in mangrove country. His son Danny is at pole. Bass boat is good choice for park waters, especially inside waters.

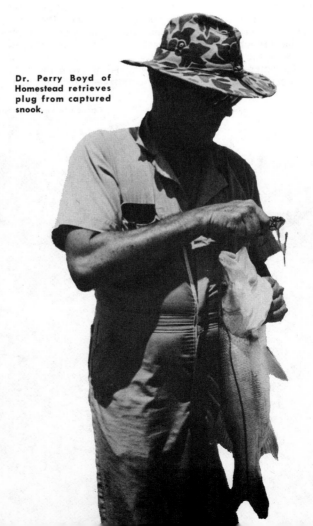

Dr. Perry Boyd of Homestead retrieves plug from captured snook.

Plugs are artfully worked out from under mangroves, usually with whipping motion making them act like injured bait.

When you get a strike you know it, and must drag the fish away from the mangroves.

Boyd caught this fair-sized snook along mangroves.

particularly in summer, are mean and spiteful.

They are also muscular. An unconfirmed rumor has it that the Flamingo mosquitoes last summer carried off two alligators and a tourist schoolteacher from Iowa. Fortunately they are vicious only at dawn and dusk. A local tradition has it that the snook bite best when the skeeters are also biting, but that's all part of the game. This writer happens to think it is true, for I have caught the most snook when I was slapping with one hand and casting with the other.

Fishing at Flamingo varies seasonally, as it does anywhere else. Redfish are thick in the autumn; late spring and early summer are good times for snook. August and September are lousy months; it is usually blistering hot, and the fish will lay in the shade and sneer at you. You can catch fish, but you'll have to work at it. As a friend once commented to me when we were casting with little success, "I bet you I catch a snook in the next hundred casts." (He didn't. It took 150 tries.) Winter months can provide fun-fishing, although the area is usually crowded with tourists.

Meantime, squirrel hunting sharpens your casting skills like no other technique. You feel downright pleased with yourself when you can park a plug in a pocket no bigger than a bucket, and do so at 75 feet or more (at 50 feet you can open a beer can).

And on those rare occasions when you go home skunked —which happens to good fishermen everywhere now and then—you can console yourself with two thoughts: You saw some of the most beautiful country the Lord ever created, still in a natural and unspoiled state; and you managed to keep your plug out of the trees.

That's the major appeal of squirrel hunting in snook country. Rare beauty, active angling, and a casting challenge rarely encountered elsewhere.

TOP BANANA
in the Bunch

by SAM VENABLE, Jr.

"Yellow banana"—plastic worm-nightcrawler rig—jigging cork—and "pole shaken" bass. Note simple crank reel at butt of pole.

AS A sporting goods dealer, H. A. LaRue doesn't always practice what he preaches.

He carries a healthy stock of firearms and ammunition, but personally prefers to do his big game hunting with bow and arrow. And while he's constantly expounding upon the virtues of the latest styles in outdoor raiment and is "more than happy to order it for you," chances are you'll find him crouched in his duck blind wrapped in the same wear-worn parka he's had for years.

So it's not too strange, then, that he also turns his back on the myriad of rods, reels, line and lures in his inventory when he hangs the "Gone Fishing" sign on his store in Knoxville, Tenn.

Instead, H.A. picks up only one piece of equipment— a tapered length of amber fiberglass rigged with a simple crank reel and stout monofilament. It's his "yellow banana." With it, he deals a powerful hurtin' on East Tennessee's bass population.

The stick is a jig pole, an item of fishing tackle which is being seen more and more frequently each year in the Tennessee Valley region. Of hollow construction, they usually measure 12 to 14 feet in length. The lightweight— but backboned—poles are eyeless, so the line must be threaded through the center. A snap-on reel at the butt serves only to keep the heavy (20-pound-test or better) line coiled and out of the way.

Jig poles began to appear in this area about 15 or 20 years ago, but like bootleg whiskey, they stayed pretty much under the counter. Only when a guy was 5 miles up the lake and in the presence of his closest fishing buddy would he dare unearth it. After a successful day of bass snatchin', the pole would again be covered with burlap on the floor of the craft as the tight-lipped jiggers made their way back to the landing, conventional gear in full display.

Fortunately for the palates of fishermen, as well as their success ratings, illegal bourbon whiskey and secrecy about jig poles have both become a thing of the past.

Properly used under the right conditions, the banana is possibly the most lethal weapon an angler can draw upon for bass. I've seen "pole shakers," as they're called locally, string limits before fishermen with spinning or casting equipment even get into the ball game.

On a trip to nearby Douglas Lake last February, I elected to cast a jig and pork rind strip, a traditional cold water bass slayer, while H.A. stubbornly stuck with his banana. Within an hour, he had picked up three largemouths to my one unproductive strike. By the time his fourth bass came flopping into the boat, I was eyeing the bow-mounted jigging platform enviously. When number five came aboard, I could take no more embarrassment. H.A. yielded the seat under threat of bodily harm.

On that particular jaunt, we were jigging with a wad of plastic worms and nightcrawlers threaded onto a 6/0 lead-head hook and suspended several feet under a large cork bobber. That's the "standard" way to use the banana and the method is simple, indeed:

Slowly and quietly, scull your boat along the shoreline, shaking the concoction via wrist and forearm action around stumps, tree limbs, rocky ledges and other typical bass hangouts. The figure-eight sculling and up-and-down jigging can be a bit tiring at first, but it only takes a few hours of practice to fall into the routine.

Once a tap is felt, quickly drop the rod tip and let the cork sink until it is just barely in sight. Then lean into that fish with all you've got—HARD—and enjoy a one-on-one battle as bass and angler scrap at opposite ends of a 6-foot stretch of monofilament. It's literally a case of "he versus thee."

Cold weather jigging with nightcrawlers like that is by far the most popular use of the banana. Check any of the larger Tennessee Valley area reservoirs which have been stained by late-winter or early-spring runoff and I'll guarantee you'll see jiggers in action on nearly every good looking bank.

A dingy or even muddy situation is the key to the whole affair. Without mud, a nightcrawler jigger is out of business unless he wants to fish after dark.

Murky water serves a dual purpose. Naturally, it hides the angler and his boat from the fish. But just as important, its presence also indicates that rains have washed the banks thoroughly and dumped a fresh supply of goodies into the water.

The bass themselves get into the picture by moving onto the banks and other shallow areas to take advantage of the available food as well as to bask in the slightly warmer temperatures which are usually found there. Locating the

Nightcrawler jiggers work a section of likely looking bank in north Georgia's Blue Ridge Lake. Man in stern helps steady boat against wind to enable companion to work pocket effectively. Note large cork bobber used.

Several popular east Tennessee jig pole lures, clockwise from Jitterbug: Doddle-Sockr, plastic worm split for jigging, plastic worm rigged in conventional manner, and Go Devil.

realizing. In fact, the pole is commanding such year-round attention that some banana enthusiasts like H.A. have almost forgotten about their conventional gear altogether.

Once the water clears for the summer and warms up enough to drive the bass off the banks during daytime, the pole's role changes from that of shaker to buzzer. Under those conditions, the banana man normally operates under the veil of darkness unless he is lucky enough to locate water dingy enough to camouflage his presence.

Also, unlike winter jigging when silence is the rule, warm water jig-poling is a noisy affair. You've got to talk 'em into striking. Just about any large, gurgling, wave-making top water plug will work. Jitterbugs, Sputterbugs, Devils Horses and Go Devils are among the more popular selections around East Tennessee lakes.

They're tied directly to the monofilament and swished, sloshed, blooped and sputtered around any log, bush, weed bed, tree top, stump or rock that looks even remotely like a bass home. It doesn't take too long for the action to occur. Believe me, when an irritated largemouth charges your sputtering bait only a scant few feet from the boat about 3 A.M., your heart gets one hell of a workout!

I was skittering a black Devils Horse along stone rip-rap in Fort Loudoun Lake one summer night when I stopped the lure 6 inches off a stump I'd been circling with figure-eights. The bait rested momentarily in the bright moonlight, still sending out small circles as the fore and aft spinners began to slow down.

From out of nowhere a pint-sized largemouth, hardly big enough to inhale the cigar-shaped plug, churned from beneath the stump and crashed into the lure, spraying water all over me and the front of the boat.

right temperature area is vital for winter jigging, so an accurate thermometer is almost as important a piece of tackle as the banana itself.

Most confirmed jiggers start suffering erratic pulse beats when they get readings in the low to mid-50s near the bank. Give an addict that, plus a warm, late-winter shower to darken things up a bit and you'll see him start reeling off lies to the wife, boss and even to card-playing buddies in order to watch corks dip under the surface.

That brings up one other important facet of winter jigging: when the signs are right, don't wait an instant, man. GO! It's the old "eat, drink and be merry" routine modified for fishing. Tomorrow the conditions may change.

I got a graphic lesson on that point last year after Bill Nichols, a close bassing friend from Clinton, Tenn., and I picked up grapevine news that the upper portion of Norris Lake was hot for jigging. We raced to the reservoir and enjoyed an afternoon of top-notch pole shaking. We simply could not find a bad bank that day; nearly every possible hideout produced a scrappy largemouth or Kentucky bass.

Realizing that times like that are sinfully few and far between, I was right back on the scene the next day. But my heart sank as I wheeled into the launch area and stared at the reservoir. Overnight, the lake had changed into a different world. A surge of cold, clear water from upstream had put the damper on jigging in less than 12 hours. I tried in vain for half the day, then left without a strike.

Nightcrawler jigging isn't the only way a banana comes in handy, though, as many anglers in East Tennessee are

H. A. LaRue battles scrappy Norris Lake smallmouth that sucked ➤ in his plastic jigging worm as he "long-lined" on a steep rocky bank. Note jigging platform mounted on bow.

Author sputters Go Devil along promising weed bed.

Author nets a 2-pound Fort Loudoun Lake largemouth that charged buzzing lure as it kicked a fuss in shallow muddy water.

Author's wife uses jig pole to swing crappie jig into likely-looking hole.

Needless to say, I had no problem setting the hook! I was so startled, I let out a yell audible for half a mile and yanked the pole skyward all in one motion. The bass completed the 180-degree arc in seconds and landed—flopping and shaking—in the bottom of the boat. Still quivering with excitement, I unhooked the little fellow and returned him to the water.

That was 3 years ago. I don't know if my nervous system could stand an attack from that bass now if he's done any growing! I've snatched a lot of bass with a buzzer, but that one took the cake.

If jigging and skittering weren't enough, plenty of other angling possibilities exist for the banana man with an inventive mind. On steep bluffs, he can let out extra line, remove the cork and "long line" with either nightcrawlers, a plastic worm or spring lizard (salamander).

By adding a short length of light leader, he can plop small crappie jigs into brush piles and other hard-to-reach spots while casters hang up notoriously from afar. In fact, some enterprising banana enthusiasts have been killing two birds with a single rock in the early days of spring when both bass and crappies are active.

The man in front dabbles wads of meat for bass, while the fellow in the stern jiggles flies for slabsides. That's as sure-fire a method for a mixed string of fine eating as I know of.

But any way you handle it, the jig pole comes mighty close to being an all-purpose rod for the lake fisherman. Properly used, there's little it can't do.

In fact, my wife and I have discovered an off-the-lake task for the lengthy bananas. She's a high school teacher, so we're occasionally the target of student pranksters who slip into the front yard at night and drape the shrubs and trees with rolls of toilet tissue. Those poles can clean even the highest limbs with ease!

And I'll bet that's one use that even H.A. hasn't thought of yet.

◄ H. A. LaRue displays 10½-pound largemouth he caught jigging with nightcrawlers in the winter from a small, state-owned lake.

A. W. McLaughlin battles crappie that went for artificial bait in springtime. He gently leads large, exhausted fish into net when hook won't tear loose from the soft mouth tissue.

S·L·O·W GO
for crappies

by RUSSELL TINSLEY

Big spinnerbaits are the ticket for taking jumbo-sized crappies.

McLaughlin works lure along area where crappies traditionally gather in spring.

THE SUSPENSE was maddening. Take my word for that.

I was retrieving the artificial lure slowly, near the bottom, reeling as deliberately as my impatience would allow. It was a supreme test of self-discipline because a crappie was nipping at the bucktail of my spinnerbait and there was the impulse to try and anticipate the strike, jerking occasionally, rather than waiting for the feel of a bite.

"There he is! . . . missed him again! . . . he's still interested! . . . Oh, damn, another miss!"

A. W. McLaughlin laughed at me out loud.

"Settle your nerves," he chuckled. "It's going to take a spell to get your timing back."

I pitched the yellow-colored bait near the stump partly exposed above the surface, let it sink a few feet, then commenced reeling in slow motion. This time when I felt a nip I set the hook into solid resistance.

The crappie fought in tight, deep figure-eights, but the protest didn't last long. Soon I had the fish at the surface.

"Need the net?" Mac asked.

He glanced around at the crappie. "Nah," he said, answering his own question. "Pull that one aboard and go back and get a good 'un."

True, it was no bragging-sized specimen, but it was a respectable crappie, measuring about a foot long. But Mac and I weren't after just "respectable" crappies. We wanted big ones, 15-plus inches, at least in the 2-pound class.

Now a 2-pound fish might not seem like much, but it takes a lot of crappie to attain that weight. The fish's size can be deceiving. The one-dimensional view from the side gives an impression of bulk since a crappie is a deep-bodied fish. But it is narrow through the shoulders and doesn't carry much weight on its frame.

McLaughlin owns a sporting goods store in Marble Falls, in the central Texas lakes country, and he regularly weighs crappies on his state-certified scales. He says the typical "2-pounder" won't even weigh a pound. I once put one 17½ inches long on his scales and to my dismay found that it lacked an ounce of hitting the 2-pound mark. I would have guessed it would have weighed nearly 3 pounds.

Mac once had a mounted crappie in his store that truly was an impressive sight. The fish was 22 inches long and, when caught, had weighed 3 pounds, 12 ounces. Every time someone admired the fish Mac would ask him to guess what it weighed. Estimates ran from 5 pounds up. One man even remarked that he thought it would weigh 10 pounds "at least." Yet the world-record white crappie weighed only 5 pounds, 3 ounces (from Enid Lake, Mississippi) while the record black crappie went 5 pounds even (from Santee-Cooper Reservoir, South Carolina).

By the time I had my fish unhooked and securely on the stringer, Mac was battling a crappie. I waited with the net, but when Mac got the fish where he could see it, he simply windmilled it into the boat and reached for the anchor.

"They're here," he said. "Maybe we can tease Old Grandpa into hitting."

Maybe there is something to the saying about the third time being a charm. Mac and I had been out twice during the prior week and we hadn't found a cooperative crappie. Today we found 'em in the very first spot we tried.

Another one goes on the stringer after a concentration is pinpointed.

Catches like this are possible during the spring spawn on artificial lures.

Fishing a spawning area produced this hefty Kentucky Lake catch.

Mac's house perches on a rocky bluff overlooking Marble Falls Lake, one of seven man-made impoundments strung along the Colorado River of Texas. It is no great shakes as a fishing lake but it does have a fair population of crappies. Each spring, when we zero in on this species, we catch quite a few crappies from this narrow impoundment. We know about what time of year to fish and what spots to try, and once fish are located, most of the mystery is solved.

We don't fish Lake Marble Falls because it is the best. There are many other lakes which offer better crappie fishing. We spend much of our search here because of convenience. Finding cooperative crappies in the spring is largely a hit-or-miss proposition. There is a general framework—about the first week in March into April in central Texas—which is used as a basic guide, but crappies might vary their spawning season from year to year, depending on the weather. Once they move into preferred areas the action might remain good for as long as two continuous weeks. But then it might be prime for a day or two, then shut off completely, particularly if there is a sudden drop in temperature.

Much of the guesswork can be eliminated by being familiar with a lake and knowing its "pattern." That's why, with few exceptions, we fish Lake Marble Falls almost exclusively. We know generally about the time of year the crappies will move into shallow water and commence hitting artificial baits, and we know, based on where we found them before, about where the fish will be concentrated.

It isn't something that is unique with just this lake, how-ever. In many impoundments scattered around the country, catching crappies on artificial lures in the spring is popular sport. I've got a friend who, once he gets the word, takes off for Kentucky Lake, in western Kentucky, and he always brings home ice chests packed with crappies. Another friend who lives in northern Texas enjoys the same fabulous sport on huge Lake Texoma, astraddle the Texas-Oklahoma border.

There is a private lake about 120 miles drive from Mac's home where he and I go at least once each spring. This man-made reservoir is about 100 yards wide and a half-mile long. For 3 years running we visited the lake in early April and enjoyed some terrific crappie fishing. But this past spring we outguessed ourselves. Mac speculated that we were hitting just the twilight of the crappie run. If we planned our trip for maybe 2 weeks or 10 days earlier than usual, we'd get in on the beginning and catch not only more crappies, but larger ones.

It has been said that a man is stupid to tinker with a good thing, and I agree. Mac and I spent 2 days assiduously prospecting our favorite crappie holes and we didn't catch a fish. Thankfully the black bass and sunfish were obliging or it would have been a dud trip. We learned our lesson.

But just finding crappies doesn't put them on the stringer. Mac and I became aware of that salient fact as we cast near the stump and retrieved our lures slowly and had repeated strikes, yet only occasionally did we connect with a fish. Usually a crappie just nips at a bait. The angler must develop a certain "feel" to know precisely when to set the hook. Too quick or too late and he gets nothing.

McLaughlin employed tiny spinner to entice this Lake Lyndon B. Johnson crappie to hit.

Now the idea of taking crappies in the springtime on artificial lures is nothing new. When the fish migrate into their "holding" or spawning areas, they are susceptive to a myriad of baits which imitate a minnow, the crappie's primary and favorite food. The philosophy is that the smaller the bait, the more crappies a fisherman will take. Tiny 1/8-ounce or 1/16-ounce marabou jigs are universal favorites for taking spring crappies.

Yet surprisingly, Mac and I were fishing with bass-sized spinner baits. Our favorite lure is one of those safety-pin-type jobs, with a Colorado spinner on one of the wire legs, a leadhead, hook and bucktail on the other. It weighs about a half-ounce, much too large for crappie fishing in the estimation of many experts who specialize in the taking of this ubiquitous fish.

A crappie specialist in my hometown of Austin, Texas, one "Red" Cameron, gave Mac and me the idea of using large baits for large crappies. One myth that has been widely published, according to Red, is that a person must

Just about any bait which imitates a minnow will fool a springtime crappie.

use tiny minnows to catch crappies, because of this fish's small mouth. He agrees that the small minnow is the ticket if a person wants to take crappies in quantity. But for quality, big crappies, he advocates using a large minnow, one about 2 inches long.

"Each school of crappies has just a very few larger fish," he explained. "By using a large minnow, you discourage the small crappies and only the big rascals will bite. It is selective fishing."

When Red told me this, I didn't question his theory. After all, it is difficult to argue with success. He catches more large crappies than any person I know.

Mac was the one who came up with the big-artificials-for-big-crappies idea. Every spring, he told me later, he regularly picks up a few large crappies while fishing for largemouth black bass. For a long time he thought he only was taking an occasional stray. But then after hearing Red Cameron preach his big-bait philosophy at a fishing clinic, Mac put two and two together and once he'd take a crappie, he'd anchor at the spot and fish it thoroughly. Often he would catch several fish, all of them fairly large. Then he began experimenting, using various-sized baits, and when he fished small baits he caught mostly small crappies; when he switched to large lures, the number of fish he would catch would be much reduced, but the fish that he did take would be of large size.

After Mac got me started in this unique sport, I now find myself eagerly awaiting that brief but magic period each spring when crappies show a fondness for artificial baits. Why these fish are most susceptive to artificials in the spring, when they are in shallow water, than any other time of the year, I don't know. I have caught them on small jigs in summer and fall, when they are in deep water, but I've dismissed such catches as more happenchance than skill.

Being at the right spot at the right time is certainly the primary consideration. Unless fish are present and are co-operative, it is impossible to catch same, an obvious fact of life that many fishermen ignore. If you make a dozen casts into an area without a hit, you might as well move on and try someplace else. When crappies are present and cooperative, they do not keep it a secret.

That magic time comes sometime in the spring, as the water temperature nears 68 degrees, and crappies move into shallow water, 5 to 10 feet deep in most man-made impoundments, and then prepare for the spawn. This period is highly variable, depending on the locale, coming in March in the deep South, to maybe June or even early July in the far northern states. The obvious initial step, then, is to pinpoint the month when crappies spawn in your area. A letter to the freshwater fisheries division of your state game and fish department will bring the information.

But that's just the beginning. No one can give exact and accurate information. Fish are just not that predictable. Should crappies spawn in your area in mid-April, for example, then you should commence searching the first week in April and continue to the end of the month. If you're trying the right spots you should find the fish sometime during this time span. A "right spot" will be over a fairly firm bottom, relatively shallow water, and usually around some sort of obstruction such as a submerged fallen tree, a stump or a rockpile, or maybe even along a weedbed. Any lake might have just a very few of these "selected" areas, and this is another reason for becoming intimately familiar with any body of water. Once you locate such an area, remember it or, better yet, mark it on a map for future reference. Crappies use the same spawning areas each year, unless something happens to discourage them, such as a fluctuating water level.

Trolling is one method for prospecting a long and likely stretch of shoreline. Try to head into any prevailing breeze and throttle the engine as far down as it will go without stalling. The slower you move a bait for crappies, the better. Start with tiny baits since the idea is to simply locate fish. Any lure which imitates a minnow will do the trick, be it a deep-running wobbling plug, a spoon, leadhead jig or spinnerbait.

Once you catch a crappie, cut the engine and either drift fish or anchor and explore the area thoroughly. Chances are that fish wasn't alone. Crappies are school fish and where you find one you normally will find several.

A system that Mac and I sometimes use is for one of us to fish a tiny bait, the other a bass-sized lure. There are occasions when fish simply won't hit the larger baits. When that happens we go to the smaller baits with no regrets. Pride can be a terrible hindrance sometimes.

With any bait the secret is to fish it slow and evenly, sans jerks. Even with a leadhead jig, just reel steadily. At first try just a foot or so beneath the surface, then go progressively deeper with each cast, until you pinpoint the strata where crappies are holding. But generally they will be in the lower third of the water, near bottom, rather than near the surface.

One mistake most fishermen make is they employ snap swivels with their baits. Tie a lure directly to the line. A swivel, even a small one, adds too much bulk. Anyway, if you're reeling fast enough to twist your line, you are fishing much too rapidly.

Inquire in many tackle stores about the crappie fishing and you are apt to get blank stares. This fish has more aliases than a fugitive on the FBI's most-wanted list. It is likely called white perch, sac-a-lait, bachelor, bride perch, campbellite, chinaquapin perch, lamplighter, papermouth, or any of a dozen or more other nicknames, in your locale. But whatever the name, it still is the same delightful fish to catch.

After a spell Mac and I began to get the hang of things again, to wipe the rust off our technique. But while we were getting strikes on practically every cast, Mac was putting three fish in the boat to every one of mine. Finally he could stand the humor of it no longer.

"Got my old 'let-back' technique working to perfection," he said with a chuckle.

It was a bit of unorthodox strategy that Mac often uses to entice a recalcitrant crappie to take his lure. When he feels a fish nipping at the bait, he drops his rod tip and quits reeling, allowing the bait to fall freely, as if the crappie has killed the baitfish. Obviously the fish sees its meal dropping and it figures it better grab quick before it ends up in the belly of one of its compadres.

"So what's new about that?" I asked.

"Nothing except that I've been practicing," Mac confessed with obvious glee. "Came out yesterday and found the fish, right here, and I caught about a dozen nice ones in less than an hour's time. Now wasn't that a sneaky thing to do?"

I told him no, I appreciated the fact that he came out and located the crappies and saved me a lot of time and bother. Sticking the hook into another fish, I started it toward the boat.

"The joke's on you," I said.

Mac also was busy with a crappie and he turned toward me and grinned. "On both of us," he said. "And aren't we having fun?"

Fishing for crappies in spring is much like plugging for bass along shoreline.

DROP A LITTLE CHUM INTO THE SEA

by MILT ROSKO

← Captain Lionel Holley and his deckhand get a utility can full of trash from a shrimp trawler. The trash, a mixture of small fish, shrimp, crabs and squid, makes an excellent chum for all of the species found in Gulf Waters.

THE DECKHAND on the shrimp trawler was perspiring as he shoveled the trash that accumulated on the deck overboard. The accumulation was the unsalable portion of the catch made during their night of dragging nets through the Gulf of Mexico. The trash, as it is commonly referred to by shrimpers, included crushed shrimp, crabs, squid and an assortment of small fish.

In the half-light of daybreak the broad expanse of Gulf was mirror smooth, and only the generator on board the shrimper broke the silence as we tied up to her stern and took aboard a utility can full of the trash. This would serve as our chum supply once the deckhand had finished his cleaning chores.

Suddenly the water at the stern of the trawler erupted as several huge fish swarmed to the surface to gorge on the shrimper's leavings. It was still too dark for our eyes to penetrate the darkness of the water, but we knew the fish were big. There were lots of them too; we could just make out their backs as they pushed water, streaking to the trash as it dropped into the sea.

Captain Lionel Holley was hurriedly baiting up a pair of rigs equipped with floats, using several hard-tailed jacks extracted from the can of trash, while his deckhand placed whole squids on another pair of sturdy outfits.

Lionel then dipped into the can of mixed chum and tossed out a smorgasbord that brought 20 to 30 fish swarming to the surface! The hungry group included little tuna (called bonito by the local people), cobia, jack crevalle and several king mackerel. Not a fish in the melee weighed under 10 pounds, and some looked to weigh over 30!

I know it will sound like an exaggeration, but within ½-minute after our four baits hit the water all four were taken by these hungry Gulf residents. I don't remember how many we landed, or even what they were for that matter. But the action came so fast and furiously that for the next several hours we were into fish almost constantly. Some we landed, many gained their freedom, and only when the sun was high in the sky did the fish begin to become moody, having filled themselves on the free meal being dumped overboard by the trawler and the *Quicksilver,* a big charter packet from Biloxi which was our boat.

While heading north to our port on Mississippi's low seacoast, we sat in the spacious cabin of the *Quicksilver,* and enjoyed a repast of freshly boiled shrimp and a couple of cold Budweisers, all the while telling and retelling each other of our individual pre-dawn experiences. There was no need to expand the truth. Our efforts were crowned by a big king mackerel that now stretched the length of our fish box and weighed over 30 pounds.

Had we simply been anchored up, drifting or trolling baits in the Gulf, I doubt if we would have experienced the action we enjoyed that day where we employed chum to coax the fish within range of our baits. Surprisingly, however, chumming in many areas is not used as extensively as it should be to attract and hold gamefish within range of hook baits and lures.

In preparing to write this article, I perused quite a number of my log books to reread passages of exciting sport I'd enjoyed on all three of our saltwater coasts as well as off Mexico, in the Bahamas, off Bermuda and many other ports-of-call. In most cases the most consistent, torrid sport occurred when we used chum to attract both gamefish and bottom feeders within range.

For those of you who may never have heard of or tried chumming we turned to our Webster's, which defined chum simply as "chopped fish, or the like, thrown overboard

This chum is popularly called trash along the Gulf coast and is comprised of small fish, broken shrimp, crabs and squid obtained from shrimp trawlers. Lionel Holley scoops from the bucket and moments later the Gulf water will boil with hungry gamefish.

A fine albacore being gaffed for the author, who hooked it while chumming with live anchovies many miles at sea off Mexico's Baja Peninsula.

It's always wise to keep cans of catfood on board. Here Herb Schoenberg prepared to toss over the contents of several cans of Puss 'n Boots fishbase catfood while chumming aboard the Mitchell II. The chum will attract a wide variety of fish to the boat, many swimming within a rod's length of the stern.

to attract fish."

Sounds simple, doesn't it?

It is, and a technique that if properly employed will certainly enhance your score along the seacoast, regardless of whether you send a bait down to the bottom for winter flounders or codfish or seek such elusive adversaries as bonefish on tidal flats or the strong swimming tunas that roam the waters of the world.

Without question the most important consideration in attracting fish within range of your lines is to study the habits of the fish you're seeking and try to determine the spot where you can best anchor or drift to establish a chum line that will carry the chum to the fish and in turn attract the fish to you.

Obviously, if your chum is drifting through a veritable desert it simply cannot work. Hence the importance of selecting the right spot to commence chumming.

Among the more likely spots I've found for a wide variety of species are patches of broken, irregular bottom, regardless of where they are along the coast. Spots such as this hold an abundance of marine growth such as crabs, lobsters, mussels, and vegetation. Additionally, small forage fish and shrimp also seek this sanctuary which offers far more protection than open places.

You'll also find that many species will be immediately above or in proximity to coral reefs, rock ledges, offshore oil drilling platforms and various wrecks resting on the bottom.

You should always use the current to advantage when chumming spots such as these. Anchor away from your spot so that the curent carries your chum—whatever it may be—to your objective and will draw the fish. In so doing you'll hook fish away from the obstructions and have less difficulty landing them.

There are also times when fish will take up residence in kelp beds such as those found off the California and Mexico coast. Here you use the same approach: using your chum to draw the fish away from the kelp and its massive stems and leaves.

California bonito readily respond to a chum of live anchovies. Here's Harry Bonner bringing a nice one hooked while chumming off San Diego.

The Pacific barracuda often sets up residence around kelp beds, and will readily leave his sanctuary to come out for a chum of live anchovies. This one was hooked off Oceanside.

Milt Rosko used a whole pilchard drifted back in a chum line to hook this fine cero mackerel. Chumming with chunks of pilchards, he hooked this beauty off Walker's Cay, Bahamas.

There will also be occasions when you'll simply be fishing in water so deep or with currents so swift, that anchoring proves impossible. Here you will simply drift as you chum. This will be particularly true when fishing in water several hundred fathoms deep where your target may be the far-roaming albacore that are so plentiful in the Pacific, or the king mackerel in the Atlantic or Gulf, or one of the several species of tuna (including the bluefin, yellowfin, blackfin and little tuna) of the Atlantic. In these cases it's a matter of using fathometers or sounding equipment to locate the schools of fish and then employing the chum to attract the fish within range of your baits.

There is a wide variety of natural foods that may be effectively used for chum. Reduced to easiest terms, if you chum with whatever the fish are eating you just can't go wrong. Pelagic species such as the albacore, school bluefin tuna, and Pacific bonito feed extensively on anchovies, sardines and saury and all of these small baitfish are fine chum. They're best when alive, but satisfactory results may be achieved when chumming with chunks of these fish and even of ground fish. On the Atlantic the tunas and bonitos feed on mackerel, herring, butterfish and menhaden, and all these make excellent chum and hook baits. Most chumming on the Atlantic is done with ground chum as the

Native bonefish guides in the Bahamas often cut up a conch or shrimp and broadcast the small pieces on a bonefish flat. It attracts and holds bonefish there, making a good target for anglers.

The anchovy is a popular bait used by chummers on the Pacific coast. Hooked lightly through the gill collar as pictured here, it's readily taken by most species.

California party boats take aboard huge quantities of live anchovies before heading for the fishing grounds. This packet will have its live bait wells full before it sails for the albacore grounds far at sea.

forage species are more difficult to obtain and keep alive. Thus, a chum line is established with ground fish and supplemented with large chunks. The piéce de rèsistance is live baitfish or whole dead bait on the hook.

Where fish exist largely on shrimp, whether the large shrimp of the Gulf or the small grass shrimp found in protected waters of the Atlantic, use them. I've used shrimp to attract many species including striped bass, weakfish, seatrout, bluefish, tautog and sheepshead.

Ground clams and pieces of crab also coax fish within range, and both are particularly popular as chum when you're after such species as codfish, pollock, winter flounder, sea bass, porgies and other bottom feeders.

On the extremely shallow bonefish flats of Florida and the Bahamas, pieces of conch are used extensively to lure the fish within casting range. Small pieces of shrimp also do a fine job.

Some tropical species, particularly the many species of grouper and snapper, can be chummed away from the bottom simply by using small pieces of almost any fish. I've even tried cans of fish-base catfood with excellent results. The finely ground catfood disperses as it settles into the depths, and when paired with a nominal amount of fish chunks, it really arouses the interest of many fish. Because

Walt Carney used a chunk of butterfish to hook this big bluefish while chumming at famed Manasquan Ridge. He used a wire leader between hook and line, to keep the big blue from biting through the line with its sharp teeth. Chum used was ground mossbunker.

Little tuna readily respond to a chum line. They're hook shy, so use a small hook and conceal it within your bait for best results. This one was hooked while fishing in the Gulf of Mexico, Biloxi, Mississippi.

A chum of ground mossbunker works wonders in attracting Atlantic mackerel. Milt Rosko, Sr. used a diamond jig and teasers to hook three mackerel at once while chumming in the New York Bight.

All species of flounder will respond to a chum line. Indeed many anglers believe that chum will arouse the interest of fish that would otherwise simply be resting on the bottom.

of the success I've enjoyed with catfood I always have several cans of Puss 'n Boots in my kit when I head offshore. Often it's just enough to get the fish coming, after which I switch over to diced or chunked fish to hold the fish close at hand.

The beautiful part about chumming is that you can use the same equipment you would use for casting, trolling or drifting. Insofar as terminal rigging is concerned, by far the most effective is simply tying a hook directly to the end of your monofilament line! Yes, that's all you need for many species!

For those that have a lot of teeth, like bluefish, king and cero mackerel and other adversaries, you'll need a short length of either single strand stainless steel or cable leader wire between hook and line.

Of course, there are times when this basic method may have to be modified somewhat to suit a particular situation. If you're chumming in a strong current, you have to add several rubber-cored sinkers to your line to keep the bait from being swept away or held too near the surface. A word here with regard to rubber-cored sinkers. These are the finest sinkers you can employ while chumming, as the sinker is held to the line with a rubber core, and the ears of the core are twisted around the line and will not nick it. Shy away from lead clinch-on sinkers, since when bending these ears around your line you may damage it causing a weak spot and possible failure of the line at a critical time.

It occasionally happens that the current is so slight that your chum will drift away while your bait will settle di-

rectly to the bottom. When I encounter this kind of situation I use a plastic snap-on float to hold my bait at the desired level. I've also used sliding floats with good results, particularly when I wanted the bait to go deeper than a conventional snap-on float would permit.

Once you've established your chum line, one of the most important considerations is to keep it going, dispensing chum overboard at regular intervals, so that you maintain a continuous, unbroken line along which the fish can move. Even when you have fish hooked, make certain that someone is tending the chum bucket, for to neglect this task may result in losing all the fish you have attracted to the area. They may simply move out of range and not return.

Often the difference in success between two chummers using identical equipment and baits is that one permits his bait to drift out uninterrupted with the current, keeping his reel constantly in free spool or with the bail open and the bait always moving, while the other lets his bait drift out and then holds it in the current, where it often spins or hangs listlessly.

I've always scored best results when I had my bait moving with the current. This applied whether I was after blues off Long Island, king mackerel along the Florida Gulf coast, or albacore far at sea off Baja. I let the bait drift as far as I feel it should (which may be just 20 or 30 feet while chumming a tidal estuary for striped bass, or 150 feet or more when after bluefin tuna) then reel back in and let the bait drift out again, usually right in the midst of a ladle of chum. As fish swarm into the chum they're bound to notice my bait.

Strikes will come in a variety of ways. Some fish, even big tuna, will mouth a bait and move off slowly one day and the following day will strike a bait as though it were the last morsel in the sea. I've found that hesitation in striking is the best policy. When you feel a fish pick up the bait, whether a gentle nibble or a line-ripping one, just keep medium thumb pressure on the reel spool to keep the line from overrunning and permit the fish to get the bait well into its mouth. With small fish I let them move off 5 or 6 feet; big ones will often rip out 10 or 15 feet of line and I'll lower my rod tip, pointing it in the direction the line is moving. I then lock the reel in gear and lift back smartly to set the hook. It takes control to do this, and many anglers react instinctively to set the hook. But, too quick a strike will often rip the bait right from a fish's jaw.

Fish that move into a chum line in search of the tasty tidbits being ladled overboard are hungry and will often respond to a variety of lures worked through the chum line. I've caught king mackerel, cobia, the tunas and bonitos and many other species, including grouper and snapper, while casting a bucktail jig and working it vigorously through the chum line. I've also scored with plugs, especially poppers and surface swimmers, which brought strikes from stripers, blue, Pacific barracuda and bonito that had moved into the slick. I've also worked a streamer fly through a chum line with fine results, having caught several species on a tiny polar bear hair fly with a sparse dressing of Mylar to give it that glitter that hungry fish find irresistible.

By now you may be eager to rush into your favorite bait shop, purchase some chum and head for the fishing grounds! But let me caution that chumming isn't guaranteed. It is, however, a technique which every good salt water angler should master to insure a good catch on days when other techniques fail.

As for myself, I'm not adverse to saying, "pass the chum bucket, and let's catch some fish." Try it, and you too will join that select group of successful coastal anglers who regularly turn to a chum line and coax a wide variety of hungry salt water species to their hook.

Blackfin tuna, along with bluefin tuna, yellowfin tuna and little tuna, as well as the many bonitos, readily respond to a chum line. Some anglers use ground fish as chum, but small forage fish work equally well. This blackfin was hooked by the author off Bermuda on a pilchard.

I Try "Tennessee Tarpon"

by H. LEA LAWRENCE

Author Lawrence enjoys the challenge of leaping, fighting river herring, a species almost wholly ignored by most anglers.

WHAT LOOKS LIKE a tarpon, fights like a demon, leaps like crazy, hits lures with wild abandon, and is unknown to most anglers and ignored by all but a few who do?

The answer is river herring.

Both of my young boys, David and Charlie B., had fish on, and if there is any sound in the world more exciting than two eager little anglers squealing with delight at the same time, it would have to be three little anglers. I didn't completely qualify, but I had a fish on too, and I'll have to admit that it was causing me to be less than silent.

We were getting a grand-slam performance at the moment, complete with every spectacular feat that goes with tangling with these fish and what they should be famous for.

All three fish were cartwheeling at once, acrobatic marvels which are truly tarpon in miniature. Within a few seconds, David was grabbing at a flopping fish on the rocky bank, while Charlie B. was wearing a face that would have matched a sad clown. Too much pressure on the light line had caused him and the fish to part company. I landed my fish, looked at it, then carefully slipped it back into the water.

Ged Petit, a fish biologist with the Tennessee Game and Fish commission, and our host for the trip, was picking his way down the bank from the car where he had gone to get a thermos of coffee.

"Quite a show," he said, "but at least it's further proof of what I told you a couple of months ago when I first mentioned these fish. They're really something else!"

He already knew I was convinced. A short while earlier, on my first cast, a river herring had struck with a wrist-numbing jolt, then instantly tail-walked right in my face, tossing my lure back at me at the same time. The truth came to me just as quickly.

Ged had chuckled.

"Just like chain-lightning. They don't call them 'Tennessee Tarpon' for nothing!"

"And," he continued, "they're actually like tarpon in more ways than one. The appearance is unmistakable, but they also have very hard mouths, and setting a hook in them can be a tough job. You'll miss more than you take because of that. I usually try to hit them at least three times —if I have them on that long!"

The site for this action was the "boils" at the Johnsonville Steam Plant on Kentucky Lake, the place Ged had selected to introduce me to one of the most terrific and little-known sport fish in Tennessee, the river herring, or skipjack. At his suggestion, I'd brought along only ultra-light spinning tackle, since he said this was the way to get maximum fun from the fish. I also had brought along my two sons with their light outfits.

Before I was rigged, Charlie B. had already hooked and lost two fish, the result of displaying a bit too much zeal in landing them. He settled down to about a "half-haul" instead of a "full-haul" after the experience.

I cast again, bringing the lure back with a slow, twitching retrieve. It had moved less than 3 feet when a fish slammed into it. I missed the strike, then missed again on a quick repeat. The third strike gained me a brief view of the fish going in one direction, and my lure headed the other way. Ged had connected solidly, and had a fish dancing on the water in a series of split-second leaps. He howled like a banshee, and I thought for a moment he had fallen in.

"I can't help it," he said. "I'm a born yeller. I've never gotten over being excited whenever I get any kind of fish on the end of a line, and I hope I never will!" He yelled again as the fish spun in the air and shook like a wet dog.

Ged, who heads up a special project on Kentucky Lake, is one of the most unlikely people I know to make such a statement. To a dedicated fisherman his life seems utopian, since he practically fishes for a living, or at least it appears that way to those who see him on the lake regularly. My boys zeroed in on him as the target for the "what I want to be when I grow up" bit immediately, and he enjoys a spot higher than mine in their rating of "best fishermen."

Ged's yelling doubly impressed me because of his occupation. It was still that much fun to him. He was still grinning broadly as he reached down and slipped the hook gently from the fish's mouth.

David and Charlie B. continued to let out frequent yips, so I knew they were staying plenty busy. As I had discovered, it isn't uncommon to get from three to six strikes on a single retrieve, each one being worth one yip in the boys' case.

The spot we were fishing is a favorite location for many anglers, although most come to seek saugers, white bass and crappies that concentrate in the "boils." Catfish are another attraction, and some hefty specimens are taken regularly. The water discharged from the turbines is warmer than that in the lake, much more so in the winter and spring, and schools of threadfin and gizzard shad, both of which prefer higher temperatures, gather here. The game fish, in turn, move in to feed on these forage fish.

Oddly, though, while both the river herring and large shad can be taken at such times, they are paid scant attention. Catfish anglers use the guts of these fish for bait, but otherwise those taken are generally thrown up on the bank to rot. Light tackle fishermen are seldom seen with the exception of those who have discovered the fantastic action available, and those who fish for fun rather than for food.

Actually, a fisherman after river herring is considered to be somewhat of an oddity, and possibly is considered also to be a bit daffy. And unless there happens to be a number of other fish species moving into the area, the fisherman looking for just plain fun has all the elbow room he could ask for, especially since you can stand in your tracks and catch all the fish you want.

Another fish flashed behind my spoon, missed it, then took it on the next pass. I was ready and set the hook as hard as I could without snapping the light line. This time I managed to stay with it. It burrowed into the current, stripping line as it went, then instantly reversed its field and rocketed up in a beautiful, spray-showering jump. It seemed to hang there in the air for a long time before it knifed back into the water.

The "Tennessee Tarpon" are well-deserving of the name, and they keep on earning it. They possess unbelievable

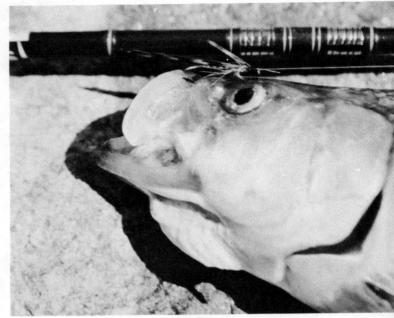

River herring is very similar in appearance to the saltwater tarpon.

strength for fish their size, make surging leaps like the true tarpon, and fight themselves almost to death before giving up. While they don't even remotely approach the tarpon in size—adult river herring range in weight between 1 and 3 pounds, with a length of 16 to 21 inches—on an ounce-for-ounce basis they measure up very well.

Since the river herring's diet is principally small minnows such as threadfin shad, they will readily take almost any type of small, shiny lure, as well as streamer flies fished with or without a spinner ahead of them. During the summer months they feed on the surface when insect hatches occur, and at such times they will hit dry flies and popping bugs as fast as you can toss them in their direction. Plenty are taken this way, but this is usually while fishermen are trying for bluegills or bass; in other words, "accidentally."

My fish wasn't going to come in easily and my wrist was getting the message. It again dug deeper into the current and had its own way for awhile. Twice it held fast in one place, bulldogging and refusing to be budged, and the 2-pound test line wasn't enough to change its mind.

Ged was yelling again, and Charlie B. and David were chiming in. All three were on to fish at once, with mine making it a foursome. Mine made another run peeling off line then suddenly came my way without further trouble, totally exhausted.

This is characteristic of "Tennessee Tarpon," going all the way in a do-or-die battle with hardly a halt in the action. Unlike bass and other game fish which take breathers now and then during a fight, and always seem to have an extra spurt of energy at the end, the river herring is a sprinter, putting everything it has on the line all at once.

Probably the main reason the river herring isn't paid much attention by most fishermen is that it isn't of any value as a food fish. Like their cousins, the shad, they're very bony, and the flesh softens and deteriorates rapidly once they're caught. Ged, who has a hobby of experimenting with various ways to prepare fish, believes there may be a way to make them palatable, but so far it has eluded him. To date his only use for them has been as bait for trot lines, but he thinks that if they could gain a reputation as a food fish, their popularity might increase.

Within a few minutes all four of us were busy with fish

Author's young sons David and Charlie B. show off their catch of "Tennessee Tarpon."

again and Ged had one on that was giving him a particularly hard time. It jumped three times, then zipped off on a long run. On the jumps it was obvious that it was larger than any we had taken so far. This time his yelling didn't bother me; in fact, I was beginning to enjoy it. It indicated a sense of pure pleasure reminiscent of those first fishing days in any of our lives. My boys, big-eyed, and with grins a mile wide, were also examples of pint-sized anglers who were in seventh heaven!

The river herring actually has a rather broad distribution. Most of the Tennessee River system has good populations, and they are found in both the Mississippi and Ohio Rivers, as well as the larger tributaries of these streams. The Gulf Coast region from Texas to Florida also has places where they are numerous. More often than not though, the river herring isn't sought by sport fishermen in any part of its range. In most cases fishermen can't distinguish them from shad, although there are definite differences. For example, the river herring has a golden sheen, which under ordinary light conditions is quite pronounced and which gives them another common name—golden shad in some areas. Too, the coloration on the back differs from that of the shad, running more to a blue-green. The river herring's lower jaw juts out, unlike the shad.

I hooked and landed three more fish, missing or losing three times that many in the process. With the spoon flashing just below the surface, I could see almost every strike and if the fish missed on the first pass, it would almost invariably come right back for another try. The rest of the crew were equally busy, hooking fish on nearly every cast. David and Charlie B. obviously were in a happy daze, since neither had ever caught so many fish on one trip. Also, Ged had told them they could string the fish for later use in making cut bait for trot lines, and they were even more elated. It's tough for little boys to throw back fish!

Just as quickly as the action had begun it stopped, and all of us went without strikes for a full half-hour. No fish were flashing and none were jumping. When river herring are in the vicinity the occasional jumping fish always make their presence known. One of the fish's names, skipjack, refers to its antics on the surface.

I noticed also, that the gulls which had been wheeling

overhead and diving to the water's surface had drifted several hundred yards away.

"The school has moved out," Ged explained, "and the gulls are following it. The river herring feeds voraciously on threadfin shad and when the schools of threadfins move, so do the river herring. The gulls take advantage of the stunned or crippled threadfins on the surface, so they follow the schools too.

"What happens is that the river herring gather under a school of threadfins, herd them to the surface, then rush in for the kill. That makes for the gull food. Keeping an eye on the birds is a sure way to locate river herring activity."

The late February day was chilly, so we sat back and drank a cup of hot coffee during the lull period. The coffee tasted good and the knot in my arm loosened up a bit. The boys had no intention of giving up, even though nothing was happening. They looked like small automatons casting and retrieving.

Ged, a native of New Hampshire, was raised as a fly rod addict, and had not the steep bank behind us prevented a decent back cast, he'd have been using that type of tackle in preference to the spinning gear. As with most devotees of the light wands, he finds the challenge of expertly handling a fish highly satisfying. Since he and his wife, Shirley, live in Eva within a stone's throw of the lake, he seldom misses getting in an hour or so of fly-rodding in the evenings. That's another reason their freezer is always loaded with fish filets.

Kentucky Lake is a mighty big piece of water, extending from just north of the Tennessee-Mississippi line all the way up across the state and into Kentucky. All told, there's 155,000 surface acres of water with a wide variety of game fish present: largemouth bass, crappies, saugers, white bass, bluegills, and channel and blue catfish.

Non-residents fishing in the Tennessee portion of the reservoir can obtain a special 3-day sport fishing license for only $1.50. A 10-day permit is available for $2. The annual sport fishing license is $5 minimum, or the fee is the same as the cost of a similar license in the visitor's state of residence. Free maps and information on Kentucky Lake can be obtained from the Tennessee Game and Fish Commission, P.O. Box 40747, Ellington Agricultural Center, Nashville, Tenn. 37220.

The gulls had drifted back and we again began spotting the river herring jumping in the turbulent water. We began casting again, with almost immediate success. Things returned to torrid from a zero level.

I could see why it would be easy to take a hundred fish in one afternoon with no trouble, or, as Ged had said, as many as one's arm could take. The fish hit recklessly, fighting just as avidly as ever. I landed and released them as fast as I could, and the others were doing the same. It was remindful of the spring runs of white bass in the rivers, but in this case the aerial displays made it even more fun.

This time the fish stayed for over an hour, and when they moved out again, we decided to call it quits. It was a unanimous vote, because the boys had slowed down after the last long spell of action. They had caught all the fish they could handle, and those that they had strung were so heavy that it took both of them to lift them. Neither Ged or I, as much as we like fishing, were at all reluctant to give it up for the day.

Besides, it was getting late and Shirley was waiting for us with a dinner of channel catfish, french fries, hush puppies and cole slaw, and that's something which shouldn't be kept waiting long!

Too, we knew that those "Tennessee Tarpon" would be right there waiting in the morning, and that we wouldn't have to worry about having any competition!

Tom Bratcher trolling for Center Hill Lake walleyes. For this, spin casting tackle is the most commonly used.

Stunt Fishing for Tennessee Walleye

by CARLOS VINSON

TOM BRATCHER and I had trolled the livelong day, but had strung less than a half-dozen walleyes. That's not too good and we couldn't figure out what was wrong.

The time of the year was right (mid-April), water conditions were perfect, and according to our fishing calendars even the moon promised jackpot fishing. Still the walleyes wouldn't cooperate.

We had been trolling the upper reaches of Center Hill Lake which is one of Tennessee's walleye hotspots. Tom and I live within easy driving distance of Center Hill so we do a big share of our freshwater fishing on this deep 15,000 acres-plus impoundment.

On the way home Tom got to thinking out loud. "The walleye can be the most stubborn freshwater fish of all," he said. "One year they'll bang the paint off certain plugs and the next year fin their snoots at the same offerings."

"Last spring," he continued, "the nightcrawler jiggers really slew them, but this spring the jiggers are not catching enough of them to stink up a skillet. There were over 40 boats of bug-eyed walleye anglers out there trolling today along the 2-mile hot stretch and I'll bet there weren't 50 walleyes caught all-told. The spring run should be at its peak but we haven't yet unlocked this year's secret of how to really catch them."

There the challenge rested until 3 days later. I couldn't sleep well at night because of it. We went around mumbling to ourselves, mostly about walleyes. The walleye fillets in our home freezers were just about down to the zero mark. Something had to be done. But exactly what was the big question. We had tried all the old tricks we knew, plus some we had just heard about, but nothing worked. We caught a few fish, sure, but nowhere near the number we usually catch during the peak of the Tennessee spring run. Somewhat half-heartedly we returned to the upper reaches of Center Hill three days later.

"Maybe we'll stumble on some way to really befuddle them," said Tom, as we eased our boat into the water at Webb's Camp Dock just before sunup.

I hadn't thought about it in that way, but "stumble" is actually what usually happens in walleye fishing. This is especially true when fishing in places where walleye moods change as often as they do here in Tennessee's artificial lake area. The walleyes become stubborn. They will not hit lures and baits which they struck during previous spring runs and no one knows why. So in desperation the spring run walleye fishermen will try all manner of tricks. Then suddenly one of the crazy stunts starts paying off with limit strings of the glass-eyed beauties and bang goes another walleye boom.

Tom and I are upper Center Hill regulars when the walleye runs get underway. But we had not discovered any of the previous jackpot secrets such as slow trolling certain plugs of certain colors, jigging nightcrawlers, or deep trolling the old spinner nightcrawler combination. Sometimes a killer trick will stay hot for two or three seasons and again a good ploy may peter out in one season or less. And these methods usually work uniformly well throughout most of the Tennessee and Kentucky artificial lake area.

Now it was mid-morning and we had strung only two walleyes. And they were nothing to crow about. When Tom gets that puzzled look on his face and starts chewing his eatin' tobacco as fast as a goat chewing briers, I know he's planning to try something unusual—in desperation. But in this case I couldn't quite believe what I saw.

Tom reeled in his medium-running plug, looked at it for a moment, and then hooked a big juicy nightcrawler on to the trebles. I didn't say anything but I figured the crawler would make the plug run wild and thereby lose most of its action. To my surprise it didn't.

Tom hadn't trolled his nightcrawler-adorned plug a hundred yards when a 4-pound walleye nailed the crazy combination. Old Tom's ears fairly wiggled. Mine did too, and I lost no time in getting a nightcrawler on to the hooks of my own plug.

As it turned out, this was the trick needed to really dazzle the Center Hill spring run walleyes. The news soon spread

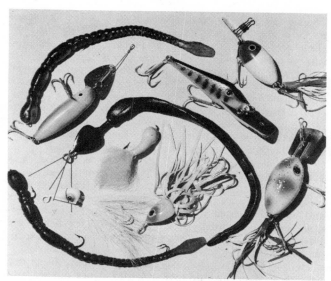

A sampling of lures which pay off from time to time on Center Hill Lake. But the appetite of walleyes constantly changes.

to other Tennessee man-made lakes. The technique worked on most of the other lakes also. It may last a couple or 3 years, it may last indefinitely, and it may be a 1-year trick. Who knows? I'll admit I don't, even after many, many moons of walleye fishing. I have stopped trying to figure out walleye moods. It is much easier to figure out some new method when an old one starts going sour.

Once the spring secret was unlocked, Tom and I and many others caught limit strings on almost every trip. A medium-running wobbling plug with a nightcrawler attached was by far the best ticket, day in and day out. And, the trick carried on into summer. We simply hooked a nightcrawler onto a deeper-running plug and trolled it through the *deeper* stretches or maybe further out from

the banks in *deeper* water. And it has paid off, not as miraculously as during the spring boom, but better than most previous summer tricks.

How long the plug-nightcrawler combination trick will hold up is anybody's guess. Center Hill and other Tennessee man-made lakes had to be restocked with walleyes during the late fifties and early sixties. For some reason as yet unknown, the original walleyes in these waters vanished after the big lakes were impounded. Various experiments to re-establish them were tried but failed. Then Tennessee biologists came up with the idea of obtaining eyed walleye eggs from New York State and to finish the hatching in a Tennessee hatchery. The plan worked like a charm.

Over 9,000,000 walleye fry were stocked in Center Hill Lake alone. The "Yankee Walleyes" caught on like nobody's business. Natural reproduction seems to be excellent. The New York walleyes are supposed to be identically the same species as the original walleyes in Tennessee waters, but why the transplants have done so well where the originals failed, no one seems to know for sure.

Back before the artificial lake days I used to catch walleyes from Caney Fork and other Tennessee rivers on live minnows. Very few were caught any other way. Now for some reason these transplanted walleyes will rarely take live minnows at all.

As soon as the first "Yankee Walleyes" grew big enough to be worth catching, fishermen started taking many limit strings on slow-trolled, rather small-size, medium-running plugs. Red was the leading plug color for walleyes with red and yellow and red and white combinations also producing. This tactic worked well for 2 years and into the third year. Then it went sour. No one knows why.

Finally someone stumbled on to a new idea. A No. 4 Hildebrandt spinner with an Eagle Claw 202 hook on it, with the hook crammed full of nightcrawlers started another boom. The rig was trolled behind a three-way swivel with a bell sinker on it to pull the baited spinner down to the desired depth. This was the walleye super-duper killer sys-

Business end of a Tennessee walleye which fell for a jointed underwater plug.

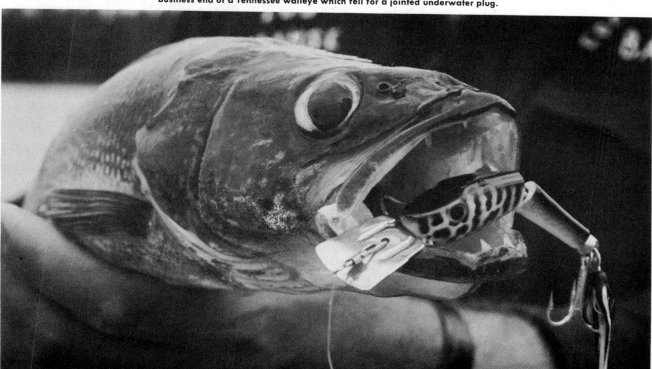

During the spring of 1970, the Bratcher and Vinson walleye team caught strings of walleyes like this one. They were living high up in hawg heaven.

Tennessee's artificial lakes, although some of the Tennessee tricks might well pay off in Michigan or New York or elsewhere. They are certainly worth a try. Spoons are good walleye catchers in some of the northern waters. These lures are of very little value in catching walleyes from Tennessee artificial lake waters. And believe me, we've tried them. They just don't pay off.

Night fishing for walleyes does very well in some parts of the country. Not so down here in Tennessee. One can catch a few at night but not nearly as many as can be caught in the daytime; this regardless of the method used.

The walleye is no glamor fish so far as acrobatics is concerned. But "Old Glass Eyes" has a lot on the ball otherwise. If there's any better fish eating than crisp, fried walleye fillets I haven't found it. And the moody stubbornness and general uncertainty of the species makes old *Stizostedion vitreum* actually a super challenge for fishermen. Here in the mid-south no other fish creates such excitement as the walleye.

Here in this vast man-made lake area walleye fishermen have to stay on their tip-toes trying to figure out ways to outwit them. The annual boom comes during the spring spawning runs and lasts for about 6 weeks. The activity starts tapering off after that and remains slow until early fall when business starts picking up again. The same methods which work successfully during the spring runs usually work during the summer also. But the summer fishing has to be in deeper water and the catches will be smaller.

Tennessee artificial lake walleyes grow to king-size. The present world's record, a whopping 25-pounder, was caught from a Tennessee artificial lake. But, like muskies, real king-size walleyes do not come to fishermen's nets often. They seem to get fat and lazy when they grow up and are far less active than the 2- to 8-pounders. But the big ones are there in Center Hill and other Tennessee artificial lakes, be assured of that. Let's hope that sooner or later someone will discover the stunt which will hook the real busters with an increased degree of regularity. Meanwhile it will continue to be a whale of a lot of fun figuring out how to outwit those moody 2- to 8-pounders. Stunt fishing for these unpredictable finny critters will probably continue to be the best bet. At least that's the way this old timer sees it.

tem for a couple of seasons. Then suddenly, without warning, this jackpot trick faded. Some walleyes could still be caught using this method but far fewer than anyone had a right to expect. Why? You tell me because I don't know. As I said, I have quit trying to figure out walleye moods.

After the spinner-nightcrawler boom came the nightcrawler jigging spree. Somebody started catching walleyes hand over fist while letting his boat drift on its own through medium current and jigging a nightcrawler off the bottom. Pop went the weasel again. Another walleye catching boom was on and soon was into high gear. The news spread like wildfire.

This one also started on Center Hill Lake. A No. 2 Eagle Claw 202 hook on the line with a No. 5 split-shot sinker about 6 inches above the hook and one nightcrawler on the hook threaded loosely so that half the crawler is left free to wiggle is the way it was done. Jig the crawler off the bottom as the boat drifts slowly along. This method created a super boom for a season or two and then started slowing down. That's when the plug-nightcrawler deal described earlier started taking over. Quite a few Tennessee walleyes are still caught by nightcrawler jiggers but nothing compared to those caught during the heyday of the trick.

Transplanting is gradually broadening the range of the walleye. But this prized member of the perch tribe is still pretty much a dweller of the eastern United States from Tennessee northward and on up into eastern and central Canada. It is true that walleyes in Minnesota and Wisconsin waters may behave quite differently from their kinfolk in

Author Vinson with an average Center Hill walleye taken on the magic (at least temporarily) plug and nightcrawler combination. That grim look indicates determination, not despair.

FISHING TACKLE MANUFACTURERS DIRECTORY

Tony Accetta & Son
932 Ave. E, Riviera Beach, Fla. 33404
Lures & Baits, Fishing Accessories

Acme Tackle Company
69 Bucklin St., Providence, R.I. 02907
Lures & Baits, Fishing Accessories

Aero Precision Engineering
7117 Point Douglas Drive
Cottage Grove, Minn. 55016
Fishing Accessories

Airlite Plastics Company
914 N. 18th St., Omaha, Nebr. 68102
Fishing Accessories

Aitken-Warner Corporation
427 Beech St., Green Camp, Ohio 43322
Lures & Baits, Fishing Accessories

Al's Goldfish Lure Company
516 Main St., Indian Orchard, Mass. 01051
Lures & Baits, Fishing Accessories

Aladdin Laboratories, Inc.
620 S. 8th St., Minneapolis, Minn. 55404
Rods & Reels, Fishing Accessories

Allan Manufacturing Company
325 Duffy Ave., Hicksville, L.I., N.Y. 11801
Fishing Accessories

Alliance Manufacturing Company
3125 N. Milwaukee Ave., Chg., Ill. 60618
Fishing Accessories

American Sportsman Bait Company
21744 Dequindre Ave., Warren, Mich. 48091
Lures & Baits

Angler Products, Inc.
868 Mercer Rd., Butler, Pa. 16001
Lures & Baits

Angler Rod Company
1426 Oakland Ave., St. Clair, Mich. 48079
Rods & Reels

Anglers' Manufacturing Corp.
7729 N. Eastlake Ter., Chg., Ill. 60626
Fishing Accessories

Angling Products Company, Inc.
2704 Skyline Dr., Lorain, Ohio 44053
Lures & Baits, Fishing Accessories

Fred Arbogast Company, Inc.
313 West North St., Akron, Ohio 44303
Lures & Baits, Fishing Accessories

Axelson Fishing Tackle Mfg. Co.
1559 Placentia, Newport Beach, Calif. 92660
Fishing Accessories

B & B Tackle Company
P.O. Box 220, Lufkin, Texas 75901
Lures & Baits, Fishing Accessories

*Members of the American Fishing
Tackle Manufacturers Association*

B & M Company
P.O. Box 231, West Point, Miss. 39773
Rods & Reels, Lures & Baits, Fishing Accessories

B & T Manufacturing, Inc.
P.O. Box 249, Ryan, Okla. 73565
Rods & Reels, Fishing Accessories

Jim Bagley Bait Company
P.O. Box 110, Winter Haven, Fla. 33880
Lures & Baits

Bait-Saver
401 N. Main St., Thiensville, Wis. 53092
Fishing Accessories

Bass Buster, Inc.
P.O. Box 118, Amsterdam, Mo. 64723
Lures & Baits

Bay de Noc Lure Company
Box 71, Gladstone, Mich. 49837
Rods & Reels, Lures & Baits, Fishing Accessories

Bead Chain Mfg. Company
110 Mountain Grove St.
Bridgeport, Conn. 06605
Lures & Baits, Fishing Accessories

Bear Paw Tackle Company
P.O. Box 177, Farmington, Mich. 48024
Lures & Baits, Fishing Accessories

Berkley & Company, Inc.
1617 Hill Ave., Spirit Lake, Iowa 51360
Rods & Reels, Fishing Lines, Fishing Accessories

Best Tackle Mfg. Co.
P.O. Box 123, Unionville, Mich. 48767
Lures & Baits, Fishing Accessories

Betts Tackle, Ltd.
Box 57, Fuquay Varina, N.C. 27526
Lures & Baits, Fishing Accessories

Bevin Wilcox Line Company
Div. Brownell & Co., Inc.
Main St., Moodus, Conn. 06469
Fishing Lines

Big Jon, Inc.
14393 Peninsula Dr., Traverse City, Mich. 49684
Lures & Baits

Bluegrass Tackle Company
205 Robin Rd., Russell, Ky. 41169
Lures & Baits

Bohn Engineering Co.
1423 Walnut St., N.E.
Grand Rapids, Mich. 49503
Rods & Reels, Fishing Accessories

Boone Bait Company, Inc.
P.O. Box 571, Winter Park, Fla. 32789
Lures & Baits

Bow-Dilly Lure Co.
206 W. Ave. B—Suite 1 (Box 1210)
Killeen, Texas 76541
Lures & Baits, Fishing Accessories

Browning Arms Company
Route 1, Morgan, Utah 84050
Rods & Reels

Brunswick Corp., Sports Div.
69 W. Washington St., Chg., Ill. 60602
Rods & Reels, Lures & Baits, Fishing Accessories

Burke Flexo-Products Company
1969 S. Airport Rd., Traverse City, Mich. 49684
Lures & Baits

Bystrom Bros., Inc.
2200 Snelling Ave., Minneapolis, Minn. 55404
Fishing Accessories

California Tackle Company, Inc.
430 W. Redondo Beach Blvd.
Gardena, Calif. 90248
Rods & Reels

Carry-Lite, Inc.
3000 West Clarke St., Milwaukee, Wis. 53245
Fishing Accessories

Challanger Mfg. Corporation
118 Pearl St., Mt. Vernon, N.Y. 10550
Fishing Accessories

Championship Tackle, Inc.
3206 Hollywood Ave., Shreveport, La. 71108
Lures & Baits

Charley's Wonderworm Company
516 Market St., Mt. Carmel, Ill. 62863
Lures & Baits

H.C. Cook Company
28 Beaver St., Ansonia, Conn. 06401
Fishing Accessories

Cordell Tackle, Inc.
P.O. Box 2020, Hot Springs, Ark. 71901
Lures & Baits, Fishing Accessories

Cortland Line Company
P.O. Box 1362, Cortland, N.Y. 13045
Fishing Lines

Creek Chub Bait Company
E. Keyser St., Garrett, Indiana 46738
Lures & Baits

Creme Lure Company
P.O. Box 87, Tyler, Texas 75701
Lures & Baits

Cuba Specialty Mfg. Company
P.O. Box 38, Houghton, N.Y. 14744
Fishing Accessories

Ed Cumings, Inc.
Box 6186, Flint, Mich. 48508
Fishing Accessories

Daisy/Heddon Div. Victor Compt. Corp.
414 West St., Dowagiac, Mich. 49047
Rods & Reels, Lures & Baits

Daisy/Heddon
P.O. Box 220, Rogers, Ark. 72756

Daiwa Corporation
14011 S. Normandie, Gardena, Calif. 90247
Rods & Reels, Fishing Lines

Les Davis Fishing Tackle Company
1565 Center St., Tacoma, Wash. 98409
Fishing Lines, Lures & Baits, Fishing Accessories

Dayton Marine Products, Inc.
7565 E. McNichols Rd., Detroit, Mich. 48234
Fishing Accessories

DeLong Lures, Inc.
80 Compark Rd., Centerville, Ohio 45459
Lures & Baits

Dep, Inc.
1116 South J St., Fort Smith, Ark. 72901
Lures & Baits

Depew Manufacturing Company
359 Duffy Ave., Hicksville, L.I., N.Y. 11802
Rods & Reels, Fishing Accessories

DeWitt Plastics
P.O. Box 400, Auburn, N.Y. 13021
Rods & Reels, Lures & Baits, Fishing Accessories

Dr. Walker's Enterprises
224 New Hope Rd., Gastonia, N.C. 28052
Lures & Baits

Dragon Fly Company
P.O. Drawer 1349, Sumter, S.C. 29151
Lures & Baits, Fishing Accessories

E.I. du Pont de Nemours & Co., Inc.
1007 Market St., Wilmington, Del. 19898
Fishing Lines

Dynaflex Manufacturing Corporation
1075 W. 21st Place, Hialeah, Fla. 33010
Rods & Reels

Earlybird Company
P.O. Box 1485, Boise, Idaho 83701
Lures & Baits, Fishing Accessories

Lou J. Eppinger Mfg. Company
6340 Schaefer Hwy., Dearborn, Mich. 48126
Lures & Baits

F. B. Spinning Reels Div. Feurer Bros.
77 Lafayette Ave.
North White Plains, N.Y. 10603
Rods & Reels

Falls Bait Company
1440 Kennedy Rd., Chippewa Falls, Wis. 54729
Lures & Baits, Fishing Accessories

Famous Keystone Corporation
1344 W. 37th St., Chicago, Ill. 60609
Rods & Reels, Lures & Baits, Fishing Accessories

Featherweight Products
3454-58 Ocean View Blvd., Glendale, Calif. 91208
Rods & Reels, Fishing Accessories

Flambeau Plastics Corporation
801 Lynn St., Baraboo, Wis. 53913
Fishing Accessories

Fly Fish Kit Company, Inc.
612 N. Mantua St., Kent, Ohio 44240
Lures & Baits, Fishing Accessories

Fo-Mac, Inc.
Box 6217, Tulsa, Okla. 74106
Lures & Baits, Fishing Accessories

Frabill Manufacturing Company
2018 S. First St., Milwaukee, Wis. 53207
Fishing Accessories

Isaac Franklin Company, Inc.
620 N. Pulaski St., Baltimore, Md. 21217
Fishing Accessories

G & R Industries, Inc.
P.O. Box 18, Purdy, Mo. 65734
Lures & Baits

The Gaines Company
Box 35, Gaines, Pa. 16921
Lures & Baits

Gapen Tackle Company
Highway 10, Big Lake, Minn. 55309
Lures & Baits, Fishing Accessories

The Garcia Corporation
329 Alfred Ave., Teaneck, N.J. 07666
Rods & Reels, Fishing Lines,
Lures & Baits, Fishing Accessories

Generic Systems, Inc.
620 W. Main St., Rockaway, N.J. 07866
Fishing Accessories

Gladding Corporation
South Otselic, N.Y. 13155
Rods & Reels, Fishing Lines,
Lures & Baits, Fishing Accessories

Gladding Corp. (Executive offices)
P.O. Box 260, Syracuse, N.Y. 13201

Great Lakes Products, Inc.
312 Huron Blvd., Marysville, Mich. 48040
Rods & Reels

Gudebrod Bros. Silk Co., Inc.
12 South 12th St., Philadelphia, Pa. 19107
Fishing Lines, Lures & Baits, Fishing Accessories

H & H Development
909-A North Lake, Burbank, Calif. 91504
Lures & Baits

Harrison-Hoge Industries, Inc.
104 Arlington Ave., St. James, N.Y. 11780
Rods & Reels, Fishing Lines,
Lures & Baits, Fishing Accessories

Heb Manufacturing Company
Box 115, Chelsea, Vt. 05038
Fishing Accessories

John J. Hildebrandt Corporation
P.O. Box 50, Logansport, Indiana 46947
Lures & Baits, Fishing Accessories

The Hofschneider Corporation
848 Jay St., Rochester, N.Y. 14611
Lures & Baits

Hopkins Fishing Company
1130 Boissevain Ave., Norfolk, Va. 23507
Lures & Baits

Ideal Fishing Float Company, Inc.
2001 E. Franklin St., Richmond, Va. 23203
Fishing Accessories

Indian Head Sporting Goods, Inc.
Ripley, Miss. 38663
Rods & Reels, Fishing Accessories

Inventors Products Company
541 West 79th St., Minneapolis, Minn. 55420
Fishing Accessories

It, Inc.
693 N. Main St., Torrington, Conn. 06790
Lures & Baits, Fishing Accessories

Jamison Tackle Corporation
3654 W. Montrose Ave., Chicago, Ill. 60618
Lures & Baits

Luhr Jensen & Sons, Inc.
P.O. Box 297, Hood River, Ore. 97031
Lures & Baits

Jeros Tackle Company, Inc.
111 16th St., Brooklyn, N.Y. 11215
Fishing Lines, Lures & Baits, Fishing Accessories

Louis Johnson Company
1547 Old Deerfield Rd., Highland Pk., Ill. 60035
Rods & Reels, Lures & Baits, Fishing Accessories

Johnson Reels Company
1231 Rhine St., Mankato, Minn. 56001
Rods & Reels

Kane Fiber Fisherman
1102 Bull St., Savannah, Ga. 31402
Rods & Reels

Keating Floating Sinker Company
3901 High St., Denver, Colo. 80216
Fishing Accessories

Kebek Industries, Inc.
Box 2381, Knoxville, Tenn. 37901
Fishing Accessories

Keel Guard Lures, Inc.
Box 181, Bowerston, Ohio 44695
Lures & Baits

Kent Sales & Mfg. Company
501 Dodge St., Kent, Ohio 44240
Fishing Accessories

Kinney Company
6448 Fireside Dr., Centerville, Ohio 45459
Fishing Accessories

Knotmaster Industries
Box 23201, San Diego, Calif. 92132
Fishing Accessories

Kodiak Corporation
Box 467, Ironwood, Mich. 49938
Rods & Reels

L & S Bait Company
148 S. Vasseur Ave., Bradley, Ill. 60915
Lures & Baits

La Push Lures, Inc.
P.O. Box 429, Ellensburg, Wash. 98926
Lures & Baits

Lake Products Company
Box 116, Utica, Mich. 48087
Lures & Baits, Fishing Accessories

Lakeland Industries
Isle, Minn. 56342
Fishing Accessories

Land-O-Tackle, Inc.
4650 N. Ronald St., Chicago, Ill. 60631
Fishing Accessories

Lazy Ike Corporation
512 Central Ave., Fort Dodge, Iowa 50501
Lures & Baits, Fishing Accessories

Leben Laboratories, Inc.
Suite 333, 100 Park Ave. Bldg.
Oklahoma City, Okla. 73102
Fishing Accessories

Lenjo Industries, Inc.
208 Market St., Philadelphia, Pa. 19106
Rods & Reels

H. L. Leonard Rod Company
P. O. Box 393, Central Valley, N.Y. 10917
Rods & Reels, Fishing Accessories

Lindy's Manufacturing Corporation
Route 7, Brainerd, Minn. 56401
Lures & Baits, Fishing Accessories

Little Beaver Manufacturing Co.
1244 Lafayette Ave., Terre Haute, Ind. 47804
Lures & Baits

Long Lure Company
P.O. Box 6, Savannah, Tenn. 38372
Lures & Baits, Fishing Accessories

Lure Corporation
20800 Chesley Dr., Farmington, Mich. 48024
Lures & Baits

Mac-Jac Manufacturing Co., Inc.
Box 116, Muskegon, Mich. 49443
Lures & Baits, Fishing Accessories

Major Rod Mfg. Co. (U.S.) Ltd.
Demars Blvd., Tupper Lake, N.Y. 12986
Rods & Reels

Marathon Bait Company
Rt. 2, Hwy. XX, Mosinee, Wis. 54455
Lures & Baits, Fishing Accessories

Marine Metal Products, Inc.
1222 Range Rd., Clearwater, Fla. 33515
Fishing Accessories

Marlynn Lure Company
Box 296, Blue Springs, Mo. 64015
Lures & Baits, Fishing Accessories

Martin Reel Company, Inc.
P.O. Drawer 8, Mohawk, N.Y. 13407
Rods & Reels

Mason Tackle Company
Otisville, Mich. 48463
Fishing Lines, Fishing Accessories

Master Fishing Tackle Corporation
13813 So. Main St., Los Angeles, Calif. 90061
Rods & Reels

Maxwell Manufacturing Company
P.O. Box 649, Vancouver, Wash. 98660
Rods & Reels, Fishing Lines
Lures & Baits, Fishing Accessories

Maybrun Manufacturing Company
2250 Clybourn Ave., Chicago, Ill. 60614
Fishing Accessories

Memphis Lure Company
208 N. Evergreen St., Memphis, Tenn. 38104
Lures & Baits

Men-Go Dot Line Mfg. Company
Box 364, Silver Lake, Wis. 53170
Fishing Accessories

Mercer Tackle Company, Inc.
2416 Gore Blvd., Lawton, Okla. 73501
Lures & Baits, Fishing Accessories

Mid-Lakes Manufacturing Company
3300 Rifle Range Rd., Knoxville, Tenn. 37918
Lures & Baits, Fishing Accessories

Mildrum Manufacturing Company
230 Berlin St., East Berlin, Conn. 06023
Fishing Accessories

Mill Run Products Company
1360 W. 9th St., Cleveland, Ohio 44113
Lures & Baits, Fishing Accessories

Mille Lacs Manufacturing Company
P.O. Box 27, Isle, Minn. 56342
Lures & Baits, Fishing Accessories

Minno-Matic Sales Company
23539 Aviva, Mt. Clemens, Mich. 48043
Fishing Accessories

Mit-Shel Company
640 South Fifth, Quincy, Ill. 62301
Fishing Accessories

National Expert, Inc.
2928 Stevens Ave., South
Minneapolis, Minn. 55408
Lures & Baits

National Fiber Glass Products, Inc.
52 St. Casimir Ave., Yonkers, N.Y. 10701
Rods & Reels

Nature Faker Lures, Inc.
108 Benton St., Windsor, Mo. 65360
Lures & Baits, Fishing Accessories

Nickelure Line, Inc.
1526 S. Dixie Ave., Vero Beach, Fla. 32960
Lures & Baits

Nicki Rig Co.
3409 S. Whitnall Ave., Milwaukee, Wis. 53207
Lures & Baits

Nor-Mor, Inc.
P.O. Box 893, Lewisville, Texas 75067
Lures & Baits, Fishing Accessories

North American Sports Products, Inc.
18320 John R., Detroit, Mich. 48203
Fishing Accessories

Nutron Plastic Company
7975 W. 20th Ave., Hialeah, Fla. 33014
Fishing Accessories

The Oberlin Canteen Company
P.O. Box 208, Oberlin, Ohio 44074
Fishing Accessories

The Orvis Company
Union St., Manchester, Vt. 05254
Rods & Reels, Lures & Baits, Fishing Accessories

P.C. Fishing Tackle, Inc.
2974 Cheyenne Dr., Owensboro, Ky. 42301
Lures & Baits

Padre Island Company, Inc.
Box 5310, San Antonio, Texas 78201
Lures & Baits

Palmer's Manufacturing Company
R.D. #1—P.O. Box 222, West Newton, Pa. 15089
Fishing Accessories

Parrish Industries
1312 W. Lee St., Greensboro, N.C. 27403
Lures & Baits, Fishing Accessories

E. H. Peckinpaugh Company
P.O. Box 15044, Baton Rouge, La. 70815
Lures & Baits

Pedigo Pork Rind Co., Inc.
500 W. 10th St., Bowling Green, Ky. 42101
Lures & Baits

Penn Dart Lure & Equipment Co., Inc.
5223 E. Simpson Ferry Rd.
Mechanicsburg, Pa. 17055
Lures & Baits

Penn Fishing Tackle Mfg. Company
3028 W. Hunting Park Ave.
Philadelphia, Pa. 19132
Rods & Reels

J. F. Pepper Company
Box 445, Rome, N.Y. 13440
Fishing Accessories

Pequea Fishing Tackle, Inc.
19 Miller St., Strasburg, Pa. 17579
Rods & Reels, Lures & Baits, Fishing Accessories

Perfection Tip Company
3020 E. 43rd Ave., Denver, Colo. 80216
Fishing Accessories

Peterson Manufacturing Company
P.O. Box 3709, Sarasota, Fla. 33578
Fishing Accessories

Phillips Fly & Tackle Company
P.O. Box 188, Alexandria, Pa. 16611
Lures & Baits, Fishing Accessories

Phillipson Rod Company
2705 High St., Denver, Colo. 80205
Rods & Reels

Plano Molding Company
P.O. Box 189, Plano, Ill. 60545
Fishing Accessories

Plas/Steel Products, Inc.
P.O. Box 176, Walkerton, Indiana 46574
Rods & Reels

Plastilite Corporation
Box 12235, Omaha, Neb. 68112
Fishing Accessories

Play-mor Products, Inc.
P.O. Drawer 740, Cape Girardeau, Mo. 63701
Rods & Reels, Lures & Baits, Fishing Accessories

Point Jude Lures, Inc.
451 Main St., East Greenwich, R.I. 02818
Lures & Baits

Eddie Pope & Company, Inc.
25572 Stanford Ave., Valencia, Calif. 91355
Lures & Baits, Fishing Accessories

Praid, Ltd.
1121 University Blvd., Silver Spring, Md. 20902
Lures & Baits

REB Manufacturing Company
P.O. Box 179, Pontiac, Mich. 48056
Lures & Baits

Recreational Development, Inc.
Box 4029, Tallahassee, Fla. 32303
Rods & Reels, Lures & Baits

Reel-Assist Corporation
430 E. First St., Casper, Wyo. 82601
Fishing Accessories

Reel Power Equipment, Inc.
3530 First Avenue, North
St. Petersburg, Fla. 33713
Rods & Reels, Lures & Baits

Ribbon Lure Company
53 Leitch Ave., Skaneateles, N.Y. 13152
Lures & Baits

The Don Rich Company
372 Franklin Ave., Redlands, Calif. 92373
Lures & Baits

Riley Company
Box 1108, Grand Rapids, Mich. 49501
Fishing Accessories

Riviera Die & Tool Mfg. Company
2819 West 28th St., Grand Rapids, Mich. 49509
Rods & Reels, Fishing Accessories

Robfin Industries
7000 E. Camelback Rd., Suite 20
Scottsdale, Ariz. 85251
Lures & Baits

Romeek Devices, Ltd.
3104 Tyre Neck Rd., Portsmouth, Va. 23703
Fishing Accessories

RTC Industries, Inc.
920 W. Cullerton St., Chicago, Ill. 60608
Fishing Accessories

J. A. Runge Company
415 "A" St., Seminole, Okla. 74868
Fishing Accessories

St. Croix Corporation
9909 South Shore Dr., Minneapolis, Minn. 55441
Rods & Reels

Sampo, Inc.
North St., Barneveld, N.Y. 13304
Lures & Baits, Fishing Accessories

Sanford's Float-a-Lite Kit, Inc.
1215 S. Central Ave., Fairborn, Ohio 45324
Fishing Accessories

Santee Lure & Tackle Company, Inc.
730 East Trade St., Charlotte, N.C. 28202
Lures & Baits, Fishing Accessories

Scientific Anglers, Inc.
Box 2001, Midland, Mich. 48640
Rods & Reels, Fishing Lines

Seneca Tackle Company
P.O. Box 2841, Providence, R.I. 02907
Lures & Baits

Sevenstrand Tackle Mfg. Company
14799 Chestnut St., Westminster, Cailf. 92683
Rods & Reels, Fishing Lines,
Lures & Baits, Fishing Accessories

Shakespeare Company
241 E. Kalamazoo Ave., Kalamazoo, Mich. 49001
Rods & Reels, Fishing Lines,
Lures & Baits, Fishing Accessories

Shakespeare Co. (Executive Offices)
P.O. Box 246, Columbia, S.C. 29202

Shellee Industries, Inc.
2516 Atlantic Ave., Brooklyn, N.Y. 11207
Fishing Accessories

Siberian Salmon Egg Company
4660 E. Marginal Way South
Seattle, Wash. 98134
Lures & Baits

Space Age Plastics
P.O. Box 9188, Knoxville, Tenn. 37920
Fishing Accessories

Sportsman's Products, Inc.
841 E. 38th St., Marion, Indiana 46952
Lures & Baits

Steffey Manufacturing Company
404 Martin Dr., Irwin, Pa. 15642
Lures & Baits

Stembridge Products, Inc.
Box 90756, East Point, Ga. 30344
Lures & Baits, Fishing Accessories

Still Fish Reel Company
4006 Vermaas Ave., Toledo, Ohio 43612
Rods & Reels

Stratton & Terstegge Company
1520 Rowan St., Louisville, Ky. 40201
Fishing Accessories

Strike Master, Inc.
411 N. Washington Ave.
Minneapolis, Minn. 55401
Lures & Baits, Fishing Accessories

Subria Corporation
P.O. Box 113, Montclair, N.J. 07042
Lures & Baits, Fishing Accessories

Sunset Line & Twine Company
Box 691, Petaluma, Calif. 94952
Fishing Lines, Fishing Accessories

Symonds & Company
1414 S. Michigan Ave., Chicago, Ill. 60605
Fishing Accessories

T.M.T., Inc.
P.O. Box 92, Birmingham, Mich. 48012
Rods & Reels, Fishing Accessories

Tack-L-Tyers
939 Chicago Ave., Evanston, Ill. 60202
Lures & Baits, Fishing Accessories

Thompson Fishing Tackle Co., Inc.
P.O. Box 275, Knoxville, Tenn. 37901
Lures & Baits

Tiki Lures, Inc.
1805 E. Eleven Mile Rd.
Madison Heights, Mich. 48071
Lures & Baits

Titan Corporation
3620 N. Central, Indianapolis, Ind. 46205
Lures & Baits

Tri Mi Lures, Inc.
711 East 16th St., Cheyenne, Wyo. 82001
Lures & Baits, Fishing Accessories

Trophy Products
9712 Old Katy Rd., Houston, Texas 77055
Fishing Accessories

True Temper Corporation American Tackle Division
1623 Euclid Ave., Cleveland, Ohio 44115
Rods & Reels, Fishing Accessories

U.S. Line Company
22 Main St., Westfield, Mass. 01085
Fishing Lines

Uncle Josh Bait Company
P.O. Box 130, Fort Atkinson, Wis. 53538
Lures & Baits

Union Manufacturing, Inc.
54 Church St., LeRoy, N.Y. 14482
Fishing Accessories

Universal Freeze Dried Products, Ltd.
41 Decker St., Copaigue, N.Y. 11726
Lures & Baits

Vari-Lure, Inc.
1605 Cedar Ridge, N.E.
Albuquerque, N.M. 87112
Fishing Accessories

Varmac Manufacturing, Inc.
4201 Redwood Ave., Los Angeles, Calif. 90066
Fishing Accessories

Vlchek Plastics Company
P.O. Box 97, Middlefield, Ohio 44062
Fishing Accessories

Walton Products, Inc.
P.O. Box 456, Atlantic, Iowa 50022
Fishing Accessories

Water Gremlin Company
4370 Otter Lake Rd.
White Bear Lake, Minn. 55110
Fishing Accessories

Weber Tackle Company
1039 Ellis St., Stevens Point, Wis. 54481
Rods & Reels, Fishing Lines,
Lures & Baits, Fishing Accessories

Erwin Weller Company
2105 Clark St., Sioux City, Iowa 51104
Lures & Baits, Fishing Accessories

Western Cutlery Company
5311 Western Ave., Boulder, Colo. 80302
Fishing Accessories

Whale Enterprises, Inc.
204 Dailey St., Piedmont, Ala. 36272
Fishing Accessories

Wood Manufacturing Company
Box 486, Conway, Ark. 72032
Lures & Baits

Woodstock Line Company
83 Canal St., Putnam, Conn. 06260
Fishing Lines

Woodstream Corporation
P.O. Box 327, Lititz, Pa. 17543
Rods & Reels, Fishing Lines,
Lures & Baits, Fishing Accessories

The Worth Company
P.O. Box 88, Stevens Point, Wis. 54481
Lures & Baits, Fishing Accessories

Wright & McGill Company
Box 16011, Denver, Colo. 80216
Rods & Reels, Fishing Lines,
Lures & Baits, Fishing Accessories

Yakima Bait Company
Box 310, Granger, Wash. 98932
Lures & Baits, Fishing Accessories

Zebco Division—Brunswick Corp.
Box 270, Tulsa, Okla. 74115
Rods & Reels, Lures & Baits, Fishing Accessories